"This book fills a tremendous void in tl
both a structured theoretical explication
well as practical guidelines and concrete ir
It uniquely combines faith and science, cı
mental health providers in providing thei
context."

Harold G. Koenig, Duke U ... Medical Center, USA

"This is a fascinating and impressive book—theologically, philosophically, and theoretically. The book also contains many helpful insights for the practice of Islamic spiritually integrated psychotherapy. It makes an outstanding contribution to the growing literature about the role of religion and spirituality in mainstream psychology and psychotherapy. I enthusiastically recommend it."

P. Scott Richards, Brigham Young University, USA

Applying Islamic Principles to Clinical Mental Health Care

This text outlines for the first time a structured articulation of an emerging Islamic orientation to psychotherapy, a framework presented and known as Traditional Islamically Integrated Psychotherapy (TIIP).

TIIP is an integrative model of mental health care that is grounded in the core principles of Islam while drawing upon empirical truths in psychology. The book introduces the basic foundations of TIIP, then delves into the writings of early Islamic scholars to provide a richer understanding of the Islamic intellectual heritage as it pertains to human psychology and mental health. Beyond theory, the book provides readers with practical interventional skills illustrated with case studies as well as techniques drawn inherently from the Islamic tradition. A methodology of case formulation is provided that allows for effective treatment planning and translation into therapeutic application. Throughout its chapters, the book situates TIIP within an Islamic epistemological and ontological framework, providing a discussion of the nature and composition of the human psyche, its drives, health, pathology, mechanisms of psychological change, and principles of healing.

Mental health practitioners who treat Muslim patients, Muslim clinicians, students of the behavioral sciences and related disciplines, and anyone with an interest in spiritually oriented psychotherapies will greatly benefit from this illustrative and practical text.

Hooman Keshavarzi, Psy.D is currently an assistant professor at Ibn Haldun University (Istanbul, Turkey), adjunct faculty at Hartford Seminary, a fellow of the International Association of Islamic Psychology and the Executive Director and Founder of Khalil Center.

Fahad Khan, Psy.D is a faculty member at Concordia University Chicago and College of DuPage, a fellow of the International Association of Islamic Psychology, and serves as an editor for the *Journal of Muslim Mental Health*.

Bilal Ali is a religious consultant and president of the Board of Directors at Khalil Center and the liaison for the Department of Hadith and academic advisor at Darul Qasim.

Rania Awaad, MD is a clinical associate professor of psychiatry at Stanford University School of Medicine, the director of the Muslim Mental Health Lab and Wellness Program, and co-director of the Diversity Clinic. She is also the clinical director of Khalil Center Bay Area.

Applying Islamic Principles to Clinical Mental Health Care

Introducing Traditional Islamically Integrated Psychotherapy

Edited by
Hooman Keshavarzi, Fahad Khan,
Bilal Ali, and Rania Awaad

Routledge
Taylor & Francis Group
NEW YORK AND LONDON

First published 2021
by Routledge
52 Vanderbilt Avenue, New York, NY 10017

and by Routledge
2 Park Square, Milton Park, Abingdon, Oxon, OX14 4RN

Routledge is an imprint of the Taylor & Francis Group, an informa business

Library of Congress Cataloging-in-Publication Data
A catalog record for this title has been requested

ISBN: 978-0-367-48887-1 (hbk)
ISBN: 978-0-367-48886-4 (pbk)
ISBN: 978-1-003-04333-1 (ebk)

Typeset in Garamond
by Newgen Publishing UK

Image 0.1

Contents

Contributors

Aneeqa Abid is an undergraduate student at Stanford University pursuing a bachelors degree in psychology. At Stanford, Aneeqa is actively involved with the Muslim community. Serving her local Muslim community is very important to Aneeqa and it is something she hopes to incorporate into her work as she aspires to become a psychiatrist. Aneeqa is passionate about Muslim mental health and Islamic Psychology and cares deeply about meeting the dire psychological needs surrounding mental health and emotional well-being, especially for Muslims living as a targeted minority in the West.

Shaykh Tameem Ahmadi engaged in a rigorous curriculum of religious knowledge, studying under some of the foremost scholars of North America, Africa, and South Asia. After completing the highly regarded *dars nizami* curriculum and being granted the *shahadah alimiyya* (recognition of Islamic scholarship), Shaykh Tameem immersed himself in the study of the Islamic Spiritual Sciences of the Heart under the private tutelage of one of the most honorable Spiritual Masters of our time, focusing on the subject of *tazkiyah* and *tarbiyah* (Purification of the Heart). Being granted the mantle of authorization to teach and transmit, he returned to the Bay Area of California under the advice and suggestion of his Shaykh.

Dr. Sara Ali, MD, MPH is a third-year psychiatry resident at the University of New Mexico Psychiatry and Behavioral Sciences Department. Prior to residency, she completed a masters degree in Public Health at University of New Mexico and worked as the lab manager and post-doctoral researcher at Stanford Muslim and Mental Health Lab. Her research interests include studying sociocultural, historical, and religious determinants of mental health and how they shape help-seeking behaviors and patterns of mental health service utilization by Muslim Americans. Her research work includes resynthesizing and examining historical Arabic mental health manuscripts and comparing them to contemporary methodologies.

Heba Elhaddad, MA received her undergraduate degree from University of California Irvine in Psychology of Social Science, later earning a Masters degree in Clinical Psychology, and is currently pursuing her doctorate degree in Clinical Psychology. She worked at OMID Multicultural Institute for Development, a mental health institute, for three years, where she completed her practicum hours and gained a variety of experience working with the Muslim population from different ethnicities and backgrounds. Heba is an affiliate of the Stanford Muslim Mental Health Lab which focuses on providing resources for clinicians, researchers and community leaders working with the Muslim population.

Danah Elsayed is an MSc student in the department of Family Relations and Human Development at the University of Guelph and a B.A. student at Al-Azhar University, pursuing a degree in Arabic and Islamic Studies. Danah earned her undergraduate degree in Psychology from the University of Toronto, where she currently studies the social-emotional resilience of Syrian newcomer children. She works with Dr. Rania Awaad and others at the Stanford Muslim Mental Health lab in the historical line of Islamic Psychology research.

Dr. Khalid Elzamzamy, MD is the Chief Psychiatry Resident at Hamad Medical Corporation, Qatar. He is also currently completing a Masters Degree in Islamic Thought and Applied Ethics at Hamad Bin Khalifa University, Qatar. Khalid serves as a Research Fellow at the Family and Youth Institute, USA. He received his medical degree from Ain Shams University, Egypt, and served as a research assistant at Yale University. Dr. Elzamzamy's interests include psychiatry training and education, the history of psychology and mental health practice among Muslims and Arabs, as well as the interplay between mental health, ethics, spirituality, and religiosity.

Donald Fette, PhD earned his doctorate in comparative literature from the University of Chicago, where he also worked as assistant director of the Writing Program. Beyond this, he served as director of writing at the Institute for Clinical Social Work in Chicago and writing advisor at the University of Chicago Medical Center, and has worked professionally with students from a host of national and international institutes and universities. On a non-professional note, he is a poet and guitarist who has performed in various capacities at a number of locations in North America and Europe.

Dr. Syed (Salman) Jafri, MD is a general neurologist in private practice in Southern California. He obtained his medical degree from the Western University of Health Sciences in Pomona, CA. He completed his neurology residency at the Medical College of Wisconsin in Milwaukee, WI.

He has an interest in traditional Islamic knowledge and has studied various traditional Islamic texts alongside his medical practice over the last decade. In particular, his interests span theology, philosophy, and spirituality. He also has an interest in narrative medicine, bioethics, and the intersection of these areas of study with neuroscience.

Paul M. Kaplick, MSc has a background in clinical psychology (BSc), cognitive neuroscience (MSc), and behavioral neuropharmacology. He is currently training as a clinical neuropsychologist in a Phase B neurological rehabilitation facility in the Rhine-Main area of Germany. He has co-authored various papers on preclinical models of stress-related disorders and believes that translational and interdisciplinary training is pivotal for state-of-the-art patient care that integrates cutting-edge research on brain–behaviour relationships. He heads the Islam and Psychology research group at the Islamic Association of Social and Educational Professions in Germany. When not working, Paul loves walking the Rheingau hillsides with his wife and son.

Sara Keshavarzi, MA is a doctoral candidate in the adult track of the Clinical Psychology program at the University of Windsor, Ontario, Canada. She holds a Master of Arts in Clinical Psychology from the University of Windsor. She is trained in various therapeutic modalities including Emotion Focused Therapy and Psychodynamic Psychotherapy. Her research interests include immigrant and refugee stress and coping, identity development, culture, religion, and spirituality.

Amin Loucif, MSc has a background in Psychology with a specialization in clinical psychology. Currently, he is finishing his postgraduate training in behavioral psychotherapy and schema therapy. He is a certified muslim chaplain and studies Islamic sciences at the University of Novi Pazar. In his practice, he mainly works with Muslim clients, both local and based online. Amin has given seminars in culturally and religiously sensitive psychology and counselling for professionals and non-professionals in Germany, Saudi Arabia, Serbia, and Morocco. His main goal is to reach out to the Muslim community and to raise awareness about the stigma around mental health.

Shaykh Rami Nsour, MA is an Islamic scholar, counselor, public speaker, teacher, and translator of Islamic texts. Spending seven years in Mauritania studying Islamic studies at some of the foremost Islamic colleges, Shaykh Rami received licensure (*ijaza*) to share his wisdom with students. Further enhancing his extensive study of *fiqh*, Nsour completed an extraordinary "in-residence" experience, allowing him to research questions (*fatawa*) of Islamic faith, law, and practice. Rami Nsour cofounded the Tayba Foundation, the first organization in the

United States to offer a distance-learning program in Islamic Education to incarcerated men and women. Shaykh Rami holds a BA in Human Development with a focus on Early Childhood. He also obatained an MA in Educational Psychology.

Dr. Aasim Padela, MD is the Director of the Initiative on Islam and Medicine, Associate Professor of Medicine in the Section of Emergency Medicine, and a faculty member of the MacLean Center for Clinical Medical Ethics and Divinity School at the University of Chicago. Dr. Padela holds an MD from Weill Cornell Medical College, completed residency in emergency medicine at the University of Rochester, and received an MSc in Healthcare Research from the University of Michigan. His Islamic studies expertise comes from part-time seminary studies during secondary school, and tutorials with traditionally trained Islamic scholars.

Dr. Faisal Qazi, DO has been practicing Neurology since 2006 in the greater Pomona Valley and the Inland Empire area of California since 2010, and more recently cross-covering St. Jude Hospital in Fullerton with outpatient offices in Pomona and Upland, CA. Dr. Qazi is from southern California and finished his residency training at Henry Ford Hospital in Detroit in 2005. He subsequently finished the Neurophysiology fellowship at University of California, San Diego in 2006. He is currently also the president of MiNDS (Medical Network Devoted to Service), a charitable organization with focus on specialty health care services to underserved families. Dr. Qazi's research interests include Neuroethics and Islamic Bioethics.

Dr. Abdallah Rothman, PhD obtained his MA in Psychology from Antioch University and his PhD in Psychology from Kingston University London. He is a Licensed Professional Counselor (LPC) and a Board Certified Registered Art Therapist (ATR-BC) with 15 years' experience as a practicing counseling psychologist. Abdallah was an adjunct faculty member at George Washington University and he established Shifaa Integrative Counseling, a private practice offering Islamically integrated psychotherapy to the Muslim community in Washington DC. Abdallah currently serves as the executive director of the International Association of Islamic Psychology and currently resides in the UAE.

Dr. Mohamed Omar Salem, MBChB, DPM, BCPsych, FRCPsych is an Associate Professor in Psychiatry, Consultant and Head of Department of Psychiatry, Al-Ahli Hospital, Doha, Qatar, and Middle East Representative of the International Association for the Study of Dreams (IASD). His main interests are dream research, CBT, and philosophical and cultural aspects of psychiatry.

Shaykh Dr Asim Yusuf, MD is a Fellow of the Royal College of Psychiatrists and a practicing clinician with a special interest in Mental Health and Spirituality. He is acknowledged as one of the leading figures in Islamic psychological studies in the UK. He received twenty years of rigorous theological training, and has been granted *ijazat* (formal religious authorizations) to instruct students in the art and science of Islamic thought by over thirty scholars from four continents. He is an authorised Shaykh of the Chishti and Qadiri spiritual orders, and has been teaching traditional Islam for nearly two decades, including an ongoing complete read-through of the Ihya Ulum al-Din of Imam Ghazali.

Foreword

Muslims have produced a very rich scholarly legacy on human psychology since the rise of the Islamic civilization and for more than fourteen centuries, and which extended geographically from Uyghuristan (East Turkestan) in Eastern China to the Balkans and North Africa. Muslims produced literature in diverse languages including Arabic, Persian, Turkish, Urdu, and many others. Unfortunately, most of this literature remains as manuscripts in libraries and very few have been published. Among these few, only a small number have been translated into English.

The first task required of specialists wanting to draw from the Islamic tradition in the field of mental health is to unearth this literature without negligence, publish them in their original language, translate them into other commonly used languages, and analyze their content. The second task, which is more challenging, is to put this rich and diverse literature into a dialogue with modern psychology and build bridges between them. The third and more practical task is to integrate the methods used in the classical Islamic literature on psychology with the modern standards of psychotherapy. This is an extremely daunting task because it requires mastery of the classical Islamic literature, modern academia on clinical psychology, and clinical expertise combined with an analytical ability to integrate them for the purpose of revolutionary alternatives to the existing models of psychotherapy. Only then would people appreciate this effort.

The present book authored by Hooman Keshavarzi and his colleagues aims to achieve this aim precisely. To my knowledge, it is perhaps the first and the only serious academic and groundbreaking effort of its kind by a team of well-qualified scholars who have explored different dimensions of the issue. I have no doubt that it will promote interest in the field and pave the ground for future research. Many scholars have realized the need for such a project, but Hooman Keshavarzi and his associates had the courage and determination to undertake this daunting and risky task, and have managed to complete it with great success.

The present book deserves great attention and appreciation because it builds a bridge to fill the gap between modern psychology and the traditional Islamic literature on human psychology. It does not only cover the conceptual dimensions of the issue but also demonstrates how it can be practiced today to complement the existing approaches and methods used in various areas of psychotherapy. It does this by providing a structured holistic conceptualization of patients that allows for the ease of integration of many existing techniques and strategies of care within its framework. It also provides specific Islamically derived therapeutic suggestions for practicing cognitive, emotional, behavioral, and spiritual interventions, with complementary case illustrations as practical demonstrations.

It is noteworthy at the outset to mention that the classical Islamic literature on psychology is not homogeneous, as various chapters in this book demonstrate (see Chapter 3 in particular). It is possible to classify this literature into three major genres with distinct methods. The first, the richest, and the most commonly read genre is the literature produced by Sufis. The second genre is the literature produced by medical doctors. The third genre is the literature produced by philosophers as part of practical philosophy under the title of self-management, *tadbīr al-nafs*. All these genres from the pre-modern period are pertinent today to psychology and psychiatry. Finally, though more indirectly related to psychology, discursive theology (*kalām*) provides very important foundational creedal concepts that inform Islam's theological assumptions as they pertain to the subject matter of human psychology and belief.

The Sufi literature on human psychology focuses on the health of the human soul or spiritual heart, with the purpose of changing the attributes of the heart and resultant social actions and relationships. This is because Sufis assume that human action is a manifestation of the state of the heart. If the heart is ill, human behavior will also deviate from virtuous conduct. If the heart is healthy, then human behavior will follow suit. Put another way, the ultimate goal of Sufis in studying the heart and analyzing its states is to engender a healthy heart that will in turn produce upright and ethical behavior. Towards this aim, they use experiential and rational methods, as well as spiritual methods commonly called *tasfiyah* and *tazkiyah*, or purification. Among numerous others, the works of al-Ghazālī may be seen as the most commonly used representative of this perspective.

The literature by Muslim medical doctors in the classical period, on the other hand, focuses on physical/mental health within the context of the health sciences. They rely on empirical methods in detecting pathology and offering treatment interventions. Among others, Abū Zayd al-Balkhī's treatise on the Sustenance of the Body and Soul, translated into English by Malik Badri, serves as a paradigmatic example of this perspective and methodology.

The classical literature on self-management as part of practical philosophy relies on rational methods to identify maladies in human behavior and attempts to change them through appealing to human reason and rational discourse. It is based on changing mental convictions and perceptions about one's own self and behaviors. This is the reason why this genre of literature is broadly referred to as "Ethics".

In sum, we can say that the three classical perspectives (the spiritual-Sufi, the empirical-medical, and the rational-ethical) on human psychology produced distinct literatures reflecting the particular methods they used. Yet they all share a multiplex human ontology involving the levels of human existence, body, mind, and soul, despite their divergent understandings, analytical focuses, and research methods. Without considering this multiplex human ontology, which is the common ground for all classical Islamic schools of thought on human psychology, it is impossible to understand the classical Islamic psychology. This book provides a good illustrative sampling of this multiplex nature as a demonstration of the richness of these Islamic discourses. Certainly, it serves as a great catalyst to inspire further inquiry and mining of the treasures of this tradition.

With regard to human ontology in Islam, I would like to draw attention to a less explored dimension in this work, the *latā'if* (plural of *latīfa*). Though some chapters make brief mention of this, a fuller exploration of this particular conceptual framework of the human being may prove enriching for future explorations. According to the Sufis, in particular those who subscribe to the Naqshibandi school, the human soul is the house of the following subtle or completely metaphysical (non-physical) faculties: *qalb* (heart), *rūḥ* (soul), *sirr* (secret), *khafi* (hidden), *akhfa* (the most hidden). The Sufis emphasize that these *latā'if* need to be cleansed through the usage of behavioral and spiritual methods that include abstention, seclusion, selfless service to the creation of Allah, *dhikr*, and other religious practices. Although the common classical Islamic psychological discourse focuses on the heart, the interest in the *latā'if* takes the discourse and practice to a further and deeper level. This level is beyond the empirical and rational domain and can be accessed and cleansed only through specific spiritual exercises. The purpose of this process is to help engender higher morality and character, and to ensure they become truly rooted and completely entrenched in the deeper levels of the human soul. While such a discussion may be beyond the scope of this particular work, I wanted to offer it as an additional demonstration of the depths of richness and potential limitless opportunities to enrich the modern psychological literature through the contributions of Islamic scholars.

I would like to conclude by congratulating Hooman Keshavarzi and his colleagues for opening a new area of study for those who are interested in bridging the gap between the classical and the present literature on human psychology from an integrative perspective. Such an integrative approach, if successfully turned into practice applications, will help practitioners better understand human psychology and contribute to solving their problems with the purpose of reducing human suffering and elevating human happiness.

Recep Şentürk, Ph.D

Preface

The main objective of the authors of this book is to show how an Islamic approach can be applied in clinical mental health issues, and to introduce readers to their valuable research that has culminated in a model of Islamic psychotherapy named Traditional Islamically Integrated Psychotherapy (TIIP). The authors are among the new generation of Muslim psychologists and psychiatrists who, unlike previous generations, are able to free their thought and beliefs from the hegemony of the secular worldview upon which Western psychology was created and is still sustained. The intellectual and ideological battle for mainstream acceptance of an Islamic psychology in a world dominated by reductionistic science situated within a secular background has been long and at times demanding.

The earliest attempts to harmonize psychology and Islam were artificial efforts to reduce the cognitive dissonance that afflicted some Muslim psychologists who realized the secular nature of their specialization and felt uneasy about submissively accepting its Eurocentric theories and practices. A good and widely held example at the time was their proposition that the Freudian seminal theory of the three structures of personality—namely the id, ego, and superego—are the same as the three spiritual ego states of the soul that are mentioned in the holy Qur'ān. They claimed that the commanding soul *nafs ammārah* stands for the id, the soul *nafs* is exemplified by the ego, and the tranquil soul *nafs muṭma'innah* stands for the superego. This undermined the richer and metaphysical nature of these Qur'ānic concepts. In the late 1950s I personally witnessed many Muslim psychologists strongly defend this false belief as if Freud were a spiritually motivated scholar!

As they matured and gained more self-confidence, Muslim psychologists abandoned this artificial search for similarities and came up with the holistic approach of "Islamization". This new endeavor gained popularity and professional momentum through the support of the International Institute of Islamic Thought (IIIT). However, as many leading Muslim psychologists realized, much of what is researched and written on Islamization was mainly an effort to give the "edifice" of Western psychology an Islamic "paint" without touching the secular worldview on which it was built. Islamizers of psychology were thus trapped within the concepts of Western paradigms. Additionally, the term "Islamization" itself began to face serious criticisms.

This led to the final development of "Islamic psychology". Though Islamic psychology endeavors to free Muslim psychologists from the chains of mental slavery to the secular worldviews of their discipline, it considers making use of whatever is useful or supported by rigorous research by non-Muslim psychologists as a gift from Allah, Most High, who allowed this knowledge to be acquired by secular researchers. This is brilliantly expressed by Hooman Keshavarzi and his colleagues in the book that I am prefacing. They draw attention to the Ḥadīth of Prophet Muḥammad (peace and blessing be upon him) that this knowledge can rightfully be claimed by Muslims as well, since they are urged to seek knowledge and wisdom (*hikmah*). Since true knowledge does not have a "western" or "eastern" aspect, there is no need for a feeling of inferiority in benefiting from this knowledge. Thus, as pursuers of truth we are indeed entitled to it.

Furthermore, Islamic psychology aims at unearthing the gems of the psychospiritual theories and practices developed by early Muslim scholars such as al-Ghazālī (d.510 AH/1111 CE), al-Balkhī (d.322 AH/934 CE), al-Rāzī (d.314 AH/925 CE), and similar scholars, and it strives to integrate their contributions into our modern Islamic therapeutic models and practical therapies. As a psychotherapist practicing in the twenty-first century, I have been greatly influenced by the cognitive behavior therapy of Abū Zayd al-Balkhī. His manuscript on the sustenance of body and soul is a shining example for the value of the works of early Muslim scholars. My clients may be surprised that the psychospiritual techniques I am using in treating them came from a Muslim scholar who lived 12 centuries ago!

Thanks to Allah, Islamic psychology is spreading far and wide. University courses on Islamic psychology are not only being taught in Muslim countries, they are also offered in distinguished universities in the UK, the US, Australia, and other non-Muslim countries. Societies and associations of Islamic psychology are established everywhere: in Indonesia, the US, UK, Russia, Sudan, Australia, and other places. Muslim psychologists are very happy about the international recognition of an Islamic orientation; some are elated. However, the authors of this book are among the few who did not merely join the bandwagon. In addition to such widespread recognition and acclaim, they drew attention to the importance of establishing an Islamic reorientation of psychology upon traditional mainstream Islam, i.e. Sunni (*ahl al-sunnah wa al-jamā'ah*). Muslims have different schools of law, sects, and beliefs, and thus it is important to construct a traditional Islamic psychology upon a commonly agreed set of beliefs and religious methodology shared by the majority of Muslims internationally.

The powerful social media of our modern age has reinforced a religious hotchpot. So, according to these authors, Muslim psychologists in general and clinical psychologists and counselors in particular should be mindful of conflating different religious beliefs. To help achieve this objective, the authors have come up with an Islamic model of the human psyche based on Islamic tradition that can Islamically adapt contemporary psychological therapies to the needs of clients. They named this new therapeutic intervention Traditional Islamically Integrated Psychotherapy (TIIP). I urge Muslim psychotherapists to read this book and to adapt TIIP to the specific needs of their patients and clients.

Malik Badri, Ph.D

Editors' Introduction

Hooman Keshavarzi, Fahad Khan, Bilal Ali, and Rania Awaad

In the name of Allah, the Beneficent, the most Merciful. All praise is due to the Source of all knowledge, the Fashioner of the human being, in spirit and body, in an organized, efficient and systematic order whose perfection can be attributed to none other than Him. The One to whose attribute of being the Creator all elements of creation point. Knowing this reality necessitates the glorification of His names and the humbling of creation before their Supreme Majestic Fashioner, who sent His perfect revelation to free humanity from the shackles of mere physicalism and temporalism. May the salutations and blessings of Allah be upon our Master and Prophet Muḥammad who came to impart the wisdom of revelation, to embody it and to perfect human character, restructure human beliefs, reform human behaviors and elevate human spirits in the best possible manner. The epitome of perfection in character belongs to him and he serves as the ultimate example of holistic human health. May peace and blessings be upon his family, progeny, wives, companions and those who follow him until the Last day.

Islamic Intellectual Heritage and Mental Health

Although human psychological functioning had been discussed in the philosophical writings of the early Greek philosophers, the seminal publication of *Sustenance of the Soul* by the polymath Abū Zayd al-Balkhī in the ninth century is one of the earliest documented manuscripts specific to mental and spiritual health (al-Balkhī, 2013). In fact, Awaad and Ali's (2016) recent comparative analysis yielded a complete convergence between the current symptomology for obsessive compulsive disorder (OCD) according to the Diagnostic and Statistical Manual of Mental Disorders (DSM V) and Abū Zayd's original manuscript.

The Muslim community experienced a significant era of growth and development between the ninth and eighteenth centuries, during which landmark religious philosophies pertaining to the relationship between spirituality and well-being flourished. During this time period, an explosion of literature on human behavior, character reformation (*tahdhīb al-akhlāq*), Spiritual Medicine (*ṭibb rūḥānī*) and Prophetic medicine (*ṭibb nabawī*) with varying ontologies were seen (Ragab, 2018). For example, the writings, and in some cases scholarly written responses to their contemporaries or predecessors such as Abū Bakr al-Rāzī (d.313 AH/925 CE), Ibn 'Alī b. Miskawayh (d.421 AH/1030 CE), Abū 'Alī alḤusayn b. Sīnā (d.428 AH/1037 CE), Abū alWalīd b. Rushd (d.594 AH/1198 CE), and later Abā Ḥāmid al-Ghazālī (d.510 AH/1111 CE), contributed to the diversity of Islamic intellectual discourse in addressing the physical (*ḥissī*), metaphysical (*ghaybī*) and rational (*'aqlī*) branches of knowledge. These conversations demonstrated the intersect and sometimes clashes between theology (*kalām*), law (*fiqh*), philosophy (*falsafah*), medicine (*Ṭibb/Ḥikmah*) and spirituality (*taṣawwuf*) contributing to the abundance of literature related to human cognition, behavior, emotions and spirituality despite the absence of a distinct field of psychology. More specifically, some of these discussions are found in al-Ghazālī's writings regarding the composition of the human psyche into *'aql*, *rūḥ*, and *nafs* (Keshavarzi & Haque, 2013). Meanwhile others such as Ibn Qayyim al-Jawziyyah discussed whether the *nafs* and *rūḥ* were truly distinct entities (al-Jawziyyah, 2002). *Ash'arīs* from among the theologians (*mutakallimīn*) discussed the role of the *'aql* and whether it was distinct from the *rūḥ*, and also whether it was physically localized in the heart. Some legal jurists maintained that the mind is localized to the brain (al-Bayjūrī, 2002).

As a result of this rich scholarship, developments in the Muslim world led to a diversification of health systems that included conversations between the various sectors of human services, including the formation of the *zāwiyah*, *khānqah*, *madrasah*, *ḥakīms* and hospitals (*bīmāristāns*) (Koenig & Shohaib, 2014; Ragab, 2015). This carried on into the Ottoman era, where even the architectural designs of Ottoman hospitals were carefully constructed to elicit a positive experience conducive to healing and promoting psychological relief (Sengul, 2015) and the traditional *madrasah* (Islamic seminaries) contained medical colleges within them. These hospitals were funded through the central treasury (*bayt al-māl*) and through charitable contributions and endowments (*awqāf*) serving as the training clinics adjacent to these medical colleges. Complementary to this, in the Indian subcontinent the works of Aḥmad al-Fārūqī al-Sirhindī (d.1033 AH/1624 CE) and Shāh Walī Allah al-Dihlawī (d.1175 AH/1772 CE) continued to focus on the role of spirituality in perfecting human well-being.

European Advancements in Clinical Psychology and Secularization

While the Muslim world was developing a rich body of literature and scholarship that integrated the core Islamic sciences with psychosocial well-being, European intellectual heritage was emerging from the Dark Ages and entering the Renaissance. Eventually, developments in the pre-modern era, headed by positivists and British empiricists, led to the precursors of contemporary modern medical practice rooted in scientific advancement and separation of religion. Throughout the Enlightenment and into the modern era there were a number of significant scientific achievements and advances. Specializations within the sciences gave rise to discoveries in medical practice that surpassed the science of the medieval period. However, the greatest loss during such intellectual growth was the discarding of theology from the contextual or worldly sciences. An inability to reconcile the mind–body problem ultimately led to the loss of Christian scholastic theologians and the eventual abandonment of metaphysics in exchange for the dominance of a physicalist monism (see Chapter 4). In this climate, the merits of psychology/psychiatry were evaluated through the medical model rooted in reductionist secular empiricism and more recent post-modernist reforms that marginalized the spiritually adherent. In fact, Sigmund Freud purported that religion was a psychologically imaginative way of being able to cope with the anxiety of life (Chapman, 2007). Later B. F Skinner and John B. Watson, leading the behavioral revolution, followed suit in taking on an extreme rejection of anything that could not be studied through observation, thereby completely abandoning discussion of the metaphysical (Badri, 1979). Additionally, Prest and Keller (1993, p. 139) said: "Priests should stay out of therapy and therapists should stay out of spirituality." Even with the post-modern era challenges to reductionism, influential post-modern theorists such as Carl Rogers maintained a disdain for religion within psychological practice (Rogers, 1961).

Response to the Secularization of Psychology and Behavioral Sciences by Muslim Psychologists in the Modern Era

In 1979 Malik Badri published *The Dilemma of Muslim Psychologists* as a response to the exclusion of faith from the field of psychology and behavioral sciences. Badri (1979), continuing the conversation started by Isma'īl Rājī al-Fārūqī (d.1986) on Islamic thought and knowledge, highlighted the incompatibility of a reductionist, ultra-behavioral, secular tradition among some other theoretical orientations with Islamic belief, particularly in a science that dealt with the human psyche once translated as the "soul". Such modalities were also imported into the Muslim world and rapidly became stigmatized, they psychopathologized Muslim culture and were rejected by a large segment of the communities they attempted to serve, contributing to the stigma of mental health left over from the colonial era.

Some of these Muslim proponents of Islamic psychologies highlighted the historical Muslim eras that demonstrated the absence of an irreconcilable dilemma between science, reason and faith. Despite historical tension at times between physicians and theologians, their respective domains were largely respected, and at times accommodations (*rukhaṣ*) were made for medically proven interventions that would not be acceptable for recreational use to be utilized medicinally. For example, permissions were granted by Jurists (*fuqahā'*) for normatively sanctioned music therapies to be utilized in hospitals treating the mentally ill. In the fifteenth century Edirne Mental Hospital in Turkey, music therapies were utilized in a treatment facility located next to a *madrasah* (Sengul, 2015), resulting in juxtaposition of the contemporary sciences and traditional Islamic disciplines. Such interactions between the scholars of the sacred tradition (*'Ulamā'*) and scholars of contextual sciences led to the benefits of addressing human health within the spiritual context of its adherents. It also demonstrated the robustness and capacity for the Islamic tradition to handle and respond to the various contextual and societal developments and challenges of human civilization.

In the late twentieth century there were several Muslim psychologists who made attempts at the "Islamization" of modern psychology. These attempts led to other academic endeavors such as the creation of an Islamically oriented psychology program at the International Islamic University in Kuala Lumpur, Malaysia and emerging publications from the International Institute of Islamic Thought (IIIT). Though much of these efforts often remained at the theoretical level, Badri and others paved the way for the emerging interest among Muslim psychologists to advance and champion their own traditions.

Meanwhile in Western Europe, and even more so in the United States, since the beginning of the twenty-first century, there has been an emergence of spiritual psychologies that has led to an openness to explore faith-based modalities and frameworks for application with the religiously observant (Pargament, 2007; Richards & Bergin, 2014). This has led to spiritual psychology concentrations in some graduate training programs in the US as well as the addition of the psychology of religion (division 36 of the American Psychological Association) in 1976. For Muslims, the International Association of Muslim Psychologists (IAMP), as well as the recent establishment and success of the International Association of Islamic Psychology (IAIP) headed by Malik Badri, bears witness to this shift. In this more open climate, investigations by Muslim psychologists and theologians have begun to explore Islamically oriented theoretical models of mental health care that are rooted in Islamic belief, though such an undertaking is significantly underdeveloped despite the growing need for mental health care (Haque, Khan, Keshavarzi, & Rothman, 2016).

Current State of Islam and Psychotherapy Research

There are two substantial reviews that have aptly summarized the current state of Islam and psychology publications. Haque, Khan, Keshavarzi and Rothman (2016) conducted a 10-year review (2006–2015) of the state of Islam and Psychology publications, and identified five major themes: (1) unification of Western theories with Islamic practices, (2) historical accounts of early Muslim scholarly writings on psychology, (3) development of Islamic theoretical models, (4) development of practical interventions and techniques, and (5) psychological scales and instruments normed on Muslim populations. In this review, the authors outlined an abundance of publications in the first two categories while evidencing a shortage of publications on themes 3 and 4. This review demonstrates what Badri (1979) originally pointed out, that many discussions of Islamic psychology are carried out within the context of modern Western paradigms, and thus are stuck in the "lizard's hole". Many of the contemporary "Islamic" models in theme 1 fall victim to the ills of being framed within the context of secular, post-modernist and reductionist empiricism.

In 2017 Kaplick and Skinner provided an alternative review that dated back a further 40 years and highlighted three major approaches to the topic in the literature: (1) the Islamic filter approach, (2) the Islamic psychology approach, and (3) the comparison approach. In Kaplick and Skinner's review, the comparison approach is similar to theme 1 in Haque et al. (2016), which further reinforces the dilemma of Muslim psychologists working with the parameters of Western psychological thought. Kaplick and Skinner described the filter approach as a modality of critiquing Western paradigms, while the Islamic psychology approach seeks to offer some kind of substantial response, although they agree with Haque et al. in their identification of the limited discussions around what such a response would entail, coupled with insufficient theoretical models and access to traditional Islamic sources.

Both reviews recognize the academic space and momentum created for Islamic psychology and the necessity among Muslims to create efforts designed to define and solidify Islamic psychology.

Traditional Islamically Integrated Psychotherapy (TIIP)

Traditional Islamically Integrated Psychotherapy was initiated in a publication by Keshavarzi and Haque (2013) that outlined a theoretical model of care as a uniquely Islamic and Muslim contribution by providing an integrative framework for psychological practice. It was originally published because the chief editor of this book ultimately penned his general orientation to psychotherapy, through his informal workgroups with Islamic theologians, to help fill a void in the literature and provide an appreciation of the Islamic tradition. This framework outlined an Islamic model of the human psyche rooted in Islamic foundations that allowed for contemporary psychological tools to be adapted and adopted into this framework.

TIIP is rooted in the prophetic principles that state: "Wisdom is the lost property of the believer, so wherever he finds it, he is most entitled to it" (al-Tirmidhī, 1970, 2687; Ibn Mājah, 2007, 4169). This prophetic tradition is very important in understanding TIIP's approach to contemporary secular psychologies. According to Islam, the fashioner of all created objects of observation is God Himself. Therefore, all created things follow a system or order that has been laid down by God (*Sunnat Allah*). The Qur'ān exhorts humanity to reflect and to observe the cosmos and nature (al-Qur'ān, 41:53; trans. Hammad), as seen in this verse: "Indeed, in the creation of the heavens and the earth and the alternation of the night and the daylight are signs of God's creative power for a those who are endowed with discretion and understanding and so heed admonition" (Qur'ān, 3:190; trans. Hammad). Muslims have been motivated by such Qur'ānic injunctions and have been engaged in discovering, observing and reflecting upon the creation of God for centuries, leading to countless discoveries (see Chapter 3). Thus, in understanding these verses and the prophetic tradition together, it is apparent that empirical or observational knowledge is an acceptable objective source of knowledge in Islam, and that irrespective of who observes scientific truths, Muslims can adopt, utilize and benefit from this knowledge since it is simply a descriptive observation of the will of God.

Additionally, the second part of the prophetic narration also leads us to conclude that not only can Muslims benefit from it, but, rather, they are most entitled to lay claim to that knowledge. They are most entitled to it on account of the fact that people of faith can appropriate that knowledge within an epistemological framework that reconciles empirical knowledge or signs (*āyāt*) mentioned above with the signs (*āyāt*) of revelation, since the source of both is God Himself (see Chapter 1). This alludes to the necessary and inseparable connection between the metaphysical and physical. These sources of knowledge have been articulated by Sunni discursive theologians and it is upon this foundation that TIIP rests (see Chapter 1). Therefore, TIIP draws upon Islamic core principles while integrating those aspects of behavioral science that are established empirical truths and filtering the admissibility of non-empirical truths through Islamic theology. This is what makes TIIP integrative, as it contains the flexibility and robustness to draw upon the behavioral sciences while remaining loyal to an Islamic orientation.

The qualification of "traditional" in TIIP is in reference to the *ahl al-sunnah wa-l-jamā'ah*. This is not for divisive purposes but rather academic honesty in labeling the foundations of the Islam that TIIP is referring to. Islamically integrated psychotherapy, as evidenced by a publication by Carrie York al-Karam (2018), is a broader and more general term that encompasses a diversity of approaches to and models of Islamic psychotherapy. Carrie York al-Karam's publication provides a still general, yet denominational approach to the subject matter with chapters from various Muslim practitioners that have described their general approach to the integration of spirituality into psychotherapy. The publication does not aim to provide any specific framework that organizes all chapters. Keshavarzi and Khan (2018), two editors of the present volume, are also contributing authors to York al-Karam's edited publication, providing a general case illustration of TIIP.

The present volume provides the first comprehensive discussion of TIIP's theoretical underpinnings and therapeutic assumptions/goals. It provides Muslim practitioners with a specific, theoretically organized, structured and unified approach for the practice of psychotherapy within an Islamic context. Therefore, the initial chapters lay heavy emphasis on the philosophical and theoretical aspects of this model that define and provide justification for its foundations, prior to presenting case illustrations. It should be kept in mind that this publication does not provide a manualized approach to TIIP; such endeavors and empirical support for this model may emerge over time. The qualification of a Sunni framework allows TIIP to coherently outline its sources, such that generalizations of TIIP's assumptions cannot be assumed across other sects of Islam. Many Muslims' utilization of the term "Islam" may include shi'ite, Ismā'īlī, and modernist approaches to religion, and thus may not agree with some of our sourcing or the stream of knowledge within the Islamic intellectual heritage that we draw from, on account of the diversity of the global Muslim community. Therefore, the "traditional" aspect of TIIP sets the parameters of this model of psychotherapy or Islamic psychology within the Sunni classical scholarly tradition. Having said this, it is important to note that the Sunni tradition is also not monolithic, and there is considerable diversity of scholarship and perspectives that contribute to the richness of this legacy, as demonstrated above.

While TIIP's epistemological framework is an agreed upon foundation of Sunni theology, its ontological framework is one that has been selected and extracted from Sunni scholarship and relies heavily on the dominant positions of the *Ahl al-Sunnah wa-l-Jamā'ah*. Therefore, the ontological framework adopted in TIIP is not the only human ontological framework, but rather there are many within the Sunni tradition that have been theorized differently. The authors have attempted to adopt a framework in the interest of providing clinicians and academics with a common language within this framework that would assist us in conducting follow-up research to this book, permit case conceptualizations, and help with training students and professionals.

Overview of the Chapters of the Book

The book is divided into three larger segments. Part I provides the basic foundations of TIIP. Chapter 1 is perhaps the most important chapter, providing the core foundations of an Islamic epistemology and the mechanisms for evaluating the strength of evidence. It provides a classification of different types of sources of knowledge and later moves on to provide the ontological schema of the human psyche adopted by TIIP. Chapter 2 builds upon this foundation and provides a discussion of the role and scope of practice for a TIIP practitioner. It also discusses proposed core competencies for mental health providers aspiring to provide TIIP.

Part II provides an overall appreciation of the Islamic intellectual heritage. Chapter 3 provides some illustrations and sampling of the ideas and writings of early Islamic scholars, particularly of the medieval medical tradition on the subject matter of human psychology. Chapter 4 addresses the historic mind and body dilemma and provides some potential reconciliations to this dilemma in light of Sunni theology. This chapter provides the richness of the oft-omitted Islamic scholarly discussions on the mind–body problem that is rarely discussed or presented.

Part III deals with assessment and case conceptualization. Chapter 5 provides a qualitative as well as quantitative assessment methodology along with treatment planning of TIIP across sessions. This format is designed to assist practitioners and trainees in assessment of domains according to TIIP. Chapter 6 provides an examination of the role of dreams and dream interpretation in both understanding the psyche of the patient, as well as its potential role in therapeutic intervention. The chapters in Part IV address the ontological schematic domains of the human psyche outlined in Chapter 1. Though it is impossible to completely separate all of these aspects from each other given overlap and the fact that a human being exists as a whole, these sections are designed to help readers understand the conceptual differences between *ʿaql*, *rūḥ*, *nafs* and *iḥsās*, and accompanying interventions that work on these domains of the human psyche. Each of these chapters provides an overview of these terms, with their respective usages, definitions and conceptualizations. Following a description of the "what", the authors of these chapters have provided practical strategies and techniques that can be implemented in psychotherapy, concluding with a concrete case illustration of one of these types of techniques.

Conclusion

It is hoped that this book will be a means of assisting many of our colleagues, students, researchers, academics and professionals in providing a coherent model of care that can be translated into practical clinical application. We hope that this will be a catalyst for research-oriented practitioners to advance TIIP by conducting empirical investigations of interventions that are rooted in TIIP. TIIP is still an emerging, evolving and growing theoretical orientation to psychotherapy, and we see it as a movement in which all can partake. It is through the collective investment in contributing this line of research that will advance TIIP's scientific and clinical rigor. We pray that Allah the Sublime accept this book from us as a service for His sake, and as a demonstration of the beauty of the illumination of our scholarly works whose source of light is the light of our Master Prophet Muḥammad (may the peace and blessings of Allah be upon him), thereby enlightening anyone whom his blessed light of truth touches. As an Islamic tradition says: "Be mindful of the foresight of the believer, for indeed he sees with the light of God."

References

al-Balkhī, A. Z. (2013). *Sustenance of the soul*, trans. M. Badri. London: International Institute of Islamic Thought.

al-Bayjūrī, A. (2002). *Ḥāshiyat al-Imām al-Bayjūrī 'alā Jawharat al-Tawḥīd*. Cairo: Dār al-Salām.

al-Jawziyyah, I. (2002). *Kitāb al-Rūḥ*. Cairo: Dār al-Qadd al-Jadīd.

al-Tirmidhī, M. (1970). *Jāmi' al-Tirmidhī*. Riyadh: Darrusalam.

Awaad, R., & Ali, S. (2016). Obsessional disorders in al-Balkhi's 9th century treatise: Sustenance of the body and soul. *Journal of Affective Disorders*, *180*, 185–189.

Badri, M. (1979). *The dilemma of Muslim psychologists*. London: MWH London Publishers.

Chapman, C. N. (2007). *Freud, religion and anxiety*. Lulu.com.

Haque, A., Khan, F., Keshavarzi, H., & Rothman, A. (2016). Integrating islamic traditions in modern psychology: Research trends in last ten years. *Journal of Muslim Mental Health*, *10*(1), 75–100.

Ibn Mājah, M. (2007). *Sunan Ibn Mājah*, Ed. H. Khaṭṭāb. Riyadh: Darussalam.

Kaplick, P., & Skinner, R. (2017). The evolving Islam and psychology movement. *European Psychologist*, *22*(3), 198–204.

Keshavarzi, H., & Haque, A. (2013). Outlining a psychotherapy model for enhancing Muslim mental health within an Islamic context. *International Journal for the Psychology of Religion*, *23*(3), 230–249.

Keshavarzi, H., & Khan, F. (2018). Outlining a case illustration of Islamically integrated psychotherapy. In C. York al-Karam, *Islamically Integrated Psychotherapy* (pp. 175–207). West Conshohocken, PA: Templeton Press.

Koneig, H., & Shohaib, S. (2014). *Health and well-being in Islamic societies.* New York, NY: Springer.

Pargament, K. I. (2007). *Spiritually integrated psychotherapy: Understanding and addressing the sacred.* New York, NY: Guilford Press.

Prest, L. A., & Keller, J. F. (1993). Spirituality and family therapy: Spiritual beliefs, myths, and metaphors. *Journal of Marital and Family Therapy, 19*(2), 137–148.

The gracious Quran: A modern-phrased interpretation in English (2009). Trans. A. Z. Hammad. Lisle, IL: Lucent Interpretations.

Ragab, A. (2015). *The Medieval Islamic hospital: Medicine, religion, and charity.* Cambridge, UK: Cambridge University Press.

Ragab, A. (2018). *Piety and patienthood in medieval Islam.* London: Taylor & Francis.

Richards, P. S., & Bergin, A. E. (Eds.). (2014). *Handbook of psychotherapy and religious diversity*, 2nd ed. Washington, DC: American Psychological Association.

Rogers, C. R. (1961). *On becoming a person: A psychotherapists view of psychotherapy.* New York, NY: Houghton Mifflin.

Sengul, E. (2015). Edirne sultan Beyazid II hospital. *Turkish Neuro-Excursion, 25*(1), 1–8.

York al-Karam, C. (2018). *Islamically integrated psychotherapy: Uniting faith and professional practice.* West Conshohocken, PA: Templeton Press.

Part I

Foundations of Traditional Islamically Integrated Psychotherapy (TIIP)

Chapter 1

Foundations of Traditional Islamically Integrated Psychotherapy (TIIP)

Hooman Keshavarzi and Bilal Ali

Chapter Summary

This chapter introduces the basic foundations of Traditional Islamically Integrated Psychotherapy (TIIP). TIIP is a psychotherapeutic framework that is rooted in an inherently Islamic foundation. Its epistemological foundations are sourced in the Sunni Islamic intellectual and spiritual tradition and offer a reconciliatory holistic approach to the construction of a spiritually integrated psychology that draws from empirical, rational, and revelatory sources. TIIP also draws from the Islamic intellectual heritage in outlining a proposed ontological composition of the human psyche, drives, nature, health, pathology, and its treatment. Psychological interventions arise as a natural consequence of attempting to restore the health of the human psyche (psycho-spiritual equilibrium) through working on the appropriate components of the psyche that are consistent with a TIIP diagnostic formulation. This formulation includes an assessment of the dominant locus of the source of pathology in the primary components of the human psyche that include the *nafs* (behavioral inclinations), *'aql* (cognition), *rūḥ* (spirit), or secondary emotional expressions of the primary components *(iḥsās)*. Thus, interventions that target these components can either be (a) inherently Islamic interventions found solely within the Islamic intellectual heritage or (b) Islamic adaptations of mainstream psychologies that are consistent with TIIP principles and goals. The ultimate goal is the nurturance of equilibrium across all components of the human psyche that lead to an integrative whole or unity of being (*ittiḥād*) that is accompanied by a healthy heart (*qalb salīm*).

A Classical Islamic Epistemological Framework for Integrating Secular and Sacred Sciences

In a traditional Islamic epistemological framework, "Islamic" issues are divided into those that relate to faith, i.e. foundational (*aṣlī*) or theological (*i'tiqādī*) issues, and those that relate to practice, i.e. subsidiary (*far'ī*) or practical (*'amalī*) issues (al-Taftāzānī, 2000, pp. 13–14). The knowledge of the former is what defines the classical field of study called *'aqīdah* (creed) while the latter comprises the science referred to as *fiqh* (law). For both creedal and legal issues, Islamic scholastic theologians assert that knowledge of things is attainable for humans by means of three sources: reliable sensory or empirical evidence (*ḥawāss salīmah*), reason (*'aql*), and truthful reports (*khabar ṣādiq*) (al-Nasafī, 2013) (see Figure 1.1). The sense-knowledge that traditional Islamic scholastic theologians refer to is the sensory evidence acquired by means of observation that informs what is referred to today as empirical study, a cornerstone of the scientific method. The second knowledge source, reason (*'aql*), refers to the primordial, a priori human faculty that is capable – when all senses are healthy – of realizing not only the probabilistically true but also certain necessary truths (al-Taftāzānī, 2000, p. 81). When a rational conclusion is self-evident and intuitive, such as the whole of something being greater than its part, such rationally established knowledge is called necessary knowledge (*ḍarūrī*), while rational conclusions requiring deduction through evidence, such as the conclusion upon observing smoke that there must be fire, are called acquired knowledge (*iktisābī*) (al-Bazdawī, 2014, p. 23; al-Nasafī, 2013, pp. 70–71). Knowledge acquired through truthful reports (*khabar ṣādiq*) is also divisible into similar categories: (1) reports that establish knowledge necessarily (*ḍarūrī*) due to their self-evident veracity, and (2) reports that establish knowledge through evidence-based deduction (*istidlālī*), such as those reports transmitted by prophets whose prophethood is corroborated by miracles. Knowledge in this category includes divine revelation (*waḥy*) and is the sole source of knowledge available to humans which provides insight into the empirically and rationally inaccessible, i.e. the unseen (*ghayb*). Reliable and unadulterated reports of

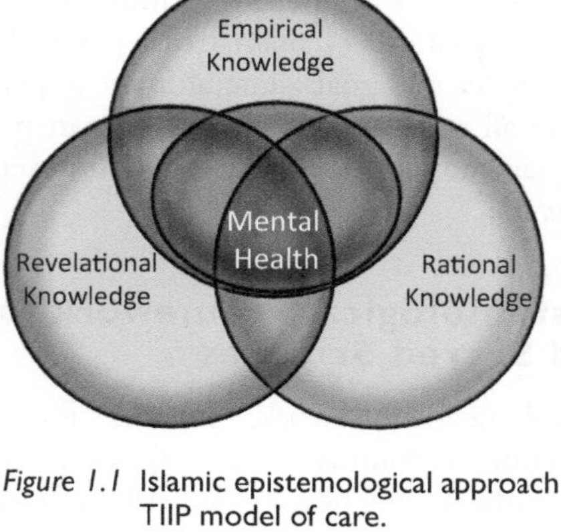

Figure 1.1 Islamic epistemological approach used to guide the development of the TIIP model of care.

revelation are accessible today in two forms: (1) the Qur'ān, or recited revelation (*waḥy matluww*), and (2) the *Ḥadīth* (prophetic tradition), or non-recited revelation (*waḥy ghayr matluww*). While both are harmonious with other sources of knowledge, and in fact provide humans access to a higher form of rationality, they also more importantly deliver otherwise unknowable knowledge, i.e. knowledge not accessible through empirical data and analytical reasoning. The utilization of this source of knowledge, namely divine revelation, represents perhaps the greatest divergence between the two epistemic frames of modern psychology and cognitive neuroscience on the one hand and Islamic theology on the other, whereby the former dismisses the admissibility of such information in both the building of models and in methods of practice.

In an Islamic epistemology, all of the three above sources of knowledge are understood to be legitimate and harmonious knowledge sources. Any contradictions (*taʿāruḍ*) between conclusions originating in these sources are understood to be only apparent and demand resolution through (1) reconciliation (*taṭbīq*), (2) abrogation (*naskh*), or (3) interpretation (*ta'wīl*) (Farfūr, 2002, ʿAbd al-Laṭīf, p. 155). Such interpretive methods and harmonization between the various knowledge sources are in fact inherent to the Islamic intellectual tradition. For example, classical Qur'ānic exegetes had few qualms about proposing that the Qur'ānic verses that mention Allah's creation of the universe in six "*ayyām*" (lit. days) denote in their use of the term *ayyām* not the customary 24-hour cycle of day and night or simply daytime (as opposed to nighttime) (Ibn ʿĀbidīn, al-Ḥaṣkafī, & al-Nasafī, 2006), but broad and ambiguous "periods" of time due to the rational unlikelihood that *ayyām* is restricted to earthly, normative time. The classical attempt at synthesizing Qurʾānic texts with reason in a way that is accommodated by the language additionally allows for the accommodation of scientific theories on the timespan of the known universe (Usmani, n.d.). Thus, in an Islamic epistemology objective facts do not have a particular cultural origin. Scientific findings that can be safely regarded as objective fact, regardless of their Eastern or Western origin, are not to be disputed or hastily assumed to be at odds with divine revelation. As such, Muslim scholars should not find the task of synthesizing empirical findings on the brain's role in cognition with Islamic theologians' understandings of the heart and the spiritual self an impossible one. In fact, some Muslim jurists had no problem in suggesting that the metaphysical *ʿaql* is physically located in the brain on account of cognitive faculties being impaired through brain damage, despite the Qur'an's apparent attribution of cognitive faculties to the heart in Sūrat al-Ḥajj, verse 22 (al-Bāyjūrī, 2002, p. 273). Exegetes have offered several potential meanings to this verse that consider empirical information and reason. Meanwhile, the majority (*jumhūr*) of discursive theologians have maintained that the metaphysical *ʿaql* is localized to the heart, but its metaphysical light stimulates the cognitive faculties in the brain, thereby reconciling the conflict between empirical information, rationality, and revelation (al-Bāyjūrī, 2002, p. 273).

Another critical Islamic epistemological understanding to the process of integrating Islam and psychology is the hierarchic arrangement of knowledge into (1) the definitive/certain (*qaṭʿī*) and (2) the probabilistic/inferential (*ẓannī*). While both categories of knowledge may contribute to discussions of what is "Islamic", it is only evidence that is indisputably established (*qaṭʿī al-thubūt*) (such as reports transmitted through widely dispersed chains of narrators, or *tawātur*) and that lack ambiguity in their indication (*qaṭʿī al-dalālah*) that are considered definitive and objective "fact" (Farfur, 2002, pp. 17–30). Even statements sourced in divine revelation that do not meet the criterion of being both certain in establishment and in indication are to be considered *ẓannī*, and thereby disbelief in them does not constitute blasphemy or departure from the religion. A great number of claims made in Islamic texts, be they theological, legal, or ethical in nature, are in this category. While they contribute to definitions and understandings of what is "Islamic", issues of a *ẓannī* nature are open to contention. This does imply that probabilistic proofs do not constitute *ḥujjah*, or proof, in Islamic epistemology, only that the category of *ẓannī* is to be evaluated according to its degrees of probability, and that it affords a degree of flexibility in determining what is true and Islamic that *qaṭʿī* proofs do not.

This demarcation between the certain and probabilistic is critical in discussions of what defines "Islamic", especially in defining an Islamic psychology. The vast corpus of Islamic literature produced by Muslim theologians, exegetes, historians, jurists, and spiritual guides comprises a wide spectrum of both *qaṭʿī* and *ẓannī* issues. In theological discussions, for example, definitive claims of God's unity and the falsehood of polytheism may accompany subsidiary and probabilistic discussions of the nature of God's attributes. Similarly, Muslim theologians considered the existence of the *rūḥ* (soul) as certain, but discussions of its exact nature and its relation to other metaphysical components of the self to be probabilistic at best. Imam Shihāb al-Dīn Yaḥyā al-Suhrawardī (d.632 AH/1244 CE), an ascetic scholar, in his *ʿAwārif al-Maʿārif*, offers that it is permissible to discuss the nature of the *rūḥ* or metaphysical essence of the human being. However, it must be considered as a possible meaning (*ta'wīl*) and not an interpretation (*tafsīr*) of the Qurʾānic term asserted with certainty (*qaṭʿī*) (al-Suhrawardī, 1993, p. 243). Therefore, although ontological discussions of the relationship between the self, the soul, and the intellect have been proposed by Muslim philosophers throughout Islamic history and their models can be properly labelled as "Islamic", it would hardly be justified to consider such potentially falsifiable and probabilistic models as incontrovertible, or to consider any contention with such models as un-Islamic. While *ẓannī* discussions, even basic ethical considerations of everyday social behavior, have always been meaningful in defining Islam's civilizational code, a careless placement of issues within the Islamic epistemic hierarchy and the conflation of the certain with the probabilistic would put the confidence of Muslims in the "Islamic" tradition at risk. Further, such conflations would betray the flexibility of the traditional Islamic intellectual inclusivity of various bodies of knowledge, i.e. scientific, inductive, theoretical, philosophical, and theological, since considerations of its admissibility and context of its usage varies based upon strength of evidence (the *ẓannī* vs. the *qaṭʿī*). For example, usually only definitive (*qaṭʿī*) proofs are admissible in issues of creed, while predominant probable (*ẓannī*) truths can be readily considered in areas of Sufism and philosophy. A traditional Islamic epistemology therefore provides a reconciliatory model for the intersectionality between modern science and Islamic theology, as well as a collaborative platform for scholars of both the behavioral and cognitive sciences on the one hand and the sacred sciences of Islam on the other to discuss the admissibility and reconciliation of disparate bodies of information as they pertain to human cognition and the soul.

Additionally, it is critical to consider the doctrine of occasionalism held by Sunni theologians with respect to empirical information. It is imperative for Muslim scientists to know that the relationship between observed signs or patterns are correlational or occasional relationships, and not causal relationships (al-Taftāzānī, 2000, pp. 74–75). For example, the visual image displayed on the retina through incoming light photons as sensory impressions from the environment and translated into neural activities by the optic nerve are occasions (*asbāb*) of seeing the image, and are neither causal nor necessary. In fact, Sunni creed holds that Allah is the essential and true cause (*mu'aththir ḥaqīqī*) and that He has preeternally ordained that the image will be perceived by the perceiver at that time, in parallel to the coincidental independent occurrence of neural activity. Therefore, these incidents typically co-occur, and are known as the *sunnah* or patterns of Allah, but they are not necessary. Such co-occurring relationships may be absent in some cases, such as miracles that break the normal pattern of events. The doctrine of occasionalism thus holds that God Almighty is the origin of patterns and to omit this association amounts to disbelief, since God is inseparable from the scientific observations that we hold.

In discussions of developing an integrative Islamic psychology, another important epistemological consideration is the distinction between subjective and objective truths. For example, in cognitive neuro-scientific brain-mapping, despite mapping of particular cognitive processes to neural circuits in the brain with a great degree of specificity, the dilemma remains that individual experiences are subjective and inferential (see Chapter 4). Similarly, subjective experiences such as dreams or religious experiences (*mukāshafāt*) are personal in an Islamic epistemic framework. It is simply not possible to validate or falsify the subjective report of an individual, nor to make binding what is acquired through subjective evidence (al-Taftāzānī, 2000). Effectively, this epistemological consideration rules out the possibility of advancing a discipline or model of care rooted in dreams or the spiritual illuminations and inspirations of the pious. In an Islamic epistemology, only empirical evidence, reason, and revelation can establish "hard" facts. Having said this, an Islamic epistemology does not entirely discredit the value and role of personal reflection, spiritual experiences, or "soft" facts. Hence, while the ability to map subjective experiences to specific brain mechanisms does not allow us to make definitive and objective knowledge claims, it is nevertheless significant in clinical psychotherapy and case applications, and personal subjective experiences carry the potential to mediate or generate psychological growth and spiritual healing for the patient. Personal truths, divine inspirations, and spiritual experiences can be powerful forms of personal meaning and guidance for patients. Contemplative meditation (*murāqabah*), for example, used as a spiritual exercise or method of healing, may lead patients to subjective personal insights that can be mapped to particular areas of the brain. However, such personal experiences are valuable in so much as they subjectively enhance the psycho-spiritual welfare of the individual and are not necessarily useful in the creation of generally applied models of intervention. Understanding the distinction between the subjective and objective will enhance our ability to appreciate the differences between disparate sources of knowledge and to appropriate, reconcile, and synthesize different pieces of information into an Islamic epistemologically sound framework.

In sum, through an acknowledgement of all three valid knowledge sources as acceptable avenues for the acquisition of knowledge, and through a thorough consideration of all rational, sacred, and empirical evidence as being congruous, an Islamic epistemology makes it possible for scholars to produce a reliable framework of psychological treatment that is both holistic and Islamically integrated. Since compelling empirical evidence is not at odds with sacred knowledge in Islamic epistemology, and rather is an important aid in understanding sacred texts and in the adjudication of Islamic ethics and law (Qureshi & Padela, 2016), in the context of the behavioral sciences, empirically evidenced modalities of treatment, understandings of the human psyche, and biological bases of psychology are critical contributors to the integration of the sacred sciences with psychotherapeutic models and methods.

Within the broad spectrum of the sacred Islamic sciences, three foundational Islamic sciences necessarily inform elements of mental health practice: (1) scholastic theology (*kalām*) and creed (*'aqīdah*), (2) law (*fiqh* or *aḥkām*), and (3) spirituality (*taṣawwuf* or *akhlāq wa ādāb*). The first science addresses fundamental issues of Islamic belief, epistemology, metaphysics, and philosophy, and because of its foundational position in the sciences is referred to by some early scholars, such as Imām Abū Ḥanīfah Nu'mān b. Thābit (d.150 AH/767 CE), the eponymous founder of the Ḥanafī school of law, as the "greater science" (*fiqh akbar*). To Abū Ḥanīfah, law, despite its role in regulating human behavior, ethics, morality, ritual responsibilities, and religious dispensations, was nevertheless of relatively lesser importance compared to theology and creed and thus deserved the title "minor science" (*fiqh asghar*), sometimes referred to by others as the "science of the outer self" (*fiqh al-ẓāhir*). Interestingly, he ranked the sacred science of Islamic spirituality, which deals directly with the reformation of human non-legal behavior and the acquisition of noble character traits, between the former two sciences. Abū Ḥanīfah referred to this field of character reformation and acquisition of sound manners as the "median science" (*fiqh awṣaṭ*), which others would also come to refer as the science of the inner self (*fiqh al-bāṭin*), or ṣūfism (*taṣawwuf*). This sort of sacred trivium is also classically extracted from a renowned prophetic tradition, called the *Ḥadīth* of Jibrīl (*Ḥadīth* of Gabriel), in which the objectives of each field are explained by the Prophet (upon him blessings and peace) in response to the angel Jibrīl's questions about the reality of (1) *īmān* (belief), (2) *islām* (surrender), and (3) *iḥsān* (excellence), each respectively referring to issues of *'aqīdah*, *fiqh*, and *taṣawwuf*. For any field to be congruent with and contributive to the Sunni Islamic intellectual heritage, it is necessary that these three sacred sciences inform its composition (Figure 1.2).

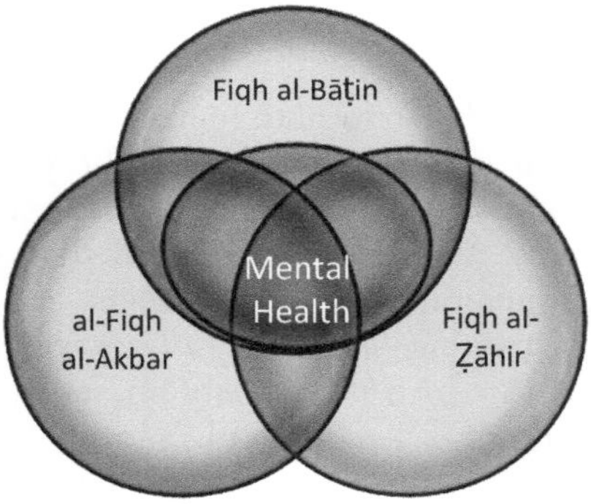

Figure 1.2 Core Islamic sciences that inform mental health care within an Islamic context.

Schema of Health and Pathology

In Islam, a person's ability to achieve true psycho-spiritual health rests on their actualization of their primordial purpose. Constructs of psycho-spiritual health in Islam assume that all human beings are created for an otherworldly purpose: To tread a path that will ultimately ensure salvation in the afterlife and the acquisition of God's pleasure. As salvation and divine pleasure are attainable only through the worship of God, health from an Islamic theological perspective is maintained by a firm adherence to a life worshipping God, and any obstacle that obstructs one's ability to tread this path of worship is detrimental to human functioning and warrants removal. There is a legal maxim that reinforces this notion that is oft-quoted: "whatever (religious obligation) cannot be fulfilled without it (i.e. its means to actualize the religious obligation) is compulsory." This legal maxim is used for several contingent actions associated with religious obligations but has also been evoked in determining whether proven medical treatment is considered obligatory to remove the obstacle of sickness, since physical and mental capacity are necessary to actualize religious aims (Qureshi & Padela, 2016). However, regardless of whether or not the absence of health meets a clinical threshold of a mental disorder or merits psychological intervention, a human being who is lacking in their ability to live a Godly life is considered psycho-spiritually unhealthy and dysfunctional. It is understood that psycho-spiritual health is akin to physical health in its variability, as the average human being oscillates from time to time between health and its absence, between optimal and suboptimal functioning. Unlike physical health, the pursuit of psycho-spiritual health is a lifelong endeavor and a human's default state is the absence of optimal health, but not necessarily sickness. The lifelong journey in pursuit of optimal psycho-spiritual health and functioning is met with occasions of spiritual or psychological impairment that result in a person's diversion from the path of God's obedience and adherence to divine directives.

Maintenance of psycho-spiritual health is critical to human functioning in Islam, more important in fact then the sustenance of the physical body. Exogenous psychological conditions that endanger psycho-spiritual health are thus to be treated seriously. A general treatment methodology articulated in the Islamic spiritual tradition is the development of resiliency by means of psycho-spiritual training (*tarbiyah*). *Tarbiyah* was traditionally conducted by spiritual mentors (*shaykhs* or *murabbīs*), individuals who themselves would have undergone a lengthy and rigorous course of psycho-spiritual training under the spiritual mentorship of their own *shaykhs*. This lengthy but often informal mentorship process resulted in their acquisition of spiritual coping mechanisms that allowed them to effectively manage the various stressors of daily life.

In modern psychiatric practice disorder is viewed quite differently from the TIIP model. The Diagnostic and Statistical Manual of Mental Disorders (DSM) (American Psychiatric Association, 2013) and the International Classification of Disorders (ICD) restrict the notion of mental illness to significant impairment of social, occupational, or familial functioning and afford marginal attention to character flaws that lie beneath the clinical threshold. Hence DSM and ICD clinical terminologies do not equate with Islamic conceptions of optimal mental health and dysfunction, and fail to speak to the impact of disorder upon a patient's spiritual, non-clinical status.

A fundamental difference between an exclusively clinical conception of dysfunction and Islamic holistic health is that Islam does not restrict dysfunction solely to the temporal world or to clinical impairment. As outlined above, character flaws that adversely impact a patient's afterlife are also taken into consideration, as well as such character traits that lead to poor functioning, even before they may become significantly impairing. Within an Islamic framework, clinical treatments are in service of the larger Islamic ethos and hence not restricted to symptom reduction or restoration of normative worldly functioning. These afterlife considerations should impact the perspectives and clinical decision-making of practitioners, including their selection of interventions. For example, while narcissistic traits may not meet the clinical threshold of narcissistic personality disorder, a practitioner using the TIIP model will nevertheless view the patient as suffering from spiritual pathological character flaws that may or may not merit treatment in a clinical setting.

The integrated Islamic therapist is ever aware of the prophetic warnings regarding the three spiritual "destroyers" (*muhlikāt*): "avarice (*shuḥḥ*) that is obeyed, material longing (*hawā*) that is complied with, and a man's admiration of himself (*iʿjāb al-mar' bi nafsihī*)" (al-Bazzār, 2009, *Ḥadīth* no. 729). (See also al-Mundhirī, 2003, *Ḥadīth* no. 394,3 in which he grades the *Ḥadīth* as fair, or *ḥasan*.) Additionally, the *Ḥadīths* inform that arrogance in the heart is an issue of critical concern as "he who has an atom's weight of arrogance in his heart will not enter the Garden" (Muslim, 2006, *Ḥadīth* no. 147 (91)). Thus, while a TIIP practitioner is aware that certain levels of self-admiration are not socially debilitating or clinical in severity, they are also aware that spiritual masters warned that self-admiration leads one down the path of arrogance (*kibr*) and that arrogance is the root of a multitude of spiritual diseases.

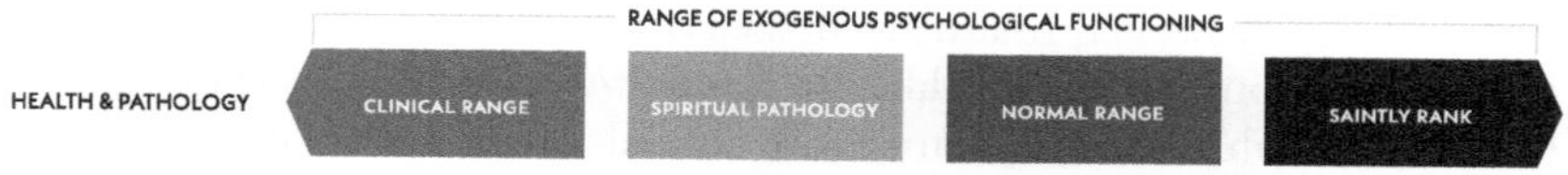

Figure 1.3 TIIP Schema of Health & Pathology.

In modern clinical practice, a formal treatment of character defects may potentially be viewed as ethically controversial. A proposed reconciliation would be to offer treatments of spiritual issues exclusively within the patient's religious frame of reference, treatments that are consistent with their self-identified treatment goals, and to avoid proselytizing or the suggestion of spiritual goals that are inconsistent with the patient's aims (Keshavarzi & Haque, 2013). The limits and scope of such a spiritually integrated practice is further discussed in Chapter 2.

Such a reconciliation is consistent with the growing trend of introducing spiritually oriented psychotherapies into mainstream health care practice (Richards, Saunders, Lea, McBride, & Allen, 2015) and the significant research that demonstrates the clinical efficacy and significantly better mental health outcomes of incorporating spirituality into psychological practice (Anderson, Heywood-Everett, Siddiqi, Wright, Meredith, & McMillan, 2015; Hook, Worthington, Davis, Jennings, Gartner, & Hook, 2010; McCullough, 1999; Smith, Bartz, & Richards, 2007; Worthington, Hook, Davis, & McDaniel, 2011; Worthington, Kurusu, McCullough, & Sandage, 1996; Worthington & Sandage, 2001). In fact, Cloninger (2004) makes the argument that people who are naturally inclined to desire deeper meaning in their lives as they face the inevitable reality of sickness, suffering, and mortality can find lasting satisfaction and health only in spiritual approaches to well-being. Through spirituality, he asserts, one can find hope and meaning in life that helps reduce vulnerability and increases resilience to clinical pathologies (Cloninger, 2004).

The TIIP Ontological Model of the Human Psyche

There is a general agreement in Islamic scholarship upon a dualistic composition of the human being into outer (*ẓāhir*) and inner (*bāṭin*) self, or the physical self on the one hand and the metaphysical or subtly physical self on the other. Scholars such as Fakhr al-Dīn al-Rāzī (d.595 AH/1210 CE) make reference to a human component that they call the *laṭīfah rabbāniyyah*, or the human divine subtle essence (the heavenly soul), and by which they appear to refer to the human metaphysical element (al-Rāzī, 2008, Sūrat al-Shu'arā', verse 78). According to the renowned scholar-mystic and Islamic reviver Abū Ḥāmid al-Ghazālī (d.510 AH/1111 CE), this metaphysical *laṭīfah rabbāniyyah* is distinct, yet has a relationship with and connection to the physical (heart) and is the general construct used to describe a unitary essence that has multiple expressions such as the metaphysical *rūḥ/qalb*, *nafs*, and *'aql*. However, Imām al-Ghazālī offers that the physical heart that is the direct home of the gas-like life force (*rūḥ*), referred to as *rūḥ ḥayawānī* by Imām al-Suhrawardī, is shared with animals and is not unique to human beings. For al-Ghazālī, the *rūḥ* that is the life force or *rūḥ ḥayawānī* is separate from the metaphysical *rūḥ* of the *laṭīfah rabbāniyyah*. Similarly, the metaphysical heart or *qalb* is separate yet interacts with the physical heart. The physical heart, fueled by the *rūḥ ḥayawānī*, governs the mobilizing human life force while the *laṭīfah rabbāniyyah* governs the human metaphysical element or "mind". Thus, the unique entity that distinguishes human beings from animals is the *laṭīfah rabbāniyyah*.

Imām al-Suhrawardī offers that the metaphysical *qalb* is the locus of the human being, and bears the resultant effects of health and dysfunction conferred upon it by the actions of the other elements of the metaphysical essence (i.e. *ʿaql*, *rūḥ*, and *nafs*). Al-Suhrawardī relates this to the etymology of the word *qalb* in the Arabic language, which means to change, turn or shift (al-Suhrawardī, 1993, p. 248). Just as the physical heart becomes physically sick due to poor lifestyle and diet, so does the metaphysical heart thrive or become sick as a result of good or bad actions. This separation between the two also resolves the potential implicit objection that the metaphysical heart (*qalb*), if it were to be synonymous with the physical heart, could be removed through a heart transplant. The nineteenth-century Ashʿarī scholastic theologian Ibrāhīm al-Bayjūrī (d.1245 AH/1860 CE) summarizes the dominant position amongst scholastic theologians in that the *laṭīfah rabbāniyyah* expresses itself in three primary forms: (1) the *rūḥ*, which serves as a person's life force, (2) the *ʿaql*, or manifestations of human rational/cognitive faculties, and (3) the *nafs*, which manifests in the form of behavioral inclinations and animalistic/survival drives (al-Bayjūrī, 2002, pp. 272–273). Regardless of its expressions (*iʿtibārāt*) in this ontology, the *laṭīfah rabbāniyyah* is part of a unitary metaphysical essence that is separate, yet connected to the physical body, which includes the physical heart and brain.

There are slight differences between the conceptualizations of al-Bayjūrī's and al-Ghazālī in that, according to the latter, the *rūḥ* of the *laṭīfah rabbāniyyah* is different than the *rūḥ* that is the life force of the human being. Al-Ghazali views the *rūḥ ḥayawānī* as the motivating life force for the physical body, while the primary governing agent of the *laṭīfah rabbāniyyah* is the *rūḥ ʿulwī samāwī*. Al-Ghazālī also views the lower *nafs* that contains predatory/hedonistic impulses as being more closely associated with the physical body, and not part of this sublime metaphysical essence, i.e. *laṭīfah rabbāniyyah*. For Ghazali, the *nafs* in general are seen more as descriptive stages of the elevation of the human soul and not true independent components. For example, the soul starts out in *nafs ammārah*, then moves to *nafs lawwāmah*, and then to *nafs muṭmaʾinnah* (see Figure 1.4). However, they both converge on the notion that the *laṭīfah rabbāniyyah* is the metaphysical essence that is embedded within and effectuates the body (al-Ghazālī, 1990, pp. 131).

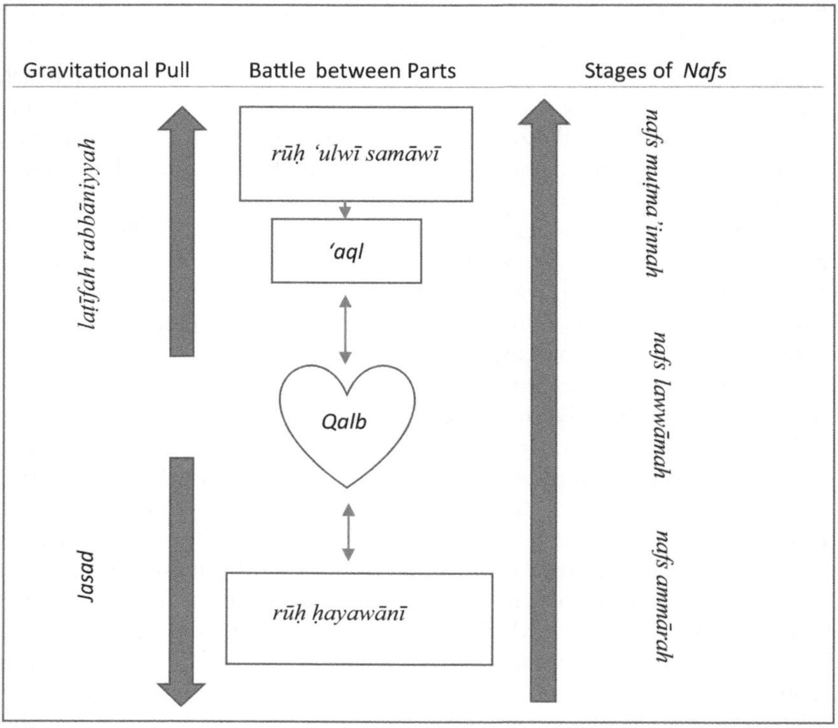

Figure 1.4 Summary of competing drives and associated psychological elements/factors.

Whether the metaphysical essence is entirely metaphysical or a subtle substance has also been debated by Islamic scholars. The position of Imām al-Ḥaramayn al-Juwaynī (d.470 AH/1085 CE), an earlier prominent Ash'ārī theologian, is that the human inner self is not entirely metaphysical but is instead subtly physical, or a subtle substance (*jism laṭīf*) (Brown, 2013, pp. 2–3). 'Aḍud al-Dīn al-Ījī (d.756 AH/1356 CE), on the other hand, asserts that it is a non-localized, completely non-physical entity (*jawhar mujarrad*). Imām al-Suhrawardī, in his *'Awārif al-Ma'ārif*, summarizes these various different positions of the discursive theologians on this topic including whether the soul is eternal (*qadīm*) or created/finite (*ḥādith*), but finally offers a bifurcation of the human being into a metaphysical life force (*rūḥ ḥayawānī basharī*) that operates at the level of the physical body, and metaphysical divine essence (*rūḥ 'ulwī samāwī*) that contains spiritual drives in the human being as an elevated spiritual essence (al-Suhrawardī, 1993, p. 247).

Imam al-Suhrawardī's conceptualization largely supports Ghazali's conceptual framework and is complementary to the one discussed by al-Bayjūrī above. Imām al-Suhrawardī categorizes the three components of the *laṭīfah rabbāniyyah* into two broad categories by associating the primitive drives (*shahwah/ghaḍab)* of the *nafs* with the *rūḥ ḥayawānī*, while the *rūḥ 'ulwī samāwī* is a more general supradivine essence that contains the faculty of the *'aql*. Al-Suhrawardī ultimately discusses this as the competing drives between the divine (*rūḥ samāwī/'aql*) and animalistic impulses (*nafs ammārah/rūḥ ḥayawānī*) of the human being. Thus *'aql* serves the cognitive and executive functions of helping actualize the aims of *rūḥ 'ulwī samāwī* through knowledge acquisition, reflection, and restraint over impulses. Ḥārith al-Muḥāsibī similarly notes that one of the linguistic connotations of *'aql* is restraint (*imtin'a*) over impulses (al-Muḥāsibī, 1971). An ascetic-scholar of the seventeenth century, Imam Aḥmad al-Sirhindī (d.1012 AH/1624 CE) emphasizes, however, that imperceptibility of truth is largely a result of the pollution of the animalistic desires. By garnering impulse control, intuitive knowledge faculties can be actualized. He believes that mere reflection and education is too narrow a pathway toward knowledge acquisition; rather, focus should be placed on restraint of the carnal desires (Er, 2016, p. 83).

As already mentioned, al-Suhrawardī seems to suggest a bidirectional influence whereby the life force (*rūḥ ḥayawānī*) and animalistic carnal desires (*shahwah*) are embedded within the physical body (al-Suhrawardī, 1993, p. 247). This is similar to al-Ghazālī's separation of *rūḥ* of the life force that is embedded within the physical body and sourced in the physical heart and the *rūḥ* of the *laṭīfah rabbāniyyah* that is divinely and heavenly sourced. Thus, actions at the level of the *nafs ammārah* operate at the primitive instinctual bodily/animalistic level and emit their negative influences on the metaphysical heart or *qalb*, consequently blackening it. The battle between the faculty of *'aql* as a tool of the *rūḥ 'ulwī samāwī* with the *nafs ammārah* as a manifestation of the influence of the *rūḥ ḥayawānī* leads to the different stages of growth. Stage-wise ascension toward *nafs lawwāmah* and *nafs muṭma'innah* is evidence of the *'aql/rūḥ 'ulwī samāwī*'s defeat of the beastly desires of the *nafs ammārah/rūḥ ḥayawānī* (al-Ghazālī, 1990, p. 131).

A seventeenth-century Ḥanafī jurist and traditionist, Mullā 'Alī al-Qārī (d.1014 AH/1605 CE) reinforces the notion of competing pulls between the celestial divine drives and the carnal drives in his *Mirqāt al-Mafātīḥ*, a commentary on the famous *Ḥadīth* collection of Imām al-Tabrayzī's *Miskhāt al-Maṣābīḥ*, wherein he states that the metaphysical (*laṭīf*) *nafs* is born out of the marriage and interconnection between the metaphysical *rūḥ* (i.e. *rūḥ samāwī*) and the body (i.e. *rūḥ ḥayawānī* as mentioned above). He states that the *rūḥ (samāwī*) is celestially oriented and the bodily drives pull toward darkness and evil ('Alī al-Qārī, 2015, pp. 376–377). He states that the *nafs* therefore contains both competing drives, and in support of this he cites the Qur'ānic verse: "and by the *nafs* and He who proportioned it (*sawwā-hā*), and inspired it with (the potential for) evil and righteousness" (98:7–8). Thus, by overcoming the hedonistic bodily drives and training it, the *nafs* can become subservient and in correspondence to the demands of the *rūḥ samāwī/ 'aql* and elevate above its beastly impulses to *nafs muṭma'innah*. Inversely, just as the carnal drives can blacken and neglect the celestial drives, spiritually radiant energies emerging from the metaphysical *qalb* can positively affect the body/brain which arises out of the *rūḥ 'ulwī samāwī* aspect of the *laṭīfah rabbāniyyah*. Thus, there exists a battle and tension between the pulls of carnal drives and desires within the body competing with divine directives and the desire for transcendence.

However, irrespective of whether the *laṭīfah rabbāniyyah* is considered to be purely metaphysical or physical, eternal or created, all of the Muslim theologians seem to agree in considering this essence as distinct from the physical body, despite being connected and inseparable from it. What follows is that the *'aql*, or cognition, in traditional Islamic understandings cannot be the function of the physical brain alone, even if some Muslim physicians and jurists seem to assume this (al-Bayjūrī, 2002, pp. 272–273). It would appear that the soundest understanding of human cognition (*'aql*) is that it originates in the *laṭīfah rabāniyyah* and is a vessel or tool of *rūḥ samāwī*, which may be situated in the vicinity of the heart (*qalb*). However, as empirical evidence and cognitive neuroscience demonstrates, its executive cognitive capacities are expressed through the brain. How would Islamic scholastic theologians reconcile this understanding with the dominant Māturīdī and Ash'arī conceptualization of the *'aql* as a distinct element from the brain while also asserting that the *'aql* is the central locus of cognitive capacity?

For those physicians and jurists who say the *'aql* is synonymous with the brain, this question is not an issue and they utilize such empirical proof to form the basis of their conclusion that the *'aql* is the brain. However, those who hold the dominant position, and maintain that the *'aql* is a distinct metaphysical element from the brain, acknowledge that the brain is related to the *'aql* but that it is merely a prerequisite for the expression of the *'aql*'s cognitive capacities (al-Bayjūrī, 2002, pp. 272–273). Al-Ghazālī further supports this by offering that the brain is merely an instrument that is used by the metaphysical essence, created to actualize its primary aim of gnosis or awareness of the Divine through the medium of contemplation, thinking, memory, imaginative capacities, and other cognitive activities (al-Ghazālī, 2011, pp. 24–25). In the same way that sexual drives (*shahwah*) are manifested through the sexual organs, cognition is manifested through the brain. Just as the heart pumps blood to the sexual organs, it also pumps blood to the physical brain, fulfilling the anatomical conditions for the full expression of cognitive capacities. Thus, through such a unified understanding of *laṭīfah rabbāniyyah*, the dilemma typically encountered by proposing that cognition is situated in the heart is curbed. It can be said that although the heart may be the proximate place of the metaphysical essence that communicates cognitive expressions through the *ʿaql*, the brain is a requirement for and the location of the manifestation of these cognitive faculties (al-Bayjūrī, 2002, p. 273).

It must be appreciated that the existence of an inner metaphysical self is a matter of certainty in Islam, while the specifics of its nature is probabilistic (*ẓannī*). Sometimes this inner self is expressed simply as a person's *rūḥ*, and the Qurʾān makes clear the human inability to access its exact nature in the sūrah of al-Isrā', verse 85. Thus, the TIIP adoption and specification of a particular ontological framework provides us with a schema for conceptualizing the human psyche while maintaining its probabilistic nature. Similarly, despite the ambiguity as to its nature and the inability of humans to make definitive claims as to its parts, scholars throughout Islam's history have proposed plausible ontological models of this inner self. Shāh Walī Allah, for example, has even attempted to localize and specify greater aspects of the metaphysical components of the human being in his discussion of the *laṭāʾif* or sutble essences (Walī Allah, 2010).

For our TIIP model, we propose that the human psyche comprises the following components, as adopted by the majority (*jumhūr*) of the discursive theologians who maintain a unified metaphysical essence of a *laṭīfah rabbāniyyah*. However, the nuance added by Imām al-Suhrawardī and Imām al-Ghazālī in drawing a distinction between the *nafsānī* and *rūḥ ḥayawānī* animalistic drives embedded in the body that compete with the divine directives of the *laṭīfah rabbāniyyah* through its *rūḥ ʿulwī samāwī* is adopted. The aspects of the human psyche that have been identified are as follows: (1) *ʿaql* (cognition), (2) *nafs* (behavioral inclinations), (3) *rūḥ* (spirit), (4) *qalb* (heart), and (5) *iḥsās* (basic emotions). The interaction between these components is illustrated in Figure 1.5.

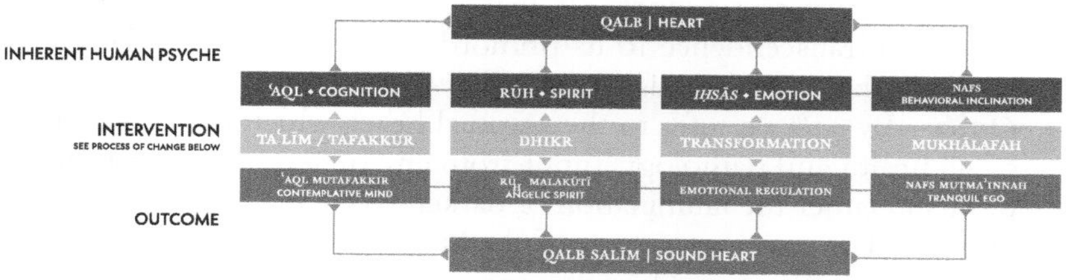

Figure 1.5 TIIP Ontological Model of the Psyche.

1. ***Nafs*** – Keshavarzi and Haque (2013) opt to semantically translate the term *nafs* as behavioral inclinations. Based upon the conceptualization provided by al-Ghazālī, Mullā 'Alī al-Qārī, and al-Suhrwardī, the *nafs ammārah bi-l-sū'* or the *nafs* inclining toward evil is contained within the aspect of the human being as a social animal with survival/aggressive instincts (*quwwat ghaḍabiyyah*) and appetitive/carnal drives (*quwwat shahawiyyah*). Therefore, in its untrained state, the *nafs* is hedonistic and can expand its appetite. It is possible to liken the *nafs* in this sense to Freud's conceptualization of the id. However, through refinement and training the *nafs* is capable of advancement, nurturance, and development through various stages (i.e. *lawwāmah* and *muṭma'innah*) that elevates it beyond its animalistic lowly aims toward the divine directives of the *laṭīfah rabbāniyyah or rūḥ 'ulwī samāwī.* The central mechanism for achieving this aim is through *mukhālafat al-nafs* or going against its animalistic instincts.
2. ***'Aql*** – The *'aql* is a rational faculty by which humans are capable of attaining knowledge and reasoning. According to al-Taftāzānī, when human internal and external senses are functioning properly, the *'aql* is what provides human beings with the ability to realize certain and intuitive knowledge (al-Taftāzānī, 2000, pp. 104; see also al-Farhārī, 2012). It is a metaphysical light that emanates from the *laṭīfah rabbāniyyah* that provides the faculty of reasoning, knowledge acquisition, appreciation of consequences, and ability to distinguish truth from falsehood (al-Bayjūrī, 2002; al-Ghazālī, 1990, p. 137). It allows individuals to appreciate the consequences of their actions and mediates and subjugates the harmful whims of the *nafs* (Ibn 'Ābidīn, al-Haskafi, & al-Nasafi, 2006). It is a faculty of reasoning that is necessary for ethical accountability and its absence would permit exclusion from liability and accountability under Islamic law.
3. ***Rūḥ*** – The *rūḥ* can be divided into two components: (a) the human being's spirit and life force (*rūḥ ḥayawānī*) and (b) the spirit's inclination (*rūḥ 'ulwī samāwī*) toward the sacred and longing for reconnection and remembrance of the divine. The former is a drive that is the origin of putting the drives of the *nafs ammārah* into motion. The latter is the portion of a person's inner self that thirsts for deeper meaning, purpose, and transcendence to its primordial state of aspiring for divine presence that corresponds to the *nafs muṭma'innah.*
4. ***Qalb*** – By *qalb* we refer to the spiritual heart, which is the receptacle of all health and pathology. Input from any of the other components results in either the illumination or darkening of the heart.
5. ***Iḥsās*** – The *iḥsās* component of the human inner experiential experience is what we refer to loosely as an individual's basic emotions. This is a secondary aspect of the human experience and may not warrant admissibility as a separate and distinct aspect of the human psyche.

However, it has been included for conceptual purposes that are conducive to clinical case conceptualization. It can be seen as a byproduct of the interaction between *nafs*, *rūḥ*, and *'aql*. Emotions can have adaptive or healthy manifestations, or become dysregulated and unhealthy, such as innate anger, which is positive when it produces assertiveness and dysfunctional if it produces aggression.

All of the four human inner domains are inevitably interconnected. Thus, a change in any one domain will be expected to have an accompanying impact on the rest of the system. Take, for example, a person suffering from hedonistic behavioral addictions. Such addictions can be expected to lead to cognitive rationalizations that will engender distortions in a person's belief system, or may result in emotional dysregulation such as despondency, and hence a reduction in ritual religious practices that affect the spiritual heart. Illustrations and explication of each component of the psyche is discussed in its own right in Part IV of this book. It is also noteworthy that, as mentioned above, the *'aql* may be seen as a subcomponent of *rūḥ 'ulwī samāwī*, and *iḥsās* as a secondary component that is the result of *'aql*, *ruh*, and *nafs*. While these elements are placed next to each other in Figure 1.5, they are **not** to be viewed as equivalent, given that the diagram does not denote a hierarchical structure. Rather, it provides a conceptual map conducive for therapeutic conceptualization and application.

TIIP Drive Theory

Human beings are all born with a primordial, inherently good nature, referred to in the prophetic traditions as the *fiṭrah*. Individuals who maintain and nurture their *fiṭrah* are able to retain an inherent capacity to comprehend and appreciate universal truths, both good and evil. This of course includes the recognition of God and the moral value of certain human acts, such as the virtue of charity and the vice of theft or murder. Despite the inherently human innocent disposition, human beings also contend with competitive drives that govern behavior. Amongst such competing drives are what Shāh Walī Allāh called the dichotomy of man's angelic (*malakūtī*) and animalistic (*bahīmī*) natural drives (Hermansen, 1982) (see Figure 1.6). These animalistic drives arise out of the pleasure-seeking (*quwwah shahawiyyah*) and destructive (*quwwah ghaḍabiyyah*) instinct. Al-Suhrawardī alternatively labels them as

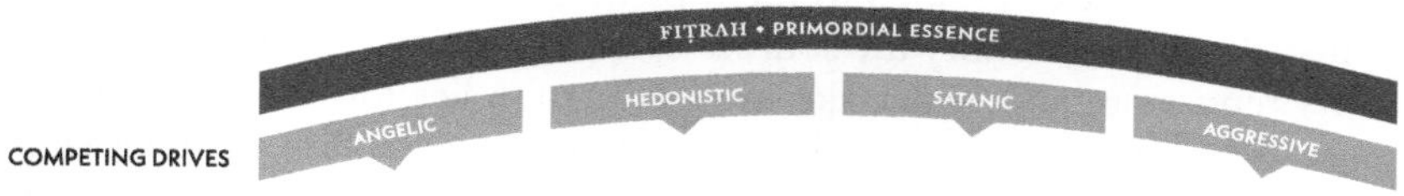

Figure 1.6 TIIP Drive Theory.

the competing drives between the *rūḥ ḥayawānī basharī* and *rūḥ ulwī samāwī*ʿ. Human animalistic drives of hedonistic pleasure-seeking and aggression must be tamed and trained. They become entrenched in the untrained *nafs ammārah* (behavioral inclinations), but if controlled through *inkishāf* (introspective awareness) and *tarbiyah* (spiritual training) it is possible to reorient the *fiṭrah* towards its angelic tendencies and spiritual elevation (*taraqqi*). This embrace of the *rūḥ samāwī* and its nurturance leads to tranquility, whereby the tension between the competing drives is released. However, if left unchecked, the lower carnal desires drive the person towards their bestial nature and render them vulnerable to the inculcation of evil traits and a satanic orientation (al-Ghazālī, 1990, p. 137).

Core Interventions Corresponding to Components of the Human Psyche for Positive Health Outcomes

We propose four core interventions for health outcomes corresponding to the four elements of the human psyche. The purpose of these foundational interventions is to achieve psycho-spiritual health across all four domains by nurturing a contemplative mind/intellect, gravitation toward the *rūḥ samāwī*, *nafs muṭma'innah*, or tranquil ego, development of emotional regulation, and ultimately a healthy heart.

We have extracted the four primary modalities of intervention outlined below in reliance upon the directives and recommendations of the scholars of the spiritual sciences. In particular, Imām al-Birgivī (2011), in his *Ṭarīqah Muḥammadiyyah*, outlines a general approach to the rehabilitation of the human soul/psyche in producing excellent character, which we have designated the phase of *ittiḥād* for the embodiment of good character as the final mechanism of reformation. Imām al-Birgivī outlines that the patient must attempt to gain awareness of the reality of their pathology. He suggests that the patient must identify the negative inclinations (*ghawā'il*) of their sickness, its sources, its opposite, what secondary benefits they derive by it, and its causes. Patients must attempt to psychoanalyze themselves and conduct deep reflection/introspection (*ta'ammul*) in order to identify their internal psycho-spiritual world. Imām al-Birgivī recommends adopting and finding a truthful companion, or in the case of TIIP a practitioner, to help identify the nature of the pathology. In this process, patients should explore their interpersonal interactions with others, and even consider the feedback provided to them by their enemies. After this process, patients will then identify the sources of their pathology and the pathways to its remission, and undertake the virtue of reversion therapy. Patients must develop motivation and impose this responsibility of rehabilitation upon themselves, since typical rehabilitation of pathology entails the adoption of the intervention of its positive opposite. Inclining toward the positive opposite and remission of unhealthy behaviors can be extremely challenging. Thus, patients must continue to maintain firm determination at all times until they start to remit toward the positive opposite, ultimately becoming inclined toward the path of moderation by engaging in resistance training (*riyāḍāt*), such that the resistance slowly dissipates and the alternative healthy psychological and behavioral expressions become second nature and easy.

In consideration of the above, a primary intervention among the core interventions is that of providing individuals with education of a psycho-spiritual nature (*ta'līm*) to help inform them of the process of change. This is furthered through the application of some of the aforementioned education in the form of encouraging reflection upon their intrapsychic state and its exploration in therapy. In addition, this contemplation (*tafakkur* and *ta'mmul*) is combined with a commitment and strategic opposition (*mukhālafahah*) to their impulsive/pathological behavioral impulses. The goal of such opposition is to nurture a tranquil ego that inclines toward moderation (*i'tidāl*) with relative ease, and that becomes oriented toward automatic self-serving adaptive behaviors. Additionally, intermittent scheduling of spiritual litanies or Godly remembrances (*dhikr*) is assigned in order to nourish the spirit, to bring peace to the heart, and to enable effective emotional regulation.

Overarching Therapeutic Goals

Process of Change (Patient)

Based upon the above, the TIIP approach articulates four overarching patient goals of the psychotherapeutic encounter (see Figure 1.7). It is noteworthy that the mechanisms of change listed below go hand in hand with the patient goals listed hereunder, as the therapist employs those mechanisms of change in order to induce the patient goals at each phase of the therapy. These phases are sequential and follow one another in a stage-wise manner.

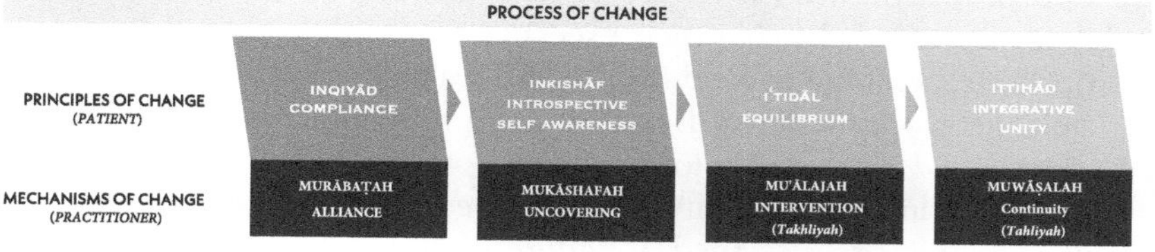

Figure 1.7 TIIP Drive Theory.

1. *Inqiyād* or compliance: A strong therapeutic bond must be engendered in order for the patient to develop trust and commitment to the treatment process. Given that the patient will be requested to undergo difficult therapeutic tasks and endure an uncomfortable process of facing their intrapsychic issues, their motivation and willingness to engage in this process is necessary. In fact, the lack of motivation or noncompliance can compromise treatment, even if the most skillful practitioner equipped with the most effective interventional tools were to work with the patient. This commitment to comply with interventions is required to ensure the efficacy of treatments that are co-constructed by the therapist and patient. Thus, through the therapeutic vehicle of *murābaṭah* or the formation of the therapeutic alliance, the patient will be more likely to embrace the demands and enthusiastically participate in this process.
2. *Inkishāf* or introspective self-awareness: Introspective self-discovery is the next goal for the patient to experience. This is facilitated via the mechanism of *mukāshafah* or the guided self-examination, through which the patient may start to gain insight into their cognitive, emotional, behavioral, and spiritual tendencies. Empathic exploration and evocations of internal experiences are central to this process (see Chapter 7). An awareness of the internal psychological processes at play and sources of tension or distress is essential to creating an accurate and effective conceptualization of the patient and accompanying treatment plan. Imām al-Ghazālī states that *inkishāf* must be engendered within the context of a psycho-spiritual relationship with a spiritual mentor as it can be very difficult to uncover one's own blindspots without the mirror of a practitioner, who can help the patient uncover their internal psycho-spiritual world.
3. *Iʿtidāl* or equilibrium: An overarching process goal of the TIIP therapeutic modality is for patients to achieve *iʿtidāl* or a state of balance and equilibrium among all of the composite parts of their psyche (i.e. *'aql*, *rūḥ*, *nafs*, *iḥsās*, *qalb*). An internal struggle will emerge during this process whereby the patient must be willing to endure the discomfort required for change to facilitate psycho-spiritual equilibrium (*iʿtidāl*). If, for example, a patient harbors excessive fear (*khawf*), they may suffer from a psycho-spiritual imbalance that leads to symptoms of anxiety. The patient will require therapeutic intervention, not only to gain insight into the nature of their anxiety, but also to help direct them towards balancing their excessive fear with healthy doses of its opposite, i.e. hope in God (*rajā'*). This was referred to above as reversion therapy by Imām al-Birgivī and is a tool employed in the process of *mu'ālajah* described below.
4. *Ittiḥād* or integrative unity: All therapeutic strategies and sequence of sessions are designed to address these three aforementioned

overarching goals, toward engendering the fourth and final goal of integrative unity, or *ittiḥād*. This is facilitated through *muwāṣalah* or continuation of the therapeutic process beyond the removal of clinical pathology or psychological imbalance. After balance has been achieved across each of the elements of the psyche, an integration of each of these elements is desired, such that they serve a unity of purpose. There should be a unification of the different parts of the psyche that aid one another in the psycho-spiritual journey. In fact, disintegration is one of the central problems that many psychological theories address.

Whether it is through parts therapy, treatment of trauma and dissociation, aspirations for congruence in humanistic therapies, gestalt therapy, or something else, pathology is often characterized by some form of internal psychological disintegration. Thus, integration of the disparate parts of the human psyche can contribute to intrapsychic dissonance. A unity of purpose that allows one to move beyond the mere survival needs of the human experience can engender psychological resilience. By *ittiḥād*, we intend the integration of the interconnected parts of the psyche and the formation of an internal unity that allows the person to holistically serve their primordial goal of connecting with God (*maʿrifah*) and actualizing their full spiritual potential. Through achieving this state of integration, the believer achieves a synthesis of their total being with the will of God such that their actions become directed by God's desires. The previous step of *iʿtidāl* has primed them to rid themselves of clinical pathologies (*takhliyah*) through *muʿālajah* in order to be prepared for the further development of their psycho-spiritual capacities and the inculcation of positive virtues and traits (*taḥliyah*). The restoration of a holistic balance is intended to provide a patient with an insight into themselves that can eventually allow them to function as their own therapists and to independently identify when they are deviating from this unity or previously achieved equilibrium.

Core Mechanisms of Change Corresponding to the Process of Change (Practitioner)

These are the core mechanisms that the TIIP practitioner will employ in order to help their patient move across the developmental phases of psychotherapy and rehabilitation. Each of these therapeutic mechanisms that are utilized by the practitioner are the facilitators of the patient processes of change outlined above: for example, *mukāshafah* utilized by practitioner should engender *inkishāf* in the patient.

Murābaṭah or Alliance and Therapeutic Connection

Many of the spiritual ascetics engage in a form of contractual bond (*bay'ah* or *'aqd*). Although this is beyond the scope of the TIIP psychotherapy, the process of identifying the objectives, scope, and mutual responsibilities of any human relationship is necessary. In psychotherapeutic practice this is known as informed consent. However, in an Islamically oriented psychotherapy it is necessary for the patient and therapist to recognize the spiritual mandates of this relationship, which includes ethical conduct with one another and a bond built on shared faith and spiritual kinship. Thus, Chapter 2 highlights the internal and external aspects of the relationship that are instrumental for effective treatment.

In short, a strong therapeutic relationship is critical in establishing a psychological forum conducive to introspective self-awareness, in addition to the appropriate training and knowledge base of human psychology. Imām al-Ghazālī emphasizes the internal characteristics of righteousness while Imām al-Birgivi outlines the characteristic of genuineness (*ṣidq*). Imām al-Bayjūrī mentions that in the process of enjoining the good and removal of evil (*amr bi-l-ma'rūf wa-l-nahy 'an al-munkar*) the practitioner must: (1) possess knowledge of what they are enjoining upon the recipient, (2) ensure that the intervention does not generate greater harm, and (3) ensure that the intervention is effective in leading the recipient to good behavior or to ceasing pathological behavior (al-Bayjūrī, 2002, p. 329). If the first two conditions are not found, then it is prohibited for the practitioner to intervene, while in the final scenario it is permissible to intervene, though not mandated. Typically, spiritual practitioners' advice is that in the early phases of forming the relationship, empathic following techniques should be utilized. This should include working on reducing patient defensiveness, developing trust, increasing comfort, engendering motivation to change, and gently challenging the patient until the therapeutic relationship is adequately established. Once this relationship is established, a more directive process can be employed that would enhance the efficacy of the interventions.

Mukāshafah or Uncovering

Classical Islamic scholars and physicians, such as Abū Zayd al-Balkhī (d.322 AH/934 CE), Abū Bakr al-Rāzī (d.313 AH/925 CE), Abū 'Alī b. Miskawayh (d.421 AH/1030 CE), and ascetic scholars like Shāh Walī Allah, insist on the centrality of seeking assistance in order to gain awareness of one's cognitive, behavioral, emotional, and spiritual self (Arberry, 1979; Badri, 2013; Hermansen, 1982; Keshavarzi & Haque, 2013). This is achievable through the patient's surrender to the supervision of a mentor, who leads the patient to a self-awareness of their personal faults, virtues, and intrapsychic dilemmas. The TIIP model sets this as a critical mechanism for change by providing an introspective forum conducive to the unveiling of the psycho-spiritual realities of the patient's self. The role of the practitioner is to create interventions designed to help facilitate the goal of self-awareness and collaboratively assess the patient's psyche.

Mu'ālajah or Intervention

Mu'ālajah is the process of facilitating change or reformation in a patient. The therapist performs the role of both practitioner and spiritual guide (*murabbi*) by employing Islamically integrated interventions targeting the four elements of the human psyche in the interest of engendering psycho-spiritual equilibrium (*i'tidāl*). The first part of the interventional process is to work on eliminating the internal psycho-spiritual imbalance and provide treatment that incorporates opposites (*mukhālafah*). This entails identifying the intrapsychic imbalances of the elements and applying resistance training to reduce extremes in order to restore the balance. This approach essentially uses the concept of *mujāhadah* or spiritual struggle against the inclination to avoid this process. For example, for avoidance behaviors, confrontation of feared or disliked actions will have to be implemented in order to counteract the unhealthy aversion to their positive opposites. If the alliance between therapist and patient has been adequately formed, then it is likely that the patient will have been primed and prepared to undergo this process, as this phase is tantamount to psychological transformation.

The ultimate goal of this phase is to free the patient from major psycho-spiritual sicknesses (*takhliyah*) in order to move on to the next phase. Certainly, the practitioner needs to utilize any of the therapeutic tools within their possession and within the therapeutic forum carefully toward helping counterbalance the maladies of any of the components of the psyche. It is important for the therapist to identify the primary area(s) that drive the pathology and address this component of the psyche first. For example, if the patient demonstrates an emotional dysregulation that underlies their trauma, then it is important to start working on the emotion as opposed to addressing thoughts or behaviors, as these can be addressed in later sessions.

Muwāṣalah or Continuity of Treatment

The second phase of intervention helps to direct the patient toward the goal of *ittiḥād* or integrative unity. It is directed toward the consolidation of gains made as well as a review of therapeutic strategies employed to develop *i'tidāl* so that the patient can reassess the knowledge acquired in the facilitation of change. Additionally, higher aims are set for the patient in respect of the acquisition of character virtues once the core sickness has been eliminated (*takhliyah*). Other avenues and modalities of increasing spiritual growth and resilience are also explored as the therapist moves toward termination of psychotherapy. For example, if the patient had overcome social anxiety that initially inhibited them from being able to meet the rights of their family members, then at this stage they will work toward strengthening those bonds through service and stronger familial connection. At this stage working on the inculcation of virtues (*tahliyah*) that can serve as resilience building for the patient would be most suitable.

Conclusion

Traditional Islamically Integrated Psychotherapy (TIIP) provides an overarching framework for the intersection of the modern behavioral sciences and the Sunni Islamic intellectual heritage. The various aspects of the human psyche discussed above are laid out in greater detail in later chapters, which provide more specificity as well as providing a demonstration of its practical clinical utility. In particular the core mechanisms employed by the practitioner is discussed in Chapter 2, while Part IV of the book outlines the components of the ontological framework of the psyche.

References

al-Bayjūrī, A. (2002). *Ḥāshiyat al-Imām al-Bayjūrī 'alā Jawharat al-Tawḥīd*. Cairo: Dār al-Salām.

al-Bazdawi, A. (2014). *Usūl al-Bazdawiyyah*. Beirut: Dār al-Bashā'ir.

al-Bazzār, A. A.(2009). *Musnad al-Bazzār/al-Baḥr al-Zakhkhār*. al-Madīnah al-Munawwarah: Maktabat al-'Ulū m wa-l-Ḥikam.

al-Birgivī, M. (2011). *al-Ṭarīqah al-Muḥammadiyyah wa-l-Ṣirāṭ al-Aḥmadiyyah*. Damascus: Dār al-Qalam.

al-Farhārī, A. (2012). *Nibrās: Sharḥ Sharḥ al-'Aqā'id*. Istanbul: Maktaba Yāsīn.

al-Ghazālī, A. H. (1990). *Mukhtaṣar: Iḥyā' 'Ulūm al-Dīn*, Beirut: Mua'ssas al-Kutub al-Thaqāfiyyah.

al- Ghazālī, A. H. (2011). *Iḥyā' 'Ulūm al-Dīn*. Vol. 5. Saudi Arabia: Dār al-Minhāj.

al-Muḥāsibī, H. (1971). *Al-'Aql wa Fahm al-Qurān*. Beirut: Dār *al-Fikr*.

al-Mundhirī , A. (2003). *Al-Targhīb wa-l-Tarhīb*. Beirut: Dā r al-Kutub al-'Ilmiyyah.

al-Nasafi, A. N. (2013). *Shurūh wa al-ḥawāshi al-'Ā qa'id al-Nasafiyyah*. Beirut: Dār al-Kutub al-'Ilmiyyah.

al-Rāzī, F. (2008). *al-Tafsīr al-Kabīr*. Damascus: Dar al-Fikr.

al-Suhrawardī, S. (1993). *'Awārif al-Ma'ārif*. Cairo: Dār al-Ma'ārif.

al-Taftāzānī, A. H. (2000). *Sharḥ al-'Aqā'id al-Nasafiyyah*. Karachi: Maktabat al-Bushrā.

'Alī al-Qārī, M. (2015). *Mirqāt al-Mafātīḥ, Sharḥ Mishkāt al-Maṣābīḥ*. Beirut: Dār al-Kutub al-'Ilmiyyah.

American Psychiatric Association (2013). *Diagnostic and statistical manual of mental disorders*, 5th ed. https://doi.org/10.1176/appi.books.9780890425596.

Anderson, N., Heywood-Everett, S., Siddiqi, N., Wright, J., Meredith, J., & McMillan, D. (2015). Faith-adapted psychological therapies for depression and anxiety: systematic review and meta-analysis. *J. Affect Disorders*, *176*, 183–196.

Arberry, A. J. (1979). *Sufism: An account of the mystics in Islam*. New York: Harper & Row.

Badri, M. B. (2013). *The dilemma of Muslim psychologists*. London: MWH.

Brown, J. (2013). The problem of reductionism in philosophy of mind and its implications for theism and the principle of soul: framing the issue for further Islamic inquiry. *Tabah Paper Series*, *7*, 1–30.

Cloninger, C. R. (2004). *Feeling good: the science of well being*. New York: Oxford University Press.

Er, M. E. (2016). *al-Mukhtārāt min Maktūbāt al-Imam al-Rabbāni al-Sirhindī*. Istanbul: ISAR.

Farfūr, M. A. (2002). *al-Zād min Uṣūl al-Fiqh al-Islāmī*. Beirut: Maktabat Dār al-Bayrūtiyyah.

Hermansen, M. K. (1982). Shah Wali Allah's arrangement of the subtle spiritual centers. *Studies in Islam*.

Hook, J. N., Worthington, E. L. Jr., Davis, D. E., Jennings, D. J. II, Gartner, A. L., & Hook, J. P. (2010). Empirically supported religious and spiritual therapies. *J Clin Psychol.*, *66*, 46–72.

Ibn ʿĀbidīn, M., al-Haskafi, M. A., & al-Nasafi, M. (2006). *Sharhu sharh al-manar*. Karachi: Idaratal Quran.

Keshavarzi, H., & Haque, A. (2013). Outlining a psychotherapy model for enhancing Muslim mental health within an Islamic context. *Int. J. Psychol. Relig.*, *23*(3), 230–249.

McCullough, M. E. (1999). Research on religion-accommodative counseling: review and meta-analysis. *Journal of Counseling Psychology*, *46*, 92–98.

Muslim, M. (2006). *Ṣaḥīḥ Muslim*. Riyadh: Dār Ṭaybah for Publishing and Distribution.

Qureshi, O., & Padela, A. (2016). When must a patient seek healthcare? Bringing the perspectives of Islamic jurists and clinicians into dialogue. *Zygon*, *51*(3), 592–625.

Richards, P. S., Sanders, P. W., Lea, T., McBride, J. A., & Allen, G. E. K. (2015). Bringing spiritually oriented psychotherapies into the health care mainstream: a call for worldwide collaboration. *Spiritual Clin. Pract.*, *2*(3), 169–179.

Smith, T. B., Bartz, J., & Richards, P. S. (2007). Outcomes of religious and spiritual adaptations to psychotherapy: a meta-analytic review. *Psychotherapy Research*, *17*, 643–655.

Usmani, M. U. (n.d). *Ma'ārif al-Quran*. Karachi: Dar al-Ma'ārif.

Walī Allah, S. (2010). *Al-Qawl al-Jamīl fī Bayān Sawā' al-Sabīl*. Cairo: Dār al-Jawdiyyah.

Worthington, E. L., Jr., & Sandage, S. J. (2001). Religion and spirituality. *Psychotherapy, Theory, Research, Practice, Training*, *38*, 473–478.

Worthington, E. L., Hook, J. N., Davis, D. E., & McDaniel, M. A. (2011). Religion and spirituality. *J Clin. Psychol.*, *67*, 204–214.

Worthington, E. L. Jr., Kurusu, T. A., McCullough, M. E., & Sandage, S. J. (1996). Empirical research on religion and psychotherapeutic processes and outcomes: a 10-year review and research prospectus. *Psychol. Bull.*, *119*, 448–487.

Chapter 2

The Role of the TIIP Therapist

Scope of Practice and Proposed Competencies

Fahad Khan, Hooman Keshavarzi, and Abdallah Rothman

Chapter Summary

This chapter provides a discussion of the role of the Traditional Islamically Integrated Psychotherapy (TIIP) practitioner and where they are situated within the professional psychotherapeutic encounter. The authors provide some guidelines as to the therapeutic competencies required by a TIIP practitioner that are demonstrated by: (1) the possession of therapeutic skill, knowledge of theory and case conceptualization, (2) familiarity with basic Islamic spiritual interventions and the Islamic tradition, and (3) internal qualities such as sincerity and investment in the well-being of the patient that serve as core ingredients for change within an Islamic spiritually oriented approach. The broader role and scope of the psychotherapist is contrasted with an Islamic spiritual scholar (Ṣūfī) by situating the TIIP practitioner within the context of Imām al-Ghazālī's conceptualization of the two potential types of transformative relationships necessary for psycho-spiritual awareness. It is proposed that the TIIP practitioner's central role is to alleviate psychological distress and dysfunction through the adaptation of mainstream psychological interventions within an Islamic framework, as well as the utilization of inherently Islamic spiritual remedies leading to a holistic conceptualization of the human psyche. Though subclinical character and spiritual development may also be within the purview of the TIIP practitioner, these are seen as secondary aspects of potential treatment. Thus, the TIIP practitioner is situated between a 'clinician' and a 'spiritual' healer. Overall, the TIIP practitioner possesses the competence and capacity to provide psychospiritual relief by integrating behavioral science into an Islamic conceptual framework.

Introduction

Many models of mental health care rely heavily, if not entirely, on the practitioner's knowledge and mastery of clinical technique (Fairburn & Cooper, 2011). Consequently, in the process of "administering" treatment to patients, sometimes through the implementation of manualized or mechanized protocols, therapists' internal characteristics are often ignored. Even the use of fake sincerity has been proposed within the practice of psychotherapy as a tool for treatment (Morstyn, 2002). However, overlooking the impact of the therapist's internal aspects of character on the psychotherapeutic process can lead to an overemphasis on the effectiveness of the therapeutic modality (Kim, Wampold, & Bolt, 2006).

Historically, Islamic scholars have recognized the importance of practitioner variables to the impact of intervention, and have placed a great degree of attention on the necessity for practitioners who are facilitating change in others to acquire, retain, and demonstrate particular traits (al-Bayjūrī 2002; al-Ghazālī, 1993). A practitioner providing psycho-spiritual reform in others (*tarbiyah*) needs not only a solid knowledge base but also to have received psycho-spiritual training and remain actively engaged in spiritual growth and retention of the resulting gains (Usmani 2001; Walī Allah & Hermansen, 1996). Many of the scholars of Islamic spirituality highlight particular indicators of God-consciousness (*taqwā*) and qualities to look for in a spiritual healer, and urge potential seekers of help to utilize such criteria in the process of selecting psycho-spiritual mentorship (Thānwī, 1971; Walī Allah & Hermansen, 1996). Thus, choosing a mentor, in a relationship where patients grant significant influence to the practitioner over their intrapsychic world, requires an appropriate degree of caution and investigation into the internal qualities of that service provider.

It is equally necessary for providers to ensure that they are actively engaged in developing the requisite qualities that will help them facilitate growth in others. Thus from the perspective of a traditional Islamically integrative approach, the position and relative state of the therapist become important factors. Therapists need to demonstrate a grounding in the knowledge of TIIP and its resulting skills, as well as their internal qualities and intentions, as these are of critical significance in developing the foundation for the therapeutic relationship. A review of the variables most commonly related to symptom relief within psychotherapy demonstrates that the therapeutic relationship is a primary factor in the promotion of mental health (Horvath, Del Re, Fluckiger, & Symonds, 2011). Thus, the role of the TIIP therapist is a dynamic one that merits further scrutiny to elucidate both the relative position that the practitioner occupies and the qualities that a practitioner must possess.

This chapter focuses on describing the essential variables of education, skill, and internal character traits necessary for the practitioner. To begin, a specification and elaboration of the relative responsibilities, objectives, and scope of the therapist within a TIIP setting is provided. An exploration of the importance of the therapist's internal characteristics and spiritual state then sets the stage for mapping the terrain within which the TIIP therapist is situated to provide psycho-spiritual care for Muslim patients. Finally, some core competencies for the psychospiritual practitioner are outlined.

Scope of Practice

Al-Ghazālī (2011, p. 227), in his *Iḥyā' 'Ulūm al-Dīn*, quotes an Islamic tradition: "When Allah wishes good for the servant, He grants him insight into his/her deficiencies." He states that most people are not aware of the full range of their deficiencies, and that such awareness can be achieved primarily through two major types of relationships:

1. To adopt a traditional spiritual guide (i.e. a Ṣūfī master) by forming a Master–Disciple relationship and remaining in their company in order to acquire psycho-spiritual awareness. This, according to al-Ghazālī, is the noblest method within the Islamic tradition as it is the sacred pathway that has been passed down through a chain of transmission that contains spiritual significance and blessings.
2. Alternatively, to appoint to oneself a companion who is upright in his/her character and who possesses expertise in facilitating insight and psycho-spiritual awareness. This individual observes his/her own states and actions and aids in detecting the faults and defects of the individual. Al-Ghazālī quotes the saying of 'Umar b. al-Khaṭṭāb (may Allah be pleased with him), a companion of the Prophet (peace and blessings be upon him), who said that "May God have mercy on the one who directs me towards my deficiencies" (al-Ghazālī, 2014).

Al-Ghazālī's (2014) second relationship seems to serve as an alternative to the traditional relationship with a Ṣūfī master. This lays a potential platform and terrain for the role of an expert with both the inner quality of God consciousness and the skills of facilitating psycho-spiritual awareness and change. Although al-Ghazālī's writing predates the modern field of psychology, the TIIP framework seeks to advance this notion as the potential scope and domain of the TIIP practitioner, who possesses psychological expertise in an independent and specialized field that did not exist historically as a discrete science. Historically, such a role was likely more closely aligned with the broader field of medicine, or *ṭibb*, where a patient would go to see a *Ḥakīm* or a *Ṭabīb*, a medical practitioner who would treat physical ailments as well as taking account of the psyche or the soul by utilizing a holistic treatment approach (Ragab, 2018). In medieval times, this would entail practices that involved the humors, or energies in the body, and would attempt to bring *i'tidāl* (balance) to the system as an integral whole: "body, mind, and soul" (Pormann, 2007).

Therefore, within the modern era of an increasingly specialized health care industry and advancement of the behavioral sciences, an integrated approach to mental health care situated within Islamic conceptions of health and healing necessitates the conceptualization of the role of the TIIP therapist by bridging several branches of knowledge (i.e. Islamic theology, spirituality, and behavioral science). An integrative approach rooted in the Islamic tradition seems to be a genuine orientation to such an endeavor, whereas post-colonial tendencies have led many modern Muslims to uncritically embrace reductionistic medicine and secular psychology (Badri, 1979). Thus, an integrative approach challenges the overly physicalist assumptions of human nature in its assertion of the human being as an interconnected integral system composed of both metaphysical and physical aspects.

Before proceeding to a discussion of the necessary therapeutic competencies of a TIIP therapist, it is imperative to define the TIIP scope of practice. It is important to understand that a TIIP therapist is not the first type of healer that al-Ghazālī mentions, i.e. a Ṣūfī *shaykh*. Nor is he/she solely a generic clinician who treats medical illnesses, but is rather a combination of both domains. Relatedly, even though Muslim physicians in the medieval era explicitly assumed the existence of a metaphysical mind or soul, they utilized an epistemic approach that was predominately guided by reason and empirical evidence. This is evident in the writings of many celebrated Muslim physicians such as Abū Zayd al-Balkhī (d.322 AH/934 CE), Abū Bakr al-Rāzī (d.313 AH/925 CE), and Abū 'Alī al-Ḥusayn b. Sīnā (d.428 AH/1037 CE) (Arberry, 1979; Badri, 1979; Hermansen, 1982; Keshavarzi & Haque, 2013). Although implicit, there is very little explicit reference to revelation or citations of Islamic scripture that informs these classical scholars' medicine. For this reason, some of the physicians were criticized as overly relying on reason and Greek medicine for their medical practices. The details of such accounts are complex and beyond the scope of this chapter, but we do propose an epistemic focus for the TIIP practitioner that relies on all three sources of knowledge (see Chapter 1) to inform their practice. Using al-Ghazālī's (2014) classification of the two roles, the TIIP practitioner would best fit into the second role, what Imām al-Ghazālī labelled as a *Rafīq*. This is illustrated in Figure 2.1. The differences between the roles are outlined in the following section and summarized in Table 2.1.

Ṣūfī Shaykh

Taṣawwuf, Sufism, or Islamic mysticism, is not a separate branch of Islam; rather it is the actualization of Islamic belief into practical application. Just as conformity to the outer rules of Islam (*sharī'ah*) is necessary, Sufism is the science of the inner qualities (*fiqh al-bāṭin*). It emphasizes introspection

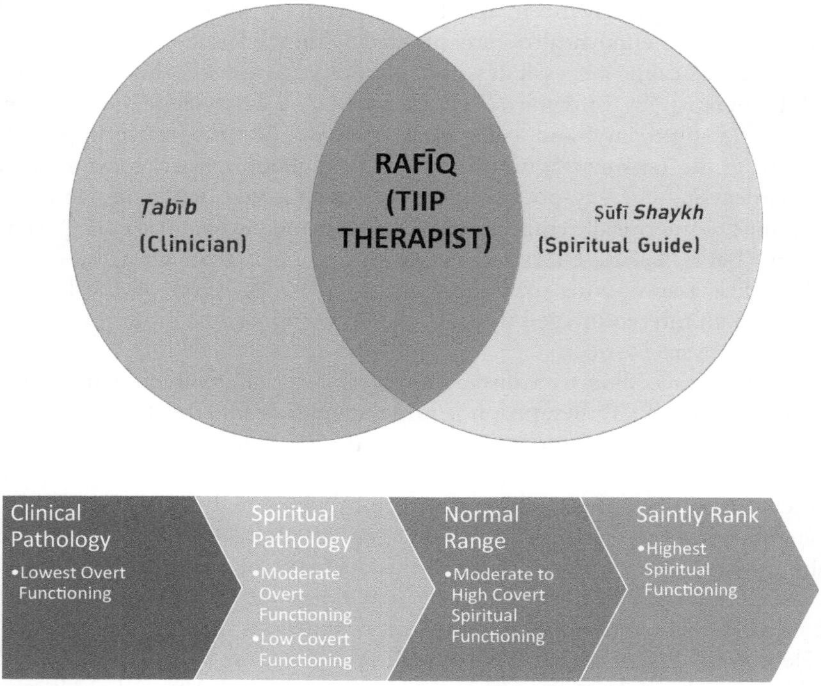

Figure 2.1 The scope of practice and focus of treatment.

and correction of spiritual diseases (pride, envy, etc.), and aims to bring the believer closer to Allah through advanced spiritual practices. Ṣūfīs aspire to internalize a constant state of God-consciousness and awareness of His presence within their own self (Durrani, Hankir, & Carrick, 2018). Traditionally, Ṣūfīs have established orders or organized groups in order to achieve the aforementioned goals. There are many Ṣūfī orders (*ṭuruq*) that have existed throughout history, most notable of whom are the Chishtī, Qādirī, Suhrawardī, Shādhilī, and Naqshbandī orders. All Ṣūfī orders believe that their teachings have been passed down in a legacy that goes back to the Prophet Muḥammad (peace and blessings be upon him) and his teachings.

A Ṣūfī aims to experience communion with God through acquisition of *ʿilm* (knowledge) and its manifestation in *aʿmāl* (actions) (Chittick, 1989). Those who adhere to strict Ṣūfī practices must have a Ṣūfī Master/guide or *Murshid* who assigns and instructs them in such practices (Ernst, 2011). A *Murshid* serves as a mentor, a guide, a teacher, and a directive discipliner for his *murīd*, the follower, in his/her development on the spiritual path.

Table 2.1 Distinctions between the domains of a *Shaykh*, clinician, and TIIP therapist

Domains	*Clinician* (Ṭabīb)	*TIIP Therapist* (Rafīq/Khalīl)	*Ṣūfī Shaykh*
Religious Authority	- No	- Some with formal education	- Yes
Credentials (authority)	- State licensure, formal academic/ clinical training	- State licensure, formal academic/ clinical training and certification in TIIP (still formative)	- *Ijāzāt* or authority/ permission granted by their Spiritual Master
Problems Primarily Treated	- Clinical problems	- Clinical with appreciation of and understanding of spiritual problems	- Spiritual problems
Treatment Modality Utilized	- Varies (biomedical, humanistic, psychodynamic, etc.)	- Psycho-spiritual integrative approach	- Spiritual reformation
Goals	- Generally: reduce symptoms, increase functioning - Specifically: varies from orientation to orientation	- Reduce symptoms - Increase functioning - Travel together on the transcendental path through collective contemplation with a righteous *Rafīq*	- Journey towards the Creator through *dhikr* (contemplation), *suḥbah* (righteous companionship), *rābiṭah* (intimate bond with *shaykh*), and *riyāḍāt* (contemplative exercises) - Spiritual reformation - Reduction of spiritual symptoms
Style/Approach	- Non-directive/ directive based on orientation	- Authoritative and collaborative	- Directive/ authoritarian
Developmental Focus	- Increase functioning to normal within the context of worldly existence (i.e. birth to death)	- From pre-natal to the post-mortem spiritual existence with a focus on improvement of present functioning	- Direct the focus to the primordial goal of attaining success in this life and in the afterlife

(*continued*)

Table 2.1 Cont.

Domains	*Clinician* (Ṭabīb)	*TIIP Therapist* (Rafīq/Khalīl)	*Ṣūfī Shaykh*
Interventions	- Evidence-based behavioral science interventions	- Adaptation of evidenced-based interventions along with interventions drawn from the Ṣūfī tradition with supportive evidence	- Inherently drawn from the Islamic intellectual heritage (i.e. Qur'ān and Sunnah) - Based on experiential knowledge
Nature of Contract	- Secular and fiduciary	- Psycho-spiritual agreement upon an integrative treatment approach	- Master/disciple - Formal pledge (*bay'ah*) and discipleship
Required Indicators for Pathology	- Biomedical - Psychosocial functioning - Thought disorder - Emotional imbalance	- Psychological functioning along with attention to spiritual sicknesses that significantly impacts current functioning	- Covert indicators of spiritual illnesses - Overt concerns related to ritual and non-ritual behaviors
Types of Pathologies Addressed	- Medical and psychological disorders within the context of functioning	- Psychological disorders along with spiritual diseases of the heart within the context of mental health and well-being	- Aspirations towards spiritual perfection (*Kamāl*) - Sickness of the heart
Educational Prerequisites	- Formal secular degree with licensure	- Academic education as well as Islamic education	- Islamic education and mentorship by a senior *shaykh*
Relationship and Boundaries	- In most cases, formal relationship with strict boundaries	- Therapist serves as a *murabbī* (mentor) and *ṭabīb* (clinical therapist), as well as an *ustādh* (teacher) - Mutual respect and authority	- Formal relationship with strict boundaries - Respect and authority reserved for the *Shaykh* - Handing over self in totality to the *Shaykh*

In most cases, seekers would select an order among the numerous Ṣūfī paths, forming an intimate bond with their spiritual master to be guided on a disciplined regimen toward advancing themselves across the stages of spiritual development (*maqāmāt*). Although the ultimate goals of character development and spiritual completion (*kamāl*) for these different spiritual paths are largely the same, the varying methods of achieving them arose on account of slight conceptual differences in areas of emphasis, experiences, and approaches to actualizing these goals. For example, while one tradition may focus on the inculcation of love as the core feature of change, another may focus more on a structured regimen of spiritual exercises (*riyāḍāt*) to nurture change (Buehler, 2011; Chittick, 2005).

There are several criteria that have been considered as prerequisites for an individual to be considered a Ṣūfī *shaykh*. One important criterion is that the *shaykh* belongs to a *ṭarīqah* and has been authorized to teach the tradition by his own spiritual master or *murshid*. This connects him to the chain (*silsilah*) within his Ṣūfī order and he passes down the spiritual authority from his teacher. This is a status not easily obtained, regardless of the individual's education and experience, since the spiritual master grants this authorization after his ascertainment of the disciple's spiritual readiness to facilitate this experience in others.

This discipline of *taṣawwuf* is perhaps the greatest resource for inherently Islamic methods of psycho-spiritual change and has a rich and long history. While these spiritual methods may converge with behavioral psychology, the ultimate aims of a TIIP psychotherapist and Ṣūfī *shaykh* will likely differ. The *shaykh* will strive to nurture spiritual perfection or integrative spiritual unity (*ittiḥād*). Although the psychotherapist desires to see integration and equilibrium in their patients, the lofty goals of reaching spiritual perfection and the final principle of *ittiḥād* in the spiritual sciences is not what is intended by the usage of *ittiḥād* in the TIIP model. What we mean by *ittiḥād* in a TIIP framework is a reintegration after psychological fragmentation that can be seen across various mental disorders. Often patients complain of a sense of disunity between their beliefs and actions, or emotions and beliefs. This is the type of integration and congruence intended by TIIP, to bring together all of the disjointed parts of the psyche into balance and unison, because the primary focus of a psychotherapist still remains the alleviation of psychological distress and engendering psychological resilience to future dysfunction. This is especially critical for work with patients whose suffering relates to more foundational aspects of day-to-day functioning, ranging from severe clinical pathologies to subclinical populations who struggle with life's trials and tribulations that knock them off-balance (see Figure 2.1). More advanced spiritual perfection (*kamāl*) and advanced spiritual development lies within the domain of the Ṣūfī *shaykh*. The danger of working outside of one's scope of experience can cause a conflation of one's aims and/or blurring of the respective roles of each practitioner, with each possessing different domains of expertise.

Certainly, there is common ground between the two areas of practice, particularly in the struggle (*mujāhadah*) to reform the unrefined impulsive drives of the *nafs*, faulty beliefs and perceptions of the *'aql*, emotional overreactions of *iḥsās*, and spiritual gaps in the *rūḥ*, where it becomes necessary for one to develop psycho-spiritual balance (*i'tidāl*) and engender congruence/unison (*ittiḥād*). However, an ultimate aim from a *taṣawwuf* perspective is to strive for the reunification of the human life force (*rūḥ hawa'ī*) with the primordial soul (*rūḥ malakūtī*) in order to realize the Divine unity of the cosmos and to witness His *tawḥīd* (Walī Allāh & Hermansen, 1996). The *ittiḥād* of the Ṣūfīs thus remains a superior goal of more advanced work on the self, and it may remain aspirational for many. Thus, al-Ghazālī recognizes that this deeper, more focused work of *inkishāf* is for those who are willing and able to exert the required effort and continuous growth that bears no limits, given the unlimited nature of the ocean of the Divine realities (al-Ghazālī, 1993). This more advanced level of pursuit therefore constitutes a specialized branch of knowledge within the domain of *taṣawwuf* that accepts an appreciation of the depth of the Islamic spiritual path, even though it may remain outside the realm of the TIIP therapist.

Clinician (Ṭabīb/Ḥakīm)

Clinicians require a combination of knowledge and skills with a primary epistemic focus on the rational/philosophical and empirical basis of understanding human behavior. This is in stark contrast to the Ṣūfī scholar, whose primary epistemic focus is metaphysics/revelation and passed-down experience (*tajrībāt*). Although these roles have been considered distinct, their focus on human psychology and behavior is what unites them. This integrated space between a Ṣūfī *shaykh* and a clinician is the proposed role for the TIIP practitioner.

Within the modern clinician/therapist framework, an individual who obtains a high level of expertise and proficiency is sometimes referred to as a "master" therapist. This involves "an encompassing, procedural kind of knowledge that can be modeled impressively for others or used as a basis for supervisory shaping of the practice of others" (Orlinsky, 1999, p. 13). Modern definitions of psychotherapy expertise place significant importance on the process of therapy and the ability of the clinician to be aware of what happens moment to moment within the therapeutic encounter with high levels of "precision, subtlety, and finesse" (Orlinsky, 1999, p. 211). These are measured through the domains of cognitive, emotional, and relational expertise (Jennings & Skovholt, 1999). Despite an emphasis on education and technique, Skovholt and Jennings (2016, p. 33) offer 11 characteristics that include internal attributes in their definition of an ideal "master" therapist:

1. They are voracious learners who are enthusiastic about learning and further increasing their knowledge.
2. They utilize accumulated experiences with many years of professional experience to draw from.
3. They value cognitive complexity, ambiguity and embrace the grey area, instead of considering all processes to be linear and logical.
4. They have emotional receptivity with increased openness and self-awareness. They reflect on their own selves and nondefensively seek feedback. They are likely to engage in their own personal therapy and seek consultation and supervision from other professionals.
5. They are healthy and nurture emotional well-being allowing them to be honest, authentic, and congruent. They can continue to meet the need of others without experiencing burnout by taking care of themselves. They can model emotional well-being.
6. They possess awareness of how their own emotional health affects professional work with patients, specifically in the context of therapy. They maintain healthy boundaries.
7. They acquire and maintain highly developed relational skills of listening, responding, and caring.
8. They cultivate strong working therapeutic alliances that they work to maintain. They believe in the patient's capacity to heal and change.
9. They excel in using exceptional therapy skills beyond just providing support and encouragement.
10. They trust that their patients possess sufficient capacity to make positive change.
11. They are culturally competent and use their knowledge to provide services to diverse populations (Jennings et al., 2003).

TIIP Therapist (Rafīq/Khalīl)

As previously mentioned, al-Ghazālī's presentation of the paths of psycho-spiritual change and expertise occupies a respected space and position within the Islamic tradition for the domain of the Muslim mental health specialist. He suggests this as one pathway for embarking on the process of *inkishāf* or introspective self-awareness. Al-Ghazālī highlighted some of the practitioner characteristics that should be present in such a facilitator of change, which include (1) uprightness in character, (2) *rifq* or companionship, denoting a more collaborative rather than hierarchical relationship, and (3) scholarship, possessing strong foundational knowledge in the intricate process of facilitating change (al-Ghazālī, 2014, p. 257). While we recognize that al-Ghazālī is a pre-modern writer and that his expression of the role of a *rafiq* did not extend to a modern psychotherapist, we view his conceptualization as creating the space that we feel today's TIIP practitioner can occupy. Furthermore, we propose that although the TIIP practitioner is working on both psychological and spiritual health, his/her main function is to both engender relief from psychological dysfunction and build necessary psycho-spiritual resilience that would protect against its recurrence. Therefore, he/she must be cautious to not attempt to focus solely on spiritual aims or goals of achieving spiritual perfection (*kamāl*), a goal more appropriate for a Ṣūfī *shaykh*. The TIIP practitioner operates from a belief in the metaphysical and draws upon the Ṣūfī tradition, while maintaining his/her focus on current psychological functioning and developing resilience. Conversely, the overemphasis of empirical evidence and the underappreciation of the metaphysical rooted in Islamic scripture is a critical differentiating feature between the clinician described above and the TIIP therapist. Thus, the TIIP practitioner ultimately bridges both spheres and contains aspects of both a clinician and spiritual mentor, while also differing in their role from each of these (see Table 2.1).

In this rich psycho-spiritual therapeutic relationship (*murābaṭah*) of the patient with the TIIP therapist, the hidden aspects of the psyche can be unveiled. To help facilitate a psycho-spiritual equilibrium of health requires insight that can be gained by an outside observer, who can serve as a mirror for bringing to the surface one's intrapsychic tensions. Thus, to truly gain access to the insight beyond the layers of veils that an overly outward-oriented existence creates, the idea is that one must have an outsider's perspective, since the familiarity of one's own behaviors resides too close to the self—sometimes below immediate consciousness—to be subject to objective examination (Badri, 1979). Al-Ghazālī states that, at times, the practitioner may point out psychological or behavioral tendencies that the person was not aware of, or that the practitioner may prescribe exercises to facilitate personal insight (al-Ghazālī, 2014).

Just as one on a journey in an unknown land would want a seasoned guide who is knowledgeable of the particular terrain being traversed, this is even more the case when it comes to one's inner self. Thus, even the TIIP therapist requires a degree of psycho-spiritual development, such that the reflection they offer to their patient is not tainted or colored by any immense disease or unresolved intrapsychic tensions that reside in the psyche of the therapist. As the common expression among psychotherapists goes, "a therapist can only take a person as far as they have gone themselves." The TIIP therapist shall be one who has traveled on the path of *inkishāf* or psycho-spiritual awareness and has achieved a level of spiritual development that embodies a relative degree of *i'tidāl* or psycho-spiritual equilibrium through *mujāhadah*, and who is well versed in facilitating the therapeutic process of change. In this way, the TIIP therapist operates as a *khalīl* (close confidant) or *rafīq* (a gentle companion or partner) to his patient. The Prophet Muḥammad (peace and blessings be upon him) is reported to have said: "a person is upon the way of his *khalīl* so each one of you shall be mindful of whom he makes his *khalīl*" (Abū Dāwūd, 2009, *Ḥadīth* 4833). This further emphasizes the importance of the internal qualities and aspects of the TIIP therapist. Thus, this role can be very different than the role of the conventional therapist, who keeps "professional distance" and whose personal life and value systems may be seen as irrelevant or bracketed within a therapeutic relationship. The TIIP therapist operates and offers a shared value system, whereby patients can seek out therapy that is consistent with their spiritual orientations and religious values. The need to bracket conflicting values is therefore mitigated, while at the same time the TIIP therapist continues to maintain a watchful eye on his/her responses that may be more self-serving than in the best interests of the patient.

As presented previously, the TIIP therapist serves a role that is an overlap between a clinician and a *shaykh*. A Ṣūfī *shaykh*, through his *silsilah* and high knowledge and understanding of Islamic teachings and principles, holds a level of authority not enjoyed by the TIIP therapist, which provides for a more egalitarian relationship with the patient, aiding them in a journey to self-realization and integrating spiritual strategies to provide psychological relief. In contrast, a secular clinician's primary focus is on symptom relief or secular psychological processing. While the TIIP therapist role is compatible with a spiritually adapted framework of modern psychology and their role as a mental health provider, there are a number of additional factors that make the TIIP therapist's role unique within an Islamic paradigm of psychology. Within this model, therapeutic interventions reflect both Islamic and clinical methods, but are delivered within an Islamic worldview and are consistent with Islam's foundational principles of change. Modern behavioral research is integrated into the model inasmuch as it is consistent with these Islamic principles. Therefore, it is a matter of the TIIP therapist:

> committing on a deep level to their own intimate knowledge and practice of the Islamic science of the soul and connecting it directly with notions of psychology, reorienting the Western paradigm while maintaining useful Western techniques, and adopting a new outlook and relationship to both psychology and Islam that embraces an indigenous Islamic paradigm.
>
> (Rothman, 2018, p. 53)

Moreover, we conceptualize the center of the human being as the heart; as the Prophet (peace and blessings be upon him) said: "there is a piece of flesh in the body, if it is sound the whole body is sound and if it is corrupt the whole body is corrupt, and that surely is the heart" (al-Bukhārī, 2010, *Ḥadīth* 52). By laying emphasis on the spiritual heart, Islam gives significant attention to the essence of the humanness residing in the nourishment of the human eternal metaphysical self. Thus, unlike conventional modern models of psychology that may conceive solely of the cognitive or emotional aspects of mental health, the TIIP model of care is broader and supposes that the subjective unseen essences (*rūḥ*, *ʿaql*, *nafs*, *iḥsās*) of the psyche are predominately metaphysical and situated at the center of the human spiritual heart (see Chapter 1). For this reason, the role of the therapist in the TIIP therapeutic encounter necessarily involves and centers around an awareness of and attunement to the state of the heart, as it is a place of manifesting health and dysfunction for both the patient and the therapist.

Perhaps where the role of the TIIP therapist, who is operating within an Islamic paradigm, differs significantly from that of a conventional psychotherapist is that the inner world they are inviting the patient to explore is not limited to human consciousness through mental processes and cognition, but is also a holistic picture of the human being that very much involves the exploration of its metaphysical essence (Rothman & Coyle, 2018). The TIIP therapist must become familiar with aspects of Islamic spiritual traditions that can be appropriately adopted in psychotherapy. Extraction of some of these inherently Islamic practices of change for use in the therapeutic encounter serve as powerful mechanisms of psychological relief, given the richness of the Ṣūfī traditions. However, it is critically important to note that being a TIIP therapist does not merely entail the use of overt religious vocabulary or Islamic spiritual interventions. In fact, mainstream psychological interventions may readily be employed with no overt reference to Islam at all. In cases where patients may be averse to "Islamic" interventions, no explicitly Islamic interventions need to be employed in order to meet the patient in the position or condition in which they find themselves. In such cases, the major defining feature of the TIIP therapist is in their understanding of the mechanism of change and conceptual framework in explaining the psychological process and treatment, as is illustrated throughout this book.

Proposed TIIP Therapist Competencies

The role of the TIIP therapist is an important consideration in this model of care and its delivery. Considering the above-mentioned distinctions between the roles of clinician and Ṣūfī *shaykh*, the authors propose the following competencies for the TIIP therapist. It must be remembered that these proposed competencies do not constitute a fully exhaustive and comprehensive list. A summary of the list of competencies that follows is provided in Table 2.2.

Table 2.2 Core competencies for a TIIP practitioner

Competencies	*Essential Components*	*Behavioral Anchors*
1. Strong foundational knowledge and skills with a yearning for further improvement and development	- Formal academic education in the fields of human ontology from an accredited and respected educational institute (college, university, etc.) - Formal Islamic education from an accredited and respected institute (*madrasah*, seminary, etc.) - Formal training in the Traditional Islamically Integrated Psychotherapy (TIIP) Model	- Has graduated from accredited and respected institutes and demonstrates the capacity through verbal and non-verbal communication - Has good knowledge and understanding of the Islamic intellectual heritage - Understands the TIIP model of treatment and is able to guide patients through the process of *inqiyād*, *inkishāf*, *i'tidāl*, and *ittiḥād*
2. Robust moral and ethical principles based on a guided understanding of the Islamic tradition	Objectives of Shariah (Ibn Ashur, 2006): - Protection of faith or religion - Protection of life - Protection of lineage - Protection of intellect - Protection of property Duties towards patients: - Relieve burdens - Ease difficulties - Maintain confidentiality - Continued support - Addresses their own psycho-spiritual development - Has a developed identity and recognizes their role	- Adheres to, and demonstrates understanding of the objectives of *sharī'ah* - Is able to apply these objectives to their professional as well as their personal life - Understands their obligation towards those under their care - Recognizes the importance of the role of their work and how it transcends beyond personal desires and motives - Has awareness of their own deficiencies and is able to further develop their inner state
3. Possesses relational qualities with a strong ability to develop a therapeutic alliance	- Qualities of assertiveness, strong will, and justice, trust in the patient and their ability to heal, hope for change - Has a value-based system grounded in the Islamic tradition	- Portrays such qualities in everyday interactions inside as well as outside of the therapy context

(*continued*)

Table 2.2 Cont.

Competencies	*Essential Components*	*Behavioral Anchors*
	- Possesses the ability to direct in the therapist–patient relationship when needed	
4. Flexibility and balance in thoughts and emotions, and an ability to observe, learn, reflect, understand, and empathize with others	- Ongoing educational drive to improve themselves - Has an understanding of behavioral presentations of various problems - Has developed and practices a holistic and contextual mode of treatment	- Is able to use personal real-life experiences to identify with the patient - Values and incorporates alternative medicine as well as indigenous and traditional healing practices found in many cultures
5. Seeks out mentors, collaborators, consultants, and supervisors for continued support and development	- Has ongoing mentorship with another, more developed TIIP practitioner, or a Ṣūfī *shaykh* who also possesses psychological understanding	- Has a *shaykh* or a mentor from whom they continually seek help - Consults with other professionals inside as well as outside of the profession of psychology
6. Desire to model perfection in character	- Thorough study of the life of Prophet Muḥammad - Self-awareness through a mentor (see #5 above) - Sound moral standing within the community	- Seeks out continued support from others for self-development - Maintains good character in all settings (home, work, community, etc.) - Can apply the *sunnah* in most aspects of daily life
7. Familiarity with the Islamic intellectual heritage and being anchored in an Islamically-derived perspective	- Proficiency in Arabic - Prerequisite courses in Islamic studies - Basic Islamic law (*Mukhtaṣar al-Qudūrī* or its equivalent) - Basic Islamic theology (*Sharḥ al-ʿAqīdah al-Ṭaḥāwiyyah* and *Badʾ al-Amālī*) - *Ḥadīth* studies (*Riyāḍ al-Ṣāliḥīn* and *Mishkāt al-Maṣābīḥ*) (the latter being taught for therapists specifically) - Qurʾān studies (*Tarjumat al-Qurʾān* and *Tafsīr al-Jalālayn/al-Nasafī*) (the latter being taught for therapists specifically)	- A foundational grounding in the core Islamic sciences - A capacity to "think" or "formulate" Islamically oriented interventions within the appropriate bounds and understanding of Islamic theology - A capacity to creatively draw upon and utilize Islamic concepts for therapeutic application - Seeks out this Islamic education at Islamic seminaries where this is offered.

1. Strong Foundational Knowledge and Skills with a Yearning for Further Personal Development

The TIIP therapist must obtain academic and clinical training of high quality. The Prophet (peace and blessings be upon him) states that wisdom is the "lost commodity of the believer and wherever he finds it, he is most entitled to it" (al-Tirmidhī, 1970, *Ḥadīth* 2687). Therefore, as mentioned in Chapter 1, the Islamic epistemology can absorb any knowledge or strategies that are consistent with the overall Islamic ethos. Obtaining a strong academic foundational education and training in the behavioral sciences is necessary given the scope and vocation of the TIIP therapist. It is hoped that educational opportunities that offer an Islamically integrated approach will become available over time. However, in the absence of such resources, current mental health training programs are a reasonable, albeit suboptimal substitute. It is recommended that therapists obtaining such academic training should supplement it with TIIP certification training.

Formal mental health training is imperative, given that the attainment of purely religious education such as a seminary education is insufficient if one wants to serve as an integrated practitioner of mental health care. For example, a therapist who works with married couples in helping them through their marital concerns must possess expertise in marital counseling and be a process expert in resolving marital disputes, whereas the study of the jurisprudence of marriage may prove minimally relevant or helpful in facilitating marital therapy. In addition to these competencies, the TIIP therapist should be able to construct an effective case formulation for their patient that demonstrates knowledge of an Islamic ontology of human nature and attempts to uncover the aspects of the patient's psyche that are being expressed in order to arrive at appropriate treatment goals, in charting a path for the patient to become aware of their deficiencies. Additionally, therapists should be familiar with the behavioral science literature on the psychology of spirituality, such that they are well acquainted with spiritually oriented interventions that enhance or are harmful to psychological well-being (Vieten et al., 2013).

Given this wider context and broader definition of health and well-being that includes the soul of the human being, there is considerable weight and gravity to the role of the therapist as defined by this model, which should come under closer scrutiny for those who consider occupying such a role. Unlike conventional Western models, where it may seem that the therapist earns their position simply because they have received a degree and have trained in certain techniques, the TIIP role requires more of the therapist than mere academic certification. Working in this arena is much more of a personal commitment to an individual calling or spiritual path, a hallmark of which is a commitment to self-work. This role is not necessarily something one "decides" to do based on professional aspirations, but rather may be more about embarking on a deeply committed journey of self-mastery and service to others (*khidmah*), and as a result of this commitment, wanting to or feeling drawn to be with others on that journey in a supportive, inspirational, and reflective capacity (Rothman & Coyle, 2018).

Once this identity and commitment is established, then a person can choose to refine their skills as a guide in this process and be even more diligent about their own work, for God's sake in being most effective in their role as a *khalīl*, but ultimately still benefitting individually from that deepened inner work on the self. As Edwards and Bess (1998, p. 98) said, "the development of a therapist's self-awareness must carry at least as much weight in his or her professional education and training as the accumulation of knowledge about theories and methodologies." The therapist then embarks on this journey to learn to step into the role that al-Ghazālī defined as the second: *Rafīq*. How this role is defined within the *ummah* (global Muslim community) or larger context of the Islamic paradigm is something that this emerging field is now defining and developing. And the TIIP model is one model of care for giving structure to the definition of the role of the therapist.

2. Robust Moral and Ethical Principles Based on a Guided Understanding of Islamic Tradition

Inner State of the TIIP Therapist

With the focus of TIIP being on the *qalb* (heart), it goes without saying that the state of the therapist's own heart, as discussed above, is of critical importance to the position that the therapist takes and contributes to the quality and efficacy of any treatment offered. There is therefore a significant focus on the state of the therapist as a primary concern in the conception of the therapist's role. It is recognized in many schools of Western therapy, particularly in Jungian therapy and the experiential schools of theoretical thought (Rowan, 2013), that the competent therapist must continually be engaged in doing work on themselves. Baldwin (2000) talks of the conception of the therapist's "self as instrument" and others expound upon the merit of continued therapeutic growth of the therapist (McWilliams, 2004; Orlinsky & Ronnestad, 2005).

The concern with the state of the heart of the therapist distinguishes TIIP as a truly Islamic approach with the therapeutic treatment goal of psycho-spiritual health and resilience, as opposed to a mechanistic administering of technique to reduce or eliminate symptoms. The TIIP places considerable emphasis on learning techniques that are consistent with the model, and the most important component of TIIP therapy is its formulation of a patient based on the model's conception of health and suffering. Additionally, the unique role of the therapist within this model of care places great emphasis on the therapist's characteristics and the state of the therapist's own heart, as this is an important aspect of attempting to provide a clear mirror to effectively reflect the patient's nature toward *inkishāf*. The Prophet Muhammad (peace and blessings be upon him) is reported to have said: "a believer is the mirror of a fellow believer" (al-Bukhārī, 2010; al-Adab al-Mufrad, *Ḥadīth* 12, 238). Therefore, companions must have the ability to reflect to each other the other's true nature, as we are all made of and come from the same source. The therapist's role is to help the patient gain knowledge of the self and to reflect this insight as a clear mirror. Thus, in order for the TIIP therapist to provide a clear reflection for their patient, they must take great care to polish the mirror of their own heart, for a turbid mirror reflects a distorted picture. This process of polishing the mirror is maintained through a constant engagement in rigorous study of the knowledge of the soul and the practices of *tazkiyah* or purification of the therapist's inner states, removing the urge to judge others, jealousy, envy, desire for attention, fame, or pride, or other diseases of the heart (see Chapter 9). The therapist must be a well-wisher for the patient and attempt to facilitate treatment that is in the genuine best interests of the patient, while seeing themselves as simply a vessel or medium of healing that ultimately comes from God.

Ethical Considerations, Value Conflicts and Pushing the Professional Practice Boundaries

Having clear ethical boundaries is important in any therapeutic relationship if the relationship is to remain in the best interests of the patient. Meanwhile, the role of the righteous companion or *Khalīl/Rafīq*, in context of the Islamic tradition and the TIIP paradigm, inherently contains a dual relationship by virtue of being brethren in faith. Therefore, it is important to consider Islamic cultural norms of a fluid and human connection even within a professional relationship. Thus, sanctioned aspects of a conventional therapeutic relationship may not need to be rigidly subscribed to, or at least carefully examined for potential value conflicts, if the therapist is practicing or bound by professional ethics within Western countries. It is important to consider that the ethical guidelines outlined by many Western professional associations like the American Psychological Association (APA), are constructed upon social conventions that are consistent with the cultural interpretations of the meanings of certain types of behaviors in those contexts. For example, while shaking hands with a patient is seen as a benign way of greeting a patient, irrespective of gender, within Muslim cultures any contact with a patient may be akin to the hesitation or conflict that non-Muslim American therapists may feel about hugging their patients. Conversely, gift giving is a normative and even prophetically recommended act to show gratitude and connection. It is reported in *Ḥadīth* that the Prophet Muḥammad (peace and blessings be upon him) readily accepted gifts from people (al-Bukhārī, 2010, 2585) and even recommended gift giving to one another. Other actions that are acceptable within general Islamic etiquette, but which are at best a gray area for Western mental health professional ethics and often frowned upon, include praying with your patient, thinking about them in your personal prayers, and attending their funeral service or marital ceremonies.

We propose that therapists exercise a greater willingness to broaden the way that they think critically about these ethical guidelines and consider defining the relationship within a less secularized or industrial schema. Practitioners should consider the potential intentions, secondary or instrumental gains, they desire from such "Islamically" normative behavior. As a good clinician, such assessments are continual and should be considered both at the outset and in ongoing conceptualization. However, the overly psychodynamic influence on these professional ethical issues, which arises out of a need to have distance from and authority over the patient and propels clinicians to overly symbolize or potentially pathologize such behaviors, can risk rupturing the therapeutic alliance. While boundaries such as keeping to limits on timed sessions are important, especially in some cases, it is also important to honor the more polychronic orientation (Hofstede, 1980) to time that is part of the way of Islam. Again, aspects of this can be cultural; however, there is an aspect of this polychronic orientation that is about honoring people and their feelings over arbitrary notions of orienting to time constraints. For example, if a patient's situation genuinely requires more time than the allotted 50 minutes, it can be reasonable and therapeutically effective for the therapist to spend more time in a session, to prioritize helping the patient in their time of need, as a brother or sister, while at the same time balancing and embodying a professional demeanor. Ultimately, while the TIIP practitioner must work within a professional role with clear boundaries and scope of practice, they may also be called to resist the overly industrialized nature of a monetized helping profession.

3. Possesses Relational Qualities with a Strong Ability to Develop a Therapeutic Alliance

While the therapist is familiar with the general realm of psychology and is experienced in guiding individuals through this inner experience of the self, part of good clinical practice is the ability to build strong therapeutic rapport (Leach, 2005). The Prophet Muḥammad (peace and blessings be upon him) stated that:

> Whoever relieves a Muslim of a burden from the burdens of the world, Allah will relieve him of a burden from the burdens on the Day of Judgement. And whoever helps ease a difficulty in the world, Allah will grant him ease from a difficulty in the world and in the Hereafter. And whoever conceals (the faults of) a Muslim, Allah will cover (his faults) in the world and the Hereafter. And Allah is engaged in helping the worshipper as long as the worshipper is engaged in helping his brother.
>
> (al-Muslim, 2006, *Ḥadīth* 2699)

This saying of the Prophet (peace and blessings be upon him) conceptualizes the most important qualities needed by a therapist, especially one practicing within the TIIP framework. First, the therapist must have the desire to help others effectively by relieving them of their "burden" or psycho-spiritual pain. He/she must focus on easing the patient's difficulties through effective therapeutic techniques. He/she must also maintain the confidentiality between him/herself and the patient, honoring the relationship and preserving this trust (*amānah*). Lastly, the focus on the patient is not just during the clinical session; the TIIP therapist should also make it a habit to pray for the well-being of his patients.

The relational factors proposed by Carl Rogers and person centered therapy, and later extended by other experiential therapies such as emotion focused therapy (see Chapter 7), are a very effective basis for helping nurture a strong therapeutic alliance. They include empathic understanding, warmth and positive regard, congruence, and authenticity (Rogers, 1959). These qualities, along with the ability to deal with ruptures in the therapeutic relationship and having mutual agreement on the goal of therapy, lead to a strong therapeutic alliance (Lambert & Barley, 2002). Whatever the approach or the therapeutic style of the therapist may be, the above-mentioned aspects play a key role in the process of healing (Spencer & Rhodes, 2005). Just as in most, if not all, contemporary psychological theories/practices, the relationship and connection between a TIIP therapist and patient is among the most important aspects of treatment. Through this relationship, the guide can model sincere inward character and beautiful outward behavior for the patient (Buehler, 2011). It is important to remember that Islamic knowledge and values have historically been transmitted through human-to-human or heart-to-heart connection, such as the sacred relationship between a spiritual master and his disciple.

4. Flexibility in the Process of Treatment and Case-Specific Conceptualization

When it comes to the field of psychology and the practice of psychotherapy, effectiveness of treatment varies and depends on many factors. It is important to be able to incorporate inherently Islamic concepts where these are warranted, since the religiously devout may benefit more from traditional and indigenous healing practices rather than modern medicine and psychotherapy at times (Moodley & West, 2005). At the same time, a TIIP therapist must develop a flexible mind and approach to treating his/her patient. This includes acceptance of alternative hypotheses related to the nature of the problem as well being open to incorporating alternative healing practices. According to Frank and Frank (1991), all major forms of healing, including psychotherapy, share certain characteristics, such as an emotionally invested relationship between patient and healer, an appropriate setting for the healing process, an explanation for the symptoms experienced by the patient, and an agreed-upon process of healing determined and accepted by both patient and healer.

Just as the TIIP therapist is constantly engaged in this process of *tarbiyah* both within themselves and in their relationship with either their own *shaykh* or "righteous companion", as in al-Ghazālī's suggestion, so too do they employ this process as a central principle in their role as a therapist in working with each patient. After initial assessment and identifying on which parts of the psyche the therapist needs to focus their attention, and a few sessions of establishing the relationship (*murābaṭah*), the therapist works with the patient to design a treatment plan or program of *mu'ālajah* to target and train those psychic aspects through an internal struggle (*mujāhadah* or *jihād al-nafs*) toward *i'tidāl*.

5. Seeks Out Mentors, Collaborators, Consultants, and Supervisors for Continued Support and Development

It is also important to take into consideration that both the TIIP therapist and the patient are on their own independent yet parallel journeys to seek spiritual guidance for themselves. Many contemporary theories (e.g. psychodynamic, insight-oriented) see personal therapy for the therapist as an important, and in some cases a necessary training requirement (Macran & Shapiro, 1998). It is similar within Islamic Ṣūfī practices, where every *shaykh* must have had a *shaykh* themselves. A famous story about Rūmī states that once he was sitting with his spiritual guide, Shams al-Dīn Tabrayzī, when someone rushed in to inform them that a nearby village was in need of a *shaykh*. Rūmī, upon hearing this, exclaimed to his teacher, "Whew, that was a close one. If they had asked for a seeker one of us would have had to go" (Buehler, 2011, p. 148).

Mentorship by peers and supervisors has been found to play an important and valuable role in the development of clinical competencies, and it has been utilized as an effective training tool in various fields of practice (Brown & Sheerin, 2018; Newman, Nebbergall, & Salmon, 2013). At times, this relationship may have a power dynamic that is appropriate for supervision, while in other instances it can be a mutual exchange of reflective accountability. In any case, it is important for the TIIP therapist to have educated and spiritually healthy individuals from whom he/she may seek guidance and mentorship.

Because of competing human drives and their tendency to cloud the ability to look at oneself from a distance, psycho-spiritual mentorship is essential. Abū Zayd al-Balkhī discusses the immense need for all individuals to adopt the mentorship of a wise one to help monitor one's psychological functioning (Badri, 1979). As the Arabic proverb goes, "whomsoever does not have an advisor, *shayṭān* [the devil] becomes their advisor." As it has historically been imperative for Muslims to seek assistance from the wise or learned, many of the Islamic scholars of the past (*mashāyikh*) would have considered it an essential part of becoming a cultured and civilized being. Abū Bakr al-Rāzī, Abū 'Alī Ibn Miskaweh, al-Ghazālī, and Abū Zayd al-Balkhī have all emphasized the need for this supervision and have advised against charting the spiritual path alone (Arberry, 1979; Badri, 1979; Hermansen, 1982; Keshavarzi & Haque, 2013).

6. Desire to Model Perfection in Character and Usage of Creativity in the "Art of Therapy"

In addition to the most obvious qualities needed in the form of skills and training, what perhaps best defines the role of the therapist are the character qualities needed to fulfill this position. The first and the most important of these qualities is that of *ikhlās* (sincerity). While *ikhlās* is translated as sincerity, its meaning conveys a higher purpose, intention, or, one could say, "calling" to this work. It is about being driven to help people for the sake of God. It requires a careful, invested commitment to selflessly learn about the experience of another and to provide undivided attention in the way that the Prophet of Islam made each person who was in his presence feel as though they were the most important person to him. While one can certainly make a career out of such a role, it is almost impossible to envisage a person who truly embodies this quality if their primary objective for doing this work is financial gain or status, two things often fueling career drive or occupation choices. One can make a living as a TIIP therapist and take on the identity of this as a career path, but these really cannot be the motivating factors for getting into this line of work. Unlike many careers that primarily serve the purpose of making money as a means of providing one's *rizq* (provision), the TIIP therapist's role is about doing God's work. Thus, the therapist should see him or herself as being positioned to help those who come to him or her as an instrument of Allah's *qadr* (destiny) for this person and be grateful and humbled for having been given this role. Although modern manualized treatment approaches may encourage pseudo sincerity, it is important to understand the significance of true sincerity and its positive effects on healing.

The therapist should be softhearted and sensitive to the needs and feelings of those who have been placed in his or her care as an *amānah* (trust) from God. This was the quality of the Prophet (peace and blessings be upon him), as it says about him in *Sūrah al-'Imrān* of the Holy Qur'ān: "it was by the Mercy of Allah ﷻ that you have been gentle with them; and if you had been harsh and hard-hearted, they would have broken away from round about you" (Qur'ān 3:159). And the Qur'ān says in the continuation of the above *āyah* (verse), "so pass over their faults and ask Allah's Forgiveness for them" (Qur'ān 3:159). TIIP therapists need to invoke the gentle Prophetic ways of interacting with people and to ask themselves "what would the Prophet Muḥammad (peace and blessings be upon him) do?"

Another essential quality that the therapist must have is creativity. Therapy is as much an art as it is a science. Each patient is a unique individual with a unique set of circumstances and who therefore requires a bespoke treatment approach that fits the specific nuances of their experience to best meet their needs. The more tools a TIIP therapist has in their toolbox and the more confident and creative they are in using these tools to respond to their patient's needs, the better equipped they are to truly help this person achieve transformation and heal at a core level.

Creativity is central to therapeutic healing because of the moment-to-moment experience of the process itself (Hecker & Kottler, 2002). Hecker and Kottler identified the importance of convergent and divergent thinking as well as intuition in fostering creativity. It is better to think of Islamic psychotherapy as a paradigmatic framework than a singular therapeutic approach with a specific set of techniques. There certainly are such things available to use as resources within the Islamic tradition, but what is more important is that the therapist is there to help the patient in front of them transform, find balance, and come closer to Allah in their journey of self-knowledge. As long as that is the ultimate goal, there are endless pathways to get there, as numerous as the permutations of each therapist's intention, imagination, and interaction with each patient's need, imbalance, and response to therapeutic interventions. This is the integrative aspect—the second "I" of TIIP—and successful integration requires creativity and flexibility. Thus, it is important for the therapist to focus more on connecting with and harnessing such creativity and the ability to "dance in the moment" (Kimsey-House, Kimsey-House, & Sandahl, 2011) than solely practicing the delivery of technique. There is a saying: "if you want a job done right, send an intelligent person and don't tell them what to do." An obedient person follows instructions that were given prior to the actual event and which were thus determined based on assumptions, formulas, or expectations. On the other hand, an intelligent person, or rather a person using their creativity intelligently, can respond to the specific and/or unexpected aspects of the given situation in the moment within the reality of the context. Each patient and each situation is unique and a new creation is experienced within the dynamic of the therapeutic relationship. The therapist must see him or herself as a creative agent of change and the process of Islamic psychotherapy as an art.

And finally, the therapist should be a spiritual person and bring spirituality into the therapeutic encounter where appropriate. What this means is that in order to truly practice TIIP within an Islamic paradigm, the therapist must understand and conceive of their role as including the spirit (*rūḥ*) in their work, along with cognitive (*'aql*), emotional (*iḥsās*), and behavioral (*nafs*) aspects. While all of these are important parts of the treatment and of the reality of the human experience, Islamic psychology is particularly concerned with the state of the soul (Rothman & Coyle, 2018). Thus, the therapist should make an effort to orient the patient toward this spiritual identity of the soul. As the famous saying goes, "we are not human beings having a spiritual experience, we are spiritual beings having a human experience". And in the event that a therapist cannot bring spirituality into their sessions with patients overtly, then they should bring it within their own selves, within their own heart. The TIIP therapist needs to cultivate their own spirituality and do the work of therapy from this place.

7. Familiarity with the Islamic Intellectual Heritage and Being Anchored in an Islamically-Derived Perspective

It is critical for the TIIP practitioner who endeavors to provide Islamically oriented treatment to be intimately familiar with the Islamic intellectual heritage. This includes not only internal qualities and practices as mentioned above, but also a strong knowledge base that forms an intuitive Islamic understanding or *Mafhūm Islāmī*. According to Shāh Walī Allah al-Dihlawī's (2010) *al-Qawl al-Jamīl*, the prerequisites for a spiritual guide (*shaykh*) or one who is offering Islamic psycho-spiritual treatment include a formal study of Qur'ān and *Ḥadīth* under a qualified teacher, which he recommends through the likes of al-Maḥallī and al-Suyūṭī's *Tafsīr al-Jalālayn* or al-Nasafī's *Tafsīr al-Madārik* for Qur'ānic study, and al-Baghawī's

Maṣābīḥ al-Sunnah. In studying the Qur'ān, he requires a development of proficiency in recognizing the meanings of the verses, the explanation of their challenging vocabulary, the background of their revelation, their syntactic analysis, and the significance of Qur'ānic stories, among other things. Similarly, for the study of the *Ḥadīth* he requires that mentors should be able to recognize the meanings, explain the vocabulary, break down the syntax, and interpret the challenging reports in light of the positions of the jurists (Walī Allāh, 2010).

Shāh Walī Allah states that it is not necessary for the spiritual guide to have memorized the Qur'ān nor to be able to critically analyze *Ḥadīth* chains. Nor does he stipulate the study of Islamic legal theory (*uṣūl*), Islamic discursive theology (*kalām*), the particulars of Islamic law (*juz'iyyāt al-fiqh*), or legal judgments (*fatāwā*) (see Walī Allāh, 2010, p. 34). Near the end of his work, Shāh Walī Allah provides other useful comments on the requisites of a *shaykh* which will contribute to the following proposed subjects of study that comprise the TIIP curriculum of Arabic and Islamic studies.

1. Proficiency in Arabic
   i. Arabic reading and comprehension (*Qaṣaṣ al-Nabiyyīn/Zād al-Ṭālibīn*)
   ii. Arabic morphology (*Min Kunūz al-Ṣarf/Taṣrīf al-ʿIzzī*)
   iii. Arabic syntax (*Tashīl al-Naḥw/al-Ajrūmiyyah/al-Tuḥfah al-Saniyyah/Hidāyat al-Naḥw/Iẓhār al-Asrār*)
2. Prerequisite introductory (short) courses in Islamic studies
   i. prerequisites in Qur'ānic studies
   ii. prerequisites in *Ḥadīth* studies
   iii. prerequisites in Islamic law studies
   iv. prerequisites in Islamic theology studies
3. Basic Islamic law (*Mukhtaṣar al-Qudūrī* or its equivalent)
4. Basic Islamic theology (*Sharḥ al-ʿAqīdah al-Ṭaḥāwiyyah* & *Bad' al-Amālī*)
5. *Ḥadīth* studies (*Riyāḍ al-Ṣāliḥīn* & *Mishkāt al-Maṣābīḥ*) (the latter being taught for therapists specifically)
6. Qur'ān studies (*Tarjumat al-Qur'ān* and *Tafsīr al-Jalālayn/al-Nasafī*) (the latter being taught for therapists specifically)

Conclusion

In sum, the TIIP practitioner plays a very important and expansive role. While the TIIP practitioner is predominately working with psychological dysfunction as a spiritually oriented mental health practitioner, his/her professional identity is informed by the Islamic tradition. We recognize that the proposed competencies listed above set a high bar. However, we also highlight the importance of such competencies due to the nature of the work of a TIIP therapist, a role that serves the nobility of human belief and identity. The primary competencies listed above in essence are composed of possessing therapeutic skill/training, Islamic education, and positive internal character traits. We are optimistic that the global climate of interest and receptivity for the intersection of spirituality and psychology among Muslims and non-Muslims alike will lead to the formalization and formulation of graduate training programs that prepare students for this endeavor. In the absence of such institutional programs, it is proposed that both practitioners and students utilize the above-mentioned guidelines as motivation to acquire them through seeking out mentorship by senior figures in this emerging field to work on their own professional and spiritual development.

References

Abū Dāwūd, S. (2009). *Sunan Abu Dawud.* Beirut: Dār al-Rasā'il al-'Ā lamiyyah.

al-Bayjūrī, A. (2002). *Ḥāshiyat al-Imām al-Bayjūrī 'alā Jawharat al-Tawḥīd.* Cairo: Dār al-Salām.

al-Bukhārī (2010). *Saḥīḥ al-Bukhārī.* Darussalam: Riyadh.

al-Ghazālī, A. H. (1993). *Revival of the religious sciences*, trans. F. Karim. Karachi: Dar al-Ishā'ah.

al-Ghazālī, A. H. (2011). *Iḥyā' 'Ulūm al-Dīn.* Vol. 5. Riyadh: Dār al-Minhāj.

al-Ghazālī, A. H. (2014). *Mukhtaṣar: Iḥyā' 'Ulūm al-Dīn*, trans. M. Khalaf. Lympia, Cyprus: Spohr Publishers.

al-Muslim, M. (2006). *Saḥīḥ Muslim.* Riyadh: Dār Ṭaybah for Publishing and Distribution.

al-Tirmidhī, M. (1970). *Jāmi' al-Tirmidhī.* Riyadh: Darrusalam.

Arberry, A. J. (1979). *Sufism: An account of the mystics in Islam.* New York, NY: Harper & Row.

Badri, M. (1979). *Abū Zayd al-Balkhī's Sustenance of the Soul: The cognitive behavior therapy of a ninth century physician.* London: International Institute of Islamic Thought.

Baldwin, M. (2000). *The use of self in therapy.* 2nd ed. New York, NY: The Haworth Press.

Brown, C. E., & Sheerin, K. M. (2018). The role of graduate students as mentors in health service psychology programs. *Training and Education in Professional Psychology, 12*, 22–28.

Buehler, A. F. (2011). *Revealed grace: The juristic Sufism of Ahmad Sirhindi (1564–1624).* Louisville, KY: Fons Vitae.

Chittick W. C. (1989). *The Sufi Path of Knowledge: Ibn Al-Arabi's Metaphysics of Imagination.* New York, NY: State University of New York Press.

Chittick, W. C. (2005). *The Sufi Path of Love: The spiritual teachings of Rumi.* Lahore: Sohail Academy.

Durrani, K. K., Hankir, A. Z., & Carrick, F. R. (2018). History and Principles of Islam and Islamophobia. In H. S. Moffic, J. Peteet, A. Hankir, & R. Awaad, *Islamophobia and Psychiatry: Recognition, Prevention, and Treatment* (pp. 33–40). Cham: Springer.

Edwards, J. K., and Bess, J. A. (1998). Developing effectiveness in the therapeutic use of self. *Clinical Social Work Journal, 26*, 89–105.

Ernst, C. W. (2011). *Sufism: an introduction to the mystical tradition of Islam*. Boulder, CO: Shambala Publications.

Fairburn, C. G., & Cooper, Z. (2011). Therapist competence, therapist quality and therapist training. *Behavior Research and Training, 49*(6–7), 373–378.

Frank, J. D., & Frank, J. A. (1991). *Persuasion and healing: a comparative study of psychotherapy*. 3rd ed. Baltimore, MD: Johns Hopkins University Press.

Hecker, L. L., & Kottler, J. A. (2002). Growing creative therapists. Introduction to a special issue. *Journal of Clinical Activities, Assignments & Handouts in Psychotherapy Practice, 2*(2), 1–3.

Hermansen, M. K. (1982). Shah Wali Allah's arrangement of the subtle spiritual centers. *Studies in Islam.*

Hofstede, G. (1980). *Culture's consequences: International differences in work-related values.* London: Sage.

Horvath, A. O., Del Re, A. C., Fluckiger, C., & Symonds, D. (2011). Alliance in individual psychotherapy, *Psychotherapy, 48*(1), 9–16.

Ibn Ashur (2006). *Treaties on Maqāṣid al-Sharī'ah.* Herndon, VA: IIIT.

Jennings, L., & Skovholt, T. M. (1999). The cognitive, emotional, and relational characteristics of master therapists. *Journal of Counseling Psychology, 46*(1), 3–11.

Keshavarzi, H., & Haque, A. (2013). Outlining a psychotherapy model for enhancing Muslim mental health within an Islamic context. *International Journal for the Psychology of Religion, 23*(3), 230–249.

Kim, D. M., Wampold, B. E., & Bolt, D. M. (2006). Therapist effects in psychotherapy: A random-effects modeling of the National Institute of Mental Health Treatment of Depression Collaborative Research Program data. *Psychotherapy Research, 16*, 161–172.

Kimsey-House, H., Kimsey-House, K., & Sandahl, P. (2011). *Co-active coaching: Changing business, transforming lives.* Boston, MA: Nicholas Brealey Publishers.

Lambert, M. J., & Barley, D. E. (2002). Research summary on the therapeutic relationship and psychotherapy outcome. In J. C. Norcross (Ed.), *Psychotherapy relationships that work: Therapist contributions to responsiveness to patients* (pp. 17–32). New York, NY: Oxford University Press.

Leach, M. J. (2005). Rapport: A key to treatment success. *Complementary therapies in clinical practice, 11*(4), 262–265.

Macran, S., & Shapiro, D. (1998). The role of personal therapy for therapists: A review. *British Journal of Medical Psychology, 71*, 13–25.

McWilliams, N. (2004). *Psychoanalytic psychotherapy: A practitioner's guide*, New York, NY: Guilford Press.

Moodley, R., & West, W. (Eds.) (2005). *Integrating traditional healing practices into counseling and psychotherapy.* Thousand Oaks, CA: Sage Publications.

Morstyn, R. (2002). The therapist's dilemma: Be sincere or fake it? *Australasian Psychiatry, 10*(4): 325–329.

Newman, D. S., Nebbergall, A. J., & Salmon, D. (2013). Structured peer group supervision for novice consultants: Procedures, pitfalls, and potential. *Journal of Educational & Psychological Consultation*, *23*, 200–216.

Orlinsky, D. E. (1999). The master therapist: Ideal character or clinical fiction? Comments and questions on Jennings and Skovholt's "The cognitive, emotional, and relational characteristics of master therapists." *Journal of Counseling Psychology*, *46*, 12–15.

Orlinsky, D. E., & Ronnestad, M. H. (2005). *How psychotherapists develop: A study of therapeutic work and professional growth*. Washington, DC: American Psychological Association.

Pormann, P. E. (2007). *Medieval Islamic medicine*. Washington, DC: Georgetown University Press.

Ragab, A. (2018). *The medieval Islamic hospital: Medicine, religion, and charity*. Cambridge, UK: Cambridge University Press.

Rogers, C. R. (1959). A theory of therapy, personality and interpersonal relationships. In S. Koch (Ed.), *Psychology: A study of a science* (pp. 184–256). New York, NY: McGraw-Hill.

Rothman, A. (2018). An Islamic theoretical orientation to psychotherapy. In C. York Al-Karam (Ed.), *Islamically integrated psychotherapy: Uniting faith with practice* (pp. 25–56). West Conshohocken, PA: Templeton Press.

Rothman, A., & Coyle, A. (2018). Toward a framework for Islamic psychology and psychotherapy: An Islamic model of the soul. *Journal of Religion and Health*, *57*(5), 1731–17444.

Rowan, J. (2013). *The reality game: A guide to humanistic counselling and psychotherapy*. 2nd ed. London: Routledge.

Skovholt, T. M., & Jennings, L. (2016). *Master therapists: exploring expertise in therapy and counseling*, 10th anniversary edition. New York, NY: Oxford University Press.

Spencer, R., & Rhodes, J. E. (2005). A counseling and psychotherapy perspective on mentoring relationships. In D. DuBois & M. Karcher (Eds.), *Handbook of Youth Mentoring*. Thousand Oaks, CA: Sage Publications.

Thānwī, A. A. (1971). *Anfās-e-Ī sā*. Deoband, India: Idārah Ta'līfāt-e-Awliyā'.

Usmani, M. T. (2001). *Spiritual discourses*. Karachi: Darul Ishat.

Vieten, C., Scammel, S., Pilato, R., Ammondson, I., Pargament, K. I., & Lukoff, D. (2013). Spiritual and religious competencies for psychologists. *Psychology of Religion and Spirituality*, 1–16.

Walī Allāh, S. (2010). *Al-Qawl al-Jamīl fī Bayān Sawā' al-Sabīl*. Cairo: Dar al-Jawdiyyah.

Walī Allāh, S. D., & Hermansen, M. K. (1996). *The conclusive argument of God: Shāh Walī Allāh of Delhi's Ḥujjat Allah al-Bāligha*. Leiden: Brill.

Part II

Introducing the Islamic Intellectual Heritage

Chapter 3

Islamic Psychology

A Portrait of its Historical Origins and Contributions

Rania Awaad, Danah Elsayed, Sara Ali, and Aneeqa Abid

Chapter Summary

Muslim scholars from Islam's rich intellectual history wrote about therapeutic rapport, psychiatric aftercare, and cognitive strategies for the treatment of depression centuries before their European counterparts. Many of these scholars drew inspiration and motivation for their contributions to psychology from Islamic sources in addition to empirical and rational sources. After providing a working definition of Islamic psychology, this chapter explores its historical and methodological origins, suggesting that its early success was due to Islamic scriptural motivation and inspiration, as well as to some intertwining socio-political factors. The legacies of ten Muslim scholars from 622 to 1492 CE (a time period in Islamic history when there was great emphasis on scientific production) are described, with particular attention paid to their impressive scholarly contributions to psychology and to their methodological foundations. The chapter concludes by discussing the current state of and future directions for the modern field of Islamic psychology, delving into the perhaps exclusive foundations of mainstream psychology as a distinct, academic discipline and the ensuing efforts for the revival of Islamic psychology. Understanding the origins and historical contributions of the study of Islamic psychology can serve as a first step towards providing holistic, spiritually integrated care to the oft-marginalized Muslim community and towards facilitating the revival of Islamic psychology as a holistic, spiritually integrated discipline of practice and research.

Introduction

Medieval Muslim scholars from Islam's rich intellectual history studied, documented, and practiced early forms of holistic psychotherapy, utilized ancient medical (herbal) management for non-remitting conditions, and employed cognitive strategies for the treatment of exogenous psychological conditions (Awaad & Ali, 2015; Farooqi, 2006; Haque, 2004; Tbakhi & Amr, 2007). Many of these scholars drew inspiration and motivation for their contributions to psychology from Islamic scriptural sources in addition to empirical and rational sources (Ivry, 2008). Despite psychology's initial involvement in the debate over the mind and body problem (which was largely couched in metaphysical language), modern psychology eventually broke from metaphysics and adopted monistic physicalism (see Chapter 4). The introduction of a secular psychology to the Muslim world was largely untenable for Muslim patients, practitioners, and researchers, who were unable to fully accept or trust a discipline with principles that dismissed such an integral source of guidance in their lives (Haque, 2004). This is likely one of several reasons why many Muslims today are not likely to access mental health services (Keshavarzi & Ali, 2018).

In recent years, however, the doors of spiritually integrated psychological care and research have reopened (Keshavarzi & Ali, 2018; Pargament, 2011). Practitioners and researchers are beginning to rediscover the early contributions of Muslim scholars and are exploring and demonstrating its applicability and relevance to a modern, spiritually integrated Islamic psychology. Understanding the origins and historical contributions of the study of Islamic psychology, then, can serve as a first step towards providing holistic, spiritually integrated care to the oft-marginalized Muslim community.

Terminology and Historical Origins

Defining Islamic Psychology

The modern term "psychology" comes from the Greek roots *psyche* (meaning breath, spirit, or soul) and *logia* (meaning the study of) (Kleinman, 2012). Similarly, the Arabic equivalent of the term psychology, *'Ilm al-Nafs*, translates to English as "knowledge of the soul". Modern psychology has shifted away from philosophizing about the soul (a metaphysical entity) and has adopted a strictly empirical and rational approach to investigating the psyche and the physical aspects of human behavior. In contrast, Islamic psychology utilizes empirical, rational, and scriptural sources to study both the physical and metaphysical facets of the human psyche and behavior (see Chapter 1). Drawing on the Qur'ān (Islam's holy book, the word of God), the Sunnah (the Prophet Muḥammad's statements, actions, and tacit approvals, peace and blessings be upon him), and Islam's intellectual heritage, Islamic psychology is the empirical, rational, and revelatory study of human cognition (*'aql*), emotions (*iḥsās*), behavioral inclinations (*nafs*), and spirit (*rūḥ*) (Keshavarzi et al., Chapter 1 of this volume).

Historical and Methodological Origins of Islamic Psychology

Long before the term "psychology" was coined, scholars and thinkers from the Hellenistic period and later were studying it (Ivry, 2008). What remains of their foundational work was preserved and built upon largely because of the large-scale translation efforts (from Greek to Arabic) and interdisciplinary knowledge hives that developed during the seventh to fifteenth centuries CE (such as the Bayt al-Ḥikmah in the Abbasid capital of Baghdad), which led to the flowering of Islamic health care (*ṭibb*) and to the beginnings of an Islamic psychology (Haque, 2004). It is likely that three elements were responsible for this: (1) Muslim religious motivation, (2) inspiration for the pursuit of knowledge, and (3) the socio-political factors resulting from (and co-occurring with) this motivation and inspiration (Haque, 2004; Ivry, 2008). These elements are discussed below.

Muslim Religious Motivation

Throughout the Qur'ān, Muslims are encouraged to reflect and to carry out introspection (41:53, 50:6, 51:21, 88:17), travel and discover (29:20, 30:42), ask questions about their origin (52:35, 52:36), nurture their curiosity about the natural world (2:164), and remain intellectually honest (17:36). In fact, Muslims believe that the very first verse of the Qur'ān revealed to the Prophet Muḥammad (peace and blessings be upon him) was: "Read, in the Name of your Lord who created" (96:1) (Faizal, Ridhwan, & Kalsom, 2013). The first word of this verse, *iqra'*, also connotes knowledge, understanding, and exploration (Ibn Manẓūr, 1955 pp. 128–133).

A second important revelatory source for Muslim motivation can be found in the Sunnah, or the life of the Prophet Muḥammad (peace and blessings be upon him). During his life, the Prophet Muḥammad (peace and blessings be upon him) endorsed learning and teaching (al-Tirmidhī, 1970, *Ḥadīth* 2685; Ibn Mājah, 2007, *Ḥadīth* 224), looking for solutions (Muslim, 2006, *Ḥadīth* 2204), and criticality/objectivity (al-Tirmidhī, 1970, *Ḥadīth* 5129). He is narrated to have said, "Whoever takes a path upon which to obtain knowledge, Allah makes the path to paradise easy for him" (al-Tirmidhī, 1970, *Ḥadīth* 2646).

In addition to their focus on learning in general, the Qur'ān and Sunnah direct Muslims to pay particular attention to their inner selves (Ivry, 2008). Rich with principles that guide the development and purification of the self, the Qur'ān encourages Muslims to study it in order to understand it. By doing so, the Qur'ān posits that they will attain certainty and discover truth. This is demonstrated in the following verse: "We will show them Our signs in the horizons and within themselves until it becomes clear to them that it is the truth" (41:53). The exegete-historian Ibn Kathīr (d.774

AH/1373 CE) states that the verse may mean that Allah demonstrates the truth of the Qur'ān and Islam through reflection on the "composition of man, its components (*mawādd*), humors (*akhlāṭ*), and marvellous conditions (*hay'āt 'ajība*)" through which one is able discover the infinite wisdom of the Creator (*Tafsīr Ibn Kathīr*, 41:53).

Islamic scholars also demonstrate the importance of studying and preserving the psyche within the Islamic legal tradition. A fundamental and universal objective of Islam is the acquisition of what is good and beneficial (*jalb al-maṣāliḥ*) and the rejection of what is evil and harmful (*dar' al-mafāsid*) in nations, in communities, and particularly in individuals. One of the five larger objectives of Islamic law (*maqāṣid al-sharī'ah*) designed to achieve this is the preservation and optimization of one's mental capacity or intellect (Awaad, Mohammad, Elzamzamy, Fereydooni, & Gamar, 2018). Muslim legal theorists posit that this is a necessary principle of the Sharī'ah because it is only possible to achieve righteousness (*ṣalāḥ)* in the world and remove corruption from it when humanity preserves its rational and spiritual capacity. Correct thinking leads to proper reflection on international, national, communal, and individual affairs. Thus the optimization of the human psyche and soul is a primary objective of Islam, as evidenced by the Prophet's statement (peace and blessings be upon him), "Verily there is a piece of flesh [*mudghah*] in the body. If it is sound, the entire body remains sound, but if it is corrupted the entire body is corrupted. That is the heart" (al-Bukhārī, 2010, ḥadith 25). This, coupled with the Prophet Muhammad's (peace and blessings be upon him) famous saying "For every illness, there is a cure", helps to explain why scholars in the Muslim world paid special attention to understanding the psyche, the way that it affects human behavior, how and why it becomes ill, and finding cures for its illness (Awaad et al., 2018; Ibn Mājah, 2007, *Ḥadīth* 3438).

It may be argued that Muslim scholars were motivated mainly by basic curiosity or because they wanted to follow in the footsteps of their Greek predecessors. However, upon reading their works more closely, it becomes clear that this was not the case. For example, in his *Faṣl al-Maqāl*, Abū al-Wālid Muḥammad ibn Aḥmad ibn Rushd (d.594 AH/1198 CE; also known as Averroes) highlights five of the Qur'ānic verses listed above to make a case for the necessity of studying philosophy (one of the precursors to psychology) (Ibn Rushd, 1986). He describes the work of the philosopher as "nothing more than investigating and reflecting upon what exists ... for the more that we know about what exists, the more that we know about the One that caused it to exist" (Ibn Rushd, 1986, p. 27). Further, after beginning his famous book, *Tahdhīb al-Akhlāq* (Refining Manners) with "In the Name of Allah, the most Compassionate, the most Merciful" (as many scholars did at that time), the Buyid era ethicist Abū 'Alī Aḥmad ibn Miskawayh (d.421 AH/1030 CE) says:

> Our purpose in writing this book is to equip ourselves with manners that lead to the most beautiful actions … And the path to this is to first know our self: what it is and what it is of, what completes it, what it desires, what strengthens it and what limits it. For God says, *By the soul and the One who fashioned it, then with knowledge of right and wrong inspired it, successful indeed is the one who purifies their soul, and failed indeed is the one who corrupts it.*
>
> (Ibn Miskawayh, 1882, p. 2, original emphasis)

These examples, and many others like them throughout the works of the Muslim scholars, reveal a scholarly motivation fuelled by revelation.

Islamic Inspiration and Methodology

Unlike many of their ancient predecessors and non-Muslim contemporaries, Muslim and Islamic psychologists—or rather philosophers, physicians, and theologians (as they were known before psychology had a name)—drew from revelatory sources (i.e. the Qur'ān and Sunnah) in addition to empirical, rational, and observational sources for inspiration for their scholarly work (Nasr, 2015). While some Muslim scholars were heavily influenced by Greek works, at times in ways that diverged from classical understandings of Islamic law, (Awaad et al., 2018), others placed revelatory sources in their own elite category (Bakar, 2015; Tibi, 2006). They believed that the purpose of inquiry in their respective fields was to unravel the truths of the universe. They also believed that ultimate truths (*ḥaqīqah*) lay in revelatory sources and they called upon those sources (if not always explicitly) in the formulation of their theories (Campanini, 2015; Nasr, 2015).

Although Muslim scholars like Ibn Miskawayh and Abū ʿAlī al-Ḥusayn ibn Sīnā (d.428 AH/1037 CE, also known as the "doctor of doctors" and anglicized as Avicenna) rarely quoted these sources in their writing, examining their theories alongside their commentaries on the Qur'ān may elucidate their use of scripture (however implicit) in their work (Nasr, 2015). For example, Ibn Sīnā is known to have supported the presence of individual differences in terms of his patients' capacity for and reactions to medicine (Saad, 2014), emotional experiences (Awaad et al., 2018), and teaching or learning (Salleh & Embong, 2017). In his commentary on the 87th chapter of the Qur'ān (Sūrat al-ʿAlaq), Abdul Haq states that Ibn Sīnā highlights three themes present throughout the chapter (Abdul Haq, 1988). Later in his analysis, he comments on the eighth verse in the chapter: "And We will make it easy and simple for thee." He says that this verse "implies that … there are some people for whom chastity is easier and who are instinctively more inclined to it" (as cited in Abdul Haq, 1988, p. 51). Although it is possible that Ibn Sīnā's existing theories about the world informed his interpretation of the Qur'ān and not the other way around, here we see that he notes (and, though not explicitly stated here, accepts) the Qur'ān's position on the presence of individual differences in capacity and reaction. A similar pattern with Ibn Miskawayh's theory of virtuous alternatives is outlined later in this chapter.

Additionally, scholars often deferred to revelatory sources where other sources were unclear or unable to guide them. For example, in contrast to the epistemological principles of Western philosophy, in many of his works, including *al-Shifā'*, Ibn Sīnā stated that he could not prove the Resurrection—he relied completely on the Qur'ān for this (Nasr, 2015). Similarly, Abū Yūsuf Ya'qūb ibn Isḥāq al-Kindī (d.260 AH/873 CE, also known as "the Philosopher of the Arabs") admitted that the intellectual tools provided by philosophy could only describe God in negative terms (i.e. God is not an accident, an element, etc.), whereas theology had the authority to describe God in positive terms (Klein-Franke, 2015). This epistemological submission to revelatory sources on the part of the scholars shows that their work was far from merely an echo of Greek philosophy. Rather, in the words of Seyyed Hossein Nasr, "Islamic philosophy is what is it is precisely because it flowered in a universe whose contours are determined by Qur'anic revelation" (Nasr, 2015, p. 84).

Socio-Political Factors

Beyond—and perhaps, because of—Muslim religious inspiration and motivation to pursue knowledge (especially knowledge pertaining to the self), several socio-political factors enabled the preservation of ancient psychological works, and in turn, the development of Islamic psychology (Haque, 2004; Ivry, 2008).

To begin, from the seventh century to the fifteenth century CE (or the first to ninth centuries AH), the Islamic world was flourishing. The Abbasids had inherited the Roman and Persian empires and decided to build the city of Baghdad at the heart of the Silk Road, a trade route that spanned the world's major economic centers (Lyons, 2010). Baghdad's strategic placement brought it prosperity, safety, and stability (Lyons, 2010). As the city (and others like it) grew, Muslim rulers had to grapple with new religious and civil questions. How could they be sure that they were praying in the direction of Mecca? How would they manage large-scale trade deals while complying with Islam's ethical economic standards? What were the best ways to carry out their Islamic duties towards treating the mentally ill in their city? These questions and others pushed them to acquire and create knowledge in the fields of psychology, astronomy, trigonometry, algebra, and more (Awaad et al., 2018).

As a result, the production and preservation of knowledge became highly incentivized. Abū al-'Abbās 'Abd Allāh ibn Hārūn al-Rashīd (d.218

AH/833 CE, also known as Ma'mūn, the seventh Abbasid Caliph), would grant scholars the weight of their work in gold for translations of foreign treatises and manuscripts into Arabic (Mehawesh, 2014; Murube, 2007). He established the famous "House of Wisdom" (*Bayt al-Ḥikmah*), an intellectual beehive dedicated to such endeavours, drawing scholars of all faiths from all over the world. Under its domes, Greek, Indian, Persian, and other ancient works related to psychology (and nearly every other discipline imaginable) were translated into Arabic, then discussed by some of the greatest minds of the time (Awaad & Ali, 2015; Bakar, 2015).

Scholars of Islamic Psychology and Their Contributions

Through examining the psyche through empirical, rational, and scriptural sources, many Muslim scholars from the seventh to fifteenth centuries CE were known to be encyclopedic in their scholarship, as their works often spanned various fields of knowledge (Farooqi, 2006). A closer look at the scholars whose academic work has contributed or may contribute to Islamic psychology reveals three main areas of scholarship from which modern attempts at developing an integrated Islamic psychology may draw: philosophy, physiology, and theology/spirituality.

The Philosophers' Perspective

AL-KINDĪ (D.259 AH/873 CE)

Known as the "Philosopher of the Arabs", Abu Yūsuf Ya'qūb ibn Isḥāq al-Kindī was an encyclopedic scholar who authored at least 231 treatises and manuscripts on a wide range of topics, including: mathematics, metaphysics, philosophy, medicine, and psychology (Adamson, 2018; Jumu'ah, 2014; Najātī, 1993). At least five of his works were related to psychology, including: *Kalām fī al-Nafs* (Discourse on the Soul), *Fī al-Qawl fī-al Nafs* (Discussions on the Soul), *Māhiyyat al-Nawm wa al-Ru'yah* (The Essence of Sleep and Dreams), *Fī al-'Aql* (On the Intellect), and *al-Ḥīlah li Daf' al-Aḥzān* (The Strategy for Repelling Sorrow (Jumu'ah, 2014; Najātī, 1993).

During his lifetime, al-Kindī was appointed by the Abbasid caliphs al-Ma'mūn and later Abū Isḥāq Muḥammad ibn Hārūn al-Rashīd (d.228 AH/842 CE, also known as al-Mu'taṣim) to the "House of Wisdom" to oversee the translation of Greek works into Arabic (Najātī, 1993). In turn, his own work became heavily influenced by the likes of Aristotle and Plato—although he refuted certain of their theories for their incompatibility with Islamic principles. For example, although he supported Plato's tripartite theory of the soul, Ivry and Janssens state that he clearly expressed that revelation from God was superior to human knowledge and reason (Ivry, 2008; Janssens, 1994). In general, his works attempted to reconcile Greek philosophy and Islamic theology in order to make the Greek ideas more palatable to Muslim readers (Adamson, 2018; Fitzmaurice, 1971; Najātī, 1993). However, according to Klein-Franke (2015) he often stretched the linguistic boundaries of both Islamic theology and philosophy in order to do so.

Al-Kindī propounded several theories related to intellectual operations, including theories on perception, sleeping and dreams, and emotional processes (Awaad et al., 2018; Ivry, 2008). Notably, al-Kindī prized cognitive strategies in the treatment of depression. In his *al-Ḥīlah li Daf' al-Aḥzān* (The Strategy to Repelling Sorrows) he suggests that the feeling of sorrow manifests itself when an individual loses loved ones or personal belongings, or fails to achieve a goal of some kind, especially goals pertaining to material gain (Haque, 2004). He says that "we must, therefore, strive to be happy and refuse to be sad by directing our desires and wants to what is attainable [i.e. by adjusting our goals] and by not grieving over what we missed out on" (al-Kindī & 'Abd al-Hadi, 1950, p. 8). It is interesting to note that in this excerpt al-Kindī borrows the same four-word phrase from the Qur'ān (57:23) used to describe grief over missing out.

IBN MISKAWAYH (D.421 AH/1030 CE)

Abū 'Alī Aḥmad ibn Miskawayh was an ethicist from the Buyid Era and a contemporary of Ibn Sīnā. His work on moral and positive psychology laid the foundation for many following theories surrounding altering behaviors, attitudes, and manners in gradual, concrete steps (Awaad et al., 2018; Leaman, 2015a). Ibn Miskawayh's work often drew from both the Qur'ān and the contemporary theories of his time (Leaman, 2015a). In addition to writing about history, chemistry, and philosophy, Ibn Miskawayh wrote several books related to psychology (Najātī, 1993), including: *al-Sa'ādah fī Falsafit al-Akhlāq* (Happiness from the Perspective of Ethical Philosophy), *Tahdhīb al-Akhlāq* (Refinement of Ethics), *al-Fawz al-Asghar* (The Minor Victory), *al-Sa'ādah* (Happiness), *Risālah fī al-Lazzāt wa al-Ālām* (A Treatise on Pleasures and Pains), *Risālah fī Jawhar al-Nafs* (On the Essence of the Soul), *Ajwibah wa As'ilah fī al-Nafs wa al-'Aql* (Questions and Answers on the Soul and the Mind), and *Ṭahārat al-Nafs* (Purity of the Soul).

Of course, Ibn Miskawayh was not the first to discuss ethics and ethical philosophy in Islamic history. Several works from the great scholars Ibn al-Muqaffa' (d.143 AH/761 CE), 'Amr ibn Baḥr al-Jāḥiẓ (d.255 AH/869 CE), Muslim ibn Qutaybah (d.276 AH/890 CE), Abū Bakr 'Abd Allāh ibn Muḥammad ibn Muḥammad Ibn Abī al-Dunyā (d.281 AH/895 CE), Jarīr al-Ṭabarī (d.310 AH/932 CE), Abū Bakr Muḥammad ibn Zakariyyā al-Rāzī (d.313 AH/925 CE), Abū Naṣr Sarrāj al-Ṭūsī (d.378 AH/989 CE), Abū Ṭālib al-Makkī, and Abū Ḥāmid al-Ghazālī (d.510 AH/1111 CE) also discussed Islamic morality, ethics, and behavior.

Many of Ibn Miskawayh's works emphasize happiness over malady. For example, in his book *al-Sa'ādah fī Falsafit al-Akhlāq* he discusses the perception of happiness, arguing that it is a relative feeling. He also stresses the importance of having a personal mission and setting individual goals, as well as the value of hard work in the pursuit of happiness (Ibn Miskawayh & Asyūṭī, 1928). In *Tahdhīb al-Akhlāq*, Ibn Miskawayh describes the "ultimate happiness", saying that it is attainable once individuals can cleanse themselves of their moral ailments. He says, "This is ultimate success, for it leads to one being prepared to meet one's Creator. Through this process of purification, one overcomes the obstacles which prevented one from attaining this ultimate happiness" (Ibn Miskawayh, 1882, p. 37).

Like Aristotle's notion of cultivating physical health by maintaining a corporal equilibrium, Ibn Miskawayh argues that our ethical health (and as a consequence our happiness) must also be cultivated through the preservation of a moral equilibrium (Leaman, 2015a). To do this, one must practice regulation of emotion and the self, and eradicate faults by swapping their ultimate causes with virtuous alternatives (Awaad et al., 2018; Leaman, 2015a). One self-regulation strategy that Ibn Miskawayh outlines is similar to modern response cost models, where an individual punishes themselves if their self-control lapses in order to eliminate undesired behaviors (Awaad et al., 2018). This practice is encouraged in Islam, with the Qur'ān commanding Muslims to free a slave if they break an oath (for example 5:89). In this instance, a moral equilibrium is achieved: When one contract is wrongly severed, another is rightfully dissolved.

IBN RUSH D/AVERROES (D.594 AH/1198 CE)

Abu al-Walīd Muḥammad ibn Aḥmad Ibn Rushd was the chief Islamic Jurist *(Qadi)* of Cordoba, the sultan's personal doctor, a philosopher, and a scientist (Urvoy, 2015). He contributed to the fields of law, medicine, philosophy, literature, physics, astronomy, politics, and psychology (Urvoy, 2015). Ibn Rushd believed that psychology carried particular importance, as its subject matter was noble and its demonstrative (rational) power made it "surpass other sciences, except for divine science" (as cited in Taylor, 1998, p. 513). He wrote several books on the topic of the self, including: the book of *al-Nafs* (The Soul), *al-'Aql wa al-Ma'qūl* (The Mind and the Rational), and his famous response to al-Ghazali's *Tahāfut al-Falāsifah* (Incoherence of the Philosophers) entitled *Tahāfut at-Tahāfut* (Incoherence of the Incoherence) (Arnaldez, 2012).

Writing extensively on mental processes (including thought, intellect, and imagination), Ibn Rushd attempted to refine the field's understanding of these internal senses (Haque, 2004; Ivry, 2008). For example, in his discussions of cognition, he argued that it is not sufficient for a person to sense an object in order for them to perceive it. Instead, imagination must be used to abstract the external input, and thus perceive it objectively (Haque, 2004). According to Haque, in the book *Faṣl al-Maqāl* (The Decisive Treatise) Ibn Rushd proposes a hierarchy of learning strategies through which a person can accept something to be true: dialectical arguments, demonstrations, and rhetorical arguments (Haque, 2004). He says that depending on a person's capacity for understanding each of these forms of arguments, they can interact with revealed Islamic scripture on two levels: the scripture's apparent (*ẓāhir*) and hidden (*bāṭin*) levels of meaning (Haque, 2004).

Ibn Rushd used these concepts of apparent and hidden meaning in scripture to balance a carefully constructed methodology of scholarship. He held revelatory sources to be flawless (using them to make arguments, as seen in the section on "Muslim Religious Motivation" and seeing flaws only in others' interpretations of them) and employed philosophical, rational, and demonstrative arguments in his analysis of those revelatory sources, as well as of the works of Aristotle, Plato, and his contemporaries (Ibn Rushd, 1986). For example, in his legal work *Bidāyat al-Mujtahid wa Nihāyat al-Muqtaṣid* (The Beginning for the Determined Seeker and the End for the Frugal Reader), he outlines a methodology of inquiry based mutually in Aristotelian logical principles and Islamic *fiqh* (jurisprudence), in which he often applies literal or metaphorical judgements to scripture to solve logical problems (for a summary see Urvoy, 2015).

AL-FĀRĀBĪ (D.340 AH/951 CE)

Abū Naṣr Muḥammad ibn Muḥammad (al-Fārābī) was born in the Farab state of Khorasan. Seeking a superior education, he moved to the then-capital of Islamic knowledge, Baghdad, to study logic, ethics, metaphysics, math, music, philosophy of religion, and science (Black, 2015; Farooqi, 2006; Haque, 2004). During his course of studies he became particularly interested in the works of Aristotle. It is said that he was so eager to understand Aristotle's theories that he reviewed Aristotle's famous book *Kitāb al-Nafs* (On the Soul) one hundred times (Najātī, 1993).

Al-Fārābī produced more than one hundred works in his lifetime, with some of his most prominent psychological writings being: *Ārā' Ahl al-Madīnah al-Fāḍilah* (Opinions of the People of the Righteous City), *Taḥṣīl al-Sa'ādah* (Attaining Happiness), *Kitāb al-Tanbīh 'alā Sabīl al-Sa'ādah* (A Guide to the Path of Happiness), *Risālah fī al-'Aql* (On the Intellect), *'Uyūn al-Masā'il* (The Depth of Matters), *al-Siyāsāh al-Madaniyyah* (Civil Policies), *Fuṣūṣ al-Ḥikmah* (The Cloves of Wisdom), and *al-Da'āwī al-Qalbiyyah* (Internal Claims) (Najātī, 1993).

In his famous book *Ārā' Ahl al-Madīnah al-Fāḍilah* (Opinions of the People of the Righteous City) he describes several tenets of social psychology using invented exemplars (Soueif & Ahmed, 2001). Through the detailed examination of the citizens of a utopia, al-Fārābī's stipulates that a person's innate psychological needs push them to be social and to conform to principles of social cohesion (Haque, 2004; Soueif & Ahmed, 2001). These principles differ, depending on whether the social group is large or small. For a large social group, al-Fārābī postulates that four factors account for cohesion: sharing physiognomic features, language, speech, and living in close proximity to one another. For a small social group, he suggests that the governing factors are frequent interpersonal contact, sharing experiences of conflict, confronting threats together, sharing food and drink, and the distribution of pleasure (Soueif & Ahmed, 2001). In this book and others, al-Fārābī also discusses the nature, causes, and interpretation of dreams, the meaning of several types of intellect, and the therapeutic effects of music on the soul (Farooqi, 2006; Haque, 2004).

Although he drew from scriptural sources, al-Fārābī also utilized and valued methodologies of experimentation and demonstration (Black, 2015; Farooqi, 2006) and used them to refute philosophers and theologians alike (Haque, 2004). In his *Kitāb al-Tanbīh ʿalā Sabīl al-Saʿādah* he comments, "It is apparent that we need to return to the observable and rational realities that we have come to know through clear evidence" (al-Fārābī, 1985, p. 18). In fact, al-Fārābi argued that philosophical sciences were superior to religious sciences because they could use the method of demonstration for evidence, whereas religious sciences were limited to dialectical proofs (Bakar, 2015). His work attempted to reconcile Greek philosophy and Islamic theology, which at times made his definitions of the soul appear somewhat contradictory. Influenced by Aristotle's work, he described the soul as the completion of an organic body that potentially has a life (Najātī, 1993). He avoided using the rest of Aristotle's definition, in which Aristotle considers the soul to be a reflection of the body. In an attempt to align with Islamic theology, he would sometimes use the Platonian definition instead, which considers the soul to be a separate entity from the body (Najātī, 1993). According to Leaman (2015b), al-Fārābī also tried to present Greek theories as compatible with Islam by using Islamic terminology to describe them (e.g. using the word "*sharīʿah*" for the Greek word "law"). These attempts to make Greek philosophy more acceptable to Muslim audiences created inconsistencies in his work and made him the subject of much criticism within the Muslim community (An-Najār, 2004).

The Physicians' Perspective

AL-RĀZĪ (D.313 AH/925 CE)

The famed physician Abū Bakr Muḥammad ibn Zakariya al-Rāzī dedicated most of his time to music, alchemy, and philosophy until his thirties, when he decided to study medicine under the celebrated polymath Abū Jaʿfar Muḥammad ibn Jarīr al-Ṭabarī (d.311 AH/923 CE) (Tbakhi & Amr, 2008). The Abbasid caliph Abū Muḥammad ʿAlī ibn Aḥmad (d.296 AH/ 908 CE, also known as al-Muktafī) eventually summoned him to direct the largest hospital in Baghdad, including the hospital's psychiatric ward (Tbakhi & Amr, 2007).

During his time in Baghdad and beyond, al-Rāzī championed the humane treatment of the mentally ill. According to Farooqi, al-Rāzī encouraged self-analysis and awareness, feedback exchange, and reasoning, and emphasized the importance of the client–practitioner relationship (Farooqi, 2006). For example, he wrote: "The physician, even though he has his doubts, must always make the patient believe that he will recover, for the state of the body is linked to the state of the mind" (as cited in Tibi, 2006, p. 206). Here, it is clear that al-Rāzī understood the impact of client–practitioner rapport, placebo effects, and psychosomatic symptoms. Al-Rāzī is also responsible for the first recorded instance of psychiatric aftercare. Upon discharge, patients from his ward received financial assistance for the provision of immediate needs (Tbakhi & Amr, 2007).

With regard to his research and writing, Farooqi and Tibi note that al-Rāzī methodologically observed and documented over nine hundred case studies, which were collected by his students after his death and published in *Kitāb al-Tajārib* (The Book of Experience), and he used experiments to inform his work (Farooqi, 2006; Tibi, 2006). He authored *Kitāb al-Ḥāwī fī al-Ṭibb* (The Comprehensive Book of Medicine), an astonishing 23-volume work, in which he defined and described many mental illnesses, their symptoms, and their cures (Husayn & al-ʿUqbi, 1977; Tibi, 2006). Among the illnesses listed, he included memory problems, disturbed thinking, mood disorders (including both melancholic and manic symptoms), and anxiety (Mohamed, 2012). He was also the first to describe conditioned responses, approximately one thousand years before Ivan Pavlov (Muazzam & Muazzam, 1989).

Al-Rāzī wrote many manuscripts and treatises related to psychology. Most of them were lost except for two: *al-Ṭibb al-Rūḥānī* (The Medicine of the Soul) and parts of *al-Lazzah* (Desire). In his *al-Ṭibb al-Rūḥānī* he focuses on soul (or psyche) remediation—spiritually, morally, and psychologically (Najātī, 1993). The book is composed of 20 chapters that discuss psychological topics in light of the Qur'ān and the Sunnah, such as the definition of the *nafs* and its classification, treating the corrupted faculties of the *nafs*, and managing psychological diseases such as depression (al-Rāzī, ʿAbd, Kirmānī, & Abū, 1978). Throughout his work he addresses self-image, the desire to desire, and the desire for attention, and addresses widespread ideas relating to these topics. For example, he says: "as for the claim that being infatuated with someone can lead you to work on yourself to be cleaner, more fit, more presentable, and better-dressed, what good is a beautiful body hosting an ugly psyche?" (al-Rāzī, 1978, p. 63).

ABŪ ZAYD AL-BALKHĪ (D.322 AH/934 CE)

Abū Zayd Aḥmad ibn Sahl al-Balkhī was a precocious psychological genius who categorized and treated mental illnesses in a manner similar to that used by psychologists nearly a millennium after him (al-Balkhī & Badri, 2013; Awaad & Ali, 2015). He also used rational and revelatory arguments to dismantle social barriers to mental health services and deliberately communicated much of his knowledge in a way that was accessible to the general public (Awaad & Ali, 2015; Haque, 2004).

Originally from Balkh (a small town in modern-day Afghanistan), al-Balkhī travelled more than 1600 miles to Baghdad to learn the scholarly methodologies of his time (al-Balkhī & Badri, 2013). He became a student of al-Kindī and immersed himself in the rational and theological sciences, in the art of constructing rational, philosophical arguments, and in deep theological discussions. More than any other system of knowledge, however, al-Balkhī prized revelation. In one of his poems, he wrote, "Religion is the greatest of philosophies; therefore, man cannot be a philosopher until he becomes a worshipper" (as cited in al-Balkhī & Badri, 2013). Throughout his life, he contributed to the fields of psychology, geography, philosophy, science, literature, Islamic theology, and theoretical medicine (al-Balkhī & Badri, 2013; Nasr, 2015).

Al-Balkhī's greatest surviving gift to psychology is likely his book *Maṣāliḥ al-Abdān wa al-Anfus* (Sustenance of the Body and Soul) (Awaad et al., 2018). In it, he is possibly the first to systematically distinguish between psychosis and neurosis (Haque, 2004). He is also likely the earliest in history to describe, classify, and distinguish the illnesses now known as obsessive compulsive disorder (OCD) and phobias from other mental illnesses (Awaad & Ali, 2015). He writes: "Obsessive whispers are among the most intrusive psychological symptoms that linger deep within the core of the human being, triggering echoing thoughts that cage the person within themselves" (al-Balkhī, 2007, p. 127).

Prior to al-Balkhī's work, phobias were considered to be a symptom of "melancholy" (an ancient category similar to depression) or mania (Awaad & Ali, 2016). Their physical symptoms (e.g. paleness, trembling hands) were thought to be unrelated and were classified elsewhere. Al-Balkhī grouped the cognitive and psychosomatic symptoms under the distinct category of *faza'* (meaning panic or intense, disproportionate fears) (Awaad & Ali, 2016). His descriptions of phobias and OCD are a near-perfect match to the DSM-5 criteria for both illnesses (see Awaad & Ali (2016) and (2015) for side-by-side comparisons).

Throughout his book, al-Balkhī offers cognitive and spiritual therapies that can be self-administered (Awaad & Ali, 2015; Haque, 2004). For example, in the treatment of a phobia, al-Balkhī suggests a technique he calls *riyāḍat al-nafs* (psyche-training) (al-Balkhī, Misri, & al-Hayyat, 2005; Awaad & Ali, 2016). In this training, the afflicted individual gradually exposes their senses and psyche to the object of the phobia. Ideally, the individual simultaneously elicits feelings of pleasure to ward off anxiety, a technique now called, "reciprocal inhibition", coined by Joseph Wolpe in the twentieth century (Wolpe, 1968). Al-Balkhī's ideas are largely in line with exposure therapy, the modern-day treatment for illnesses such as OCD and phobias (Awaad & Ali, 2016).

Maṣāliḥ al-Abdān wa al-Anfus also carries a social mission. Al-Balkhī mentions in the introduction to the book that he deliberately wrote it in non-technical, simple Arabic to facilitate access by the general public (al-Balkhī, Misri, & al-Hayyat, 2005; Awaad & Ali, 2015). Al-Balkhī also uses scientific and religious sources to earn the trust of his readers, and to encourage them to seek treatment. For example, he explains OCD as either whispers from the devil or the result of black bile (the dominant psycho-physiological explanation of that time) (al-Balkhī et al., 2005; Awaad & Ali, 2015). Then, using a famous prophetic saying, he reminds his readers that God has created a cure for every illness, and that afflicted individuals should seek treatment and remain optimistic. To normalize the mental illnesses and demonstrate the efficacy of his proposed treatments, he gives examples of common-place instances where they can be used successfully. For example, he mentions that his psyche-training technique has often been used successfully to train horses to not be afraid of harmless objects. After several exposures to the initially feared object, the horse becomes accustomed to it and is thus no longer afraid (Awaad & Ali, 2016).

IBN SĪNĀ/AVICENNA (D.428 AH/1037 CE)

Abū Alī al-Ḥusayn ibn Sīnā, also known as Avicenna and the "doctor of doctors", combined his talents as a philosopher and as a physician to deliver innovative treatments and cutting-edge commentaries to the fields of psychology, medicine, geometry, chemistry, poetry, and theology (Farooqi, 2006; Haque, 2004). From an early age Ibn Sīnā was exposed to a wide range of religious, philosophical, and scientific ideas. Equipped with an unusually precise memory, he memorized both the Qur'ān and Aristotle's *Metaphysics* (Inati, 2015). He is estimated to have written between 100 and 250 works, including his famous writings *al-Shifā'* (The Healing), *Risālah fi-l-Nafs* (Treatise on the Soul) (Awaad et al., 2018; Inati, 2015), and *al-Qanūn fī al-Ṭibb* (The Canon of Medicine), which remained the primary textbook taught in medical schools throughout Europe until the sixteenth century (Lim & Khan, 2017).

One of Ibn Sīnā's most interesting psychological theories is his discussion of the relative motivational powers of physical desires (e.g. eating, sexual activity), cognitive desires (e.g. immersion in a game of chess), and virtuous desires (e.g. modesty, altruism, and dignity). In his book *al-Ishārāt wa-l-Tanbīhāt* he organizes these desires into a crude, two-level hierarchy, vaguely resembling Maslow's hierarchy of needs (Ibn Sīnā, al-Ṭūṣī, & al-Rāzī, 1916; see also Maslow, 1943). He says: "The greatest physical pleasures may seem to come from eating and sexual activity. Yet, the human being may put these desires aside in search of a more meaningful psychological activity" (Ibn Sīnā et al., 1916, pp. 334–335). Here, he notes the intuitive and expected direction of the hierarchy of needs, but then challenges it, acknowledging some important exceptions. He gives examples of individuals ignoring their need for food or sexual activity in the pursuit of cognitive stimulation in the form of a chess game, moral satisfaction in satisfying the hunger of others, and social satisfaction in preserving one's dignity or modesty. He concludes that "all of these [examples] point to the reality that psychological desires or values may be greater than physical or material desires" (Ibn Sīnā et al., 1916, pp. 334–335).

Ibn Sīnā was also acutely aware of the mind–body connection (i.e. chronic emotional stress leading to somatic symptoms or lowered immunity, which could exacerbate mental health problems) (Awaad et al., 2018; Farooqi, 2006). In *al-Shifā'* he details how he observed physically sick people heal through sheer will-power, and mentally ill people lose their physical health because of unhealthy obsessions and other mental illnesses. He also lists the ways through which the mind can influence the body on three levels: voluntary movements (i.e. moving a limb), on an inwardly emotional level (i.e. strong feelings of fear could lead to the body collapsing), and on an externally emotional level (i.e. feeling such strong emotions that another person's body is affected) (Farooqi, 2006; Haque, 2004).

As discussed in the section on Islamic inspiration and methodology, Ibn Sīnā used combinations of empirical, rational, and revealed sources to come to his conclusions (e.g. philosophical analyses of both the Qur'ān and Hellenistic treatises, empirical trial-and-error with medical clients, and belief in resurrection based completely in scripture) (Abdul Haq, 1988; Bakar, 2015; Farooqi, 2006; Ivry, 2008; Nasr, 2015). When challenged with a particularly difficult case or question, Ibn Sīnā would go to the mosque and pray (Nasr, 2015).

Using such diverse sources allowed Ibn Sīnā to access a multitude of treatment techniques. He often recommended meditation, self-awareness, dialogue, reflection, imagery, and conditioning to treat mental illnesses (Farooqi, 2006). His therapeutic techniques in the treatment of hysteria, mania, epilepsy, anxiety, and depression are not unlike those used today, more than a thousand years after him (Avicenna, 1877). First, he would search for the source of the client's emotional conflict, sometimes using crude bio-feedback techniques to do so (Awaad & Ali, 2016; Farooqi, 2006). For example, when treating a prince suffering from anorexia nervosa, he constructed a hierarchy of anxiety-inducing words, then spoke each of the words while measuring the prince's pulse with his thumb. A quickened pulse meant that the word just spoken was closer to the prince's trigger area than the word spoken previously. After identifying his client's emotional difficulties, he would often expose the client to those difficulties, while inducing a state of antagonistic relaxation (Awaad & Ali, 2016; Farooqi, 2006). Ibn Sīnā believed that it was impossible to simultaneously experience anxiety and relaxation because of the autonomic nervous system's role as an antagonist. Thus, by stimulating a relaxation response in his client, he expected that the learned nervous response would eventually be extinguished (Avicenna, 1877; Farooqi, 2006).

The Theologians' Perspective

Muslim theologians contributed to the development of an "Islamic psychology" through their work in three fields: (1) Islamic creed, (2) Islamic law, and (3) Islamic spirituality. The list of scholarly figures with significant contributions in each of these fields is far too large to include here. For brevity, longer discussions of Islamic legal history and its most important figures have been presented in Chapter 1.

Many of the great Muslim theologians whose contributions we have highlighted here in one or more fields were recognized polymaths who contributed to the development of a variety of sciences. Al-Ghazālī, Ibn al-Qayyim, and Shāh Walī Allāh, for example, were renowned not only for their unique contributions to Islamic philosophy, but also for their impact on our understanding of Islamic spirituality, medicine, and the social sciences.

AL-GHAZĀLĪ (D.510 AH/1111 CE)

Abu Ḥāmid Muḥammad al-Ghazālī was an Islamic scholar, jurist, mystic, and one of the greatest philosophers of Islam (Campanini, 2015). He drew upon a variety of sources to study the self, its ultimate purpose, and the moral, behavioral, and cognitive factors that lead to its felicity and suffering (Awaad et al., 2018; Bakar, 2015; Haque, 2004). He argued that "even though much attention has been given by physicians to refining the craft of treating diseases of the body, such diseases compromise an already fleeting life. More attention should be directed to treating diseases of the heart [psyche], which has an infinite lifetime" (al-Ghazālī, 2005, p. 929).

In his lifetime, al-Ghazālī wrote approximately seventy books, including: *Iḥyā' 'Ulūm al-Dīn* (Reviving the Religious Sciences), *Kīmiyā -e-Sa'ādat* (Alchemy of Happiness) (al-Ghazālī & Sharīf, 2011), and *Tahāfut al-Falāsifah* (Incoherence of the Philosophers) (al-Ghazālī, 1974; Haque, 2004). In his book *Fayṣal al-Tafriqah bayna al-Islām wa al-Zandaqah* (The Decisive Criterion for Distinguishing Islam from Clandestine Unbelief), al-Ghazālī supports the application of non-Muslim theories, provided that they do not contradict revelation or rationale (Griffel, 2014). Al-Ghazālī also accepted and applauded scientific methods of demonstration in every field except for metaphysics (Bakar, 2015). In the introduction to his *Tahāfut al-Falāṣifah* (Incoherence of the Philosophers), he says that those who contest proofs derived from this method using a literal interpretation of revelation damage religion, as religion and the natural sciences have different methodologies (Campanini, 2015).

Al-Ghazālī affirmed and elaborated on the spiritual diseases of the heart, including arrogance, miserliness, ignorance, envy, and lust (Haque, 2004). He encouraged individuals to engage in *tazkiyat al-nafs*, or the purification and training of the self (including its cognitions and behavioral inclinations) to cure these diseases. He said: "If behavior could not be changed, there would be no value to advice, reminders, and discipline … How can we deny that a human is capable of change when we see the possibility of change in animals?" (al-Ghazali, 2005, p. 937). By highlighting the fact that animals could be domesticated and trained, he makes a case for behavioral rehabilitation in humans.

In *Iḥyā 'Ulūm al-Dīn* he outlines six steps for self-purification: *mushāraṭah* (making a contract with oneself to meet set goals), *murāqabah* (self-monitoring), *muḥāsabah* (self-examination; holding oneself accountable), *mujāhadah* (self-penalization; implementing consequences for breaking the self-contract), *mu'āqabah* (self-struggle; working diligently to overcome sinful inclinations), and *mu'ātabah* (self-admonition; regretting breaking and re-committing to upholding the contract) (Keshavarzi & Haque, 2013).

Examining the self through a cognitive lens, al-Ghazālī believed that individuals suffering from delusional thoughts could be treated using negative reinforcement, modeling, labeling, and shaping (Farooqi, 2006). He classified cognitive mental processes according to their functions (e.g. *takhayyul*, or imagination, enabled people to retain images from their experiences or reflections), locating these cognitive abilities in different anatomical areas and lobes of the brain (e.g. imagination in the frontal lobe) (Haque, 2004).

SHIHĀB AL-DĪN ABŪ ḤAFṢ 'UMAR AL-SUHRAWARDĪ (D.632 AH/1234 CE)

Shihāb al-Dīn al-Suhrawardī was born in Suhraward and was raised by his paternal uncle, the renowned ascetic and eponymous founder of the

Suhrawardī spiritual order, Abū al-Najīb 'Abd al-Qādir al-Suhrawardī, from whom he learned Islamic law, the science of oration, *Ḥadīth*, and also Islamic spirituality (*taṣawwuf*). Shihāb al-Dīn was considered one of the most recognized spiritual teachers in Baghdad in his time. His most celebrated work, *'Awārif al-Ma'ārif* (The Excellent Benefits of Knowledge), provided guidelines for the seeker of the spiritual path of righteousness, defining terms such as Sufism and outlining the conditions of the proper "Sufi". Al-Suhrawardī believed that Spiritual Perception was the purview of the heart and not the mind. Unlike empirical and rational knowledge, spiritual knowledge was intuitional and could only be realized fully when experienced. He likens this experience to tasting the sweetness of sugar, which can be described thoroughly, but never truly appreciated and realized until it is tasted (al-Suhrawardī, 1993, p. 43).

Like other spiritual theoreticians, al-Suhrawardī believed that souls have two modalities: (1) the animal-human soul (*rūḥ ḥayawānī basharī*), which is the source of human bodily movements and sensations, and (2) the sublime, heavenly soul (*rūḥ 'ulwī samāwī*), which has the potential to connect to the realm of divine commands (*'ālam al-amr*) and allows the animalistic soul to rise above its limitations by acquiring rationality or receiving inspiration (*ilhām*) (al-Suhrawardī, 1993, pp. 320–321). Al-Suhrawardī followed his predecessors in asserting that the source of undesirable impulses, such as avarice and rage, is the *nafs*, or appetitive self, which is developed in three stages drawn from the Qur'ān: (1) the prompting self (*ammārah*), (2) the repentant self (*lawwāmah*), and (3) the satisfied self (*muṭma'innah*) (al-Suhrawardī, 1993, pp. 258–259). The *qalb* (heart), he believed, is neither the *rūḥ* nor the *nafs*, but a subtle essence (*laṭīfah*) whose locus is in the physical heart and results from the connection between the *rūḥ* and the *nafs*. As for the *'aql* (intellect), al-Suhrwardī explained that it is the vehicle of expression of the heavenly soul as well as its guide (al-Suhrawardī, 1993, p. 321).

Al-Suhrwardī also provided a detailed elaboration of the operations of the spiritual path, including etiquette of the spiritual lodge, certain spiritual interventions (such as spiritual songs, or *samā'*), the 40-day spiritual retreat, the spiritual guide and student relationship, and the everyday protocols for the spiritual aspirant (including mundane daily acts such as eating, sleeping, time management, etc.), which provide a rich source to draw from when developing Islamic spiritually integrated interventions today.

IBN TAYMIYYAH (D.728 AH/1328 CE)

Growing up under the constant threat of Mongol invasions, Taqī al-Dīn Abū al-'Abbās Aḥmad bin 'Abd al-Ḥalīm al-Ḥarrānī (also known as Ibn Taymiyyah) dedicated his life to defending Islam and Muslims from foreign forces both by the pen and by the sword (Bazzano, 2015). When he was 7 years old, Ibn Taymiyyah's family fled to Damascus to escape Mongol invasions from the East. There he mastered the Islamic sciences and began to teach Qur'ān exegesis, Islamic jurisprudence, *Ḥadīth*, Arabic, and political theory before he was 20 years old (Bazzano, 2015).

Ibn Taymiyyah is documented to have been able to produce a complete volume of work in one day and write 40 pages in one sitting (Bazzano, 2015). He authored more than five hundred manuscripts and short treatises on various branches of the Islamic sciences, three of which are related to psychology: a chapter on the diseases and treatments of the heart (*'ilm al-sulūk*), published in his encyclopedic fatwa collection *Majmū' al-Fatāwā*, a treatise on the soul and intellect (*Risālah fī al-'Aql wa al-Rūḥ*), and lastly *al-'Ubūdiyyah* (Obedience).

Although Ibn Taymiyyah is perhaps best known for his contributions to the sacred sciences, the imprint of his work on other fields (like psychology) can be seen in one of his best students, Shams al-Dīn Abū 'Abd Allāh Muḥammad ibn Abī Bakr ibn Ayyūb al-Zur'ī al-Dimashqī al-Ḥanbalī (d.751 AH/1350 CE, also known as Ibn al-Qayyim), who was known to have mainly taught and build upon what his teacher had taught him, but in a simpler and more accessible manner (see below) (Qadhi, 2010). One direct example of Ibn Taymiyyah's psychological work is his discussion of emotion. Whereas many of his peers and predecessors focused on the value of happiness and its pursuit (e.g. Ibn Miskawayh, see above), in his collection of *fatāwā* (religious rulings) Ibn Taymiyyah delves into the realm of moral emotions, discussing the merit of an empathetic sadness. He says: "As for sadness that does not bring about a benefit nor displace a harm, there is no benefit in it, and God does not command that which has no benefit … However, some forms of sadness are divinely rewarded … including sorrow over the calamities of the Muslims in general" (Ibn Taymiyyah, 2004, pp. 13–14). Here, he highlights the difference between productive and unproductive sadness, subtly using scripture to encourage his reader to down-regulate sadness that is without a productive purpose.

Ibn Taymiyyah's most important goal, however, was to build an Islamic framework for psychology (and other sciences) from the ground up, free from the influence of foreign ideas, which he felt often threatened Islamic tenets of faith (An-Najār, 2004). He heavily criticized the likes of al-Fārābī, al-Kindī, and Ibn Sīnā for breaking away from the fundamentals of Islam in their pursuit of knowledge, saying that they were dressing up Greek thought in Islamic clothing. Ibn Taymiyyah felt that the philosophers raised reason above its place in epistemology, and that they failed to recognize its limitations as a human faculty (An-Najār, 2004). He explored the relationship between cognitive and emotional states and how some thoughts have emotional underpinnings even if they appear to be rational (e.g. prejudice leading to confirmation bias). He argued that only by examining the world through revelation could we rid ourselves of the limitations to human rationality and emotions in order to acquire ultimate truths (An-Najār, 2004).

IBN AL-QAYYIM (D.751 AH/1350 CE)

Shams al-Dīn Abū ʿAbd Allāh Muḥammad ibn Abī Bakr ibn Ayyūb al-Zurʿī al-Dimashqī, or as he was more commonly known Ibn al-Qayyim, was one of the most important students of the famous scholar Ibn Taymiyyah (Livingston, 1992). He mastered many Islamic sciences including *Ḥadīth*, Islamic jurisprudence, Arabic, and Qurʾānic commentary (Krawietz, 2006). He was also well versed in several branches of the natural sciences (Livingston, 1992). Ibn al-Qayyim authored close to one hundred books, with six related manuscripts : *al-Ruh* (The Soul), *Tuḥfat al-Mawdūd fī Aḥkām al-Mawlūd* (*The* Gift of the Beloved Regarding Laws Dealing with the Newborn), *Miftāh Dār al-Saʿādah* (The Key to the Abode of Happiness), *Rawdat al-Muhibbīn wa Nuzhat al-Mushtāīn* (The Garden of the Lovers and the Retreat of the Lovesick), *Ṭarīq al-Hijratayn wa Bāb al-Saʿādatayn* (The Path to Two Migrations and the Door to the Two Forms of Happiness), and *Risālah fī Amrāḍ al-Qulūb* (A Treatise on the Disease of the Heart) (al-Mubarak, 2017; Najātī, 1993; Qadhi, 2010).

Unlike his great predecessors al-Kindī, Ibn Sīnā, and Ibn Rushd, who had defended philosophy using Islam, Ibn al-Qayyim defended Islam using philosophy's descendants, namely mathematics, astronomy, physics, and logic (Livingston, 1992). In his book *Miftāh Dār al-Saʿādah*, Ibn al-Qayyim launches an attack against pseudosciences (including astrology and augury), which he believes are an insult both to Islam and to contemporary science. He refutes them historically (by providing examples of Islamic leaders whose court astrologists advised them according to a horoscope and were wrong), technologically (citing reputable scientists who deemed the astrological tools and methods of observation imprecise), and scientifically (unveiling astrology's contradictory principles and arbitrary rules) (Livingston, 1992). Outside of such refutations, Ibn al-Qayyim's writings were almost exclusively drawn from the Qur'ān and Sunnah—only taking from the contemporary sciences what could be supported with revelatory sources (Najātī, 1993).

In terms of his psychological contributions, Ibn al-Qayyim highlighted the importance of meditation, reflection, and introspection in the pursuit of happiness. He said: "The righteous among our predecessors used to say that mindful reflection for an hour is better than worshipping for sixty years" (Ibn al-Qayyim, n.d., p. 516). He also described a sequential stage-theory of cognition and behavior (perhaps building upon the work of al-Ghazālī before him) based on terms used in the Qur'ān to describe thinking (Abdul-Rahman, 2017a; Badri, 2000). According to his stage-theory, an individual first has an involuntary thought. If the individual chooses to deliberate over this thought, it becomes an emotional motivation to act. If the individual continues to feed the emotional inclination, it will turn into a firm decision to act, and then into an action, and then finally into a habit (Abdul-Rahman, 2017a; Badri, 2000). Ibn al-Qayyim then offers some practical advice, suggesting that it is easier for one to monitor and halt negative thoughts before they grow into strong emotions, and to resist those emotions before they become actions, and to halt actions before they become habits (Badri, 2000). As with many Islamic scholars, he advises treating a negative inclination or action with its opposite (see Ibn Miskawayh, above).

Finally, just as he supported cognitive behavioral interventions, Ibn al-Qayyim also advocated for the importance of mental health. In his *Ighāthat ul-Lahfān fī Maṣāyid al-Shayṭān* (Rescuing the Fool Caught in the Trap of Satan), he states:

> The second category of diseases of the heart are based on emotional states such as anxiety, sadness, depression, and anger. This type of disease can be treated naturally by treating the cause or with medicine that goes against the cause … and this is because the heart is harmed by what harms the body and vice versa.
>
> (Ibn al-Qayyim, 2011, p. 26)

This demonstrates Ibn al-Qayyim's balanced approach to treatment centuries before his Western counterparts thought to combine somatic and cognitive therapies (Abdul-Rahman, 2017b).

The Modern Field of Islamic Psychology

Barriers to Entry for Muslims in Modern Mainstream Psychology

In the early nineteenth century, psychology as a distinct discipline, was born into a largely secular world established on the shores of colonialism. Both colonialism and secularism created ideological (and sometimes physical) barriers, preventing many Muslims from participating in psychology as an academic discipline or as a therapeutic service.

By the nineteenth century colonialism had taken hold of the Muslim world, imposing a lack of infrastructure and instilling a lack of confidence in combining revelatory and empirical or rational methods of study. For example, when Mohamed Ali (d.1266 AH/1849 CE), commonly regarded as the founder of modern Egypt, took charge of Egypt, his goal was to modernize the country according to colonial standards (Iqbal, 2007). He established training colleges where modern sciences were taught by foreign teachers in foreign languages. Replacing Arabic with colonial languages inserted a linguistic fissure between religion and science, because Arabic (unlike many other languages) evolved in a manner that allowed for scientific and revelatory terms to co-exist. This change also divided Muslims along linguistic lines. Before this, Arabic was commonly spoken in many lands, and was recognized as the formal language of academia (Iqbal, 2007). Now, scholars were less able to share ideas and resources, and being thus divided, were conquered.

Additionally, modern mainstream psychology's roots in secularism meant that it had methodological foundations that opposed the Islamic worldview, upon which revelation also holds ultimate truths and guidance (Haque, 2004). These foundations resulted in a lack of trust and acceptance of mainstream psychology by many Muslims, as it often ignored (and even rejected) such an important source of knowledge and healing for them (Haque, 2004; Keshavarzi & Ali, 2018). This trend continued until the early 1970s, when Muslims began calling for the revival of Islam's rich scholarly heritage of developing psychological theories that are rooted in Islamic principles (Kaplick & Skinner, 2017).

Current Developments, Future Directions, and Limitations for Islamic Psychology Research

Since the re-emergence of Islamic psychology, scholars have worked diligently to nurture its growth (Kaplick & Skinner, 2017). However, there are several areas that have been identified to be of particular importance to the field's continued development (Kaplick, Chaudhary, Hasan, Yusuf, & Keshavarzi, 2019). The first is to develop a shared nomenclature and methodology between traditional Islamic and contemporary psychological scholarship in order to form the basis of interdisciplinary work between Islamic scholars and psychologists (see Kaplick et al. (2019) for more thorough discussion). The second is to establish scholarly "adequacy" (i.e. educational standards in the Islamic and psychological fields that set the credentials for participation in the field of Islamic psychology (Kaplick et al., 2019). Lastly, only a tiny fraction of the classical works from the rich history of Islamic psychology are available in English. Many scholars also believe that thousands more are as yet undiscovered or unexplored in libraries, such as those recently uncovered in Timbuktu (Nobili & Mathee, 2015). Translation and rediscovery efforts, such as those underway at the Stanford Muslim Mental Health Lab and elsewhere, will help facilitate the revival of the field of Islamic psychology and reinstate it in its proper place as a holistic, spiritually integrated discipline of practice and research. Examples of upcoming efforts include a deeper dive into historical texts such as Al-Balkhī's book *Maṣāliḥ al-Abdān wa al-Anfus*, Ibn al-Qayyim's *Risālah fī-al-Nafs*, *al-Qanūn fī al-Ṭibb* by Ibn Sīnā, *al-Ṭibb al-Rūhānī* by Abū

Bakr Muḥammad ibn Zakariya al-Rāzī, and *Ta'dîlü'l-emzice fî hıfzi sıhhati'l-beden* by Şuûrî Hasan Efendi.

In addition to these exciting developments, greater documentation and a deeper understanding of the historical factors, figures, and their psychological contributions during the Ottoman era and beyond are warranted in order to more fully grasp the richness of Islamic intellectual heritage that could not be encompassed in this chapter. For example, further study of the contributions of Ottoman scholars such as Imam Muhammad Birgivi, Mulla Fenari, Sadr al-Din al-Qunwani, Ahmet Cevdat Pasha, Ibn al-Mubarak, and Harith al-Muhasibi, scholars from the Indian subcontinent such as Imam Sirhindi, Shah Abdul Aziz, and Ashraf Ali Thanwi, as well as institutions such as the Ottoman zawhiyahs or khanqahs, could bridge gaps in our understanding of this important time period in Islamic intellectual history.

Conclusion

Muslim scholars during the seventh to fifteenth centuries applied the methodological framework of Islamic psychology (i.e. the empirical, rational, and revelatory study of human cognition, emotions, behavioral inclinations, and spirit) with great success. They developed cognitive behavioral therapy techniques and discussed strategies to defeat the social stigma surrounding mental health centuries (and in some cases a millennium) before their European counterparts (Awaad & Ali, 2015; Haque, 2004). If it were not for their religious motivation and inspiration, as well as investments made by their leadership to advance scholarship, it is unlikely that Muslims would have reached such heights in intellectual achievement (Chen, 2014). With the advent of spiritually integrated mental health practices and the return of Islamic psychology, modern psychologists and researchers must ensure that contributors to this field are sufficiently well versed in its Islamic and empirical roots. Leaders in the field of Islamic psychology must also solidify the methodological frameworks as suggested by Kaplick and colleagues (2019), and continue to explore and understand the depths of Islamic history in order to reclaim Islam's formidable intellectual heritage and to contribute once again to the advancement of psychology, and more broadly, to society.

References

Abdul Haq, M. (1988). Ibn Sina's interpretation of the Qur'an. *The Islamic Quarterly*, *32*(1), 45–56.

Abdul-Rahman, Z. (2017a, September 20). The lost art of contemplation: Spiritual psychology series. Retrieved from https://yaqeeninstitute.org/zohair/the-lost-art-of-contemplation-spiritual-psychology-series/.

Abdul-Rahman, Z. (2017b, March 13). Islamic spirituality and mental well-being. Retrieved from https://yaqeeninstitute.org/zohair/islamic-spirituality-and-mental-well-being/.

Adamson, P. (2018, April 11). Al-Kindi. Retrieved from https://plato.stanford.edu/entries/al-kindi/.

al-Balkhī, A. Z. (2007). *Maṣāliḥ al-abdān wa al-anfus.* (M. Badrī, Ed.). Riyadh: King Faisal Centre for Islamic Studies and Research.

al-Balkhī, A. Z., & Badri, M. (2013). *Abū Zayd al-Balkhīs Sustenance of the Soul: The cognitive behavior therapy of a ninth century physician.* London: International Institute of Islamic Thought.

al-Balkhī, A. Z., Misri, M., & al-Hayyat, M. (2005). *In taḥqīq wa-dirāsat Maḥmūd al-miṣrī, taṣdīr Muḥammad Haytham al-Khayyāṭ.* (Masālih al-abdān wa-al-anfus, Eds.) (1st ed.) Al-Qāhirah: Ma'had al-Makhṭūṭāt al-'Arabīyah.

al-Bukhārī (2010). *Sahih al-Bukhari.* Riyadh: Darussalam.

al-Farābī, M. (1985). *Kitāb al-tanbīh 'alá sabīl al-sa'ādah.* (J. Āl Yāsīn, Ed.) (1st ed.). Beirut: Dār al-Manāhil.

al-Ghazālī, A. M. (1974). *Al-Ghazali's Tahafut al-Falāsifah: [Incoherence of the philosophers].* Lahore: Pakistan Philosophical Congress.

al-Ghazālī, A. M. (2005). *Iḥya' 'ulūm al-Dīn.* (Z. A. al-'Irā qī, Ed.) (1st ed.). Beirut: Dār ibn Ḥazm.

al-Ghazālī, A. M., & Sharīf, M. M. (2011). *Revival of religion's sciences: Ihya' ulum ad-din = Iḥyā' 'ulūm al-dīn.* Beirut: Dar Al-Kotob Al-ilmiyah.

al-Kindī, A. Y., & 'Abd al-Hādī, M. (1950). *Rasā'il al-Kindī al-falsafiyah.* Cairo: Dār al-Fikr al-'Arabī.

al-Mubarak, T. (2017). Ibn Qaiyyim al-Jawziyya. In *The architects of Islamic civilization* (pp. 197–203). Kuala Lampur: Pelanduk Publications.

al-Rāzi, A. (1978). *Al-Ṭib al-Rawḥāni.* ('A. Al-'Abd, Ed.) (1st ed.). Cairo: The Library for Egyptian Revival.

al-Rāzī, A. B. M. Z., 'Abd, A.-L. M., Kirmānī, H.-D. A. A. A., & Abū, H.-R. A. H. (1978). *Al-Ṭibb al-rūḥānī.* Al-Qāhirah: Maktabat al-Nahḍah al-Miṣrīyah.

al-Suhrawardi, S. (1993). *Awarif al-Ma'rif.* Cairo: Dar al-Ma'rif.

al-Tirmidhī, M. (1970). *Jāmi' al-Tirmidhī.* Riyadh: Darrusalam.

An-Najār, F. Q. (2004). *Al-Dirāst al-Nafsiyyah 'ind al-Imām ibn Taymiyyah.* Riyad: Fahrasah Katabat al Malik Fahd al Waṭaniyyah.

Arnaldez, R. (2012). Ibn Rushd. In *Encyclopaedia of Islam* (2nd ed.). Edited by P. Bearman et al., http://dx.doi.org/10.1163/1573-3912_islam_COM_0340.

Avicenna (1877). *Kitāb al-Qanūn fī al-Ṭibb.* Bulaq.

Awaad, R., & Ali, S. (2015). Obsessional disorders in al-Balkhī's 9th century treatise: Sustenance of the Body and Soul. *Journal of Affective Disorders, 180,* 185–189. doi:10.1016/j.jad.2015.03.003

Awaad, R., & Ali, S. (2016). A modern conceptualization of phobia in al-Balkhī's 9th century treatise: Sustenance of the Body and Soul. *Journal of Anxiety Disorders, 37,* 89–93. doi:10.1016/j.janxdis.2015.11.003

Awaad, R., Mohammad, A., Elzamzamy, K., Fereydooni, S., & Gamar, M. (2018). Mental health in the Islamic golden era: The historical roots of modern psychiatry. *Islamophobia and Psychiatry,* 3–17. doi:10.1007/978-3-030-00512-2_1

Badri, M. (2000). *Contemplation: An Islamic psychospiritual study.* Herndon, VA: International Institute of Islamic Thought.

Bakar, O. (2015). Science. In O. Leaman & S. H. Nasr (Eds.), *History of Islamic philosophy* (pp. 1656–1692). London: Routledge.

Bazzano, E. A. (2015). Ibn Taymiyya, radical polymath, Part I: scholarly perceptions. *Religion Compass*, *9*(4), 100–116. doi:10.1111/rec3.12114

Black, D. L. (2015). Al-Fārābā. In O. Leaman & S. H. Nasr (Eds.), *History of Islamic philosophy* (pp. 334–371). London: Routledge.

Campanini, M. (2015). Al-Ghazzālī. In O. Leaman & S. H. Nasr (Eds.), *History of Islamic philosophy* (pp. 477–509). London: Routledge.

Chen, J. T. (2014). Re-orientation: The Chinese Azharites between Umma and Third World, 1938–55. *Comparative Studies of South Asia, Africa and the Middle East*, *34*(1), 24–51. doi:10.1215/1089201x-2648560

Faizal, P. R., Ridhwan, A. A., & Kalsom, A. W. (2013). The entrepreneurs characteristic from al-Quran and al-Hadis. *International Journal of Trade, Economics and Finance*, 191–196. doi:10.7763/ijtef.2013.v4.284

Farooqi, Y. N. (2006). Understanding Islamic perspective of mental health and psychotherapy. *Journal of Psychology in Africa*, *16*(1), 101–111. doi:10.1080/14330237.2006.10820109

Fitzmaurice, R. G. (1971). Al-Kindī on psychology [unpublished master's thesis]. McGill University Montreal, Quebec, Canada.

Griffel, F. (2014, September 22). Al-Ghazali. Retrieved from http://plato.stanford.edu/entries/al-ghazali/

Haque, A. (2004). Psychology from Islamic perspective: Contributions of early Muslim scholars and challenges to contemporary Muslim psychologists. *Journal of Religion and Health*, *43*(4), 357–377. doi:10.1007/s10943-004-4302-z

Husayn, M. K., & al-'Uqbi, M. A. (1977). *Tibbal-Raẓi: Dirasah wa-tahlil li-kitab al-hawi*. Beirut: Dār al-Shūrūq, al-Qāhirah.

Ibn al-Qayyim, M. I. A. B. (2011). *Ighāthat ul-laḥfaan fī maṣāyid ash-shayṭān*. (M. 'U. Shams, Ed.). Vol. 1. Mecca: Dār 'ālim al-Fawā'id.

Ibn al-Qayyim, M. I. A. B. (n.d.). *Muftāḥ dār al-sa'āda*. ('A. Ibn Qā'id & B. Abu Zayd, Eds.). Vol. 1. Mecca: Dār 'Alam al-Fawā'id.

Ibn Mājah, M. (2007). *Sunan Ibn Mājah*. (H. Khaṭṭāb, Ed.). Riyadh: Darussalam.

Ibn Manẓūr, M. (1955). Iqra'. *Lisān al-'Arab*. Vol. 1. Beirut: Dar Ṣādir.

Ibn Miskawayh, A. M. (1882). *Hātha kitāb tahdhīb al-akhlāq wa taṭhīr al-a'rāq*. (H. R. Al-Mashhadī, Ed.). Cairo: Maṭba'ah Wād al-Nīl.

Ibn Miskawayh, A. M., & Asyūṭī, 'Alī -T. (1928). *Al-sa'ādah fī falsafat al-akhlāq*. Cairo: al-Maṭba'ah al-'Arabīyah.

Ibn Rushd, M. (1986). *Kitāb faṣl al-maqāl wa taqrīr ma bayn al-sharī'ah wa al-ḥikmah min al-ittiṣāl*. (A. Nādir, Ed.). 2nd ed. Beirut: Dar El-Machreq.

Ibn Sīnā, A. 'A., Al-Ṭūṣī, N. A.-D., & al-Rāzi, Q. (1916). *Al-Ishārāt wa al-tanbihāt*. Vol. 3. 2nd ed. Al-Qudṣ: Al-Nashr al-Balagha.

Ibn Taymiyyah, T. A. (2004). *Majmū'it al-fatāwā*. (A. Al-Jazzār & A. Al-Bāz, Eds.). Vol. 10. Medina: King Fahd Complex for the Printing of the Holy Quran.

Inati, S. (2015). Ibn Sīnā. In O. Leaman & S. H. Nasr (Eds.), *History of Islamic philosophy* (pp. 430–457). London: Routledge.

Iqbal, M. (2007). *Science and Islam*. New Delhi: Pentagon Press.

Ivry, A. (2008, April 18). Arabic and Islamic psychology and philosophy of mind. Retrieved from https://plato.stanford.edu/entries/arabic-islamic-mind/

Janssens, J. (1994). Al-Kindī's concept of God. *Ultimate Reality and Meaning, 17*(1), 4–16. doi:10.3138/uram.17.1.4

Jumu'ah, M. L. (2014). *Tārīkh Falāsifah al-Islām*. Cairo: Hinddawi Foundation for Education & Culture.

Kaplick, P. M., & Skinner, R. (2017). The evolving Islam and psychology movement. *European Psychologist, 22*(3), 198–204. doi:10.1027/1016–9040/a000297

Kaplick, P. M., Chaudhary, Y., Hasan, A., Yusuf, A., & Keshavarzi, H. (2019). An interdisciplinary framework for Islamic cognitive theories. *Zygon, 54*(1), 66–85. doi:10.1111/zygo.12500

Keshavarzi, H., & Ali, B. (2018). Islamic perspectives on psychological and spiritual well-being and treatment. *Islamophobia and Psychiatry*, 41–53. doi:10.1007/978-3-030-00512-2_4

Keshavarzi, H., & Haque, A. (2013). Outlining a psychotherapy model for enhancing Muslim mental health within an Islamic context. *International Journal for the Psychology of Religion, 23*(3), 230–249. doi:10.1080/10508619.2012.712000

Klein-Franke, F. (2015). Al-Kindi. In O. Leaman & S. H. Nasr (Eds.), *History of Islamic philosophy* (pp. 308–333). London: Routledge.

Kleinman, P. (2012). *Psych 101 psychology facts, basics, statistics, tests, and more!* Cincinnati, OH: F W Media.

Krawietz, B. (2006). Ibn Qayyim al-Jawziyah: His life and works. *Mamlūk Studies Review*, 19–64. doi:10.6082/M13X84RM

Leaman, O. (2015a). Ibn Miskawayh. In O. Leaman & S. H. Nasr (Eds.), *History of Islamic Philosophy* (pp. 466–476). London: Routledge.

Leaman, O. (2015b). Introduction. In O. Leaman & S. H. Nasr (Eds.), *History of Islamic Philosophy* (pp. 27–42). London: Routledge.

Lim, B., & Khan, A. (2017). *Avicenna: Leading physician and philosopher-scientist of the Islamic Golden Age*. New York: Rosen Publishing.

Livingston, J. W. (1992). Science and the occult in the thinking of Ibn Qayyim al-Jawziyya. *Journal of the American Oriental Society, 112*(4), 598. doi:10.2307/604475

Lyons, J. (2010). *The house of wisdom: How the Arabs transformed Western civilization*. New York: Bloomsbury Press.

Maslow, A. H. (1943). A theory of human motivation. *Psychological Review, 50*, 370–396.

Mehawesh, M. (2014). History of translation in the Arab world: An overview. *US-China Foreign Language, 12*(8). doi:10.17265/1539–8080/2014.08.009

Mohamed, W. M. (2012, December 15). *IBRO history of neuroscience* [Scholarly project]. In *IRBO*. Retrieved from http://ibro.org/wp-content/uploads/2018/07/Arab-and-Muslim-Contributions-to-Modern-Neuroscience.pdf.

Murube, J. (2007). Hunain's Eye: The oldest preserved scientific image of the ocular surface. *The Ocular Surface, 5*(3), 207–212. doi:10.1016/s1542-0124(12)70611-0

Muslim, M. (2006). *Ṣaḥīḥ Muslim*. Riyadh: Dār Ṭaybah for Publishing and Distribution.

Najātī, M. U. (1993). *al-Dirāsāt al-nafsānīyah 'inda al-'ulamā' al-Muslimīn*. Cairo: Dār al-Shurūq.

Nasr, S. H. (2015). The Qur'ān and Hadīth as source and inspiration of Islamic philosophy. In O. Leaman & S. H. Nasr (Eds.), *History of Islamic Philosophy* (pp. 68–90). London: Routledge.

Nobili, M., & Mathee, M. S. (2015). Towards a new study of the so-called Tārīkh al-fattāsh. *History in Africa, 42*, 37–73.

Qadhi, Y. (2010). The unleashed thunderbolts of Ibn Qayyim Al-Gawziyyah: An introductory essay. *Oriente Moderno, 90*(1), 135–149.

Pargament, K. I. (2011). *Spiritually integrated psychotherapy: Understanding and addressing the sacred.* New York, NY: Guilford.

Saad, B. (2014). Greco-Arab and Islamic herbal medicine: A review. *European Journal of Medicinal Plants, 4*(3), 249–258. doi:10.9734/ejmp/2014/6530

Salleh, S., & Embong, R. (2017). Educational views of Ibnu Sina. *Al-Irsyad: Journal of Islamic and Contemporary Issues, 2*(1), 13–24.

Soueif, M. I., & Ahmed, R. A. (2001). Psychology in the Arab world: Past, present, and future. *International Journal of Group Tensions, 30*(3), 211–240.

Taylor, R. C. (1998). Averroes on psychology and the principles of metaphysics. *Journal of the History of Philosophy, 36*(4), 507–523. doi:10.1353/hph.2008.0844

Tbakhi, A., & Amr, S. S. (2007). Ibn Rushd (Averroës): Prince of science. *Annals of Saudi Medicine, 28*(2), 145–147. doi:10.5144/0256-4947.2008.145

Tibi, S. (2006). Al-Razi and Islamic medicine in the 9th century. *Journal of the Royal Society of Medicine, 99*(4), 206–207. doi:10.1258/jrsm.99.4.206

Urvoy, D. (2015). Ibn Rushd. In O. Leaman & S. H. Nasr (Eds.), *History of Islamic Philosophy* (pp. 602–629). London: Routledge.

Wolpe, J. (1968). Psychotherapy by reciprocal inhibition. *Conditional Reflex: A Pavlovian Journal of Research & Therapy, 3*(4), 234–240.

Chapter 4

Framing the Mind–Body Problem in Contemporary Neuroscientific and Sunni Islamic Theological Discourse

Faisal Qazi, Donald Fette, Syed S. Jafri, and Aasim Padela

Acknowledgments

Research support for AIP, FQ, and DF was covered by a grant from the John Templeton Foundation (#39623) entitled "Scientific Discoveries & Theological Realities—Exploring the Intersection of Islam and the Human Sciences". Additional time-effort for AIP and symposium support was provided by the Doha International Center for Interfaith Dialogue. In 2016 this chapter was presented in partial form at Bayan Claremont College at a symposium entitled "Dignity and Healthcare at the End-of-Life: Abrahamic Faiths in a Bioethics Conversation" and at the University of Chicago at a conference entitled "Interfaces and Discourses: A Multidisciplinary Conference on Islamic Theology, Law and Biomedicine". We are indebted to Shaykh Jihad Hashim-Brown (Jason Totten) whose lectures and writings provided much of the Islamic arguments and resources for this chapter. We would also like to thank Drs. Ahsan Arozullah, Muhammed Volkan Stodolsky, Katherine Klima, and Shaykh Mohammad Amin Kholwadia who were key interlocutors and partners in the working group project that motivated the work presented herein.

Introduction

How does the mind interact with the body? What is the connection between thoughts, emotions, intentions, and other states of mind with the body? Is consciousness a function of, or somehow dependent on, the body—or is it something entirely distinct from the body? How are "mind" and "consciousness" related? Are they synonymous or disparate entities? These are the kinds of questions which, according to philosopher Tim Crane (1999), "in effect, define the contemporary debate on the mind-body problem". For the religiously-inclined, other questions must be considered: What is the soul? How does the soul relate with the body? Are the functions of the soul identical to or analogous with the various properties attributed by modern science to the mind or consciousness?

Investigation into the connection between mind and body by modern neuroscience has fallen short of explaining the gap between the non-physical and the physical. The possibility of bridging the mind–body divide seems to some even an impossible task. Indeed, as Crane and Patterson (2000) note, science has provided "no adequate account, and in the case of consciousness at least, the problems in giving such an account are sometimes taken to be insuperable".

Part of the problem in giving such an account (of mind being an entity distinct from body) is connected to the origin of the problem in Western philosophy dating back to Plato but taking its more modern form from René Descartes (d.1650). Descartes, by categorizing mind and body as two completely distinct and incommensurable substances, created an impassable, or nearly impassable, gap between the two which haunts science and philosophers of mind to this day.

One way that modern philosophers and scientists have addressed this impasse is simply to undermine the non-physical nature of the mind and reduce it exclusively to the confines of the physical brain. In other words, there is no mind–body "problem" per se, since there is no non-physical aspect to the mind–body connection: The mind and body are, in essence, one and the same. As Schwartz and Begley (2002) note, these kinds of physicalist/reductionist approaches have been criticized by prominent philosopher of mind David Chalmers, who has dubbed them as "no-clue-science", noting that it would be impossible to reduce the entire mind solely to a physical organ such as the brain. Avoiding reductionist approaches, in this chapter we will focus on the substance dualism position, as that position provides a point of intersection between the three discourses discussed. While such physicalist/reductionist modes of inquiry in neuroscience have produced some interesting findings, this data is not only limited but it also has not addressed the dualism on which the mind–body problem hinges.

This chapter seeks to avoid the limitations of inquiry based solely on modern Western scientific and philosophical approaches as well as the scientism that they give rise to and propagate. We believe that a cross-cultural, interdisciplinary approach may provide insights that allow for addressing the mind–body problem in novel ways, and by doing so will advance our understanding of our being. What makes this approach possible is the commensurability and overlap of dualism across all three fields: modern neuroscience, Western philosophy of mind, and Islamic theology. Accordingly, this chapter, while it intends mostly to initiate the dialogue, will demonstrate that the metaphysical and the physiological hold a profound correlation which supplements, rather than dismisses or invalidates, the long-held beliefs of millions of people about the "soul" across time, culture, and place.

This study, then, calls for an examination of the connection between the philosophical (the metaphysical reality of the soul) and the neuroscientific (the soul's physiological impact) from a new perspective, by bringing into dialogue Islamic conceptions of the soul and reflections on the linkages between soul and body.[1] In other words, we propose to initiate a multi-disciplinary dialogical interaction spanning three broad categories of study: (1) philosophy of mind, (2) cognitive neuroscience, and (3) Islamic theology and metaphysics. In what follows, the position of each of these disciplines with respect to the dualism problem will be outlined and the pertinent subdisciplines highlighted.

History of the Mind–Body(–Soul) Problem in Western Philosophy

Before addressing how contemporary neuroscience addresses the mind–body problem, it will be useful to give a brief overview of the history of and approaches to the mind–body(–soul) problem in the Western philosophical tradition, not only because the problem (which continues to be debated today) began as a purely philosophical one, but also because contemporary neuroscience, being a relatively recent field, has undoubtedly inherited, intentionally or unconsciously, many of the perspectives and tenets from the philosophy of mind. The mind–body problem has enjoyed a vast and fruitful history, with schools and subschools of thought too numerous to recount for our purposes here, so we will focus on those most salient for our project.

To begin, the Western perspective on this issue has traditionally hinged upon two ontological positions: dualism and monism. Dualism and its variants divide the world into the physical and the non-physical and, based on this distinction, they endorse the notion that there is a distinct non-physical entity, i.e. the mind and/or soul, at play in human cognition, and that this entity is separate from the physical brain itself. Monism, on the other hand, maintains that there is no actual dualism at work; rather, what is held by dualists as an immaterial, distinct mind or soul is simply part of the body, as one singular fundamental entity, i.e. located and contained within the physical brain. Many contemporary monists, but not all, are materialists, and, as we will note below, much of contemporary neuroscience relies on a materialist, monistic ontological orientation. Outside of these two broad distinctions is a more recent argument popularized by the philosopher Colin McGinn and termed by Owen Flanagan as "mysterianism", which, as McGinn (2012, n.p.) himself simply states, amounts to this: "we just don't have the faculties of comprehension that would enable us to remove the sense of mystery. Ontologically, matter and consciousness are woven intelligibly together but epistemologically we are precluded from seeing how." According to mysterianism, then, there is an epistemic limitation to any surefire interrogation of the mind–body problem, and thus neither dualist nor monist arguments are satisfactory.

Before arriving at the important Cartesian and post-Cartesian dualist and monist instantiations of the problem, it will be useful to trace very briefly its ancient history by highlighting some early key ideas and figures, some of whose ideas were known in paraphrases or directly by early Arab and Muslim scholars such as al-Kindī, al-Rāzī (Rhazes), al-Fārābī, and, most famously Ibn Sīnā (Avicenna) and Ibn Rushd (Averroes). The origins of the problem in the West can be traced to ancient Greek philosophy and, namely, discussions on the nature of the soul (psyche) by the Athenian philosopher Plato and his famous pupil Aristotle. In Book IV of the *Republic*, Plato describes the soul as consisting of three components: the appetitive (ἐπιθυμητικόν), the spirited (θυμοειδές), and the rational (λογιστικόν) portions. Associated with each of these three components were the following functions or faculties: the appetites (ἐπιθυμία), passion/spiritedness (θυμός), and the mind/intellect (νοῦς). According to Plato, the soul was an incorporeal substance and, consequently, immortal. Aristotle, however, differed from his teacher, keeping "the physical aspect of psychological activities very much to the fore" (Ackrill, 1981). "The Philosopher", as he was known for over a millennium, notes in his treatise *De Anima* that the soul could not exist apart from, and thus perished along with, the body. Despite this difference, both philosophers propounded the idea that the soul was a separate entity that interacted with the physical body.

Plato's notion of an immortal soul aligned well with that of the early Church and thus held prominence well into the Middle Ages. A notable idea during this time (late second century BCE) that continued to persist for centuries was Galen of Pergamon's (d.*c.*216 BCE) contention that psychological capacities were associated with the brain and that the soul itself was anatomically related to the fluid-filled ventricles within the brain (Bennett, 2007).

For the next 1500 years the mind–body problem remained essentially unchanged until the Early Modern Era. The discourse was then largely impacted by René Descartes, who is almost single-handedly credited for creating the discipline of philosophy of mind (Kim, 2011). According to Descartes' ontological view, all of nature was divided into two discrete substances: thinking things (*res cogitans*) and things extended in space (*res extensa*). The embodied human being was no different in composition: Humans possess an extended body ruled by a non-extended, thinking mind (soul). According to Descartes, the extended body was the passive, acted-upon, flawed, and fundamentally mutable and therefore ephemeral part of the human being, while the mind (soul) was active, acted upon extended objects, perfect, and fundamentally immutable, and thus immortal. In light of this division, Descartes' famous declaration "I think, therefore I am" (*cogito ergo sum*) signalled a major shift in how mind (thought) and body (extension) were understood as being connected to each other, and to the notion of consciousness as the preliminary basis not only for our identity but also for our very existence. It would seem to most as though the tangible, extended body is the measure of who we are as human beings and the surest proof of our existence, but in reality, Descartes suggests, the opposite is quite true: The invisible, immaterial, non-measureable thinking part of us is the ultimate proof of who and what we are as humans. And thus, though the body perishes and decays, the immaterial, immortal soul endures. Indeed, Descartes' position that our essence as individual humans depended solely on our status as thinking things privileged the place of the psychological (conscious self-awareness), and maintained that the psychological (the mind/soul) was really distinct from the physical. This distinction between the two modes of substances is the essence of so-called Cartesian dualism (Descartes, 1984).

Descartes' contemporaries also made several important contributions to this newly conceived dualism. Reminiscent of the use of creative metaphors such as Descartes' comparison of the soul–body distinction to a pilot in a ship, Gottfried von Leibniz (d.1716) made a famous contribution to the mind–body problem in the so-called mill argument in Section 17 of the *Monadology* (Leibniz & Latta, 1968). In it, he asserted that no matter the degree and extent of inspection of a machine (extension), one would remain hard-pressed to find therein a perception (thought). He stated: "Assuming that, when inspecting its interior, we will find only parts that push one another, and we will never find anything to explain a perception. And so, one should seek perception in the simple substance and not in the composite or in the machine" (Leibniz & Latta, 1968). In effect, the dominant position at this time was that due to the real distinction between thought and extension, consciousness could not arise from mere matter, but that the two were nevertheless connected causally. Cartesian dualism gave rise to what is commonly referred to as substance dualism, which asserts that there are two entirely distinct *substances*—one physical (brain) and another non-physical (mind, often synonymous with consciousness and with soul)—and that the two of them interact with each other in a causal relationship. The obvious problem that remains to be resolved, apart from whether or not there are two really distinct substances at work, is *how* does the non-extended soul/mind interact with the extended body?

In part as a solution to this and other problems with substance dualism, some philosophers diverged from the two-substance model, eschewing the notion of thought being a non-extended substance, and instead posited that only one substance existed—physical, extended substance. Working within this paradigm, so-called property dualism affirms that the mind exists as a non-physical entity (although not a substance), but that it is a mere *property* of the physical brain, a kind of side-effect, and not a unique substance in itself (Gennaro, 2006). Hereafter, much could be said about the ways in which a non-physical entity (essential to both substance and property dualism) *interacts with* the physical entity. Ideas here include interactionism, occasionalism, and parallelism. Of these, the latter two are more or less historic relics, whereas the first remains (Gennaro, 2006). Interactionism asserts that a non-physical mental entity has a causal relationship with the physical.

During the mid to late nineteenth century, a new scientific methodology of investigating psychology surfaced. It was in this context that the works of Herman von Helmholtz, Wilhelm Wundt (widely considered the founder of experimental psychology), and American psychologist/ philosopher William James came to the fore. Even with the start of their investigation, the relation of consciousness to the brain remained a mystery. A famous remark by T. H. Huxley captures the thought and unresolved problem of the age: "How it is that anything so remarkable as a state of consciousness comes about as a result of irritating nervous tissue, is just as unaccountable as the appearance of the Djin, when Aladdin rubbed his lamp" (Huxley, 1986).

With regards to monism, there are two broad categories within the discourse: (1) physicalist monism and (2) non-physicalist monism. The former asserts that the only existing substance is physical, namely the brain, and thus further advances in cognitive neuroscience will ultimately uncover all explanations therein (Bennett, 2007). Although nuanced distinctions are present between them, for the purposes of this conversation, functionalism, behaviorism, and neural identity theory are all more or less physicalist monisms. Non-physicalist monisms, foremost amongst them being idealism, asserts that only mental and conscious phenomena exist, and that the physical world is a benign by-product or appearances of a primarily mental existence (Bennett, 2007).

Turning to the past several decades, the shift in the discourse regarding the mind–body problem had two closely related catalysts in the 1970s and 1980s. The first was the famous paper by Thomas Nagel entitled "What Is It Like to Be a Bat?" Nagel's essay brought to the fore the idea of a first-person, subjective consciousness that is in principle inaccessible to objective interrogation. The second catalyst was a preponderance of scientific advancements that allowed a deeper and more thorough assessment of neurobiological functions. Later, in the 1990s especially, many contemporary philosophers such as Dennett, Penrose, Crick, Chalmers, and others crafted a resurgence in conversations about the mind–body problem. A plethora of articles, books, journals, conferences, and other scholarly activities have recently appeared, as neuroscientists and philosophers alike attempt to tackle the relationship between consciousness and the brain (Kim, 2011). In fact, Jaegwon Kim has proposed renaming the mind–body problem as the consciousness–brain problem (Kim, 2011). Further, following Owen Flanagan's lead, philosopher Colin McGinn has recently popularized the notion of mysterianism—the idea that neither dualism nor monism are satisfactory arguments given the current state of knowledge in cognitive neuroscience, and that there is an epistemic gap yet to be traversed (McGinn, 2012).

Despite its rich history of philosophical refinement, scientific development, and more recent calls for paradigm shifts, the mind–body(–soul) problem indeed remains as what David Chalmers has been attributed to calling the *hard problem* of consciousness and subjective experience—one that faces a seemingly insurmountable explanatory gap or gaps in understanding of the link between mental and physical substances (from the dualist perspective) and the link between the objective physical changes in the brain and the subjective experience of the individual feeling them (from a materialist perspective). Turning to other discourses such as modern neuroscience or Islamic theology may help to bridge this seemingly Gordian gap. Thus, bringing the philosophical discourse on the mind–body problem into dialogue with other, more seemingly disparate discourses that approach the problem with points of view that are disciplinarily different yet share a common thematic scaffolding for substance dualism is in order.

Consciousness in Neuroscience

Attempts to resolve the intricate and difficult philosophical question of the mind–body connection by appealing to past philosophical works, on intense personal introspection, and, at best, on soft sciences such as psychology, have not yet provided answers that move us in any satisfactory way beyond the substance dualism introduced by Descartes. One promising way of answering the questions raised by the philosophy of mind and posed at the outset of this chapter might be by turning to contemporary neuroscience. What neuroscience (and specifically cognitive neuroscience) can offer to the traditional philosophical approach is a more data-driven approach that relies both on empirical observation/measurement as well as the scientific method. Before examining the most recent findings of the field with respect to a possible mind–body connection, including neural correlates of consciousness, we will first provide an overview of important concepts and key terms connected to the understandings of consciousness within contemporary neuroscience.

In contemporary neurological discourse, and cognitive neuroscience by extension, we find two aspects of consciousness: (1) the *level* of consciousness and (2) the *content* of consciousness. The level of consciousness refers to the degree of "wakefulness" an individual possesses—ranging from being fully awake to being in a state of sleep, which could vary from a state of delirium to brain death, with many additional states in between. The level of consciousness, in turn, has three subcategories—alertness, attention, and awareness (Blumenfeld, 2002). Each of these states is thought to have a physical/biological correlate which, if damaged, manifests as a "disorder of consciousness". For example, a lesion in an area of the brainstem referred to as the RAF (reticular activating formation) is associated with a state of coma.

The content of consciousness, by contrast, is best understood, as various components (elements and substrates) that are involved in producing an individual's "awareness of self and environment" (Blumenfeld, 2002). This is discussed in more detail in sections below, but a more technical definition of consciousness in terms of content, offered by neurologist Hal Blumenfeld (2002), is: "The unification of higher order cerebral functions, including the sensory, motor, emotional, and mnemonic (rational), into an efficient summary of mental activity which can potentially be remembered at a later time."

The most visible determinant of a functional/healthy brain is the presence of what is called global consciousness where full awareness is present. By contrast, a state of lack of global consciousness is seen, for instance, in conditions such as coma, where the opposite of an awake/alert state is evident. In this condition, however, content-consciousness by definition is deemed lacking even though the brain may retain an extremely low degree of functioning and minor brain-mediated reflexes in response to stimuli might be present. While excluded by definition, the presence or absence of conscious content in this state remains an important empirical question.

When in a coma, the patient lacks awareness of, and is thus unable to interact with, the surrounding environment. Such unresponsiveness is correlated with the absence of sleep-wave cycles and the suppression of cerebral rhythm as can be seen on electrographic studies (Young, 2000). This widespread dysfunction of the brain results in both the decreased level and loss of the content of consçiousness, although some areas of the brain, particularly those responsible for autonomic function, continue to work. Between a fully awake/alert state of global consciousness and a comatose one lies a wide spectrum of conscious/subconscious states. These include: vegetative, minimally conscious, obtunded, stuporous, and lethargic or cognitively impaired states as in dementia or traumatic brain injury. All of these states involve different levels of conscious awareness, contents of consciousness, and perceptive abilities (Tindall, 1990).

High-level cognitive functions, such as those requiring attention and executive function, are thought to rely primarily on the frontoparietal regions of the brain, though it is now known that various cognitive functions performed in this region can operate in the absence of "conscious perception of the relevant stimuli" even while functional performance is diminished (Boly et al., 2013). Somewhat surprisingly, in awake individuals metabolism is higher in the visual cortex than in the frontoparietal region of the brain—the region that is otherwise considered the seat of conscious perception. This raises the interesting question of how widespread consciousness, in terms of content and level, might be disseminated across the brain, and suggests that a process for the integration of sensory information is required for varying levels of perception. One prominent theory, the Global Workspace Theory, suggests such integration involves neuronal inputs from several brain structures. This theory, as proposed by Baars, describes coalescing of information from various areas of the brain to produce, in essence, a conscious stream by excluding contradictory or unnecessary information (Baars, 2002).

The cerebral cortex is where the content of consciousness is generated and where perceptions achieve meaning. As Negrao and Viljoen (2009) have noted, "unity of consciousness is conferred by integrative processing of these regions." This does, however, create a so-called "binding problem" requiring adequate explanation of the exact processes involved in such integration, or "binding", of all (sensory) input that results in unique perceptions and experiences (Boly et al., 2013). Specifically, the frontoparietal areas of the cerebral cortex seem to be the primary areas responsible for producing consciousness content, and without the functioning of these areas, brain activity is not integrated well enough to sustain consciousness. In addition, this area is also an important factor in cognition, a key element in perception or consciousness content. Yet cognition may occur without conscious perception, as "increasing evidence suggests that in humans, many, if not all, cognitive functions that involve fronto-parietal areas can also operate in the absence of reportable conscious perception of the relevant stimuli, even if performance is usually much diminished" (Boly et al., 2013). Indeed, a number of studies suggest that conscious perception may not be necessary for the operation of various complex cognitive processes such as attention, cognitive control, conflict monitoring, volition, arithmetic, feature binding, and semantic analysis. And while "high conscious levels are associated with an increased range of conscious contents [it remains unclear whether] or not a high level of consciousness without any conscious contents is possible" (Boly et al., 2013). In summary, conscious content allows for the development of perception as well as awareness, yet how the presence or absence of these elements correlate with various lower levels of consciousness still remains an area of investigation.

The Neural Correlates of Consciousness

Neural correlates of consciousness are the minimal measurable neural activity in the brain that "correlate" to a person's conscious, subjective state of mind. In other words, when a person is having a subjective, conscious experience in the mind, the brain will show physical, objectively measurable changes. While some measurable brain activity does not operate on or otherwise affect the conscious awareness of the individual, in the case of neural correlates of consciousness, the individual must register an experience at the conscious level, whether it be love, hunger, or even the slightest touch of a feather on the skin, that then corresponds to measurable neuronal activity.

The most comprehensive of such events, then, is that of consciousness as experience, wherein an individual's conscious experiences represent a "phenomenal quality" in their mind (Graaff, Hsieh, & Slack, 2012). The content changes in this form of consciousness allows the "subject [to] experience different things [while being] conscious in the sense of 'medically aware'" (Graaf et al., 2012). The state of being aware of these experiences is known as "phenomenal awareness" or "qualia". The information present in content-consciousness is both globally available and widely distributed across the brain, reaching "access consciousness" (Graaf et al., 2012).

In order for content-conscious experiences to occur, certain mechanisms for awareness must be employed within brain structures such as the frontal lobes. The employment of these awareness mechanisms blurs the distinction between what can be understood as mere attention and what as individual consciousness. As Graaf et al. (2012) note: "The relation between attention and consciousness is so strong, that a rather severe debate rages on whether consciousness is really nothing more than attention, or stimuli reaching attention." This leads us to ask: Is attention, then, the only prerequisite for consciousness? Following Graaf et al. (2012), attention is a necessary component of conscious awareness, but it is not necessary for other types of perceptions that may be present subconsciously.

We agree with Negrao and Viljoen (2009) in that consciousness "depends on the multitude of unconscious processes that occurs in the brain. Although they don't represent consciousness by themselves in isolation, consciousness cannot exist without these processes." We also agree on the importance of focused attention: "which of the subconscious processes will reach consciousness, appears to be focused attention. This act of deliberately bestowing attention on something specific draws attention to the enigma of free will" (Negrao & Viljoen, 2009).

In summary, models of the mental architecture of consciousness are divided. On the one hand, consciousness is thought to be widely distributed throughout areas of the brain that coalesce to produce the unified experience of being conscious; on the other hand, some models attribute consciousness to specific regions of the brain only. The latter view would suggest that these specific areas must undertake complex interactions to integrate information to produce said consciousness (Baars, 2002).

The Mind–Body Problem in Neuroscience

As can be seen from the increase in scholarly papers and commentaries over the last 30 years, neuroscience is revisiting the mind–body problem. This increase in interest may be due to concerns about the effects of technology on holistic health care, which can, in effect, contribute to the "dehumanizing" of patients. In response to this sense of dehumanization, scholars such as Brian Dolan (2007) have noted that the "soul is what makes a person more than a machine". Elaborating on his anti-mechanistic position, Dolan (2007) continues: "As an organ of reflection, meditation, and memory, the brain becomes synonymous with what defines the self through the existence of consciousness—of mind."

With twentieth-century advancements in identifying the brain's circuitry, a focus on localizing the cognitive functions of the brain has led to a physicalist-dominant approach to the mind–body discussion. According to Dolan, the question of the seat of the soul did not "disappear from the discourse", but instead medical humanism became more concerned with how to replace what he calls "classic Christian dualism" (the view that there is a metaphysical reality beyond the physical which is demanded by beliefs about a creator and creation) without engaging in a necessarily pure "reductionist materialism", which at once does away with any notion of a creator distinct from or beyond the material, physical world and thus precludes the possibility of mind (or soul) as being anything other than an entity reducible to material reality (Dolan, 2007).

On the other hand, some have argued that consciousness (and thus rationality) evolved in such a way that the mind is contingent on the body. Neurologist Antonio Damasio (1994) is a major proponent of this position, arguing against what he calls Descartes' "error" of separating reason (mind) from emotion (body). Damasio (1994) holds that our seemingly rational decisions may actually be guided and informed by—and thus not distinct from—our emotions. The basis of this hypothesis is rooted in the belief that "there can be no separation between mind and body, as all thought is grounded in" body-representing neural structures (Dolan, 2007). Advances in neurosciences as noted above, however, have been able to identify elaborate systems in the brain that produce and sustain consciousness and cognition, and also sustain attention, making Damasio's argument somewhat less viable within the framework of a working physiological model. Yet further research is required to advocate any specific position regarding how consciousness and rationality are connected, if at all, and whether functions we attribute to the "mind" supervene on brain structures.

In modern neuroscience, despite the ability to localize experiences using functional MRI and other advanced imaging techniques, Joseph Levine's (1983) so-called "explanatory gap" argument has continued to undermine experimental findings. Levine's argument aims to demonstrate our inability to explain away conscious experiences such as pain by relying solely on descriptions of the physical processes that occur in the brain at the time of those experiences. In other words, Levine is clarifying that physicalist theories will inevitably face difficulty insofar as purely physiologic knowledge does not lend insight into the correlative subjective experience. He famously stated in 1983 that "pain is the firing of C fibers", referring to the gap between identifying the neurophysiology as an objective entity and the actual reality of experiencing, in the subjective sense, that very thing. This insolubility of the explanatory gap requires more thought in any reframing of the mind–body–soul problem. As limitations of a purely scientific interrogation of consciousness are felt in the broader discourse, theorists would do well to broaden the epistemes under which they presently operate. The persistence of an explanatory gap is indication enough that physicalism is less tenable a view, and that in substance dualism, as an example, an explanatory gap does not even exist, because the presence of a non-physical substance (soul) renders the whole issue more congruent.

According to Kurthen, Grunwald, and Elger (1998), science can address the problem of the explanatory gap, not by trying to solve the problem, but, instead, by redefining the way it is framed, thus *dis*solving the problem: "The explanatory gap cannot simply be closed by achieving a better understanding of the neural correlates of consciousness. What is required instead is an approach that somehow undermines the explanatory-gap intuition itself."

Consequently, the big question for the field of neuroscience and empirical approaches is whether modern scientific investigative methods can study the soul while maintaining the paradigm of the mind–body nexus. This idea may appear difficult but, according to Dolan, at least one British research group has recently provided cause for cautious optimism. In their resolve to use advanced imaging techniques on the prefrontal cortex to understand paraspsychotic grief, this group has suggested "the soul will be elusive but not an impossible concept to study with neuroimaging" (Dolan 2007).

An Islamic Theology of the Soul

One approach that may be useful in reframing the explanatory gap problem lies in turning to the discourse of Sunni Islamic theology. While this discourse also resolves itself into a view generally commensurate with substance dualism,[2] it is distinct from the other two approaches, which hinge on the Weltanschauungen of the secular, materialist, and scientific/scientistic culture of the Western modern world. In the following, we will outline some essential features of the Sunni Islamic conceptualization of the soul, and also point to two major areas where the Islamic position may be placed into fruitful dialogue with contemporary neurological/ philosophy of mind perspectives (the two Western discourses have begun to overlap), namely the so-called "binding problem" in neurology and Levine's "explanatory gap", while pointing out more generally several other areas of potential dialogue.

In Islamic thought, the soul is a necessary entity as it serves as the basis for a number of essential theological views, which include its role as the diagnostic of life, the locus of moral accountability and the explanatory principle of post-mortem existence. It also allows for access to understandings from the Divine realm (Brown, 2013). The term "soul", however, can apply to a number of significant theological terms, which can, consequently, be a source of confusion for researchers. The two most common and certainly most easily conflated of these terms are *al-rūḥ* and *al-nafs*. The first term, *al-rūḥ*, while meaning "soul", might perhaps best be translated as "spirit". As its root is r-w-ḥ, it is, at a deep etymological level, connected with the verb "to breathe" or the noun "breath".[3] The second term, *al-nafs*, also translated as "soul", carries with it a sense of soul as "mind" or "psyche", and can also often be translated as "self".[4] In theological discussions the term most commonly used to refer to the human soul is *al-nafs*.

Despite the similarity between these two fundamental terms, there is an important distinction between them, which may also connect Islamic thought to the binding problem in neuroscience. As noted by al-Ghazālī:[5] the spirit "is the subtle divine essence (*al-laṭīfah al-rabbaniyyah*) – knowing, thinking, and percipient, abiding in human beings" (Sachedina, 2009); as such, it is essentially synonymous with other terms that can be used to denote various facets or functions of the spirit via the body, such as "the heart (*al-qalb*), the soul (*al-nafs*), and the intellect (*al-'aql*). The bodily parts are the tools of the spirit, which, infusing the body, enables the organs to perform different tasks" (Sachedina, 2009). In other words, the body and soul, while closely linked, as evidenced in the spiritual functions expressed via the body, are distinct entities, which separate at death. As al-Ghazālī himself notes, "Just as the onset of an incapacitating disease may mean that the hand is no longer *a tool* of which use is made, so death is an incapacitating disease spread throughout all members" (Sachedina, 2009, emphasis added). Al-Ghazālī's notion of a singularly bounded, coherently unified soul that is at once connected with ostensibly disparate functions or "tasks" may serve as a starting point to reframe or open a dialogue with contemporary neuroscience and the problem of "unity of consciousness" noted by Negrao and Viljoen (2009) above.

This view of the interconnectedness yet distinction between soul and body ultimately finds its roots in verses of the Qur'ān. These verses appear to substantiate an eschatological doctrine that holds there to be an immaterial, non-physical entity that constitutes the essence of the human experience (namely a soul or spirit, words that are interchangeable for our discussion in English—see above and notes 3–4 for finer distinctions), and that the body is merely a vehicle to which it is attached in the temporal world. For example, one verse recalls a primordial covenant where God asks mankind to testify to His lordship:

> And [mention] when your Lord took from the children of Adam—from their loins—their descendants and made them testify of themselves, [saying to them], "Am I not your Lord?" They said, "Yes, we have testified." [This]—lest you should say on the day of Resurrection, "Indeed, we were of this unaware."
>
> (Qur'ān 7.172–182)

Based on this verse, many Islamic theologians and Qur'ān exegetes point out that all human souls perceived God prior to bodily incorporation, and thus a type of dualism between soul and body is required.

Looking at the Islamic intellectual tradition as a whole, and the development of theological orthopraxy, it is critical to note that Muslim theologians throughout the ages have discussed and debated the nature of the soul and have held many different positions on its linkage to the body and its essential nature as substance or body. Tracing this history is beyond the scope of the present chapter; rather, our point here is to stress that speculative discussions and debates occurred within Muslim scholarly circles in full recognition of the fact that the Qur'ān conveys that mankind has been endowed with little knowledge of the soul (see verse 17:85). The essential meaning of this verse bears great significance insofar as rendering a prerequisite flexibility to any conclusive statements concerning the soul.

The flexibility mentioned above can be seen among the myriad of contentions about the ontological realities of the human soul posited by Muslim thinkers over the centuries, particularly during the Islamic Golden Age (eighth through thirteenth centuries CE). It is not the intention of this chapter to highlight each of the arguments, but rather to note the two most dominant positions, at least in Sunni theology: (1) the "subtle body" position (*jism laṭīf*) and (2) the immaterial substance position (*jawhar mujarrad*). The former stated that a physical locus of the soul is to be found somewhere in the body proper—and traditionally thought to be the heart—whereas the latter stated that the soul is by its intrinsic nature immaterial and non-physical, and has more of an "attachment" relationship with the body. Of these two positions, the latter is one that modern thinkers should build on in their contributions to the mind–body problem discourse, for it attends to critical questions and knowledge gaps that the former cannot.

The subtle body (*jism laṭīf*) position suggests that the soul is a tenuously fine and atomically dispersed body (as purported by highly renowned scholars such as al-Juwaynī, d.470 AH/1085 CE).[6]. The position is based on the notion that subtle bodies are integrated into dense bodies, i.e. corporeal ones (*jism kathīf*), and holds that when these subtle bodies leave the dense ones, a change happens. In the case of the human, then, when the soul departs, animation and cognitive as well as integrative faculties leave with it, and "death" ensues. This position is widely taught in seminaries as part of early studies of creed and doctrine, and is attested to by works such as *al-Fiqh al-Akbar* authored by the promulgator of the Ḥanafī school of law himself, Imām Abū Ḥanīfah, and is attributed to Abū Bakr al-Bāqillānī, one of the founders of the Ash'arite school of theology (al-Muntahā, 2007). This corporeality necessitates that the soul exists within the material world and must therefore be accessible to the five empirical senses (Brown, 2013). It does not explain, however, how the soul will endure after it departs the body. Additionally, this theory runs into inherent problems with unity of consciousness as well as with the "binding problem" noted above, but may indeed be brought to bear in a dialogue with the contemporary neuroscientific theories regarding the problem.

Another theory expounded by theologians such as 'Aḍud al-Dīn al-'Ījī (d.1355)[7] is that the soul is an immaterial substance (*jawhar mujarrad*). According to this theory, the soul is defined as a non-physical entity without extension or parts, and therefore it is not perceptible to the five empirical senses. It is an independent, indivisible, and non-spatial entity. It is viewed as a substratum supporting faculties (which are accidents) inhering in it; in other words, it instantiates modes and properties. As the soul in this view would not be a spatially extended entity, it would seem to follow that consciousness (more specifically intellection or thought as a faculty of the soul) cannot simply be a physical thing (Brown, 2013).

This understanding of the soul, then, provides an Islamic entry point into discussions about the relationships between the physical/material and the metaphysical/mental, which may be brought to bear on the mysterianism proffered recently in philosophy of mind or, perhaps more directly, with Nagel's "explanatory gap" problem. Indeed, since the soul cannot be interrogated by the senses and empirical experiments according to the Islamic perspective, an epistemic gap needs to be recognized. Perhaps the explanatory gap between the "objective" *description* of what is happening in the brain during various qualia or experiences of feeling and the "subjective" *experience* of those feelings could find fruitful dialogue with al-'Ījī's position. The question of how the soul and body relate within the realm of Islamic scholastic theology (*kalām*) therefore has resonances for the brain–mind relationship in philosophy of mind.

Bringing the two disciplines into conversation around a table constructed by neuroscientific data would facilitate fruitful exchange. As an example, it may be that models of interactionist mind–body causation beholden to substance dualism, such as those offered by Karl Popper, help advance arguments in Islamic scholastic theology of the soul. Similarly, it is possible that recovering arguments made by Islamic theologians about whether the soul is a simple substance and how it governs the body might nudge the field of philosophy of mind on a bit further. Lastly, perhaps in a more practical way, bringing Islamic theology, philosophy of mind, and neuroscience into conversation might allow us to think more deeply about the borders of life. What we have in mind (pun intended) is that consideration of what constitutes brain death might provide the occasion for each of these three disciplines to engage with data and models that emerge from the other fields and, by doing so, attend to the ethical, empirical, and metaphysical conundrums of biomedicine.

Conclusion

Discussion of the mind–body problem, or as Jaegwon Kim (2011) puts it, consciousness–brain problem, abounds. Physicalist positions dominate, especially as they are strengthened by ongoing advances in modern neuroscience. It should be maintained, however, that the "jury is still out" and that an entirely physical explanation for higher-order cerebral functions—consciousness in particular—do not yet exist and may not arise in the future. Karl Popper noted an idea he termed "promissory materialism", or the belief that while reductionist explanations do not suffice at present, scientific advances will inevitably confirm such beliefs to be facts. Thus it is felt by most that although consciousness (content of consciousness) has not yet been explained in physical terms, this will happen one day. To adequately and fairly address the mind–body problem, especially in light of contemporary Islamic thought, such an underlying philosophy must be highlighted and sidelined.

The "hard problem" of consciousness is noteworthy. David Chalmers, credited for coining the term, argues that, even in principle, a complete objective interrogation of the brain could not grant access to the subjective phenomena experienced by the possessor of said brain (Chalmers, 1995). That is to say, even if one were to perform every fMRI study conceivable, if all 100 trillion synapses of the human brain were to be mapped into a connectome, objective data would remain objective, and subjective experience would remain subjective. In other words: All of our advanced machinery and methods of measurement remain merely at the level of describing what happens from the outside but can never explain how or why things feel the way they do to the subject. This explanatory gap persists and the consciousness–brain problem remains un(re)solved.

Therefore, substance dualism is not outmoded, but is rather a tenable position worth revival in an age where scientism predominates. Indeed, one of the dominant positions on the soul within Islamic theology, *jawhar mujarrad* or the position of "attachment" of an immaterial substance (soul) with a particular body, may provide a fruitful starting point for engaging with the mind–body problem. While argued for theological purposes, and not empirical or philosophical ones, this Islamic vision of the soul suggests that the attachment relationship is one whereby the soul exerts governance on the body for fulfilment of duties in the worldly realm (and acknowledges that an "otherworldly" realm also exists).

What, then, should be made of the modern neuroscientific assessment of the brain, of consciousness, of deficits after brain injury such as stroke, brain tumour, and multiple sclerosis? Accounting for an Islamic conception of the soul might lead us to consider the physical brain to be the tangible intermediary between the non-physical and the physical, and injuries or defects to it negatively hinder this relay. The patient with glioblastoma multiforme experiencing cognitive disturbances (in other words disruptions that appear to be linked to faculties of the soul) does so because of a "transmission" problem—no deficiency in the individual soul exists per se, but what is manifested to us in this physical realm may appear as such. The brain is thus seen as the means of connection of the soul to the worldly realm, the place in the body where such function is most localizable, and any accumulating injury to it weakens or lessens that connection. Total brain failure, then, would signify the complete detachment of the soul from the body.

We would suggest that one who embarks on a deeper inquiry into the mind–body problem might do so with a particular framing in mind. This framing requires the simultaneous juxtaposition of (1) an understanding of the philosophical underpinnings of the mind–body problem in the West, which are inflected in modern neuroscience, (2) advances in modern neuroscience itself, and (3) frameworks from Islamic scholastic theology. Bringing into reflexive conversation these disparate bodies of knowledge might yield fruitful insights into our understanding of the essential aspects of cognition and the human being.

Notes

1 In this chapter we focus primarily on the Sunni tradition and references to "Islamic" theology and philosophy are to the Sunni tradition. For further reading on the Shī'ah tradition regarding the soul, see Ṣadrā (2003, 2008), Panjwani (2014), al-Ṭūsī (1964).
2 For a discussion of possible subtle distinctions between Cartesian dualism and dualism in Islam, see Aftab (2015).
3 The term *al-rūḥ* shares, it turns out, the same root as the Hebrew term for spirit, i.e. *ruah*.

4 It may be useful to compare these two terms *al-rūḥ* (spirit, breath) and *al-nafs* (soul, mind, self, psyche) to the familiar distinctions in the Western tradition, which include the Greek πνεῦμα (spirt, wind, breath) and ψυχή (soul, mind, psyche) as well as the Latin *spiritus* (spirit, wind) and *animus* (mind, soul, psyche).
5 For further reading on the etymology of 'soul' in Arabic, see: Ibn Manẓūr (1984, p. 326).
6 'Abd al-Malik b. 'Abd Allah al-Juwaynī is known by the honorific title *Imām al-Ḥaramayn* (the Scholar of the Two Holy Sanctuaries, i.e. the Ka'bah and the Prophet's Mosque, peace and blessings be upon him) and was a pre-eminent theologian and jurist. He authored leading texts such as *Kitāb al-Irshād 'alā Qawāṭi' al-Adillah fi Usūl al-I'tiqād*, and was the teacher of Abū Ḥāmid al-Ghazālī.
7 'Aḍud al-Dīn al-'Ījī is a renowned Sunni scholar known for the monumental theological treatise *al-Mawāqif fī 'Ilm al-Kalām*. He was a trained Shafi'ī jurist and Ash'arī theologian and served as state judge.

References

Ackrill, J. L. (1981). *Aristotle the philosopher*. Oxford/New York, NY: Claredon Press.

Aftab, M. (2015). Is Islam committed to dualism in the context of the problem of free will? *Journal of Cognition and Neuroethics*, *3*(1), 1–12.

al-Muntahā al-Maghnisāwī, A. (2007). *Imām Abū Ḥanīfah's al-Fiqh al-Akbar explained*. Santa Barbara, CA: White Thread Press.

al-Ṭūsī, N.r al-D. (1964). *The Nasirean ethics*. Trans. G. M Wickens. London: Allen and Unwin.

Baars, B. J. (2002). The Conscious Access Hypothesis: Origins and recent evidence. *Trends in Cognitive Sciences*, *6*(1), 47–52.

Bennett, M. R. (2007). Development of the concept of mind. *Australasian Psychiatry*, *41*(12), 943–956.

Blumenfeld, H. (2002). *Neuroanatomy through clinical cases*. Sunderland, MA: Sinauer Associates.

Boly, M., Seth, A., Wilke, M., et al. (2013). Consciousness in humans and non-human animals: Recent advances and future directions. *Frontiers in Psychology*, *4*, 625–20.

Brown, J. (2013). The problem of reductionism in philosophy of mind and its implications for theism and the principle of soul: framing the issue for further Islamic inquiry. *Tabah Paper Series*, *7*, 1–30.

Chalmers, D. (1995). Facing up to the problem of consciousness. *Journal of Consciousness Studies*, *2*(3), 200–219.

Crane, T. (1999). Mind-body problem. *The MIT encyclopedia of the cognitive sciences* (pp. 546–548). Cambridge, MA: MIT.

Crane, T., & Patterson, S. (2000). *History of the mind-body problem*. New York, NY/ London: Routledge.

Damasio, A. R. (1994). *Descartes' error: Emotion, reason, and the human brain*. New York, NY: G. P. Putnam.

Descartes, R. (1984). *Meditations on first philosophy*. Trans. Cottingham, Stoothoff, & Murdoch. *The philosophical writings of Descartes, Volume II*. Cambridge, UK: Cambridge.

Dolan, B. (2007). Soul searching: A brief history of the mind/body debate in the neurosciences. *Neurosurgical FOCUS*, *23*(1), 1–7.
Gennaro, R. J. (2006). Consciousness. *Internet encyclopaedia of philosophy*. Available from: www.iep.utm.edu/consciou/. [Accessed December 13, 2015.]
Graaf, T., Hsieh, P. J., & Sack, A. T. (2012). The "correlates" in neural correlates of consciousness. *Neuroscience and Biobehavioral Reviews*, *36*(1), 191–197.
Huxley, T. H. (1986). *Lessons in elementary physiology (1900)*. London: Macmillan.
Ibn Manẓūr, M. (1984). *Lisān al-'Arab*. Beirut: Dār al-Kutub al-'Ilmiyyah.
Kim, J. (2011). *Philosophy of mind*. 3rd ed. Boulder, CO: Westview Press.
Kurthen, M., Grunwald, T., & Elger, C. E. (1998). Will there be a neuroscientific theory of consciousness? *Trends in Cognitive Sciences*, *2*(6), 229–234.
Leibniz, G. W., F. von, & Latta, R. (1968). *The Monadology and other philosophical writings*. London: Oxford University Press.
Levine, J. (1983). Materialism and qualia: the explanatory gap. *Pacific Philosophical Quarterly*, *64*, 354–361.
McGinn, C. (2012). All machine and no ghost? *New Statesman*. February 20. Available from: www.newstatesman.com/ideas/2012/02/consciousness-mind-brain.
Negrao, B. L., & Viljoen, M. (2009). Neural correlates of consciousness. *African Journal of Psychiatry (South Africa)*, *12*(4), 265–269.
Panjwani, I. (2014). Soul. *The Oxford Encyclopaedia of Philosophy, Science and Technology in Islam*, pp. 267–273. Oxford: Oxford University Press.
Qur'ān. Sahih International Version. Available from: https://quran.com/7/172.
Sachedina, A. (2009). *Islamic biomedical ethics: principles and application*. Oxford: Oxford University Press.
Ṣadrā, M. (2003). *Iksīr al-'Ārifīn (The elixir of the Gnostics)*, trans. William Chittick. Chicago, IL: Brigham Young University Press.
Ṣadrā, M. (2008). *Spiritual psychology: the fourth intellectual journey in transcendent philosophy – volumes VIII & IX of the asfar*. London: ICAS Press.
Schwartz, J., & Begley, S. (2002). *The mind & the brain: neuroplasticity and the power of mental force*. New York, NY: Harper.
Tindall, S. C. (1990). Level of consciousness. In H. K. Walker, W. D. Hall, & J. W. Hurst (Eds.), *Clinical methods: the history, physical, and laboratory examinations*. 3rd Ed. Boston, MA: Butterworths. Available from: www.ncbi.nlm.nih.gov/books/NBK380/.
Young, G. B. (2000). The EEG in coma. *J. Clin. Neurophysiol.*, *17*(5), 473–85. Available from: www.ncbi.nlm.nih.gov/pubmed/11085551.

Part III

Case Formulation and Assessment

Chapter 5

Quantitative and Qualitative Assessment of the Ontological Domains of the Psyche in TIIP

Fahad Khan

Chapter Summary

Assessment of human functioning is an essential component of the therapy process. The ability to quantitatively or qualitatively assess an aspect of the human self (whether its outwards expression of symptoms or internal state) is an important step in facilitation of the process of change. The goal of this chapter is to assess the domains of human ontological psychospiritual functioning as identified in the Traditional Islamically Integrated Psychotherapy (TIIP) model. A sample case illustration is used to present how these assessments can be of benefit in the therapeutic process. Although no single methodology to assess these domains exists, the author presents previously published assessments as well as qualitative elements to help assist in the assessment process.

The Domains of Human Psychospiritual Functioning

In the TIIP model, Keshavarzi and Khan (2018) have presented a complex and merged model of the human psyche (see Figure 5.1). It includes:

1. *'aql* or cognition,
2. *nafs* or behavioral inclinations,
3. *rūḥ* or spirit,
4. *iḥsās* or emotions, and
5. *qalb* or the heart.

According to Islamic spirituality, the *qalb* or spiritual heart is the vessel for all health and pathology. The four domains (*rūḥ*, *nafs*, *'aql*, and *iḥsās*) can affect the heart in both positive and negative manners. Contrary to the popular usage of the term among Muslims, the *nafs*, by its very nature, is not intrinsically evil. It can be trained and disciplined, leading to its ultimate state: *muṭma'innah*. The *'aql*, primarily residing in

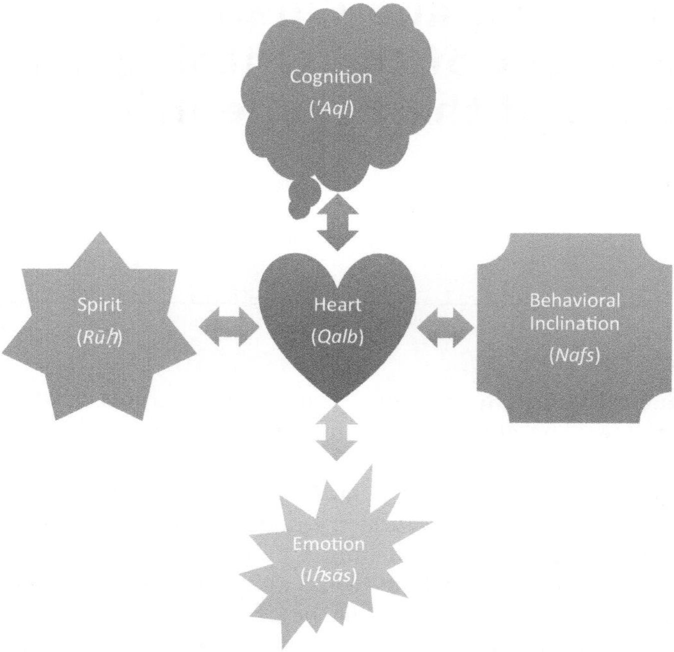

Figure 5.1 Composite elements of internal human psyche (Keshavarzi & Khan, 2018).

the human brain, contains rationality and logic. As discussed in the cognitive theory, thoughts and cognitions are coordinated through schemas built using experiences in the past. The *rūḥ* is the "spirit of the human being, its life force with an innate affinity for the sacred with a thirst for the purpose of life, finding meaning in living, and a longing for the divine" (Keshavarzi & Khan, 2018, p. 178). Finally, *iḥsās* or emotions are the inner human states resulting from physical, internal psychological elements (see Chapter 7) and social environments. All of these aspects are interconnected, so that a change in the state of one will lead to a change in the system overall.

Goals for Healthy Psycho-spiritual Functioning

According to the TIIP model, a healthy individual living a holistic life will focus not only on their internal framework of psycho-spiritual functioning, but will also take into consideration their relationship with others around them and their Creator. This is depicted in Figure 5.2.

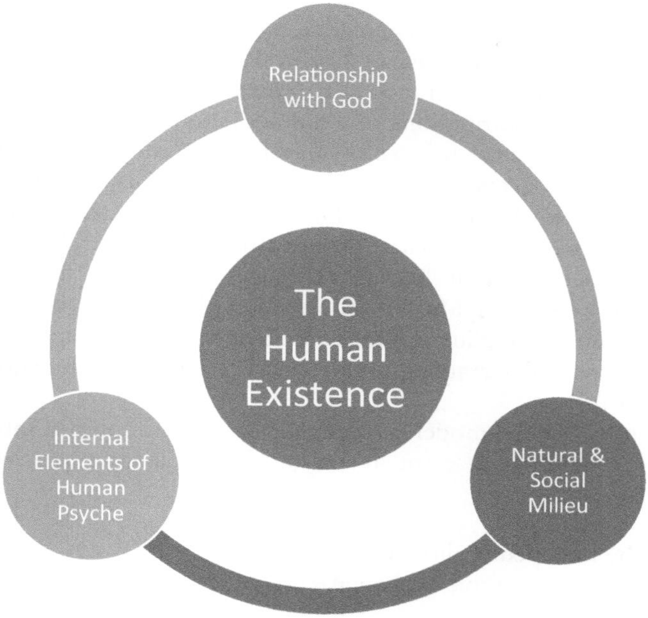

Figure 5.2 Contextual existence of the human being.

The relationship with Allah most High can be strengthened through His worship and following the tradition of His Prophet (peace and blessings be upon him), as well as being a moral and responsible individual in the natural and social environment. The human being is both interrelational and interconnected, and influences from the environment can lead to a change in inner functioning. Similarly, the spiritual connection with the Creator can also alter the inner functioning in a negative or positive manner.

Assessment of Psycho-spiritual Functioning

The process of assessment aims to categorize, compartmentalize, and quantify that which it measures. The specific definition of assessment varies depending on the type of assessment being conducted. For example, an assessment can be used to measure whether certain performance criteria or learning outcomes have been met. This process entails collection and evaluation of both facts and evidence to establish a particular level within a specified range or spectrum. This chapter will focus on assessing human psycho-spiritual functioning through such a process.

Comprehensive Spiritual Assessments and Its Goals

There has been an increase in the integration of spirituality into the practice of psychology and counseling (Cashwell, Bentley, & Yarborough, 2007). In the West, this integration was initiated in the late nineteenth century through the contributions of Francis Galton and Frank Parsons (McCormick, 2004). Since then, spirituality has become a core component of graduate-level counseling courses (Curtis & Glass, 2002), holistic wellness models (Adams, Bezner, Drabbs, Zambarano, & Steinhardt, 2000), and assessment instruments (Hall & Edwards, 2002). Historically, spirituality has been part of human existence, practice, suffering, and healing for many centuries. Muslim scholars and physicians from as early as the ninth century have incorporated the assessment of spirituality as an essential factor in determining healthy and holistic human functioning (al-Balkhī, 2013).

Since the focus of the model is essentially on psycho-spiritual integration, the psycho-spiritual assessment and initial formulation phase has six major goals:

1. building the therapeutic alliance,
2. assessment of motivation to change,
3. assessment of religiosity,
4. diagnosis and conceptualization,
5. assessment of internal and external psycho-spiritual functioning, and
6. psychoeducation and setting therapeutic goals.

From Islamic spiritual writings to modern behavioral research, the importance of building a therapeutic alliance with trust and mutual understanding is frequently highlighted. This first mechanism of change is termed *murābaṭah* (see Chapter 1, Figure 1.3). In fact, therapeutic alliance is often considered the strongest determinant variable of success in treatment (Horvath, Del Re, Flückiger, & Symonds, 2011). Formation of the therapeutic alliance is deemed necessary in order to engender treatment compliance (*inqiyād*), which is the first step of the process of change in TIIP. The assessment phase necessitates an approach that is non-directive and person-centered. Appropriate motivation for change is necessary for treatment to be effective. As highlighted by Prochaska and DiClemente's (1983) model of change, a person who is not considering or is ambivalent about change is not likely to respond well to therapy, especially to a directive stance from the therapist. Since Muslims are often likely to attach stigma to mental health problems with resultant increased barriers for seeking treatment, assessment of motivation to change is imperative. An important distinction needs to be made regarding the approach and style of therapy with Muslims. Whether or not the patient will respond well to a directive approach is irrelevant to the assessment process; the approach needs to be non-directive.

Religiosity is not an easy factor to assess and quantify; however, there are assessment tools that can help measure various factors related to one's religiosity. For instance, Psychological Measure of Islamic Religiousness (PMIR) is a comprehensive religiosity assessment that measures many factors (Abu-Raiya, Pargament, Mahoney, & Stein, 2008). Muslim Experiential Religiousness (MER) assesses the experiential religiosity of the individual, rather than focusing on rituals (Ghorbani, Watson, Madani, & Chen, 2016). Informally, the degree of usage of explicit or overt religious vocabulary, language, concepts, or religious references during the therapeutic encounter (Keshavarzi & Haque, 2013) can also aid in this assessment. Also, as part of the psychoeducation goal, the clinician must provide a brief descriptor of their therapeutic orientation, style, and general outline of the therapeutic goals.

Although diagnosis is not absolutely essential to initiate the process, it can certainly aid in determining the course of the treatment and expected outcome objectives. This includes assessment of severity, etiology, prognosis, and potential therapeutic utility of the TIIP for the individual. Since some Muslims report a preference for a more directive and authoritative approach to psychotherapy, psychoeducation can be a useful tool in providing the individual with a greater degree of confidence in the expertise of the therapist (Kobeisy, 2004). This further helps set up the expectations for the therapeutic encounter in early sessions.

Lastly, this conceptualization entails internal and external psychospiritual functioning using the approach described below. A therapist educated and trained in recognizing the functioning of the internal and external aspects of spirituality can determine its proper functioning by assessing the patient's basic thought processes, emotional functioning, behavioral and instinctual inclinations, and spiritual and social functioning, the last of which includes participation in the community and relationships with other individuals (relatives, community members, co-workers, etc.). Proper diagnosis and conceptualization can help determine therapeutic goals. These goals can be clinically focused towards the patient's psychological disorder and/or spiritually focused towards the patient's spiritual problems.

Case Introduction

Below is a case illustration with information obtained during multiple intake sessions as well as information uncovered during subsequent therapy sessions. Personal information has been manipulated to protect the confidentiality of the patient.

Patient

Muqeem was a 16-year-old, unmarried South Asian American high school student who was brought by his family to a counseling center that utilizes TIIP in the treatment it offers. He was initially very hesitant to work with a Muslim therapist; however, his hesitation decreased as the therapeutic alliance was established based on trust and unconditional positive regard. He suffered from symptoms of depression and anxiety related to many facets of his life.

History

Muqeem was born and raised in the United States in a South Asian Muslim household. He was the youngest in his family. As a child, he moved from one state to another with his family, which caused strain within his social relationships. His parents and older siblings were all religiously oriented individuals who also attended *madāris* (religious schools; singular: *madrasah*) for formal Islamic education. At the age of 14, Muqeem was sent to a *madrasah* to memorize the Qur'ān. He graduated from the *madrasah* after successful memorization of the entire Qur'ān in approximately two and a half years. After graduation, he was sent to an Islamic private school to continue his education. Muqeem said his madrasa experience was difficult. He denied being "traumatized" by it; however, it appeared to be a significant negative factor in his history. Muqeem was the youngest child and all of his siblings were a decade or more older than him. His father was always busy so there was hardly any opportunity for them to spend time together. His mother primarily focused on overt religiosity and taking care of the house. He said he felt isolated throughout his life.

Precipitating Event

Muqeem's internal symptoms (which were not observable through his behavior) did not become a concern until the day he wrote a note to his family with the intention of running away from home. The note was discovered by his teacher and subsequently reported to his mother. She became concerned and sought psychotherapy services. Due to their high level of religiosity, the family was only open to a religiously oriented therapist who would incorporate Islamic concepts into the treatment.

Assessment

His initial assessments included the Beck Depression Inventory, Beck Anxiety Inventory, Brief Symptom Inventory, Islamic Positive Religious

Coping, and Muslim Experiential Religiousness scale. The results indicated symptoms related to a very high level of depression and anxiety with hopelessness regarding the future, as well as low religiosity.

Other History

Muqeem had no medical or psychiatric history. He had previously used marijuana; however, he showed no signs of physical or behavioral dependence on it. He had once previously tried to shoplift from a store and was caught and handed over to the police. This was an isolated incident that was not repeated.

Case Conceptualization and Treatment Plan

Subsequent therapy sessions with Muqeem focused on arriving at a conceptualization of his psychological functioning within a TIIP context and specification of the most appropriate treatment plan. This conceptualizes the patient across the TIIP elements of the human psyche while mapping the treatment plan designated to treat the imbalance on each domain.

After the clinical assessment, it appeared that Muqeem's cognitive and emotional disturbances were the primary sources of his symptoms of depression and anxiety. His irrational thought processes, as well as maladaptive emotions, were a result of the trauma he had experienced during his time in the *madrasah*. It has been hypothesized that emotions are initiated after an individual evaluates emotional cues. This evaluation leads to a set of response tendencies that involve experiential, behavioral, and physical symptoms (John & Gross, 2004). For Muqeem, these negative emotions and cognitive disturbances eventually led to a disruption in his spirituality, causing him to lose faith. Although he could have benefited from *rūḥānī* (spiritual) as well as *ijtimāʿī* (social) interventions, the primary focus of the treatment was to bring *iʿtidāl* (balance) to his *ʿaqlānī* (cognitive) and *iḥsāsī* (emotional) aspects so that he could have better control of his *nafs* (behavioral inclinations), thus leading to a sound *qalb* (heart). Each component and the interventional approaches utilized are described below.

ʿAql—*Cognition*

ʿAql or cognition comprises the thoughts and schemas that exist within the patient. According to Beck (1964), a schema is a hypothesized cognitive structure that organizes information. A therapist needs to identify problematic thought processes and deconstruct any unnatural and unhealthy schemas (and core beliefs) found within the patient's cognitive apparatus (Beck, 2011). Table 5.1 provides a summary of assessment areas within this domain as well as treatment planning options.

Table 5.1 Assessment and treatment planning for *'aql*

Domain	*Quantitative Assessment*		*Qualitative Questions*	*Treatment Planning* (Mu'ālajah)
'Aql **Cognitive**	Presence of negative thoughts towards self/ others/future?	☐ Yes ☐ No	- In what areas of life does the individual present with these negative thoughts? - Are they universal or specific? - Are they negatively attributed to the self?	- Increase awareness (*inkishāf*) of thoughts (both negative and positive) through thought processing during sessions and thought records as homework.
	Cognitive Distortions?	☐ Selective abstraction ☐ Disqualifying the positive ☐ Personalization ☐ Arbitrary inference ☐ Magnification or minimization ☐ Overgeneralization ☐ Polarized/all-or-nothing thoughts ☐ Jumping to conclusions/mind reading ☐ Emotional reasoning ☐ "Should's" ☐ Labeling/ ☐ mislabeling ☐ Other	- How did these cognitive distortions develop? - How do these distortions negatively affect the individual's relationships? Functioning? Spirituality? - Is the individual aware of these problematic thought processes? - How do the thoughts and schemas disrupt the *i'tidāl* and affect the *qalb*?	- Teach the patient the ability to identify negative thought patterns and distortions. - Challenge the negative thoughts, reverse the distortions during sessions and coach the patient to continue in-between sessions. - Process with the patient how these negative thoughts create an imbalance and negatively affect the patient's overall internal psychological state (i.e. the *qalb*).
	Do thoughts manifest in dreams?	☐ Yes ☐ No	- Do the dream patterns represent the negative thoughts experienced by the individual?	- Have the patient keep a journal to write down dreams as well as negative thoughts.
	Presence of obsessive thoughts?	☐ Yes, identify obsessions. ☐ No	- What thoughts are obsessive (intrusive, repetitive, unwelcomed, and painful)?	- Utilize exposure and response prevention to treat obsessive thoughts.

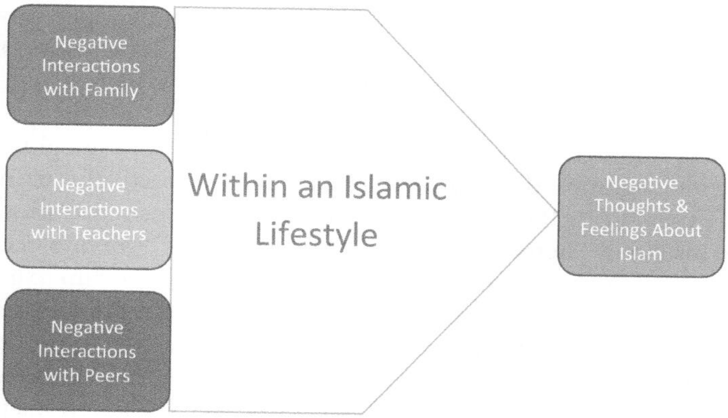

Figure 5.3 Enmeshment of thoughts due to negative social experiences.

Muqeem suffered from negative thoughts related to his family, his religion, and the Muslim community. As a result of his negative historical interactions with his family, which were characterized by an excessively critical/authoritarian parenting style with minimal warmth or positive attention, Muqeem appeared to have internalized feelings of shame and sadness due to a sense of isolation and resentment. Feelings that were accompanied by negative thoughts of others had also been generalized to other family members, the community, and even his personal religion and spirituality (see Figure 5.3). The intensity of these negative feelings evoked in him a maladaptive avoidance response that most significantly included a distancing from his own religious identity, as well as an outward distancing, that eventually lead to plans of running away from home. This overcompensation to the opposite extreme led Muqeem, a *ḥāfiẓ* (someone who has committed the entire Qur'ān to memory), to self-identify as an atheist. His feelings of inferiority and shame also led him to a sense of hopelessness about his future. This manifested in his lack of planning to attend college, as he was not confident that he would be able to graduate.

As stated in the TIIP model, after the alliance between patient and therapist has been built, the second phase of treatment is to proceed to the utilization of *mukāshafah* or therapeutic uncovering in order to induce *inkishāf* or introspective self-awareness in the patient. This required Muqeem to become aware of his internal thought processes, their origins, and how they were related to and influenced by his emotions and associated with his behavior. In the initial stage, it was important for Muqeem to realize how historical interactions with his family/peers/teachers had led to immediate emotions of disgust, shame, and anger. These emotions were instigated by confrontation with any internal or external cues that triggered his familial history, thereby leading to coping through cognitive dissociation and behavioral avoidance. Internal cues might include his thoughts related to his religious identity while external cues could include entering a mosque or opening the Qur'ān.

The most important challenge related to Muqeem's thoughts was dealing with cognitive distortions that had been created due to negative past experiences. For example, Muqeem continuously had thoughts related to his family "betraying" him and "manipulating" him into become more religious. He stated that his father would regularly take him to a local *madrasah* and ask him to play with the children there, attempting to deceptively instill the belief into his mind that *madrasah* is a fun environment with accepting and loving individuals. This idea was shattered during his first few weeks at the *madrasah*, when he was not only bullied by his peers for being Bangladeshi but was also physically abused by his Qur'ān teacher. This catalyzed intense negative emotions of fear that became associated with religion and, by extension, emotions of anger characterized by betrayal by his family, especially his father.

A key interventional tool used was to defuse and help Muqeem develop a distinction between the cognitive constructs of (1) God/religion and (2) humans/culture. This was helpful in challenging overgeneralizations of his experiences and creating the psychological space for him to develop a capacity for the formation of a healthy religious identity that was not shaped by his negative historical experiences. This was necessary because Muqeem was unable to determine whether an action or an attitude was due to Islam (commandments of Allah, most High and the teaching of His Prophet, peace and blessings be upon him) or due to cultural norms and individual interpretations and attitudes. All of these appeared to have been merged together, causing his feelings of resentment to transfer and generalize to his religious identity.

After the cognitive intervention of defusion, an emotionally oriented intervention was utilized in order for Muqeem to process the expression of emotions during treatment sessions that might not be achievable in reality with his family members. As shown in the section below, the emotion-focused chair work, along with cognitive interventions, eventually led him to soften his emotions and empathize with his father, Qur'ān teacher, and peers with regard to his negative perception of their behaviors. Since Muqeem's atheistic views primarily developed due to unresolved negative emotions or unfinished business, it was inappropriate to cognitively challenge these views in an attempt to alter them without sufficient processing and validation of his feelings. To the contrary, challenging his atheistic views may have evoked transference of these negative feelings towards the therapist, since the therapist would have personified the pathological psychological object of his father that Muqeem had internalized. By doing so, the therapist would be viewed as allied with Muqeem's family, thereby invalidating his feelings and risking rupture in the patient–therapist alliance. Therefore, at this juncture, after cognitive awareness was developed, the therapist transitioned into emotionally oriented psychotherapy.

Iḥsās—*Emotions*

Emotions are considered to be among the fundamental aspects of the psyche in constructing the self and an important determinant of self-organization (Greenberg, 2010). At their basic level, emotions are adaptive, and are helpful in determining needs, values, or goals. Certain life experiences and resulting memories form emotional schemas that can transform adaptive primary emotions into maladaptive ones. For example, sadness can cause anger to appear. Maladaptive feelings include loneliness, worthlessness, and unhealthy shame (Greenberg, 2010). Table 5.2 provides a summary of assessment areas within this domain as well as treatment planning options.

Muqeem experienced a variety of emotions due to negative past experiences. He stated that, as the youngest in the family, he felt like he was "never given any importance". Decisions were made about his life without any consultation with him. He felt "betrayed" and "manipulated" by his family. When he started the *madrasah*, he was bullied by his peers, which caused him to feel sad and socially isolated. He was physically abused by his teacher and he felt unsupported.

Muqeem's emotional functioning was conceptualized and treated using emotionally integrated psychotherapy. Figure 5.4 shows how Muqeem experienced core pain resulting in primary emotions. He felt lonely as a young child, which made him feel ashamed of himself. He further felt sadness and fear when experiencing trauma. This led to his negative treatment of the self in relation to others and behavioral avoidance. He felt the need to run away because he did not want to experience those negative emotions. Instead of addressing his sadness and fear, he chose to apply secondary emotions of maladaptive anger and feelings of betrayal.

To achieve emotional balance or *iʿtidāl*, Muqeem needed to uncover his primary emotions of sadness associated with being hurt that lay beneath the more comfortable and more easily accessible secondary or maladaptive emotion of anger. Two-chair enactment was used to help identify the core primary emotions. Given that his historical experiences centered around his father, this therapeutic marker emerged, which signaled a need to transition into "unfinished business" intervention. Most of Muqeem's emotional

Table 5.2 Assessment and treatment planning for *iḥsās*

Domain	*Quantitative Assessment*		*Qualitative Questions*	*Treatment Planning* (Mu'ālajah)
Iḥsās **Emotion**	Presence of positive emotions? ☐ Love ☐ Respect ☐ Understanding ☐ Happiness Presence of negative emotions? ☐ Sadness ☐ Fear ☐ Rejection ☐ Jealousy	+ Extreme + Quite + Very + Little ----------0---------- - Little - Very - Quite - Extreme	- Have the emotions caused adaptive actions: * Anger leading to assertiveness or defensiveness * Sadness leading to withdrawal * Shame/disgust leading to avoidance * Fear leading to fight, flight, or freeze * Joy leading to connection or engagement?	- Increase emotional awareness (*inkishāf*). - Identify unmet needs from childhood and beyond. - Track repetitive problem cycles. - Enhance emotional regulation through spiritual struggle (*mujāhadah*). - Empathically listen and reflect emotions. - Interrupt and redirect as needed. - Balance (*i'tidāl*) and transform emotions.
	Presence of primary emotions? Presence of secondary emotions?	☐ Sadness ☐ Hurt ☐ Fear ☐ Shame ☐ Loneliness ☐ Anger ☐ Jealousy ☐ Resentment ☐ Frustration	- What are the root causes of primary emotions? - How and why have the primary emotions turned into secondary emotions? - How do the primary emotions increase the quality of relationships? - How do the secondary emotions push others away?	- Access unacknowledged emotions behind actions and decisions. - Identify the adaptive/healthy primary emotions below the secondary emotions. - Utilize two-chair enactment as needed (e.g. unfinished business, self-critic)

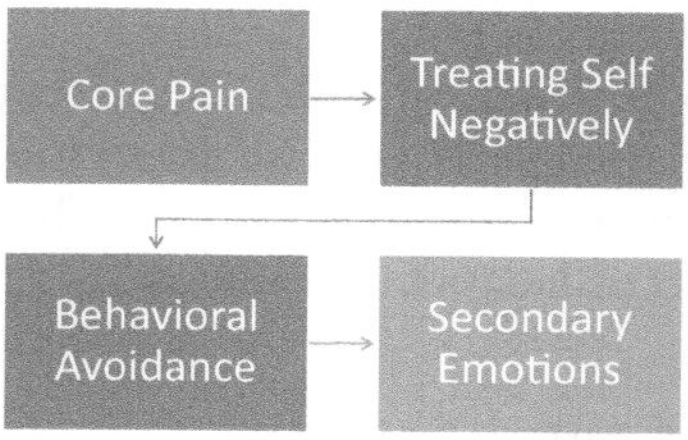

Figure 5.4 Assessment of emotions and exploration of distress.

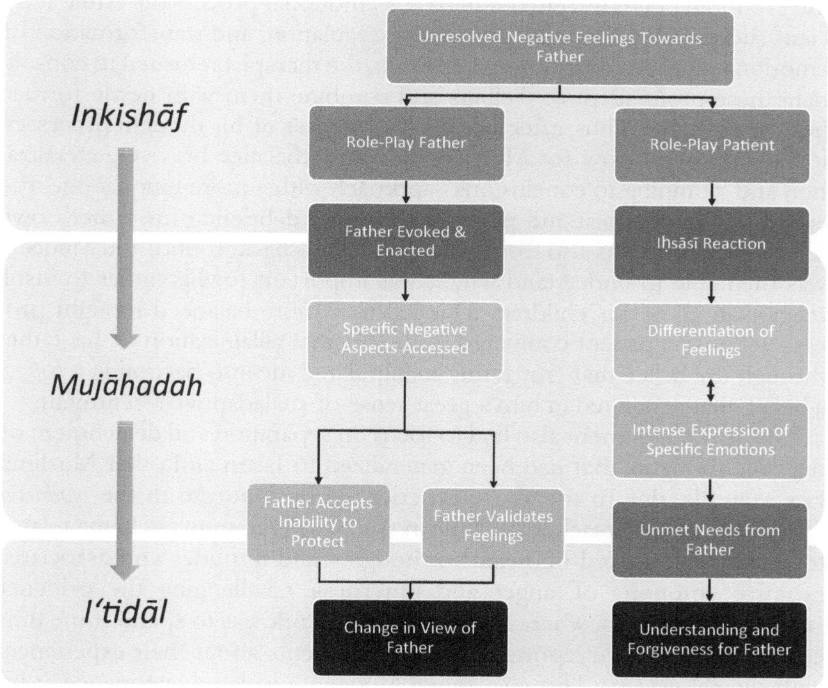

Figure 5.5 Emotion-focused therapy's two-chair enactment of unfinished business towards father.

schemas were related to his unprocessed experiences with his father; thus the therapist used a two-chair enactment in which Muqeem placed his father on the empty chair in an attempt to evoke and express his emotions, regulate and increase understanding of his emotions, and transform them through a newly enacted interpersonal experience related to "unfinished business" (see Figure 5.5). This process led to softening Muqeem's view of his father, as well as an ability to feel validation, differentiation, regulation, and transformation of his emotions toward his father.

Other emotional interventions also focused on isolated incidents of self-destructive behaviors. For instance, Muqeem once attempted to shoplift an item he did not need and was involved in a legal case. This also appeared to be a behavioral response to maladaptive emotions.

Return to the 'Aql—Cognitive Consolidation

In the above exercise, Muqeem's experiences were at the pre-cognitive level, and through several therapeutic markers (see Chapter 7 on emotional interventions) demonstrated a need for emotional processing. After sufficient successful sessions of processing, regulation, and transformation of emotions through a bottom-up approach, the therapist returned to consolidate these more adaptive feelings and combine them with newly formed healthy thoughts. Thus, after increased awareness of his thought processes, it was important now for Muqeem to counterbalance his overgeneralization and "jumping to conclusions" approach with a more rational one. For example, the therapist and patient spent time debriefing his father's own upbringing (who was also from an ultra-religious background) and Muqeem was then able to understand why it was important for his father to instill religion in all of his children. This led to a more balanced thought process within the patient compared to the original villainization of his father through the belief that "my father manipulated me into becoming a *ḥāfiẓ*," a belief that generated in him a great sense of maladaptive resentment.

The *'aqlānī* treatment also had to focus on separation and detachment of negative thoughts that had been generalized to Islam and other Muslims. For example, due to the abuse experienced by Muqeem in the *madrasah* (physically abusive teacher and bullying peers), his cognitive schema related to *madrasah* consisted of negative thoughts and attitudes and associated negative emotions of anger and bitterness. Challenging the evidence strategy was utilized, where Muqeem's homework was to spend some time collecting qualitative reports from other students about their experiences with several *madāris*. This challenged Muqeem's isolated experience at his own *madrasah*. The therapist not only had to consistently challenge these thoughts, but as sessions progressed, he played a less directive role by cuing Muqeem to notice his own thought process and to challenge himself when he started to regress to old ways of thinking. The therapist also utilized Socratic questioning during this process. For example, the therapist asked the patient whether Islam allows abuse within a family or social context. The patient disaffirmed this on account of his awareness that Islamic belief condemns abusive behaviors. This caused cognitive dissonance, generating the anxiety and desire in the patient to find a response that would bridge the incongruence he felt. A deep discussion of the meaning and interpretation of the verse "There shall be no compulsion in the religion" (Qur'ān, 2:256) was also utilized to deal with dissonance. As a result, the patient reached the conclusion that some Muslims may individually do harm while Islam as a religion promotes the good. This allowed him to feel great relief in being able to create a personal relationship with religion that did not need to be associated with fallible (albeit well-intentioned) human beings such as his parents. It opened the door for him to revisit his conflict and developmental blocks in the formation of his religious identity.

This treatment eventually led to a separation of thoughts related to social relationships and Islam. Figure 5.6 illustrates the newly formed thought processes.

Nafs—*Behavioral Inclinations*

Tahdhīb al-nafs, or the disciplining of behavioral inclinations, is an important aspect of Islamic spirituality. Keshavarzi and Haque (2013) cited al-Ghazālī's horse analogy to show how the *nafs* requires discipline in order to be controlled. Controlling the *nafs* entails that the patient embraces the discomfort felt in the process of generating healthy resistance training (*mukhālafah*) of their *nafsānī* inclinations. Table 5.3 provides a summary of assessment areas within this domain as well as treatment planning options.

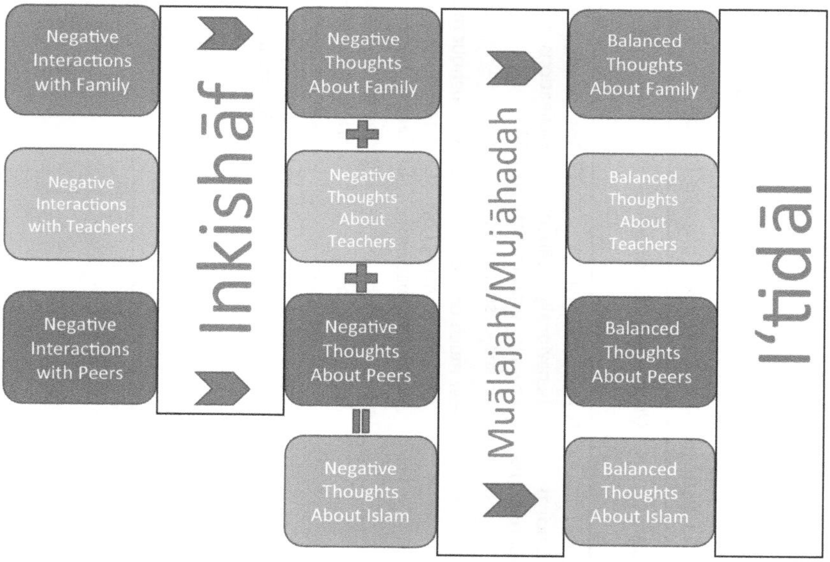

Figure 5.6 Transformation to balanced thought processes.

Table 5.3 Assessment and treatment planning for *nafs*

Domain	*Quantitative Assessment*		*Qualitative Questions*	*Treatment Planning* (Mu'ālajah)
Nafs **Behavioral Inclinations**	Is the individual behaviorally inclined towards gratification or self-destruction?	☐ Yes, identify behavioral inclinations ☐ No	- What is the driving force behind day-to-day decisions and actions? - How much of the behavior is driven by appetites and desires as compared to needs and necessities? - Which specific areas of the behavioral inclinations are most prominent in the individual? - Has the individual previously attempted to discipline the *nafs*? - If yes, what was effective, what was not?	- Increase awareness through identification of daily actions and how these acts satisfy the *nafs*. - Set goals and challenge the patient in opposing (*mujāhada*) these inclinations. - Utilize the opposite behaviors in decreasing negative behavioral inclinations (e.g. fasting when having a binge eating problem).
	How much of the behavior is driven by *nafsānī* inclinations?	☐ Throughout most of the day ☐ A few times a week ☐ Rare to none		
	Which category of behavioral inclinations are catered to (al-Ghazālīī 1993)?	☐ Cattle-like: (بهيمية) (eating, drinking, comfort, entertainment, sex) ☐ Predatory: (سبعية) (attacking, killing, stealing, controlling) ☐ Satanic (شيطانية): (plotting, lying, deceiving, cheating) ☐ Angelic (ربانية): (kindness, fairness, justice)		

For Muqeem, it was first important to identify how the different states of his *nafs* would manifest within him and drive his behavior. For example, when his behavior was driven by pleasure as well as pain (self-destructive tendency), his *nafs* was in the state of *nafs ammārah*. The avoidance of pain was also identified as a pathological behavioral response to his feelings and thoughts.

During the process of *inkishāf*, Muqeem and his therapist identified when and how his *nafs ammārah* drove both his behavior as well as his capacity to regulate his *nafs*. The self-destructive episode of shoplifting was used to identify how he was emotionally driven to cause pain to himself and others, thereby seeking retribution for his negative experiences. This can also be considered behavior that attempts to satisfy the *nafs* through getting attention, albeit for negative behavior. Another example of this could be seen when his mother asked him to sit and read Qur'ān for 15 minutes every day in front of her. Muqeem stated that he would pretend to read Qur'ān and was just moving his lips and making vocal gestures. He further indicated that he did this out of spite and to "show her" that he does whatever pleases him. These behaviors were emerging out of his sense of anger and resentment toward his parents and negative associations with religious practice (as explained above).

After creating sufficient awareness through cognitive and emotional processing, Muqeem was prepared to make adjustments to these behaviors. *Mujāhada* (struggle) and *mukhālafah* (opposition) of his *nafs* was necessary to avoid these negative behaviors. Some of this required accessing his emotions (see above section "*Iḥsās*—Emotions"). In this example, the therapist and Muqeem identified how his behavior of pretending to read Qur'ān was driven by negative emotions. Cognitive reappraisal and rational thought processing helped identify for Muqeem the following balanced thoughts (*i'tidāl*):

> I am sitting for 15 minutes and pretending to read the Qur'ān. However, since I have to sit there for 15 minutes anyway, as required by my mother, maybe I should use that time to revise a portion of the Qur'ān to build a personal relationship with the Qur'ān thereby separating my religious practice from people. This way, I will not feel "compelled" to do this because I have opted to make the God given *choice* of practicing my faith.

Such personalization of his religious practices and transition from an extrinsic religious orientation to an intrinsic one was motivational for Muqeem. These types of balanced thoughts also empowered him in a previously assumed oppressive practice. This, combined with his corrective interpersonal experiences with a religiously observant male therapist, allowed him to relate differently to his faith. In fact, Muqeem on occasion excitedly reported to the therapist an example of his success in controlling his *nafs* for greater meaning. He stated that once he was able to say "No" to a girl from his school who was interested in being sexually involved with him. The therapist positively reinforced his gains and congratulated his capacity to oppose (*mukhālafah*) his *nafs ammārah*. Furthermore, Muqeem and his therapist identified other daily occurrences where he could utilize the *mukhālafat al-nafs* to help guide his behavior.

Muqeem also had a remarkable realization in a session. He admitted to the therapist that part of his identification as an atheist also served as a rationalization for and absolved him of any religious responsibility towards Allah and others, therefore allowing more permissiveness. This was a demonstration of how part of his *nafsānī* drives of pleasure-seeking impacted his cognitions. Since Muqeem was previously able to identify that the cause of his loss of faith was due to cognitive enmeshment and an emotional response, he felt a greater sense of motivation to conquer these lower desires through a higher order purpose and meaning he had created. Muqeem began praying once a day and gradually increased it to five times a day over the span of many months.

Rūḥ—*Spirit*

Rūḥ is by far the most intricate aspect of human psyche. As God has stated: "The soul is of the affair of my Lord. And mankind has not been given of knowledge [of it] except a little" (Qur'ān, 17:85). Although it may be difficult to assess a person's spirituality (*rūḥāniyyah*), it is an area that can be improved upon. Table 5.4 provides a summary of assessment areas within this domain as well as treatment planning options. In the view of Ibn 'Arabī, the spirit which resides inside the human body, governs the body and soul, and it also corresponds to the universal spirit (*rūḥ kullī*), which controls the whole universe (Ebstein, 2014).

Perhaps one of the most intricate explanations and assessments of *rūḥ* has been provided by Shāh Walī Allah in his works. In the theory of the subtle spiritual centers (*laṭā'if*), the *rūḥ*, at its lowest level, is divided into the psychic spirit (*rūḥ nafsānī*), the vegetative/natural spirit (*rūḥ ṭab'ī*), and the animalistic spirit (*rūḥ ḥayawānī*). The psychic spirit is related to direct perception of sensible objects, the interpretation of their significance to the perceiver, and creation and storage of their schemas, and it corresponds to *'aql*. The natural spirit, according to him, corresponds to the *nafs*. The animalistic spirit focuses on reproduction, growth, and digestion. He further categorized *rūḥ* into higher positions above the material pneuma (*nasama*). These include rational soul (*nafs nāṭiqah*) and spiritual/angelic soul (*rūḥ samāwī*) (Hermansen, 1988; Horkuc, 2015).

For Muqeem, his *rūḥānī* health had deteriorated as a result of his negative experiences. He had stopped all ritual practices such as praying and

Table 5.4 Assessment and treatment planning for *rūḥ*

Domain	*Quantitative Assessment*		*Qualitative Questions*	*Treatment Planning* (Mu'ālajah)
Rūḥ **Spiritual**	Does the individual engage regularly in acts of worship?	☐ Five daily prayers ☐ Fasting ☐ Charity ☐ Reading Qur'ān ☐ Kindness towards others ☐ *Du'ā'*: supplication	- What is the purpose of life? - How do the acts of worship bring the person close to Allah? - What are the intentions of the individual behind the actions? - Does the person live a holistic life with a balanced inner self? - Is the individual able to reorganize the thoughts and seek to worship Allah in all daily acts? - Does the individual attempt to follow the Prophetic tradition in daily life?	- Identify the areas of daily life where the individual lacks spirituality. - Assess and overcome cognitive, emotional, or behavioral issues that impede in spiritual growth. - Find areas of improvement and set goals toward the ideal. - Educate the individual on the Prophet tradition and identify ways to achieve this goal.
	How active is the individual's *rūḥ* (*tab'ī*, *nafsānī*, and *ḥayawānī*)?	☐ *Ṭab'ī*—vegetative ☐ *Ḥayawānī*—animalistic ☐ *Nafsānī*—Psychic		
	Does the individual employ other spiritual practices in daily life?	☐ *Murāqabah*: contemplative meditation ☐ *Tafakkur*: deep thinking ☐ *Dhikr*: remembrance ☐ *Muḥāsabah*: accountability ☐ *Mujāhadah*: struggle to overcome desires ☐ *Mu'ātabah*: repentance		

fasting. He was not reading the Qur'ān even though he was a *ḥāfiẓ*. He had begun to lose faith in the existence of God. This was an emotional reaction; however, it was affecting his *rūḥānī* functioning.

However, after sufficient cognitive, emotional, and behavioral processing and interventions, Muqeem began to feel a greater sense of connection to himself and his faith. Additionally, his intrinsic religious orientation made him feel religiously satiated. He described this as feeling as if a spiritual light was sparked in him that previously had been put out. This light in him drove many of his behaviors and he felt an overall sense of connection to the Divine that was very personal for him. It further empowered him due to a newly gained control over his own spirituality and connection with his Creator. This was different from his previous functioning where religiosity was imposed and controlled primarily by his parents, leaving him feeling powerless.

Ijtimā'ī—*Social*

Western individualistic society does not put much emphasis on the role of community and family in individual well-being. Nonetheless, Islamic scholars such as Ibn Khaldūn have understood that it is part of human nature to feel compassion and affection for one's blood relations and relatives, and considered this as a "divine gift put into the hearts of men" (Rosenthal, 1969, p. 98). A holistic individual belongs to an interconnected community and is responsible for *ḥuqūq al-'ibā d* (the rights of the servants of God): managing their familial and social relationships (Keshavarzi & Khan, 2018). Furthermore, the relationship with the world outside one's self is not only for human beings; it also extends to the natural surroundings of the individual. Imām al-Ghazālī claimed that society exerts an influence on the inclinations that are intrinsic in human nature. Furthermore, these inclinations are constantly interacting with human feelings, thoughts, and behaviors (al-Ghazali, 1998).

Table 5.5 provides a summary of assessment areas within this domain as well as treatment planning options.

Due to Muqeem's negative interactions with his social milieu, his social and interpersonal relationships had deteriorated. He was secluded, had few to no friends living close to him, had a poor relationship with his family, and did not trust anyone. This led to feelings of isolation and he became behaviorally withdrawn. Beginning with a poor relationship with his parents, his social functioning further deteriorated when he was bullied in *madrasah*. Not only was Muqeem no longer a socializing teenager, he mostly did not want to be around Muslims on account of his negative experiences with them.

Along with the holistic TIIP approach that led to improvement in Muqueem, the focus was also towards improving his social functioning

Table 5.5 Assessment and treatment of *ijtimāʿī* functioning

Domain	*Quantitative Assessment*		*Qualitative Questions*	*Treatment Planning* (Mu'ālajah)
Ijtimāʿī **Social**	Does the individual cater to the personal factors that affect others?	☐ Appearance ☐ Hygiene ☐ Mannerisms ☐ Responding to others ☐ Reaching out to others	- How does the individual's appropriate appearance and presentation affect his inner as well as social functioning? - What does the patient consider a socially and Islamically acceptable interaction? - When others call on him, how does he respond? - How does the individual reach out to others within familial and social circles? - How often does the individual leave the house to interact with the community/society? - Is the person capable of managing their own health and finances? - Does the individual possess too few or too many belongings?	- Identify the areas in need of improvement. - Increase or decrease social functioning as needed. - Identify the need for increased social connection if the individual isolates and suffers. - Identify the need for solitude as part of spiritual growth if the individual socializes more than appropriate. - Identify the need to socially connect with family members and community members in an attempt to increase overall spirituality.
	Does the individual interact with others in a manner most beneficial and appropriate?	☐ Speech ☐ Choice of words ☐ Going out of the house ☐ Interacting with the community		
	Other socially related factors:	☐ Leisure activities ☐ Personal health ☐ Personal finances ☐ Possessions		

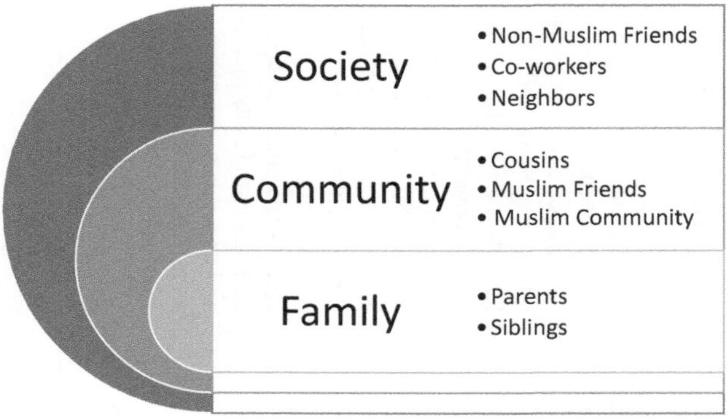

Figure 5.7 Social milieu of a Muslim teenager living in a non-Muslim country.

and interpersonal relationships. Muqeem's aversive attitudes towards Muslims were due to the negative interactions he had had with parents, peers, and teachers. However, his aversive attitudes towards non-Muslims appeared to be reactionary due to overwhelmed emotions. When an individual feels a certain emotion, it is often portrayed in all of their dealings and affairs with others around them. For Muqeem, treatment in this domain began with non-Muslim, general social improvements and moved towards improving his spiritual interpersonal relationships as well (see Figure 5.7).

Conclusion

The ultimate assessment of success in TIIP is through the evaluation of *qalb* or the heart, an epistemological and metaphysical sense that can be described as the locus of our awareness or ignorance of the Divine Presence (Duderija, 2017). One cannot quantitatively or qualitatively measure the *qalb* and its functioning. Through sinning, a heart becomes "darkened" or "blackened"; through proper *mu'ālajah* or treatment utilizing the aforementioned TIIP method, it is believed that the heart can become sound (*qalb salīm*) and restored. According to Imām al-Ghazālī, knowledge related to God can be acquired through one's heart (*qalb*). The other organs used in the process of sense perception cannot themselves provide such knowledge; rather, they are involved in the process of gathering information and sensations for the heart, which can freely dispose of them as a king disposes of his slaves (al-Ghazālī, 1998). Ibn Sīnā, in his writings, justified a sharp dualism between soul and body. Al-Ghazālī, on the other hand, insisted that there is a special connection between the "subtle" heart and the "physical" heart. Referring to Sahl al-Tustarī (d.283 AH/896 CE) and his saying that the heart is the throne and the breast the footstool, he points out that the relationship between them can be compared to that between God and His throne and footstool (Bowering, 1980; Janssens, 2011).

For Muqeem, the work through the TIIP model led to a "cleansing" of his heart. This process/state is experiential and cannot be measured. Through this process, the heart can become more receptive to good and be aligned with its *fiṭrah* (primordial disposition).

References

Abu-Raiya, H., Pargament, K., Mahoney, A., & Stein, C. (2008). A psychological measure of Islamic religiousness: Development and evidence for reliability and validity. *The International Journal for the Psychology of Religion, 18*(4), 291–315.

Adams, T. B., Bezner, J. R., Drabbs, M. E., Zambarano, R. J., & Steinhardt, M. A. (2000). Conceptualization and measurement of the spiritual and psychological dimensions of wellness in a college population. *College Health, 48*, 165–173.

al-Balkhī, A. (2013). *Abu Zayd Al-Balkhi's Sustenance of the Soul: The cognitive behavioral therapy of a ninth century physician*, trans. M. Badri. Herndon, VA: International Institute of Islamic Thought.

al-Ghazālī, A. H. (1990). *Mukhtaṣar: Iḥyā' 'Ulūm al-Dīn*, Beirut: Mua'ssas al-Kutub al-Thaqāfiyyah.

al-Ghazālī, A. H. (1998). *Minhajul 'Abideen*, trans. I. H. Ansari. Karachi: Darul Isha'at.

Beck, A. T. (1964). Thinking and depression: II. Theory and therapy. *Archives of General Psychiatry, 10*, 561–571.

Beck, J. S. (2011). *Cognitive behavior therapy: basics and beyond*, 2nd Ed. New York, NY: The Guilford Press.

Bowering, G. (1980). *The mystical vision of existence in classical Islam: The Quranic hermeneutics of the Sufi Sahl At-Tastari (d. 283 AH/896 CE)*. Berlin/New York, NY: de Gruyter.

Cashwell, C. S., Bentley, P. B., & Yarborough, J. P. (2007). The only way out is through: The peril of spiritual bypass. *Counseling & Values, 5*, 139–148.

Curtis, R. C., & Glass, J. S. (2002). Spirituality and counseling class: a teaching model. *Counseling & Values, 47*, 3–12.

Duderija, A. (2017). *The imperatives of progressive Islam*. London: Routledge.

Ebstein, M. (2014). *Mysticism and philosophy in al-Andalus*. Boston, MA: Brill.

Ghorbani, N., Watson, P. J., Madani, M., & Chen, Z. J. (2016). Muslim experiential religiousness: Spirituality relationships with psychological and religious adjustment in Iran. *Journal of Spirituality in Mental Health, 18*(4), 300–315.

Greenberg, L. S. (2010). Emotion-focused therapy: A clinical synthesis. *Focus, 8*, 32–42.

Hall, T. W., & Edwards, K. J. (2002). The spiritual assessment inventory: A theistic model and measure for assessing spiritual development. *Journal for the Scientific Study of Religion, 41*, 341–357.

Hermansen, M. K. (1988). Shah Wali Allah's theory of the Subtle Spiritual Centers (Lata'if): A Sufi model of personhood and self-transformation. *Journal of Near Eastern Studies, 47*(1), 1–25.

Horkuc, H. (2015). *God, man, and morality: The perspective of Bediuzzaman Said Nursi.* Clifton, NJ: Tughra Books.

Horvath, A. O., Del Re, A. C., Flückiger, C., & Symonds, D. (2011). Alliance in individual psychotherapy. *Psychotherapy, 48*, 9–16.

Keshavarzi, H., & Haque, A. (2013). Outlining a psychotherapy model for enhancing Muslim mental health within an Islamic context. *International Journal for the Psychology of Religion, 23*(3), 230–249.

Keshavarzi, H., & Khan, F. (2018). Outlining a case example of Traditional Islamically Integrated Psychotherapy (TIIP). In C. Y. Al-Karam (Ed.), *Islamically integrated psychotherapy: Processes and outcomes with Muslim clinicians* (pp. 175–207). West Conshohocken, PA: Templeton Press.

Janssens, J. (2011). Al-Ghazali between philosophy (*Falsafa*) and Sufism (*Tasawwuf*): His complex attitude in the Marvels of the Heart (*'Aja'ib al-Qalb*) of the *Ihya Ulum al-Din*. *The Muslim World, 101*, 614–632.

John, O. P. & Gross, J. J. (2004). Healthy and unhealthy emotion regulation: Personality processes, individual differences, and life span development. *Journal of Personality, 72*(6), 1301–1334.

Kobeisy, A. N. (2004). *Counseling American Muslims: Understanding the faith and helping the people.* Westport, CT: Praeger Publishers/Greenwood Publishing Group.

McCormick, D. J. (2004). Galton on spirituality, religion, and health. *American Psychologist, 59*, 52.

Prochaska, J., & DiClemente, C. (1983). Stages and processes of self-change of smoking: towards an integrated model of change. *Journal of Consulting Clinical Psychology, 51*, 390–395.

Rosenthal, F. (1969). *Ibn Khaldun, the muqadimah.* N. J. Davord (Ed.). Princeton, NJ: Princeton University Press, Bollinger Series.

Chapter 6

Dreams and Their Role in Islamically Integrated Mental Health Practice

Khalid Elzamzamy and Mohamed Omar Salem

Chapter Summary

While modern psychology considers dreams to be the royal road inwards into one's preoccupations, intrapsychic conflicts, and the unconscious, Muslims have additionally viewed dreams to be a royal road outward into the realm of spiritual inspiration and prophecy. Despite the significance attributed to dreams in both worldviews, dreams have become an endangered species in the mainstream practice of psychiatry and clinical psychology. In an attempt to address this gap in clinical practice, the authors provide a foundational account of the study of dreams in Islamic literature and intellectual heritage. They will also shed light on the profound tradition of dream interpretation (*ʿilm al-taʿbīr*) established by Muslim scholars. Following this theoretical foundation, they will discuss clinical applications of dreamwork within an Islamically integrated model of psychotherapy. The clinical tools provided for clinicians in this chapter include a toolkit for dream interpretation, utilization of "healing dreams" in practice, navigating through nightmares, understanding the connection between dreams and *istikhārah*, providing psychoeducation about dreams, and understanding the connection between dreams, psychopathology, and psychopharmacology.

Introduction

A dream is a "mental state that occurs in sleep and is characterized by a rich array of sensory, motor, emotional, and cognitive experiences" (VandenBos, 2013). If humans are said to spend 30 percent of their life sleeping, i.e. 8 hours a day, it is believed that people spend one third of that time, i.e. 6 years in a lifetime, dreaming (Myers, 2010). Frequently, our dreams are laden with aspects of our waking lives. For example, people who suffer from trauma report experiencing nightmares (Levin & Nielsen, 2007), people playing video games very often report seeing elements of these video games in their dreams (Stickgold, Malia, Maguire, Roddenberry, & O'Connor, 2000), and musicians experience more dreams about music than non-musicians (Myers, 2010; Uga, Lemut, Zampi, Zilli, & Salzarulo, 2006). Moreover, blind people report dreams in which they use their non-visual senses, e.g. hearing and touch (Buquet, 1988). Historically, dreams were believed to serve a prophetic function and, thus, the Ancient Egyptians, Ancient Greeks, and other civilizations developed systems of dream interpretation and dictionaries of dream symbols (Salem, 2010). Many dreams prophesized future events. It is documented that Abraham Lincoln, the sixteenth President of the United States, dreamed of his own assassination shortly before it actually occurred. He dreamed that he heard people sobbing and weeping in the White House with soldiers surrounding a coffin that contained the body of the president (Van de Castle, 1994, p. 30).

Some argue that the earliest writings we have on dreams were mainly religious treatises which examined the religious and spiritual aspects of dreams. Therefore, given this long history of working with dreams, religions and religious studies offer valuable insights into the world of dreams (Doniger & Bulkley, 1993). Many other disciplines have also heavily contributed to the fascinating world of dream study, attempting to find functions, mechanisms, and interpretations of dreams. Despite the attention dreams have received in modern psychology, Holmes (1991) considered dreams to be an endangered species in the mainstream practice of psychiatry and clinical psychology. Mitchison (1999) suggested that there is a discrepancy between the patients' interest in their dreams and the attention paid to them by the clinician. Mitchison further highlighted that clinicians, by showing no interest in patients' dreams, miss important opportunities of inquiry into the patient's world and into any potential distressing factors.

In this chapter the authors attempt to provide an overview of the study of dreams across religion, psychology, and mental health. They will delineate Islamic perspectives on dreams by examining the Islamic scriptures (Qur'ān and Sunnah) and the rich Muslim tradition of dream interpretation (DI). The authors will then discuss clinical applications of dreamwork within an Islamically integrated model of psychotherapy.

Dreams: An Islamic Perspective

Dreams in the Islamic Scriptures

The discourse on dreams in the Qur'ān and Sunnah is significantly rich. The Qur'ān mentions seven dreams with some comments on their interpretation in more than twenty verses (*āyāt*) in five chapters (*surah*) (37:101–106; 12:4–6, 36, 41, 43–49; 48:27; 8:43). The Prophet Muḥammad (peace and blessings be upon him) not only talked about dreams, their functions, types and nature, but also interpreted dreams that he and his Companions experienced. *Ḥadīth* collections dedicated entire chapters to *Ḥadīth* reports on dreams and dreaming.

According to the Islamic literature, dreams are classified into various categories. Abū Hurayrah (may Allah be well pleased with him) reported that the Messenger (peace and blessings be upon him) said that dreams are of three types: a good dream that is a glad tiding from Allah; a dream which causes distress and is inspired by Shayṭān; and a dream which is the result of one's own thoughts and self-talk (Muslim, 2006, Kitāb al-Ru'yā). This *Ḥadīth* classified dreams according to their source into divine, psychological, and satanic.

Dreams can also be looked at from a content vis-à-vis source perspective, the first category of which would be visions (*ru'yā*, prophetic dreams, true dreams), which are of divine origin and may serve multiple functions, including bringing forth glad tidings, warning and premonition, guidance, problem-solving, condolences, or a combination of all of these. *Ru'yā* also include dreams that represent a form of revelation sent by God to his prophets. The other type of dreams is that which reflects one's psychological condition, including one's concerns, preoccupations, intrapsychic processes, and emotions (ordinary or psychological dreams: *'Ḥadīth al-nafs'*).

The Qur'ān mentions a descriptive category of dreams that is not outlined in the above-mentioned tripartite *Ḥadīth* classification, *'aḍghāth al-aḥlām'*, which includes dreams that are jumbled, indecipherable, muddled, or maybe terrifying in nature. The source of *'aḍghāth al-aḥlām'* may be psychological or satanic according to Ibn Ḥajar al-'Asqalā nī (1986, vol. 12, p. 367). The Qur'ān also narrates multiple examples of visions, including the vision of Prophet Yūsuf (upon him be peace) in which he saw the sun, the moon, and 11 stars falling in prostration to him, as well as a vision of the Prophet Muḥammad (peace and blessings be upon him) in which he observed himself entering Mecca safely and circumambulating the *Ka'bah*, among other visions.

Nightmares are a type of dreams the content of which is terrifying in nature, and the source of which can be attributed to a myriad of factors (please refer to the section titled "Dreamwork").

Status of Dreams and Dream Interpretation

Visions have been viewed as a means of bringing glad tidings to the righteous. In a commentary on Qur'ān verses (10:63–64), Prophet Muḥammad (peace and blessings be upon him) said, "All that will be left of prophecy after me are the *mubashshirāt* (dreams of glad tidings)." They (the Companions) said, "What are the *mubashshirāt*, O Messenger of Allah?" He said, "A true dream which is seen by a righteous person or seen on his behalf—is a forty-sixth part of prophecy" (Mālik, 1994, Kitāb al-Ru'yā,

Bāb Mā Jā'a fī-l- Ru'yā). This highlights the special status attributed to dreams in Islam. Once revelation ceased after the death of the Prophet Muḥammad (peace and blessings be upon him), dreams continued to be a gateway into divine inspiration and prophecy (Al-'Asqalā nī, 1986, p. 391; Lamoreaux, 2002).

Highlighting the significance of DI, the Qur'ān praises the special knowledge that was given to the Prophet Yūsuf (upon him be peace) in interpreting dreams. The Qur'ān narrates, in detail, three of these dreams and his interpretation of them. In fact, the Prophet Yūsuf's ability to interpret dreams—through which he averted seven years of famine in Egypt—has been documented in both the Bible and the Qur'ān. Prophet Muḥammad (peace and blessings be upon him) also engaged in dream interpretation. He used to acknowledge and pay attention to his Companions' dreams and is reported to have had a habit of frequently asking them, "Did any of you see any vision/dream last night?" (al-Bukhārī, 2010, Kitāb al-Ta'bīr, Bāb Ta'bīr al-Ru'yā ba'd Ṣalāt al-Ṣubḥ). The Prophet (peace and blessings be upon him) would then engage in providing an interpretation of their dreams as well as any he himself may have seen. The significance of dreams is further highlighted by the Prophet's warning against lying about the content of one's dreams and visions. A *Ḥadīth* stated that the worst lie is that a person claims to have seen a dream which he has not seen (al-Bukhārī, 2010, Kitāb al-Ta'bīr, Bāb Man Kadhab fī Ḥulmihi). Al-'Asqalānī elaborated on this *Ḥadīth* and considered lying about one's dreams a graver sin than other forms of lying in speech, as it is a form of lying about Allah, because dreams could represent a form of divine inspiration, as highlighted above (al-'Asqalā nī, 1986, p. 445). The Prophet (peace and blessings be upon him) dealt with dreams as a form of a trust (*amānah*) about which someone should not lie, but rather narrate as honestly as possible only to the right people, who are expected to give insightful and knowledgeable advice or interpretation (Bulkeley, Adams, & Davis, 2009, p. 118).

Dream Interpretation in the Early Islamic Period

An interest in DI can be traced to the early days of Islam. As highlighted above, the Prophet (peace and blessings be upon him) engaged in DI. His DI relied heavily on decoding names, phrases, and concepts mentioned in dreams. For example, a dream in which names that are derived from words that mean high rank (*rāfi'*), fate (*'uqba*) and goodness (*ṭāb*) were interpreted as a glad tiding of good fortune in this life and the Hereafter for the dreamer (Muslim, 2006, Kitāb al-Ru'yā, Bāb Ru'yā Al-Nabī may Allah bless him and grant him peace). The Prophet (peace and blessings be upon him) also used to interpret dreams based on certain concepts and word associations: for example, his interpretation of a "shirt" as the

Table 6.1 Examples of dream symbols and their interpretations

Symbol	*Interpretation*
Shirt (*qamīṣ*)	Religion
Milk (drinking)	Acquiring knowledge
Cows being sacrificed	The death of some family members or companions
Sword	Companions (as they offer support and protection)
A sword being broken	The death of some family members or companions
Being in a garden	The garden represents Islam and religion
Running water spring	Ongoing good deeds
Gold ornaments worn by a man	Something that is null and void
A body part being detached and placed in the lap of a woman	A child will be born to the person and will be nursed by that woman
Choking on food	A problem faced in some important work the person is undertaking

religiosity of a person, his interpretation of a running water spring as ongoing good deeds (al-Bukhārī, 2010, Kitāb al-Ta'bīr), and his interpretation of a milk drink as knowledge (Muslim, 2006, Kitāb Faḍā'il al-Ṣaḥābah, Bāb Min Faḍā'il 'Umar).

The Companions also engaged in DI. In fact, the Prophet (peace and blessings be upon him) acted as a mentor for the Companions in DI. The Prophet (peace and blessings be upon him) one day was asked to interpret a dream in the presence of Abū Bakr al-Ṣiddīq (may Allah be well pleased with him), his most senior and excellent Companion. Abū Bakr asked to offer his own interpretation under the supervision of the Prophet and then asked if he was correct. The Prophet (peace and blessings be upon him) told him that he interpreted a part of the dream correctly but that he erred in interpreting another part of it (Muslim, 2006, Kitāb Al-Ru'yā, Bāb fī Ta'wīl al-Ru'yā). Many of the interpretations of Abū Bakr and other Companions can be found in the books of Ḥadith and Sunnah.

Based on some of the interpretations by the Prophet and the Companions, Nagati (1993) compiled a list of examples of dream symbols and their interpretation, some of which are shown in Table 6.1.

The Classical Muslim Discipline of Dream Interpretation 'Ilm Ta'bīr al-Ru'yā

The rich Islamic discourse on dreams and DI led to an unprecedented systematic interest in DI, and established the foundations, guiding concepts, and methodologies for an Islamic field of DI, i.e. *'Ilm Ta'bīr al-Ru'yā* or *al-Ta'bīr* (The Discipline of DI). This discipline was extremely popular and attracted the attention of many bright Muslim scholars and philosophers. It is of particular note that more than sixty manuals of DI were composed in the first five centuries of the Islamic civilization. In his bibliography, Fahd (1959) listed at least 171 DI manuals, most of which are written in Arabic and exist today in only manuscript form.

Ibn Sīrīn, a seventh century scholar (d.110 AH/729 CE), is one of the most prominent names in this field. Other major contributors to the field include al-Shihāb ibn N'imah (d.697 AH/1297 CE) (author of *al-Badr al-Munīr fī 'Ilm al-Ta'bīr*), Khalīl b. Shāhīn (d.893 AH/14CE 87) (author of *al-Ishārāt fī 'ilm al-'ibārāt*), and 'Abd al-Ghanī al-Nābluṣī (d.1143 AH/1731 CE) (author of *Ta'ṭīr al-Anām fī Ta'bīr al-Manām*). Their works were encyclopedic in nature and compiled wisdom from religious scriptures in addition to wisdom inherited from other cultures. The strong influence of the Qur'ān and *Ḥadīth* is very evident in the manuals that emerged in the early Islamic period. This rich inherited wisdom was utilized by Muslims who engaged in dream interpretation as an intellectual endeavor that was intuitive and relied on the analytical reasoning (*ijtihād*) of these individuals.

The DI methodology required knowledge of the symbolic underpinnings of dreams as well as the status and the background of the dreamer. In order to provide sound interpretations, authors of DI manuals also listed numerous requirements and ethics that the interpreter has to fulfill prior to qualifying as a dream interpreter (please refer to the section titled "Dream Interpretation Toolkit").

Most of the Muslim works on DI consist of two sections: an introduction offering an overview of the author's methodology followed by a list of dream symbols and their interpretation. Symbols are either classified alphabetically or by subject. Under each entry, scholars attempt to provide a variety of possible interpretations for the numerous forms in which a subject might be seen in a dream. For example, under the subject of "water", they would list interpretations for seeing the ocean, turbid water, clear water, flowing water, offering a drink of water in a cup, drinking warm water, a water spring, black water, hot or cold water, swimming in water, sitting in deep water, bathing in water, feeling thirsty, etc. In the collection of Ibn Sīrīn's interpretations of dreams, water in general was interpreted as a sign of piety, knowledge, life, and prosperity. It was also seen as being connected to reproduction (pregnancy, abortion, and miscarriage). Some of the specific forms of water were interpreted as follows: turbid water as a sickness or a hardship; filling a water container as gaining wealth, getting married, or a spouse conceiving; bathing in cold water as cure for an illness or a sign of repentance; falling in deep water as prosperity and wealth; using hot water as an affliction caused by a king or a ruler; walking on the surface of water as a sign of pride and risk-taking, or also as a sign of strong faith and certainty; salty water as grief; and someone carrying water as representing a person of piety and good deeds (al-Barīdī, Ibn Sīrīn, & al-Nabulusī, 2008).

Some of their interpretations are based on themes, analogies, and symbols mentioned in the Qur'ān and *Ḥadīth*. Examples are the interpretation of a rope as a covenant (Qur'ān 3:103), wood as a hypocrite (Qur'ān 63:4), a ship as a means of safety (Qur'ān 29:15), and bottles as women (Muslim, 2006, Kitāb al-Faḍā'il, Bāb Raḥmat al-Nabī li-l-Nisā').

Bulkeley (2002) reported that Muslims' insights and observations in their DI manuals often overlap with theories developed by Western psychologists over the past 150 years. However, there are also some major differences with how dreams were conceptualized by Freud, the founder of psychoanalysis. Freud's dream theory claimed that dreams represent the dreamer's emotional concerns and preoccupations, including those they are unaware of, often portrayed in a condensed and symbolic form. His dream theory also stresses that the "manifest dream" is a censored and disguised wish-fulfilling version of the underlying "latent dream", occurring through the processes of displacement, condensation, and other psychological processes. The manifest content is usually derived from the dreamer's daily experiences, while the latent content represents repressed unconscious meanings (Freud, 2010, pp. 147, 295–296; Salem, 2001). Some of these Freudian views have been substantially re-evaluated and developed in the twentieth century by Neo-Freudians such as Carl Jung and others. "From the Islamic perspective, both Freudian and Jungian theories of dreams represent only a small space in the broader map of dreaming" (Bulkeley, Adams, & Davis, 2009, pp. 111, 191). For example, from an Islamic perspective, a dream could carry a divine message to the dreamer about the past, present, or future, and it can, for example, be seen by a dreamer on behalf of someone else, i.e. carrying a message to the other person or other people.

In conclusion, contrary to modern psychoanalysis, Islamic DI was more concerned with how dreams can be gateways into the outer world, including divine inspiration, rather than being merely a window into an individual's psychic composition and concerns. In other words, while Freud has considered the interpretation of dreams to be "the royal road to a knowledge of the unconscious activities of the mind" (Freud, 2010, p. 604), "DI offered Muslims a royal road that led not inward but outward" (Lamoreaux, 2002, p. 4).

In order to give a flavor of what Islamic DI looked like, we offer below a synopsis of one of the important DI manuals attributed to Ibn Sīrīn.

Synopsis of Ibn Sīrīn's Treatise "Ta'bīr al-Ru'yā" (DI)

Ta'bīr al-Ru'yā (Dream Interpretation) is a DI manual that has been attributed to Ibn Sīrīn in *al-Fihrist* (the Index) of Ibn al-Nadīm (Ibn al-Nadīm, 1971, p. 378). In *Taʿbīr al-Ruʾyā*, Ibn Sīrīn starts off with the etiquette governing the interpreter and the principles of DI. A qualified dream interpreter is someone who has adequate knowledge of the Qur'ān and *Ḥadīth*, is well versed in the Arabic language and the derivations of words, and is familiar with the nature and status of people. A dream interpreter is also someone who is engaged in self-purification and *tazkiyah*, who has good morals, and who is honest in his speech and conduct. Furthermore, Ibn Sīrīn mandates familiarity with the basic principles of interpretation. These include understanding that DI depends on the condition of the dreamer as well as the time when the dream is seen. Principles of DI also include knowledge of the different ways of interpreting dreams, such as using the Qur'ān, the *Ḥadīth*, cultural proverbs, derivation of words, and other methods. In the subsequent chapters of the book, Ibn Sīrīn presents a list of dreams and dream symbols and his interpretations of them organized categorically as follows:

1. seeing Allah,
2. seeing angels, righteous people, and holy sites,
3. seeing the sky, the moon, the stars, Paradise and Hell, etc.,
4. seeing natural phenomena such as rain, thunder, oceans, etc.,
5. seeing geographical landmarks, e.g. the earth, mountains, etc.,
6. seeing plantations, trees, fruits, etc.,
7. seeing drinks such as milk, wine, and honey,
8. seeing men, women, and body parts, etc.,
9. seeing marriage, pregnancy, children, etc.,
10. seeing death and dead people,
11. seeing clothing, accessories, jewelry, utensils, weapons, etc., and
12. seeing various kinds of animals, various kinds of jobs, and other miscellaneous topics.

The above description was an overview of the discourse on dreams in Islamic scriptures and the rich heritage of Muslim DI. In the following section we will briefly look at how Muslim scholars addressed dreams in different disciplines.

Muslim Scholars' Views on Dreams Across Disciplines

This rich Islamic discourse has stimulated great attention from Muslim scholars starting with the Companions of Prophet Muḥmmad (peace and blessings be upon him). In his *tafsīr* of verse (39:42), al-Ālūsī narrates a conversation about dreams that took place between 'Umar b. al-Khaṭṭāb and ʿAlī b. Abū Ṭālib, may Allah be pleased with them:

> 'Umar expressed his surprise that some people's dreams come true as though they were walked through their experiences in their

> dreams before they actually take place while others' dreams are not, i.e. nothing comes out of them. In response, 'Alī narrated the verse, "Allah takes the souls at the time of their death, and those that do not die [He takes] during their sleep. Then He keeps those for which He has decreed death and releases the others for a specified term. Indeed, in that are signs for a people who give thought." (39:42), and explained, "Allah takes all the souls during sleep. Whatever they see while they are with Him in the heavens is true visions and whatever they see when they are sent back to their bodies is the false dream".
>
> (al-Ālūsī, 1994, vol. 24, p. 8).

Later Muslim scholars have dealt with the topic of dreams in their philosophical, spiritual, and psychological treatises. Their outlook has been wider in scope than what is usually recognized in contemporary psychological thought, as highlighted above.

Ya'qūb b. Isḥāq al-Kindī (d.259 AH/873 CE), Abū Naṣr al-Fārābī (d.340 AH/951 CE), Abū 'Al Aḥmād b. Miskawayh (d.421 AH/1030 CE) and Ibn Sīnā (d.428 AH/1037 CE) believed that dreams were a function of the imaginative faculty of the mind which processes, consolidates, and filters thoughts and images acquired during the wakeful state, sometimes based on the individual's mood or sensory state. They also believed in a symbolic nature and function of dreams as well as the role it plays in fulfilling desires. Ibn Sīnā also postulated that some dreams might be the earliest signs of underlying medical problems (al-Kindī & Abū Raydah, 1950, pp. 293–306; al-Fārābī & Nādir, 1973, pp. 68–74; Ibn Miskawayh & Fu'ad, 1901, pp. 108–110; Ibn Sīnā, 1988, pp. 173–177).

Muḥi al-Dīn Ibn 'Arabī (d.638 AH/1240 CE), in his discourse on dreams, proposed different types of dreams, including "ordinary" dreams reflecting daily waking life experiences, in addition to divinely inspired dreams, which could be either symbolic in nature and requiring interpretation or could be direct and clear revelatory dreams like the dream of the Prophet Ibrāhīm (upon him be peace) sacrificing his son (Ibn 'Arabī & 'Abbās, 2009, pp. 99–102; Landau, 1957).

Ibn Sīnā believed that true visions take place because of a connection between the soul and the heavens in which some sort of an inspiration or revelation takes place (similar to the explanation of 'Alī b. Abū Ṭālib above). According to him, other types of dreams take place as a reflection of one's preoccupations and concerns, and as a reflection of the interaction between one's imaginative faculty and internal and external bodily sensations and experiences (Ibn Sīnā, 1988, pp. 173–174; Nagati, 1980, p. 271). Ibn Khaldūn (d.808 AH/1406 CE) further elaborated on the spiritual and divine blessings that can happen in the dreaming state. He considered the sleeping state as an opportunity offered by God to humans to "lift the veil of the senses" and allow the soul to gain access to divine realities and truths. Ibn Khaldūn further argued that the stronger the spiritual connection, the less allegorical and symbolic the dream is and therefore the less interpretation is required (Ibn Khaldūn, 1967). This notion is present in Platonic and Neoplatonic thinking about dreams (Bulkeley, 2002). The Qur'ān has also clearly referred to souls being lifted from their bodies by Allah at the time of sleep (Qur'ān 39:42). Salem (2010) postulates a hypothesis that correlates this verse and Ibn Khaldūn's explanation with the fact that most dreams occur during REM (rapid eye movement) sleep. Based on the *Ḥadīth* that reports, "When the soul is taken, the sight follows it" (Muslim, 2006, Kitāb al-Janā'iz, Bāb fī Ighmāḍ al-Mayyit wa-l-du'ā' la-h idhā ḥaḍar), Salem postulates that these eye movements could be a manifestation of the eye following the movement of the soul during its spiritual journey when dreams take place.

Finally, in the legal discourse, the general rule and the consensus among Muslim jurists is that dreams do not override already established Islamic rulings and cannot establish new legislations or rulings. In other words, a dream that suggests a ruling that is contrary to what has already been established, or a ruling that has no precedence in the Islamic *sharī'ah*, should be rejected and discarded (al-Nawawī, 1996, p. 96).

Integrating Dreamwork in Clinical Practice

Introductory Case Scenario

A patient diagnosed with schizophrenia was seen by his psychiatrist for a regular assessment. During that visit the patient was deemed free of psychotic symptoms and was considered in recovery and remission. Tragically, the patient was brought in for a forensic psychiatric assessment few days later after he had murdered his 8-month-old baby. Following further assessment, it was found that the patient had been having a dream in which he saw himself slaughtering his son. This was around the time of 'Īd al-Adḥā (Feast of Sacrifice for Muslims) in which Muslims offer sacrifices in commemoration of Prophet Ibrāhīm's sacrifice of his son Ismail.

In this case, the psychiatrist who saw the patient prior to the incident screened for psychotic symptoms but did not pay attention to the aspect of the patient's mental activity which occurs during sleep, i.e. dreaming. Unfortunately, this resulted in a negative and fatal outcome.

Mental state examination (MSE) is the crux of the work of mental health clinicians. MSE is concerned with the wakeful mental state of patients such as their mood, speech, thoughts, etc. However, it does not typically include assessment of mental activity and phenomena occurring during sleep, such as dreams. Mitchison (1999) highlights the paradox and risk in such clinical practice that shows little interest in the subjective experience and content of patients' sleep, despite the attention given to assessing the quality and quantity of sleep in patients with mood disorders and other problems. Paying attention to dreams, especially puzzling or disturbing ones, offers good opportunities for personal inquiry and exploration, may be empowering to patients, may show empathy and understanding, may allow for feelings of despair and terror to be addressed, and can lead to appreciation of areas of concern.

The International Association for the Study of Dreams (IASD) is the main international body that advocates for the scientific study of dreams and its clinical applications. The IASD was established in 1983 in the USA. It holds an annual meeting and issues a peer-reviewed journal, *Dreaming*, as well as a newsletter, "Dream Times". The IASD defines dreamwork as "any effort to discover, speculate about, and explore levels of meaning and significance beyond the surface of literal appearance of any dream experience recalled from sleep" (IASD Board of Directors, 2001). Given the complexity of the task of dreamwork and the multitude of contexts in which dreams may occur, the IASD has laid some ethical foundations for professionals who are interested in engaging in dreamwork and dreamwork training. They recommend establishing well-rounded training programs in different approaches and cross-cultural perspectives of dreamwork. However, they emphasize that dreamworkers are free to adopt particular approaches, techniques, or theories over others. They recommend adequate access to personal counseling, supervision, and face-to-face work with individuals and groups, and encourage facilitating opportunities for dreamworkers to work on their own dreams. They also emphasize the necessity of having appropriate knowledge and licensing in the relevant medical, psychological, or psychiatric field.

The above principles provide a very useful framework that sets the ground for an appropriate utilization and propagation of dreamwork in clinical practice. Cultural sensitivity was a recurring theme in the principles established by the IASD. In the following section we will explore how dreamwork can be incorporated as a spiritual strategy within an Islamically integrated, culturally appropriate model of psychotherapy.

Islamic Spiritual Strategies in Psychotherapy

The Spiritually Focused Assistance (SFA) Program designed by Salem, Alhadi, and Algahtani (2012) proposed six important domains of integrating spirituality into psychotherapy. First, religious and spiritual guidance can be offered by clergy as part of a multidisciplinary team approach. The input can focus on faith revival in both theoretical and practical domains (Ali, Milstein, & Marzuk, 2005). Second, therapists and clergy can facilitate spiritual support groups around spiritual themes, e.g. meaning of life, suffering, hope, etc. Third, religious self-help through religious bibliotherapy, prayers, meditation, scripture memorization, and journal writing (diaries) may be an integral part of such an approach. Patients are encouraged to keep diaries of their dreams for further elaboration and discussion with their therapist. Fourth, praying for patients and with patients is an essential part of the Islamic tradition and could have positive impacts on the patient's well-being (Weld & Eriksen, 2007). Fifth, support from the religious community can be of great help. Finally, evidence-based psychotherapeutic interventions, such as those derived from cognitive behavioral therapy (CBT), emotion-focused therapy (EFT), or others that are conducive to working with religious themes and content are at the heart of this proposed multidimensional SFA Program (Salem & Ali, 2008).

Dream Diaries

Richards and Bergin (2005, pp. 287–288) identified a wide range of religious and spiritual interventions that reflect and represent varying degrees of integration of religious and spiritual perspectives and practices in psychotherapy, one of which was dream interpretation. Working with dreams is an essential ingredient of the aforementioned SFA program.

Given that dreams tend to be forgotten, and recognizing the significance of the cumulative knowledge of each dreamer's symbols, patients may be advised to keep dream diaries to record their dreams for regular reflection and possible correlation with future events (Salem, 2010). It is also believed that the earlier the dream is narrated or reported, the more accurate the interpretation will be. It is believed that the more intense or vivid the dream is, the clearer and more memorable its details will be. Dream diary entries should include important dream content, namely characters, emotions, setting, social interactions, activity, objects, success/failure, misfortune/good fortune. Important descriptive elements and modifiers, such as color, size, age, etc., should also be included (Hall, & Van de Castle, 1976). Entries should be dated and given a title indicating their content. Given the symbolic nature of dreams, when one records and reflects on their dreams, they may end up developing their own personal dream language based on the frequently occurring symbols in their dreams.

Dreamwork

Dreamwork may be conceptualized as referring to two levels of work with dreams. First, it refers to efforts discovering and exploring the meanings of dreams. Second, it refers to efforts utilizing dreams for therapeutic and healing purposes. A dream diary is an essential tool for both purposes, as highlighted above. When a patient records their dreams, it helps them reflect, explore, and understand those dreams, as well as differentiate meaningful and truthful dreams from other types such as psychological and jumbled ones. Such differentiation is necessary as each category serves a different function and shall be dealt with differently. For example, ordinary dreams are an important window into the individual's preoccupations, concerns, and intrapsychic tensions. A therapist may utilize this window to understand more about their patients as well as to initiate therapeutic dialogues with resistant patients. Some patients with severe mental illnesses, e.g. psychosis, may experience vivid dreams during the course of their illness that may pose potential risks to the patient or others (refer to the introductory case scenario). Therefore, it is recommended that clinicians explore their patients' dreams by using quick screening questions about any particular dreams that may be of significance or that may be a source of distress.

In addition, dreamwork may be part of various psychotherapeutic techniques in a variety of psychiatric conditions including cases of grief, mood disorders, adjustment disorders, and anxiety disorders.

Parents grieving over their deceased children sometimes present with severe and atypical forms of grief reactions. One of the authors of this chapter (Salem) has incorporated dreamwork in his interventions with grieving mothers which included psychoeducation about "dream incubation" techniques, the value of communicating with the deceased through dreaming (visitation dreams), and the positive impact that may result from such experience. The following are case scenarios of some of the patients that benefited from such techniques.

Case #1

A mother lost her beloved son, who drowned while swimming with his friends. She was in a state of shock and denial for more than a month. When she presented to the therapist, she was noted to have a flat affect and expressionless face, was not engaging with the therapist, and reported very poor sleep. She had refused any medications to assist with sleep in the previous month. She was also very resistant to therapeutic conversations or interventions. When she was asked if she had dreamt of her lost son, she denied however, she started opening up when the idea of seeing her deceased son in a dream was mentioned. She was taught "dream incubation" techniques, e.g. repeating regular prayers throughout the day and before sleeping. It was deemed necessary to prescribe her some sleeping pills, which she was now more prepared to take, because a good night's sleep was her means of seeing healing dreams. When she was seen the following week, there was a notable improvement and she reported three dreams in which she saw her son in a very good state. In the following sessions she reported more dreams about her son. In one of those dreams her son was offering her condolences and reassuring supportive words, telling her about his state and that he was in a good place. Seeing those dreams was this mother's path to healing.

Case #2

A young mother lost her son in a road traffic accident. She was referred to her gynecologist due to amenorrhea that lasted for three years. After very thorough assessments by the gynecologist, her amenorrhea, which started following the death of her son, was believed to be of a psychological origin. This was a case of prolonged atypical grief. A similar approach to case #1 was used with her. "Dream incubation" techniques helped her see profound visitation dreams within two weeks. All of the visitation dreams showed signs that her son was in a good state, which had a profound healing effect.

Case #3

A mother lost her son when he drowned in a water well. For a couple of years following his death, the mother was suspicious that his siblings were the ones who caused him to drown, although the siblings repeatedly denied that. These years of distressing thoughts were only brought to an end through a healing visitation dream in which she saw her son, who reassured her that he fell and drowned on his own and that his siblings were not responsible for his death.

Nightmares

Nightmares are another important category of dreams that clinicians may frequently encounter. Nightmares should not be confused with warning prophetic dreams or visions. Nightmares are generally fearful dreams which occur during REM sleep and may lead to sudden awakening of the dreamer with intense anxiety and good recall of the fearful dream. They also generally have repetitive themes over time. They may be due to several causes, such as the side effects of medications and medical conditions. They are also associated with various forms of psychopathology including depression, anxiety, and post-traumatic stress disorder (PTSD). Nightmares could also stem from satanic influence, as it was narrated that the Prophet (peace and blessings be upon him) said that a good dream is from Allah, while a bad dream is from Satan (al-Bukhārī, 2010, Kitāb al-Ta'bīr, Bāb al-Ḥulm min al-Shayṭān), and that he also said that some dreams are terrifying in nature and are inspired by Satan to cause distress to the son of Adam (Sunan Ibn Mājah, Kitāb Ta'bīr al-Ru'yā, Bāb al-Ru'yā Thalāth). The Prophet (peace and blessings be upon him) advised those who experience such dreams to do a few things, including seeking refuge with Allah from its evil, blowing to their left side, altering their physical state by changing the side on which they were sleeping, getting up and praying, avoiding sharing the dream with others, except a scholar or an advisor (al-Mustadrak, *'alā al-Ṣaḥīḥayn*, Kitāb Taʿbīr al-Ru'yā: al-Nayāspūrī, 2002), and after doing all this to rest assured that no harm will come to them, by the will of Allah. A clinician who is aware of these teachings can guide their patients to the right approach in handling such dreams.

Moreover, patients with nightmares that are of a psychological (not medical) nature may benefit from "imagery rescripting and rehearsal" techniques. In "rescripting and rehearsal", a bad, terrifying dream ending is replaced and rescripted with a more positive one. The patient is then asked to rehearse the rescripted version of the dream multiple times during the day and before sleep. Usually this leads to the cessation of the nightmares in a short time (Davis & Wright, 2006).

DI Toolkit

Finding meaning in truthful dreams and visions is another important form of dreamwork. DI requires mastery of basic DI principles and tools, as well as a careful examination and consideration of the dreamer's psychological, social, spiritual, and environmental contexts.

Al-Sadḥān (2003) classified dream interpreters into different categories according to the scope of their approach. He favored a holistic approach to DI in which the interpreter takes into consideration all important symbols within a dream, engages with the patient's environment and situation, and takes account of all psycho-spiritual aspects of dreams. On the contrary, less favorable approaches are those that neglect important dream symbols, rely heavily on classical interpretations, lack solid DI methodology, and/or neglect the spiritual, paranormal, and prophetic aspects of dreams. In general, the dreamer's context has to be taken into consideration, as some classical interpretations of certain symbols may be irrelevant to a twenty-first-century dreamer.

Muslim DI manuals list certain requirements that a dream interpreter should attain before engaging in DI. They consider a strong spiritual connection with Allah of utmost importance. They also encourage a thorough analysis of the dream and its symbols. They regard highly an inquisitive mind that attempts to find a connecting thread between all symbols/events occurring in a dream and the patient's circumstances. They encourage focusing on the significant message of the dream (warning or glad tiding). They also provide interpretive methods, principles, and approaches (see below for more details). An interpreter is ethically obliged to inform the dreamer if they are unable to interpret the dream. Interpreters should also offer their interpretations with an element of uncertainty or tentativeness to leave room in the mind of the dreamer for other interpretations and possibilities. A large number of them have expanded the requirements to include knowledge of the Islamic scriptures, language, and culture. Finally, DI is in some sense similar to giving a religious verdict, which is a responsibility, and thus one should not engage in it unless they have the necessary knowledge and skill (al-Barīdī, Ibn Sīrīn, & al-Nabulusī, 2008; al-Dīnūrī, 2001; al-Sadḥān, 2003). DI is a noble field of Islamic studies, the principles and guidelines of which shall ideally be taught to the public, and more importantly to Muslim mental health professionals, to allow dreamers to look into and analyze their own dreams, which they keep in their "dream diaries", in pursuit of their meaning. People can be trained in how to utilize the guidelines given by the prominent authors of DI manuals. Workshops can be offered to teach this art and serve this purpose, like the popular ones offered by Dr. Salem (co-author of this chapter).

In this section the authors will attempt to provide some principles of DI that maybe useful in providing a general framework for interpretive dreamwork, particularly with dreams that are deemed to be truthful and prophetic in nature (*ru'yā*).

Identifying Types of Dreams Based on Their Content

Visions generally refer to incidents that are yet to happen, and therefore the dream content of those visions should be interpreted as the main characters and actions of those incidents (e.g. the dreams of the two prisoners with Prophet Yūsuf). When dreams contain characters or incidents from the afterlife, they are generally considered to be true, unless something indicates otherwise. Another sign of the truthfulness of a dream is that the same dream is seen and narrated by many people around the same time. On the other hand, dreams that are related to day-to-day events, emotions, and struggles are generally believed to be of the psychological type, unless they are related to a prior supplication (*du'ā'* or *istikhārah*) (see below for more details on dreams and *istikhārah*). When a dream is seen repeatedly, it might be carrying a significant prophetic message to the dreamer, and thus they should seek an interpretation for it. Some truthful dreams are "literal" and thus do not require an interpretation (they happen and come true exactly the same way they were seen).

Dream Content Interpretation

Some dream symbols can be interpreted by their opposite. For example, seeing something fearful may be interpreted as a sign of peace, and seeing poverty may be interpreted as wealth. Moreover, dream symbols might have short-term and long-term interpretations, some of which are positive while others are negative. The interpreter, however, should favor sharing positive and optimistic outcomes as much as possible. Dreams are interpreted based on their content (characters, emotions, objects, activities, etc.) as well as the "descriptive elements/modifiers" of that content. Interpreters should take into consideration the innate dispositions of symbols as they might indicate the meaning (e.g. a palm tree is a plant that indicates prosperity and provision). Symbols have to also be interpreted within their context in the dream. For example, a bird on one's shoulder may be interpreted as someone's action or deeds, a bird on the head may represent a leadership position, while a bird coming out of someone's mouth may represent death (his soul leaving his body).

When specific words or phrases occurring in a dream are remembered, they may have different meanings for different people in different times. The dreamer's psycho-social circumstances have to be taken into consideration while interpreting such linguistic elements. For example, it was narrated that Ibn Sīrīn interpreted the same dream seen by two people in two different ways. Both dreamers saw that they were giving the Adhān (Islamic call for prayer). He interpreted it for one of them as "stealing" while for the other one as "performing *ḥajj*". Ibn Sīrīn explained that he saw some good signs in one of the people that made him favor a positive interpretation (al-Sadḥān, 2003).

Al-Shihāb ibn N'imah (d.697 AH/1297 CE), one of the prominent Muslim figures in DI, emphasized the importance of the bio-psycho-social context of the dreamer's language, time and season, job and occupation, location, customs, and state of well-being. For example, wearing an armor (1) for a soldier could be a sign of being recruited for military service, (2) for a fighter could be a sign of victory, (3) for a worshipper could be a sign of an invalid worship, while (4) for others could be a sign of dispute and unrest (*fitnah*). Another example was that of shaving one's head or beard, which could be a good sign for a person who is accustomed to and familiar with such shaving, while it could be a bad sign for a person who dislikes it. Furthermore, for a person who is accustomed to wearing black outfits, seeing that in a dream could be a sign of majesty and honor, while for a person who is not accustomed to wearing black outfits could be a sign of distress, anxiety, and sadness. He also gave the example of seeing oneself wearing thin outfits and interpreted this as a sign of distress for someone who is already sick, a sign of marriage for someone who is single, and a sign of a healthy skin for someone with skin abscesses and ulcers (al-Shihāb, 2000, pp. 149–154). These are a few examples of how the context of the dreamer may influence the process of DI.

Dreams that are about natural phenomena, public landmarks, or public figures are generally interpreted as being general and not as specific to the dreamer. However, they can sometimes have some relevance to the dreamer's personal life.

When numbers occur in one's dreams, they may indicate time units (like the dream of the king of Egypt in the story of Prophet Yūsuf) or they may hint at specific units whose numbers match the number in the dream (the dream of Prophet Yūsuf's childhood).

Parables mentioned in the Qur'ān and the Sunnah can be used as principles for DI. Examples that have been used by interpreters include interpreting dates as prosperity (Qur'ān 19:26), wood as hypocrisy (Qur'ān 63:4), sleeping as tranquility (Qur'ān 8:11), and a ship as rescue (Qur'ān 29:15) (al-Sadḥān, 2003).

Dreams and *Istikhārah*

The linguistic meaning of *Istikhārah* is seeking what is good or seeking the best course of action. Technically, *istikhārah* is an Islamic prophetically sanctioned practice of seeking the guidance of Allah in choosing the best course of action in a given matter. The Prophet (peace and blessings be upon him) is reported to have taught the Companions to practice *istikhārah* in all matters. *Istikhārah* entails praying two *rakʿāt* (two units of prayer) followed by a specific *duʿā'* (supplication) invoking the names and attributes of Allah and seeking guidance in regard to the matter at hand (see Box 6.1). Although the original teachings of the Prophet regarding *istikhārah* have not made any clear connection between dreams and *istikhārah*, *istikhārah* is believed by some Muslims across cultures and communities to reveal its guidance through dreaming (Aydar, 2009; Edgar & Henig, 2010).

Box 6.1 Du'ā' al-Istikhārah

O Allah, I ask You to show me what is best, through Your knowledge, and I ask You to empower me, through Your power, and I ask You from Your immense bounty, for You have power, and I am powerless, and You have knowledge and I know not, and You are the Knower of the unseen realms.

O Allah, if You know that this undertaking is good for me with regard to my religion, my livelihood, and can yield goodness in the long term, then decree it for me, facilitate it for me, and grant me blessing in it.

And if You know that this undertaking is bad for me with regard to my religion, my livelihood, and in the long term then turn it away from me and turn me away from it; and decree for me better than it, wherever it may be, and make me content with it.

The majority of Sunni Muslim jurists have argued against this notion of expecting a dream following the prayer of *istikhārah*, and have rather emphasized a more natural course of decision-making following the *istikhārah* based on one's evaluation of the situation, counseling of others, and feeling at ease with one choice over another (MEIA, 1983–2006; Islamweb, 2016; Ullah, Nouman, & Niaz, 2014). Perhaps it is the Islamic discourse that emphasizes the significance of dreams and DI, as well as the need for solid evidence to rely on in decision-making, that has given rise to this notion of the *istikhārah*–dream connection. In the modern study of dreams, the cultural connection between *istikhārah* and dreams is seen to fall in part under the concept of "dream incubation". "Dream incubation" refers to "the practice of going to sleep with the intention of having a dream for a specific purpose" (Henry, 2012). In other words, it is a process of evoking a dream related to a certain subject through ritualistic bedtime behavior, spiritual practice, or other means (Barrett, 1993; Henry, 2012).

That being said, and based on the agreement of the majority of Muslim jurists, it is important to delineate the fact that a dream is not always to be expected following an *istikhārah*, and that if a dream does occur, it is also difficult to totally rely on it due the difficulty of delineating the source and type of the dream. As mentioned earlier, a dream can be divinely inspired, but can also be a result of one's preoccupations, worries, and intrapsychic tensions, or can result from satanic whispers. Therefore, unless a dream meets the qualities of a true dream, one should not totally expect a dream as the outcome of an *istikhārah* or rely on its message. In fact, as highlighted earlier, *istikhārah* is a process of seeking the best course of action and best decision. A person should not expect an outcome from *istikharah* other than the facilitation of the intended matter, or otherwise being turned away from it by Allah's will. A therapist may use this to assist, empower, and educate patients when they are confronted with decisions to make. Relying on such divine intervention and permission could lift any potential future regrets regarding the decisions that were made.

Dreams, Psychopathology, and Psychopharmacology

The majority of people's dreams are of the "psychological type". Physical and psychological factors play an important role in such dreams. Dreams are also affected by different psychopathologies and psychotherapeutic interventions. In addition to a strong knowledge about the Islamic discourse on dreams, a Muslim clinician must be aware of how different mental disorders and psychotherapeutic interventions might impact dreaming.

Depression

Depressed patients have reported a decrease in the frequency and length of dreams, most of which are past-oriented with prevalent themes of failures and misfortunes. Patients' improvement was reflected in dreams and their content (Hauri, 1976; Cartwright, Lloyd, Knight, & Trenholme,1984). Suicidal depressed patients and violent patients have reported more death content and violence in their dreams than non-violent and non-suicidal patients (Firth, Blouin, Natarajan, & Blouin, 1986).

Dream content was reported to reflect the depressed state as well as the circumstances of the individual, especially in patients who attempted suicide or had gone through divorce (Firth et al., 1986; Cartwright, 1991).

Anxiety

Anxious people are reported to have more dreams with anxiety-related content and more nightmares than other people. The application of relaxation techniques reducing waking anxiety traits was accompanied by an improvement in the pleasantness of dreams (Simonds & Parraga, 1984). Moreover, systematic desensitization applied to a phobic subject can induce the disappearance of the phobic objects from dreams (Koulack, Lebow, & Church, 1976).

PTSD

The link between PTSD and dreams has been well established and studied. Kramer and Roth (1979) proposed that the disturbing dream is more the hallmark of PTSD than the sleep disturbance. Ross, Ball, Sullivan, and Caroff (1989) described the dreams of patients with PTSD as vivid, affect-laden, disturbing, outside the realm of current waking experience, and easy to recall. Such dreams may be associated with several symptoms, such as increased awakenings, increased motoric activity (Melman, Kulick-Bell, Ashlock, & Nolan, 1995) and increased sweating (Wilmer, 1996). Such disturbing dreams may last up to three to four decades after the traumatic event (Kramer, 2000). Cognitive behavioral therapy, imagery rehearsal therapy (Krakow et al., 2001), phenelzine, imipramine (Kosten, Frank, Dan, McDougle, & Giller, 1991), trazodone (Warner, Dorn, & Peabody, 2001), nefazodone (Gillin et al., 1999), and fluvoxamine (Neylan et al., 2001) appear effective for the treatment of insomnia and nightmares associated with chronic PTSD.

Psychotic Disorders

In patients with psychotic disorders, dreams tend to have themes that are a continuation of their wakeful mental state. No matter how bizarre those dreams might be, they could carry significant meaning for patients and, more seriously, could pose a risk to patients and others, as highlighted in the case scenario described earlier.

Kramer and Roth (1979) highlighted that dreams of patients with schizophrenia are more primitive, more direct, more sexual, more anxious and hostile. They also showed that the psychotic symptoms and dream contents had comparable degrees of paranoia. Lesse (1974) found that a decrease in the anxiety level in the dreams of a patient with schizophrenia was the first change seen with antipsychotic medications. Wilmer (1982) reported that discussing dreams in a group decreased the insomnia of schizophrenia patients and increased their self-understanding.

Bipolar Affective Disorders

Dream content was found to be a possible indicator of a relapse in patients with bipolar disorder (Frayn, 1991). Bipolar patients reported bizarre dreams with death and injury themes before their shift to mania. Compared to unipolar patients, they also reported dreams with more anxiety-related content (Beauchemin & Hays, 1995).

Eating Disorders

Dream content of patients with eating disorders reflects a preoccupation with food and oral activities (Brink & Allen, 1992). Anorexic patients revealed dream content related to a fear of getting fat (Wilson, 1982) and seemed more anxious in their dreams than comparison groups (Frayn, 1991).

Substance Use

Certain brain pathways have been shown to be involved in both dreaming and drug cravings (Johnson, 2001). In people with substance use disorders, dreams about drug use have been associated with relapse (Christo & Franey, 1996). In addition, alcoholic patients have reported more nightmares than control subjects, and some reported drinking to alleviate such nightmares (Cernovsky, 1986; Hershon, 1977).

Dreams and Psychopharmacology

Numerous classes of psychotropic medications have an impact on dreams and dream content. Some are reported to trigger bizarre and vivid dreams and nightmares (Nielsen & Zadra, 2000; Balon, 1996). Bedtime administration of some tricyclic antidepressants and antipsychotics leads to a higher recall of frightening dreams than when these medications are taken in twice-daily doses (Strayhorn & Nash, 1978). Moreover, withdrawals of some sedative medications (e.g. triazolam, barbiturates) was found to cause negative dream experiences (Adam & Oswald, 1989; Kales & Jacobson, 1967).

These interactions between dreams, psychopathology, and psychopharmacology are extremely important to bear in mind when patients bring up dreams in clinical encounters or when clinicians ask patients about their dreams.

Psycho-Spiritual Education

The above information provides a comprehensive foundation that can be utilized by clinicians to educate their patients about dreams and dreamwork. Patients should be educated about the different types of dreams and how to recognize and deal with each. If patients experience good positive dreams, they should be encouraged to follow the teachings of the Prophet (peace and blessings be upon him), which entail thanking Allah for the dream, showing gratitude, and reporting it to those whom they love and trust. On the contrary, if they experience a bad dream, several elements should be considered. The dreamer should explore further the different elements of the dream, as some dreams may appear bad on the surface but have a rather positive meaning in the science of *Ta'bīr* (DI). They should also follow the instructions of the Prophet (peace and blessings be upon him) by avoiding discussion of the dream, praying and seeking refuge in Allah, seeking the best outcome, and seeking protection from any negative outcomes.

Bad dreams can also carry a warning message, and thus the dreamer should be encouraged to take any necessary precautions and seek protection through *du'ā'*. If a dream brings glad tidings, the dreamer should be encouraged to show gratitude and not rely on the dream, but rather continue fulfilling their duties and obligations.

Conclusion

Despite the extremely rich Islamic discourse on dreams, modern clinicians and psychologists have either neglected dreams in their practice or reduced their function to a mere a gateway into the subconscious. Islamic scriptures and heritage laid the foundations for understanding the nature, status, and types of dreams. They also offer invaluable content of profound practical value, which can be utilized by Muslim mental health clinicians in psychoeducation and dreamwork, both of which constitute important spiritual strategies within an Islamically integrated psychotherapy.

References

Adam, K., & Oswald, I. (1989). Can a rapidly-eliminated hypnotic cause daytime anxiety? *Pharmacopsychiatry, 22*(03), 115–119.

al-Ālūsī, A. M. (1994). *Tafsīr al-Ālūsī (al-Ālūsī's Qur'ān Commentary).* Vol. 24. Beirut: Dār Iḥyā' al-Turāth al-'Arabī.

al-'Asqalā nī, A. H. (1986). *Fatḥ al-Bārī Sharḥ Ṣaḥīḥ al-Bukhārī [Commentary on Ṣaḥīḥ al-Bukhārī].*Vol. 12. Cairo: Dār al-Rayyān Publishing House.

al-Barīdī, B., Ibn Sīrīn, M., & al-Nabulusī, M. (2008). *Mu'jam Tafsīr al-Aḥlām (Dictionary of dream interpretation).* Abu Dhabi: Al-Ṣafā Publishers.

al-Bukhārī (2010). *Sahih al-Bukhari.* Riyadh: Darussalam.

al-Dīnūrī, A. M. (2001). *Ta'bīr al-Ru'yā (Dream interpretation).* Damascus: al-Bashā'ir Publishing House.

al-Fārābī, A., & Nādir, A. N. (1973). *Kitāb Ārā' ahl al-Madīnah al-Fāḍilah (Opinions of the people of the virtuous city).* Beirut: Dar al-Mashriq.

Ali, O. M., Milstein, G., & Marzuk, P. M. (2005). The Imam's role in meeting the counseling needs of Muslim communities in the United States. *Psychiatric Services, 56*(2), 202–205.

al-Kindī, Y. I., & Abu Raydah, M. A. (1950). *Rasā'il al-Kindi al-Falsafiyyah (al-Kindi's Philosophical Treatises).* Cairo: Dār al-Fikr al-'Arabī.

al-Nawawī, Y. S. (1996). *al-Minhāj fī Sharḥ Ṣaḥīḥ Muslim b. al-Ḥajjāj (Commentary on Ṣaḥīḥ Muslim).* Damascus: Dār al-Khayr.

al-Naysāpūrī, H. (2002). *al-Mustadrak 'alā al-Ṣaḥīḥayn.* Beirut: Dār al-Kutub al-'Ilmiyyah.

al-Sadḥān, A. M. (2003). *al-Qawā'id al-Ḥusnā fī Ta'wīl al-Ru'ā (The perfect principles of dream interpretation).* Al-Ta'if, KSA: Unknown Publisher. Retreived from: https://d1.islamhouse.com/data/ar/ih_books/single2/ar_Fine_Rules_in_Interpreting_the_Dream.pdf.

al-Shihāb b. N'imah (2000). *al-Badr al-Munīr fī 'Ilm al-Ta'bīr (The shining moon in the science dream interpretation).* Beirut: al-Rayyān Foundation.

Aydar, H. (2009). Istikhara and dreams: Learning about the future through dreaming. In K. Bulkeley, K. Adams, & P. M. Davis (Eds.), *Dreaming in Christianity and Islam: Culture, conflict and creativity* (pp. 123–136). New Brunswick, NJ: Rutgers University Press.

Balon, R. (1996). Bupropion and nightmares. *The American Journal of Psychiatry, 153*(4), 579.

Barrett, D. (1993). The" committee of sleep": A study of dream incubation for problem solving. *Dreaming, 3*(2), 115.

Beauchemin, K., & Hays, P. (1995). Prevailing mood, mood changes and dreams in bipolar disorder. *Journal of Affective Disorder, 35*, 41–49.

Brink, S. G., & Allan, J. A. (1992). Dreams of anorexic and bulimic women: A research study. *Journal of Analytical Psychology, 37*(3), 275–297.

Bulkeley, K. (2002). Reflections on the dream traditions of Islam. *Sleep and Hypnosis, 4*, 1–11.

Bulkeley, K., Adams, K., & Davis, P. M. (Eds.). (2009). *Dreaming in Christianity and Islam: culture, conflict, and creativity.* New Brunswick, NJ: Rutgers University Press.

Buquet, R. (1988). The dream and the visually impaired. *Psychoanalysis at the university, 13*(50), 319–327.

Cartwright, R. D. (1991). Dreams that work: The relation of dream incorporation to adaptation to stressful events. *Dreaming*, *1*(1), 3.

Cartwright, R. D., Lloyd, S., Knight, S., & Trenholme, I. (1984). Broken dreams: A study of the effects of divorce and depression on dream content. *Psychiatry*, *47*(3), 251–259.

Cernovsky, Z. Z. (1986). MMPI and nightmare reports in women addicted to alcohol and other drugs. *Perceptual and Motor Skills*, *62*(3), 717–718.

Christo, G., & Franey, C. (1996). Addicts drug-related dreams: their frequency and relationship to six-month outcomes. *Substance Use & Misuse*, *31*(1), 1–15.

Davis, J. L., & Wright, D. C. (2006). Exposure, relaxation, and rescripting treatment for trauma-related nightmares. *Journal of Trauma & Dissociation*, *7*(1), 5–18.

Doniger, W., & Bulkley, K. (1993). Why study dreams? A religious studies perspective. *Dreaming*, *3*(1), 69.

Edgar, I., & Henig, D. (2010). Istikhara: The guidance and practice of Islamic dream incubation through ethnographic comparison. *History and Anthropology*, *21*(3), 251–262.

Fahd, T. (1959). *Les songes et leur interprétation selon l'Islam: Tiré à part (Dreams and their interpretation in Islam)*. Paris: Éditions du Seuil.

Firth, S. T., Blouin, J., Natarajan, C., & Blouin, A. (1986). A comparison of the manifest content in dreams of suicidal, depressed and violent patients. *The Canadian Journal of Psychiatry*, *31*(1), 48–53.

Frayn, D. (1991). The incidence and significance of perceptual qualities in the reported dreams of patients with anorexia nervosa. *The Canadian Journal of Psychiatry*, *36*, 517–520.

Freud, S. (2010). *The interpretation of dreams. 1900.* Ed. and trans. by James Strachey. New York, NY: Basic Books.

Gillin, J. C., Smith-Vaniz, A., Zisook, S., Stein, M., Rapaport, M., & Kelsoe, J. (1999). Effects of nefazodone on sleep, nightmares and mood in PTSD. *Sleep*, *22*(suppl), S277–278.

Hall, C. S., & Van de Castle, R. L. (1976). *The content analysis of dreams.* New York, NY: Appleton-Century-Crofts.

Hauri, P. (1976). Dreams in patients remitted from reactive depression. *Journal of Abnormal Psychology*, *85*(1), 1–10.

Henry, R. (2012). Incubation of dream. In D. Barrett & P. McNamara (Eds.), *Encyclopedia of sleep and dreams: the evolution, function, nature, and mysteries of slumber.* Vol. 1. Santa Barbara, CA: ABC-CLIO.

Hershon, H. I. (1977). Alcohol withdrawal symptoms and drinking behavior. *Journal of Studies on Alcohol*, *38*(5), 953–971.

Holmes, J. (1991). The democracy of the dream. *The British Journal of Psychiatry*, *159*(6), 20–23.

IASD Board of Directors (2001). Ethics for dreamwork. https://asdreams.org/ethics/.

Ibn al-Nadīm, M. I. (1971). *Al-Fihrist (Index)*. Unknown Publisher.

Ibn 'Arabī, M. A., & 'Abbās, Q. M. (2009). *Māhiyyat al-Qalb (Essence of the Heart)*. Damascus: Dār al-Madā.

Ibn Khaldūn, A. (1967). *Al-Muqaddimah (The introduction)* Trans. Franz Rosenthal. Princeton, NJ: Princeton University.

Ibn Miskawayh, A. A., & Fu'ad, A. A. (1901). *Al-Fawz al-Asghar (The Minor Triumph)*. Beirut: Unknown Publisher.

Ibn Sīnā, A. A. (1988). *'Ilm al-Nafs fī Kitāb al-Shifa' (Psychology Section in the Book of Healing)*. Paris: Editions du Patrimoine Arabe et Islamique.

Islamweb (2016). *The Prayer of Seeking Allah's Guidance (Salat Al-Istikharah)*. Retrieved from: www.islamweb.net/en/article/88943/the-prayer-of-seeking-allahs-guidance-salat-al-istikharah.

Johnson, B. (2001). Drug dreams: a neuropsychoanalytic hypothesis. *Journal of the American Psychoanalytic Association*, *49*(1), 75–96.

Kales, A., & Jacobson, A. (1967). Mental activity during sleep: Recall studies, somnambulism, and effects of rapid eye movement deprivation and drugs. *Experimental Neurology*, *19*, 81–91.

Kosten, T. R., Frank, J. B., Dan, E., McDougle, C. J., & Giller, E. L. (1991). Pharmacology for posttraumatic stress disorder using phenelzine or imipramine. *J. Nerv. Ment. Dis.*, *1*(179), 366–370.

Koulack, D., Lebow, M. D., & Church, M. (1976). The effect of densensitization on the sleep and dreams of a phobic subject. *Canadian Journal of Behavioural Science*, *8*(4), 418–421.

Krakow, B., Hollifield, M., Johnston, L., Koss, M., Schrader, R., Warner, T. D., et al. (2001). Imagery rehearsal therapy for chronic nightmares in sexual assault survivors with posttraumatic stress disorder: a randomized controlled trial. *JAMA*, *286*(5), 537–545.

Kramer, M. (2000). Dreams and psychopathology. In M. Kryger, T. Roth, & W. Dement (Eds.), *Principles and practices of sleep medicine* (pp. 511–419). 3rd Ed. Philadelphia, PA: W. B. Saunders.

Kramer, M., & Roth, T. (1979). Dreams in psychopathology. In B. Women (Ed.), *Handbook of Dreams: Research, Theories and Applications* (pp. 361–387). New York, NY: Van Nostrand Reinhold.

Lamoreaux, J. C. (2002). *The early Muslim tradition of dream interpretation*. Albany, NY: SUNY Press.

Landau, R. (1957). The philosophy of ibn 'aarabi (1). *The Muslim World*, *47*(1), 46–61.

Lesse, S. (1974). Psychiatric symptoms in relationship to the intensity of anxiety. *Psychother. Psychosom.*, *23*, 94–102.

Levin, R., & Nielsen, T. A. (2007). Disturbed dreaming, posttraumatic stress disorder, and affect distress: A review and neurocognitive model. *Psychological Bulletin*, *133*(3), 482–528. https://doi.org/10.1037/0033-2909.133.3.482

Mālik, M. A. (1994). *Muwaṭṭā Mālik*. Dār Iḥyā' al-'Ulū m al-'Arabiyyah.

Melman, T., Kulick-Bell, R., Ashlock, L., Nolan, B. (1995). Sleep events among veterans with combat-related posttraumatic stress disorder. *Am. J. Psychiatry*, *152*, 110–115.

Ministry of Endowments and Islamic Affairs (MEIA) (1983–2006). *Al-Mawsū'ah al-Fiqhiyyah (Encyclopedia of Islamic Jurisprudence)*. Vol. 3. Kuwait City: Dār al-Salāsil.

Mitchison, S. (1999). The value of eliciting dreams in general psychiatry. *Advances in Psychiatric Treatment*, *5*(4), 296–302.

Muslim, M. (2006). *Ṣaḥīḥ Muslim*. Riyadh: Dār Ṭaybah for Publishing and Distribution.

Myers, D. G. (2010). *Psychology*. New York, NY: Worth Publishers.
Nagati, M. O. (1980). *Al-Idrāk al-Ḥissī 'ind Ibn Sīnā (Sensory Perception in Ibn Sīnā's Works)*. Cairo: Dār al-Shurūq.
Nagati, M. O. (1993). *Al-Dirāsat al-Nafsāniyyah 'ind al-'Ulama' al-Muslimīn (Psychological Studies of Muslim Scholars)*. Cairo: Dār al-Shurūq.
Neylan, T. C., Metzler, T. J., Schoenfeld, F. B., Weiss, D. S., Lenoci, M., Best, S. R., et al. (2001). Fluvoxamine and sleep disturbances in posttraumatic stress disorder. *J. Trauma Stress.*, *14*(3), 461–467.
Nielsen, T. A., & Zadra, A. (2000). Dreaming disorders. In M. Kryger, T. Roth, & W. Dement (Eds.), *Principles and practices of sleep medicine*, 3rd Ed. (pp. 753–772). Philadelphia, PA: W. B. Saunders.
Richards, P. S., & Bergin, A. E. (2005). *A spiritual strategy for counseling and psychotherapy*. 2nd Ed. Washington, DC: American Psychological Association.
Ross, R. J., Ball, W. A., Sullivan, K. A., & Caroff, S. N. (1989). Sleep disturbance as the hallmark of post traumatic stress disorder. *Am. J. Psychiatry*, *146*, 697–707.
Salem, M. O. (2001). Critical evaluation of the Freudian theories. *Psychiatry Update*, *2*(1), 1–6.
Salem, M. O. (2010). Function of dreams: An integrated approach. *Journal of the Islamic Medical Association of North America*, *42*(1), 15–22.
Salem, M. O. (2012). Islam and dreams. In D. Barrett & P. McNamara (Eds.), *Encyclopedia of sleep and dreams: the evolution, function, nature, and mysteries of slumber*. Vol. 1. Santa Barbara, CA: ABC-CLIO.
Salem, M. O., & Ali, M. M. (2008). Psycho-spiritual strategies in treating addiction patients: Experience at al-Amal Hospital, Saudi Arabia. *Journal of the Islamic Medical Association of North America*, *40*(4), 161–165.
Salem, M. O., Alhadi, A., & Algahtani, H. (2012). Cognitive behaviour therapy in the Middle East. In F. E. Naeem & D. E. Kingdon, *Cognitive behaviour therapy in non-Western cultures*. New York, NY: Nova Science Publishers.
Simonds, J. F., & Parraga, H. (1984). Sleep behaviors and disorders in children and adolescents evaluated at psychiatric clinics. *Journal of Developmental and Behavioral Pediatrics*, *5*(1), 6–10.
Stickgold, R., Malia, A., Maguire, D., Roddenberry, D., & O'Connor, M. (2000). Replaying the game: hypnagogic images in normals and amnesics. *Science*, *290*(5490), 350–353.
Strayhorn, J. M., & Nash, J. L. (1978). Frightening dreams and dosage schedule of tricyclic and neuroleptic drugs. *Journal of Nervous and Mental Disease*, *166*(12), 878–880.
Uga, V., Lemut, M. C., Zampi, C., Zilli, I., & Salzarulo, P. (2006). Music in dreams. *Consciousness and Cognition*, *15*(2), 351–357.
Ullah, H. I., Nouman, M. W., & Niaz, A. (2014). The fact of sharah-e-sadar and its need in implementation of istikhara. *Gomal University Journal of Research*, *30*(1), 56–63.
Van de Castle, R. L. (1994). *Our dreaming mind*. New York, NY: Ballantine Books.
VandenBos, G. R. (2013). *APA dictionary of clinical psychology*. Washington, DC: American Psychological Association.

Warner, M. D., Dorn, M. R., & Peabody, C. A. (2001). Survey on the usefulness of trazodone in patients with PTSD with insomnia or nightmares. *Pharmacopsychiatry*, *34*(4) 128–131.

Weld, C., & Eriksen, K. (2007). Christian clients' preferences regarding prayer as a counseling intervention. *Journal of Psychology and Theology*, *35*(4), 328–341.

Wilmer, H. (1982). Dream seminar for chronic schizophrenic patients. *Psychiatry*, *45*, 351–360.

Wilmer, H. (1996). The healing nightmare: war dreams of Vietnam veterans. In D. Barrett, (Ed.), *Trauma and Dreams* (pp. 85–99). Cambridge, MA: Harvard University Press.

Wilson, C. P. (1982). The fear of being fat and anorexia nervosa. *International Journal of Psychoanalytic Psychotherapy*, *9*, 233–255.

Part IV

Treatment of the Domains of the Human Psyche

Chapter 7

Emotionally Oriented Psychotherapy

Hooman Keshavarzi and Sara Keshavarzi

Chapter Summary

This chapter provides an overview of the role, function, and expression of emotions according to both traditional Islamic scholarly writings and emotion theories in modern psychology. Emotion-focused psychotherapy (EFT) is closely examined through a comparative analysis between the theoretical underpinnings of this theory and Islamic conceptions of the human emotional experience. A reconciliatory and filtration approach is taken to offer a Traditional Islamically Integrated Psychotherapy (TIIP) conceptual framework of working with emotions. The core principles of emotion theory are adapted and adopted into a TIIP ontological framework while offering a nuanced conceptualization and approach to its therapeutic applications.

The TIIP conceptualization of working with emotions expands dialectical constructivism to "theistic trilectual constructivism" that characterizes emotions as originating from (1) *nafs*, (2) *'aql*, and (3) *rūḥ*. Trilectual constructivism holds that emotions originate out of these three inherent sources and are consolidated within the meaning-making cognitive constructs of their sociocultural environments. These experiences become internalized as emotion schemes and can be either adaptive or maladaptive in facilitating or serving as barriers to the underlying balanced needs of their emotions. The therapeutic encounter is designed to allow for a re-expression and reprocessing of emotions, facilitating the replacement of maladaptive emotions with adaptive emotional expressions. This further leads to emotional transformation and cognitive reconsolidation of a healthier emotion scheme within the context of therapy that is believed to impact therapeutic change and lead to remission of symptoms. A case illustration of an Islamic guided imagery, *'taṣawwur'*, is provided as a practical demonstration of TIIP emotionally oriented psychotherapy.

Introduction

Emotions are a significant aspect, if not central part, of what mental health practitioners work with in psychotherapy. Patients typically seek out psychological treatment on account of emotional pain that has become intensified over time, and the need to regulate emotions that they feel are beyond their control. Traditionally, emotions in clinical psychology used to be viewed as symptoms or side effects of thinking, and the richness of experiential work in psychotherapeutic settings in modern psychology has only emerged relatively recently (e.g. Gendlin, 1974; Johnson & Greenberg, 1985). After significant research demonstrated the empirical utility and efficacy of experiential psychotherapies, even cognitively oriented therapies such as cognitive behavioral therapy (CBT) have started to incorporate experiential work into therapy, which is particularly evidenced by cognitive processing psychotherapy (CPT) (Resick, Monson, & Chard, 2016).

Islamic scholars have also offered substantial literature on cognitively oriented interventions as a primary mechanism for influencing emotion, spiritual experience, and behavior that predates modernity. For example, the polymath Abū Zayd al-Balkhī (d.322 AH/934 AD) wrote an entire treatise on preventative and interventional behavioral medicine in which he predominately employs a cognitive approach to treating psychological disorders and emotional dysregulation (al-Balkhī, 2005). However, the Islamic tradition is also rich in describing emotions and emotional states. Although emotions in the Islamic tradition are typically discussed within the context of spiritual reformation and associated with the genre of literature on character development (*tadhīb al-akhlāq*) and spirituality (*tazkiyah* or *taṣawwuf*), sections within larger works have focused on emotional states, and even a few independent works on emotions have been authored. For example, the Andalusian polymath Ibn Ḥazm (d.452 AH/1064 AD) wrote a treatise on love and its various aspects entitled *The Dove's Neck-Ring*. Similarly, Ibn al-Qayyim al-Jawzī (d.749 AH/1350 AD) authored *Rawḍat al-Muḥibbīn* or *The Garden of Lovers*, in which he goes into great detail in defining love and its subtypes, as well as terms and states that are associated with it. Imām al-Ghazālī (d.510 AH/1111 AD), in his *Iḥyā' 'Ulūm al-Dīn* or *The Revival of the Religions Sciences*, devotes a section to fear, providing cognitive strategies for inducing or reducing fear (al-Ghazālī, 1990, p. 211). These works, among many others, add to the richness of the Islamic tradition's discussion of human emotions and experience.

Defining Emotion

Islamic scholars have discussed emotion both in terms of top-down cognitively influenced responses similar to Ortony and Turner's (1990) conceptualization of emotions, as well as bottom-up biologically/psychologically primitive motivational responses as are consistent with biosocial theorists (Izard, 1992). However, Islamic scholars would extend the biosocial theorists' conceptualization to include spiritually inherent motivational drives as well (see below). But, irrespective of the origins and processes of emotions, Islamic scholars typically view them as a secondary aspect of the human experience. Rarely are emotions seen as valuable in and of themselves; rather, their adaptive utility is their ability to propel instinctual survival or facilitate spiritual connection.

The closest proximate classical Arabic terms for emotions are *iḥsās* or *sh'ūr*. These terms imply knowing through sensory information, or can be translated more loosely as emotions that vary slightly in their connotations from those typically defined by modern psychologists as subjective states that comprise feelings, associated cognitive processes, and physiological states that propel action tendencies, such as the fight or flight response (Izard, 1977, 1992; Plutchik, 1980). Typically, the term *shu'ūr* or *iḥsās* denotes knowing or becoming aware through cognitive processes or to know intuitively, particularly when it (i.e. *iḥsās*) is accompanied by the Arabic preposition '*bi*'. For example, Persian polymath Abu Naṣr Sarrāj al-Ṭūsī (d.378 AH/996 AD) in his *al-luma' fi al-taṣawwuf* describes the difference between two spiritual stations and mentions that the deeper state (*sirr al-sirr*) is one that the experiencer is not consciously aware of (*mā lā yuḥassu bihī*), while the other is known consciously (al-Ṭūsī, 1914, p. 354). A prophetic example is in the narration of Uthman ibn Abu al-As (may Allah be pleased with him), who complained to the Prophet (peace and blessings be upon him) about intrusive satanic whispers that were intervening between him and his prayers or recitation of the Qur'ān. The Prophet (peace and blessings be upon him) informed him: "That is a satan known as Khinzab and when you sense (*aḥsastahū*) him, then seek refuge in Allah from him and spit three times to your left" (Muslim, 2017, *Ḥadīth* 2203). Sometimes the term can also include subjective states or "feelings". By way of an example of the usage of the term in this way, Abū al-Qāsim Junayd al-Baghdādī (d.298 AH/ 910 AD) describes an ascetic as someone whose heart feels (*man aḥassa*) relief (*salāmah*) from the (stressors of the) world ('Aṭṭār, 1905, p. 31). There are other words that carry similar meanings with varying connotations, such as '*awāṭif* and *wijdān* (al-Taftāzānī, 2000, pp. 75–76).

Although the word 'emotion' is not a perfect translation, there is a great degree of convergence between modern psychological understandings of emotion and descriptions of particular emotional states according to Islamic scholars. For example, a definition of the emotion of fear or anxiety given by Islamic scholars is "the anticipation of an undesirable future outcome or potential loss of something valuable to the self" (al-Ghazālī, 1990, p. 211; al-Rāzī, 2008, p. 73). This is related to the definition provided by the APA dictionary: "a basic emotion aroused by the detection of an imminent threat, involving an immediate alarm reaction that mobilizes the organism by triggering a set of physiological changes … and a general mobilization of the organism to take action (available at dictionary.APA.org). Though not a perfect equivalent, the characteristic of future harm or fear of undesirable events in modern psychology is typically referred to as "anticipatory fear", or anxiety where fear is the underlying primary emotion (Barlow, 2000). While the physiological and behavioral responses described above have not been mentioned in the Muslim scholarly definition of fear, typically they are provided in the descriptive texts that follow, explaining what is associated with such emotional states. For example, ancient humoral medicine may be cited to describe physiological qualifiers (Jabin, 2011) or action potentials as outcomes of the subjective state of fear induction (al-Ghazālī, 1990, p. 211). Therefore, for our purposes "emotion" may serve as a working term to describe subjective states that impact and are influenced by cognition, have accompanying physiological reactions, and propel behavior.

The aim of this chapter is to provide a comparative analysis between modern emotion theories in the psychological literature and Islamic conceptions of human experience as it pertains to emotions. An integrative and reconciliatory approach is applied to filter and expand the scope of working with emotions within an Islamic context that includes sourcing of emotions to one or multiple parts of the human psychological elements of *nafs*, *'aql*, and *rūḥ*. The core foundations and principles of emotionally oriented psychotherapy are provided within an integrative focus, accompanied by practical interventions. A case illustration is provided in order to demonstrate this approach for psychotherapeutic application.

Utility of Emotion and Emotion Regulation

Consistent with modern emotion theory, the likes of Imām al-Ghazālī, the sixteenth-century Ottoman ascetic scholar Imam al-Birgivi, and the nineteenth-century reviver of the spiritual sciences Mawlānā Ashraf 'Alī al-Thānwī of the Indian subcontinent offered that primary emotions do contain adaptive and survival utility. Al-Thānwī (1971, p. 170) states in his *Anfas-e-Ī sā* that "being quick-tempered is natural. It is not within one's power and there is no blame for it. However, putting its demands into action by exceeding the limits is blameworthy." Mawlānā Taqī 'Uthmānī, in his *Spiritual Discourses*, expounds upon Mawlānā al-Thānwī's discussion of anger and states: "without anger man may not survive. Suppose an enemy attacks you or a wild beast targets you and you do not show anger, then you will be devoured" ('Uthmānī, 2001, vol. 3, p. 39). Furthermore, anger or *ghaḍab* serves as one of the primary drivers of the human being (see Chapter 1), though it contains a predatory/destructive potential if not regulated. However, in its primitive adaptive form it permits protection of self and progeny, and in the context of humans as a social animal it mobilizes a desire for justice. The underregulation of anger produces destructive anger, and over-regulation produces cowardice (al-Birgivī, 2011, p. 254).

Thus, in a similar way to evolutionary psychologists, Islamic scholars acknowledge the survival instincts of the human being and that human emotions contain underlying adaptive needs, while maintaining that predatory or hedonistic inclinations are destructive. Rather, the appropriate regulation of these emotions allows for healthy expression. Emotion theorists concur that the importance of emotions lies in their adaptive purpose for processing complex environmental cues and producing the actions necessary to satisfy personal needs (Izard, 1992). Emotions provide information about the current state of a patient, allowing access to their underlying needs. As patients try to make sense of experiences, emotions highlight what is important, thereby informing directions for action to alleviate distress and fulfill adaptive needs (Greenberg & Safran, 1987).

Beyond biological survival needs, such emotions also become important vehicles and motivating instruments for spiritual experiences and religious performance. This aspect of the discussion of emotions is perhaps where the greatest divergence between modern emotion theory and the Islamic discourse on emotions occurs. Emotional expression in the Islamic tradition is praiseworthy, especially when it is directed toward God, and therefore its repression can be unhealthy. For example, when a Companion expressed surprise at his grief over the loss of his child, the Prophet of Islam (peace and blessings be upon him) is known to have said, "the eyes shed tears and the heart is sad", demonstrating a healthy need to express emotion (al-Bukhārī, 2010, book 23, *Ḥadīth* 62). He is also reported to have said that "the Qur'ān has been sent down with sadness and sorrow, so cry upon reciting it and if you cannot cry, then attempt to cry" (Ibn Mājah, 2007, book 5, *Ḥadīth* 1398). This narration indicates that if one is able to reflect and contemplate upon the Qur'ān, then they would be able to bring themselves to tears, or at least attempt to do so. In fact, Ibn Abī al-Dunyā (d.281 AH/894 AD), a notable early traditionist and ascetic, wrote a book entitled *al-Riqqah wa-l-Bukā'* or "Tenderness and Crying", in which he discusses the experience of sadness and narrates experiences of the Prophet (peace and blessings be upon him) and his Companions, and early Muslim interactions with moving religious experiences that brought them to tears (Ibn Abī al-Dunyā, 1998).

However, these emotional expressions are not to be given free rein and the unregulated maladaptive expressions of even grief are not permitted, as seen in the Prophet's (peace and blessings be upon him) reprimand of a woman crying profusely and exaggeratedly over the loss of a loved one (al-Bukhārī, 2010, book 23, *Ḥadīth* 61). The balancing instrument across emotions are cognitions, through the act of *ṣabr* or patience, which is a mental act to mitigate emotional expression. In fact, human beings are predisposed to the activation of hopelessness triggered by environmental stressors. Learned cognitive beliefs develop and enlarge the orbitofrontal cortex of the brain, which serves to inhibit the tendency for an overactivated and dysregulated response (Dolcos, Hu, Iordan, Moore, & Dolcos, 2016). Thus it is commonplace to find that many of the Islamic scholars place a great deal of emphasis on the early acquisition of healthy worldviews that allow for the appropriate expression of emotions.

Cognition serves as a meaning-making lens that impacts the interpretation of environmental sensory inputs. This interplay between healthy emotional expression and cognitive regulation of emotion is the process of attempting to achieve balance. Islamic scholars have recognized that an imbalance leading to intense unregulated emotions can disrupt reasoning and decision-making. They conclude that individuals making high-stakes decisions, particularly those in authority positions, should not make these decisions while their reasoning may be impaired by a heightened degree of anger. They have deduced this from the *Ḥadīth* of the Prophet (peace and blessings be upon him) where he states "Let the judge not pass judgement over individuals when he is in a state of anger" (Muslim, 2017, book 30 *Ḥadīth* 21), and have generalized this to apply to all emotions. In fact, another *Ḥadīth* of the Prophet (peace and blessings be upon him) states that "intense love of something, can blind and deafen" (Abū Dāwūd, 2009, book 43, *Ḥadīth* 358), in reference to the impairment of rationality. Therefore, extreme and unregulated expressions of emotions are seen as maladaptive. 'Alī b. Abī Ṭālib (may Allah be pleased with him) stated: "Love your beloved moderately for he/she may become your enemy one day, and hate your enemy moderately for he/she may become your beloved one day" (Ibn Ḥibbān, 2010, vol. 1, *Ḥadīth* 351). This further illustrates the goal of achieving emotional regulation and balance across all elements, as identified in the TIIP framework.

Emotion Schemes and the Need to Balance Them

Acquiring balance in and regulation of emotional states is a goal shared by Islamic scholars and modern emotion theories, as demonstrated above. Emotions function as alarm signals that cause an individual to pay inward attention to discover or understand what these signals are calling for. Similar to other internal bodily feelings such as hunger or thirst, ignoring such emotional feelings can have negative consequences. For example, the Qur'ān states, "die with your (repressed) anger" (3:191). Exegists such as Abū al-Qāsim Maḥmūd al-Zamakhsharī (d.532 AH/1144 CE) in *al-Kashshāf*, and the late twentieth-century exegete Muḥammad b. 'Āshūr in his *al-Taḥrīr wa-l-Tanwīr*, in discussion of this verse offer that death and *ghayẓ* (repressed anger) has a causal relationship with hastening death.

This provides further indication that although repression of anger is even necessary in certain circumstances, the chronic repression of anger that turns into resentment is unhealthy. In fact, the blocking of human emotions can lead to them being channeled to different areas of the human experience. This can lead to psychosomatic symptoms, flashbacks, nightmares, and other manifestations, such that these "alarm signals" start to get louder and less easy to ignore overtime. All human emotions have the propensity for maladaptive expression and require transformation into optimal expression. This can be achieved by an emotional reprocessing that extinguishes the persistence of maladaptive expression in order to maintain healthy human psycho-spiritual functioning. This reprocessing approach is outlined later in the chapter. Table 7.1 outlines various emotions discussed by both emotion theories and Islamic scholars, and highlights their central needs, adaptive/maladaptive expressions, and the associated cognitive, physiological, and behavioral reactions.

The balancing and regulation of emotions is generally necessary. An exception to this rule, however, is that excesses in love for God, His messenger (peace and blessings be upon him), and His religion are rather seen as praiseworthy. They can be seen as adaptive strengthening drivers to spiritual realization. For example, Allah states in the Qur'ān that "the believers are most intense in their love of God" (2:165). Similarly, the Prophet (peace and blessings be upon him) is known to have said that "None of you are (complete) believers until I become more beloved to him than his parents, his children, and humanity in its entirety" (Muslim, 2017, book 1, *Ḥadīth* 76). In fact, there is a significant amount of literature written on the love for God and the Messenger (peace and blessings be upon him) (Safi, 2018).

Theoretical Underpinnings of Emotion Theories

EFT is the dominant therapeutic orientation that directly addresses and works with emotional experiences. EFT psychotherapists have demonstrated significant empirical evidence for the clinical efficacy of working with emotions directly (Elliott, Watson, Goldman, & Greenberg, 2004). Emotion theory is a secular paradigm that is rooted in evolutionary psychology, which is situated within the humanistic tradition. The evolutionary assumption holds that all emotions have an adaptive survival need and that the survival of the species is a function of its ability to express these adaptive needs. Emotions are instinctually prewired responses that are activated by environmental stimuli, which then propel a cognitive evaluation of that stimuli and an accompanying behavioral response. Emotion-focused theorists are biosocial theorists and largely rely upon the original James–Lange theory of emotion, which asserts that emotions typically occur as physiological reactions that are precognitive (Greenberg, 2004).

Table 7.1 Table of emotions

Emotion	*Need*	*Adaptive Reaction*	*Maladaptive Reaction*	*Cognitive State Reaction*	*Physiological Reaction*	*Behavioral Reaction*
Sadness (*ḥazn*/*ḥuzn*)	Meaning	Grief and grief processing Proximity to God (al-Rāzī, 2008, 10:62)	Clinical depression hopelessness, despondency (*ya's*) (al-Ghazālī, 1990, p. 213) Numbing	Past Orientation and occurrence of an undesirable past event and regret (*tadhākur*) (al-Khaṭṭābī, 2012, p. 287; al-Qasṭallānī, 2015 p. 152; Ibn al-Qayyim, 2013, p. 62 – Rawḍat; al-Birgivī, 2011, p. 320)	Psychomotor retardation and fatigue	Stop Pause Inactivity
Anger (*ghaḍab*)	Justice (Greenberg & Paivio, 1997)	Assertive expression	Aggressive drives (al-Birgivī, 2011, p. 155)	Over-exaggeration Black and white All or nothing	Adrenaline released, fight/flight system activated	Protect Defend (Greenberg & Paivio, 1997) Call to action
Shame, Chastity (*Ḥayā'*/*khajal*/*'iffah*)	Divine and social connection	Healthy guilt that propels correction or hides impropriety to protect social standing and/or place with God. Act in accordance with social norms and Islamic law (al-Birgivī, 2011, p. 155)	Hide "perceived" impropriety or globalized view of self as flawed and unforgivable (Greenberg & Paivio, 1997)	Regret (*nadam*)—starts with past orientation and regret Desire to hide and disappear	State of increased arousal, decreased motor behaviors—increase in heart rate and respiration but desire to retreat and flee (Greenberg & Iwakabe, 2011)	Resolve to correct and grow (only in adaptive) Inactivity and sense of helplessness (maladaptive)

Anxiety (*hamm*/ *Ghamm*) Fear (*khawf*)	Safety (Greenberg & Paivio, 1997)	Freeze, monitor, flee (Greenberg & Paivio, 1997)	Overgeneralized anxiety beyond optimal threshold	Anticipation of future negative event (*tawaqqu'*) (al-'Aynī, 2011, vol. 5, p. 90) Catastrophization (maladaptive)	Adrenaline released, fight/flight system activated	Action
Love (*Ḥubb*/ *Shawq*)	Attachment	Contact, strengthen bonds, loss of self in the beloved (Ibn Ḥazm, 2014; Ibn al-Qayyim, (2013), p. 52, Rawḍah). An inclination toward the Divine without much exertion. It is self-less preference to love that which your Beloved loves (al-Kalābādhī, 2001, p, 78)	Lust and passionate love (*'ishq*) that leads to potential harm Blind love—that is uninhibited impulsive and irrational (Ibn al-Qayyim, (2013), p. 60, Rawḍah)	Time/space perception is altered Fixation and attention consumed by object of love	Social bonding, oxytocin (women), vasopressin and attachment centers of cortex activated	Compliance with the demands of object of love. Behaviors intended to maintain and create greater connection
Contentment (*Qana'*/*Riḍā*)	Gratitude/ Appreciation	*Shukr* -Thankfulness, demonstration of gratitude Hope – Letting go of control and reliance in the Mercy of God (al-Birgivī, 2011, p. 323) Appreciation of one's bounties (Ibn 'Abd al-Salām, 2005, p. 12)	Excessive hope, contentment with less than one's potential, complacency, satisfaction despite lack of productivity and insufficiency in actions (al-Ghazālī, 1990, p. 213)	Sufficiency with what is present and abandoning discovering what one does not possess (al-Rāzī, 2008, p. 95; al-Birgivī, 2011, p. 342) Positive attribution bias/optimism (Seligman, 2011)	Sense of calm, relaxation of muscles, release of serotonin and dopamine	Displays of gratitude through speech or behavior (e.g. prayer)

(*continued*)

Table 7.1 Cont.

Emotion	*Need*	*Adaptive Reaction*	*Maladaptive Reaction*	*Cognitive State Reaction*	*Physiological Reaction*	*Behavioral Reaction*
Surprise, Interest, Curiosity (*Ta'jjub*)	Engagement (Greenberg & Paivio, 1997)	Explore the beneficial	Stimulation-seeking, nosiness, over-involvement in that which is insignificant and non-beneficial	Imagination and fantasy	Physiological arousal	Attend, approach, explore, engage (Greenberg & Paivio, 1997)
Disgust (*nafrah/bughḍ*)	Avoidance (Greenberg & Paivio, 1997)	Flee (Greenberg & Paivio, 1997)	Mischaracterization of the object of disgust, misattribution Dislike of spiritual objects and beings (al-Birgivī, 2011, p. 318)	Dissociation	Activation in insular regions of the brain	Flight response, grimacing response
Protective Jealousy (*ghayrah*)	Protect and preserve that which is highly valued (al-Birgivī, 2011, p. 254)	Protect	Impulsive aggressive response that does harm	Sense of honor violated All or nothing	Adrenaline released, fight/flight system activated	Fight/engage response activated

Competing theorists utilize the Canon–Bard theory, which states that physiology and cognition occur simultaneously, leading to later emotional experience or evaluation (Bear, Connors, & Paradiso, 2007). The latter theory is typically favored more by CBT-oriented psychologists, given their primary focus on changing cognitions in order to modify emotional reaction.

Emotion-focused theorists hold firm to the notion that undifferentiated physiological experiences lie in the body and are precognitive, though meaning is formed within the social contexts of the human experience. This is known as "dialectical constructivism". Thus, the process of meaning-making is inherently triggered by basic biological instinctual drives that are then consolidated and translated through social experiences. These instinctual drives may be supported and permitted expression, or may be deemed socially undesirable and thus inhibited or prohibited. Emotional expression is thus bound to the cultural contexts of the organism. Therefore, this interaction of preconceptual biological drives articulated through language and socialization influences the construction of its meaning. This works bidirectionally in that the constructed meanings of emotions can also influence emotional expression. For example, social messages such as "it is unmanly to cry" may inhibit instinctual grief impulses, thereby impacting the range of emotional expressions available to men living in those cultural contexts.

While emotion-focused therapy lays emphasis on biological drives, it is still situated within the post-modernist, humanistic school of thought. Thus, EFT theorists believe in the core human good that possesses an inherent orientation toward that which is adaptive. They believe that the human being has an inherent instinct for meaning-making and growth. Through the removal of environmental constraints and judgements to allow experiences to emerge, human beings will flourish and become fully self-actualized. The therapist must provide a phenomenological or semi-directive approach that permits and encourages emotional expressions which will lead naturally to transformation and the correction of pathology. This transformation consists of the modification of maladaptive emotions to adaptive emotional expressions that ultimately reunifies the instinctual biological drives/needs with the patient's newly acquired social context, i.e. the therapy forum. Such corrective therapeutic experiences in essence restructure the pathological emotion schemes that previously were not permitted to be expressed in an adaptive way. Thus, the therapist's role is to heighten, facilitate, and stay empathically attuned to the patient to allow for the expression of maladaptive emotion, and through this therapeutic context a restructuring of the pathological emotion scheme toward adaptive expression will emerge. There are several tools utilized to heighten and facilitate emotional expression that allow movement toward identification of adaptive needs and transformation. However, they propose that the therapist must work solely with emergent experiences and attune themselves to those provided by the patient without introducing their own motives or ideas in the meaning-making process.

Dialectical Humanistic Constructivism vs. TIIP Trilectual Constructivism

TIIP theory can accommodate the evolutionary psychological view of emotions as containing adaptive survival instincts. However, TIIP provides a greater differentiation of these drives and believes that instinctually pre-wired drives have multiple origins. That is, the instinctual human desires for adaptive expression do not lie solely within the context of a human being as an animal with biological needs expressed within a social context. Rather, these needs and instincts also include the metaphysical energies that have an affinity for the Divine and the afterlife. The inherent desire for meaning, belief in a greater power, and existential questions regarding the purpose of life are unsatisfactorily addressed by evolutionary psychology. Therefore, while the drive for the adaptive expression of needs through the vehicle of emotions is acknowledged by TIIP, the inclusion of the metaphysical aspect of human needs and drive is a salient aspect of TIIP's underlying ontological structure of the human being.

Dialectical constructivism rooted within humanistic experiential psychotherapies focus on the origins of a core goodness. Islamic belief also corroborates this idea, as expressed by the concept of the *fitrah* and inherent survival drives built into the soul (*rūḥ*). However, contrary to humanistic notions that take more of a phenomenological approach leading to an overly permissive stance that embraces any emergent experience, an Islamic psychotherapy would help make the distinction between whether unfolding articulations of needs through emotional expressions are truly adaptive or manifestations of the untrained infantile hedonistic wishes of the *nafs ammārah bi-l-sū'*. Although the art of psychotherapy would demand a nuanced approach to such differentiation, utilization of strategies found within motivational interviewing fit closer with Islamic notions of identifying and resolving incongruence between values and wishes. This may be seen as a more directive "empathic attending approach" in listening and directing attention to that which is adaptive. Since complete objectivity can never be achieved, and is a fallacy found in non-directive therapies, a semi-directive approach that is rooted in a shared theology between patient and therapist might warrant subtle and skillful direction with more attention paid to some experiences over others.

Trialectical Constructivism

Chapter 1 illustrated the TIIP ontological framework, succinctly described as the position of the majority of Islamic discursive theologians (*jumhūr*) on the human psyche by Imām al-Bayjūrī. In this chapter our focus is on the human experience as it relates to the three components of *'aql*, *rūḥ*, and *nafs*, or perhaps a trialectical constructivist paradigm.

In his *'Awārif al-Ma'ārif*, ascetic scholar Imām Shihāb al-Dīn Yaḥyā al-Suhrawardī (d.632 AH/1234 CE) offers a similar and complementary ontological structure, and describes the heart (*qalb*) as ultimately reflecting the tensions between the pulls of the spirit (*rūḥ*) and the lower *nafs*, thereby, either becoming more inclined toward the animalistic side of the self, resulting in the blackening of the heart, or showing an inclination toward the spirit (*rūḥ*) that yields its radiance and enlightenment (al-Suhrawardī, 1993, p. 248). In this treatise, Imām al-Suhrawardī discusses several different positions regarding the spirit (see Chapter 4), but ultimately offers that there are two types of *rūḥ* that are contained by the human being (al-Suhrawardī, 1993, p. 248). The *rūḥ ḥayawānī basharī* or the spirit is the spirit of the human as an organism which serves as the life force (*ḥayātī*). This *ruūḥ ḥayawānī* contains survival instincts that are not exclusively unique to human beings, but are shared with other animals. The excesses of these animalistic inclinations are expressed by the *nafs ammārah bi-l-sū'* either through carnal/appetitive desires (*quwwat al-shahwiyyah*) or predatory instincts (*quwwat al-ghaḍabiyyah*). On the other hand, the *rūḥ 'ulwī samāwī* or the exalted celestial spirit contains an affinity for the divine. Its expression can be manifested by the *'aql* that captures and articulates the knowledge that is accessed through the elevation of the *rūḥ samāwī* (al-Suhrawardī, 1993, p. 252). By this process of elevation (*taraqqī*), the *rūḥ samāwī* is capable of attaining knowledge (*'ilm*) and gnosis of Allah (*ma'rifah*). This is an experience that the lovers of Allah enjoy, finding great satisfaction in beholding the presence of the Divine. The central mechanism for unlocking the elevation and potential of the *rūḥ samāwī* is by spiritual exercises (*riyāḍāt*) designed to tame, train, and go against the lower self. By this process of inclining toward the dictates of the *rūḥ samāwī*, it becomes free of the *nafs ammārah bi-l-sū'* and the *nafs* enters the state of *nafs muṭma'innah* (al-Suhrawardī, 1993, p. 251). As a result of this internal battle between *rūḥ samāwī/nafs muṭma'innah* and *nafs ammārah* there exists the tension of *qabḍ* (constriction) and *basṭ* (expansion), the feeling of being confined and grief-stricken or free and liberated. However, this is a stage of ascendency, and once surpassed, the *nafs* sheds its carnal desires and this tension is relieved. It becomes free of the shackles of the lowly carnal/animalistic desires. The desires of the *nafs muṭma'innah* become unified with the divine will of Allah in complete submission and obedience to His demands, feeling a sense of serenity and contentment.

Imām al-Suhrawardī in his *'Awārif* further describes a unique Qur'ānic concept of the *sirr* (20:7) or the hidden secret or mystery. He describes it is a stage of gnosis of the divine that is attained through continuous elevation such that one reaches a stage of elevation that is known as the hidden secret. This concept of the *sirr* is also mentioned by the great eighteenth-century Indian reformer and traditionist Shāh Walī Allah al-Dihlawī (d.1175 AH/1772 CE), who describes an even higher state known as the *akhfā* or deeply mysterious or hidden. Imām al-Suhrawardī does not discuss the *akhfā* or the *sirr* of the *sirr* that is mentioned by others such as Abū Nasīr Sarrāj al-Ṭūsī, who differentiates the two in his *al-lama' fī al-taṣawwuf* by stating that in the stage of the *sirr* one is consciously aware of internal experiences and potential divine unveilings, while the *sirr al-sirr* or *akhfā* exists at an unconscious level for the believer (al-Ṭūsī, 1914, p. 354). The concept of the *akhfā* and *sirr* is discussed in the Qur'ān and exegetists have attempted to describe its potential meanings. The famous historian and exegete Imām Muḥammad b. Jarīr al-Ṭabarī (d.310 AH/923 CE) cites several potential interpretations of this verse (20:7) that mentions *sirr* and *akhfā*. Among them he describes the *akhfā* as reported by the famous exegete companion of the Messenger of Allah (peace and blessings be upon him) Ibn Abbās (may the mercy of Allah be upon him): "it is what Allah has put in the heart of the believer regarding that which has he/she has not done (yet)." Another position attributed to Ibn 'Abbās is "that which is to occur in the future that is only known to Allah", while another interpretation he mentions is that the *akhfā* is even more hidden than the *sirr* and it is that which is not yet contained by conscious internal self-dialogue (*Ḥadīth al-nafs*) of the psyche.

While the *'aql* is mentioned by Imām al-Suhrawardī, he sees it as a part of the *rūḥ*, rather than as an independent aspect—it bears the expressions of the *rūḥ*—whereas the early ascetic scholar Imām Ḥārith al-Muḥāsibī (d.243 AH/857 CE) offers that it is an inherent disposition (*gharīzah*) that permits cognitive conception and awareness of consequences of actions (al-Muḥāsibī, 1986, p. 61). It provides the faculty for understanding necessary self-evident (*ḍarūrī*) truths, and through reflection, acquisitional truths or knowledge (*'ilm naẓarī*) can be attained (al-Bayjūrī, 2002, p. 363). Al-Muḥāsibī further states that it contains the capacity for conscious reflection, and through exercising of this faculty for contemplation (*tafakkur*), it attains lessons (*i'tibār*) that lead to true knowledge (*'ilm*). Through this process one can arrive at gnosis (*ma'rifah*) and even the perception of true existential divine reality (*haqīqah*). Thus, Imām al-Muḥāsibī is highlighting a conscious, deliberate process whereby emotions and the human experience can be impacted by conscious thought processes. He describes this by saying, "when he consciously realizes that none possesses harm nor benefit to him, neither in this world nor the hereafter except Him, he solely fears Him and puts his sole hopes in Him, feeling secure/safety in Him" (al-Muḥāsibī, 1986, p. 222).

Imām al-Ghazālī puts forward a similar approach, where he discusses how to induce emotions such as an appropriate level of fear (*khawf*) for someone who does not possess enough of it (al-Ghazālī, 1990, p. 214).

Imām al-Ghazālī recommends bringing to mind statements of revelation regarding punishment in the hereafter or the day of reckoning, and that through this one can increase adaptive fear for those who struggle with complacency. The *sirr*, on the other hand, appears to be more of an unlocking of deeper suprarational realities through intuitive cognition that can be captured after spiritual elevation and "tasting" or *dhawq* of the high planes of spiritual existence (al-Suhrawardī, 2000). *Ma'rifah*, or gnosis, occurs for the more advanced and spiritually ascended, since *'ilm* is knowledge of the apparent, while *ma'rifah* is the unfolding of its subtleties (al-Kalābādhī, 2001, p. 43); some have said that *'ilm* is within the grasp of the common man, while *ma'rifah* is exclusively attainable by the spiritually advanced (*awliyā'*) (al-Kalābādhī, 2001, p. 43). Through spiritual elevations a believer may even acquire foresight or *firāsah*. This is the capacity to see into the future, know inner realities, or have a strong intuition or sense that guides one's decision-making that is typically spot-on, as has been narrated from the speech of the early generations: "beware the foresight of the believer, for verily he sees with the light of Allah" (al-Kalābādhī, 2001, pp. 113–114; al-Tirmidhī, 1970, *Ḥadīth* 3127). Imām al-Bayjūrī outlines a type of *'aql* that is *kasbī* or acquisitional, through reasoning and learning, while the *'aql* that is *'atā'ī* is that which is given as divine guidance and enlightenment that is not subject to acquisition and is gifted (al-Bayjūrī, 2002, p. 362). Perhaps it is this subtle cognitive consciousness or intuition that is being described by this type of non-volitional *'aql*, *akhfā*, or aspects of the *sirr* that all point to the presence of an intuitive or experiential cognition that lies below the immediately accessible cognitive consciousness, in contrast to more deliberate rational processes.

In summary of the above, a mapping of the different aspects of experiences is provided that occur and can be expressed in the form of emotions is provided in Figure 7.1. This mapping outlines human experiences as emerging out of the *nafs*, *rūḥ*, or *'aql*.

Nafs and Rūḥ

Origins of emotions can thus arise out of the *nafs ammārah*, that feels a sense of happiness and pleasure upon confronting sensual desires and anger with the denial of attaining these aims. The denial of these lowly aspects is directed by the *nafs lawwāmah*, which serves as a moral compass that induces shame in an effort to shape and develop the *nafs ammārah*. During the process of disciplining the *nafs ammārah*, and the ensuing battle between listening to the lower self or attempting to reform it, the individual moves between the experiences of *qabḍ* (contraction/constriction) and *basṭ* or expansiveness. During *qabḍ*, the individual has emotional experiences of grief and feeling down, while during the stage of *basṭ* there is relief and great degrees of joy. The vacillation between these two poles

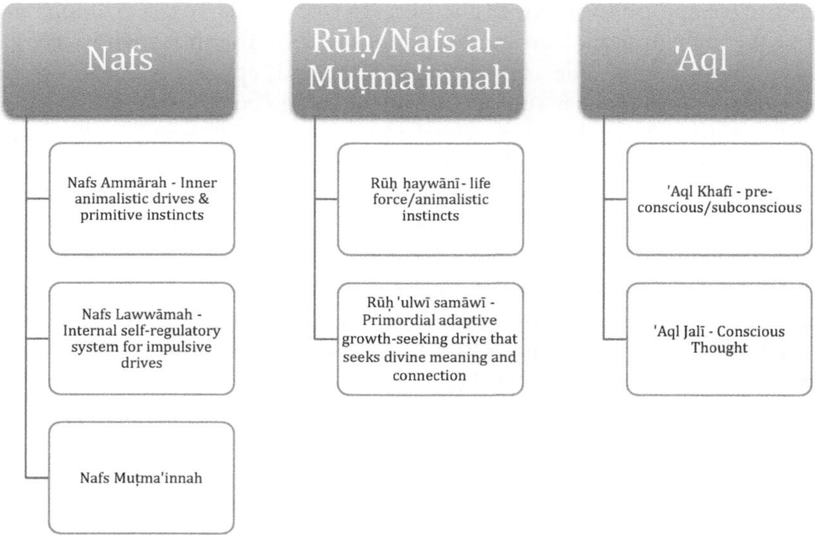

Figure 7.1 The potential origins of emotional experiences.

continues until the tension is resolved and moves into the stage of more constancy, which is felt when in the state of *nafs muṭma'innah* and which is in tune with the pull of the *rūḥ samāwī* (al-Suhrawardī, 1993, p. 251).

Thus, emotional experiences can emerge out of any of the three aspects of the *nafs*. Ibn al-Jawziyyah, in his *kitāb al-rūḥ*, contrasts emotional experiences that can seem to be similar but may be expressed differently, depending on whether they are experienced by the *nafs ammārah* or *nafs muṭma'innah* (al-Jawziyyah, 2002, p. 340). He gives the example of the fear/humility (*khushū'*) experienced as part of one's consciousness of God on account of faith that arises out of the *nafs muṭma'innah* in contrast to the superficial or instrumental expressions of humility of a hypocrite that arise out of the *nafs ammārah*. Another example he gives is assertiveness (*ḥamiyyah*) for the protection of the self or for the sake of Allah in contrast to selfish aggression (*ghaḍab*). Thus, any emotion, such as anger or happiness, can be rooted and sourced in a different element of the psyche.

'Aql

Emotions can also arise out of conscious, deliberate conceptions of the *'aql* that is acquisitional (*kasbī*). Conversely, they may be due to non-volitionally (*'aṭā'ī*) inspired insights/thought processes that are expressions of spiritual elevation and *tafakkur* (contemplation), i.e. the *sirr*. For example, as mentioned previously, al-Ghazālī cites an approach of inducing fear by reflecting on verses of scripture that discuss the punishments in the afterlife. In contrast, emotions can also arise out of more subtle and unconscious thought processes that influence human emotional experience. For example, belief in one's superiority over others (*kibr*) or self-fascination (*'ujb*) can serve as a subtle influence and source of feeling angry when other people pay little attention to such an individual (al-Birgivī, 2011, p. 259). Another example could be the gratification that one may feel on account of being perceived as pious and being observed while praying in public (*riyā'*). Alternatively, reaching the higher planes of spiritual ascension can unveil realities (*ma'rifah*) that can be accompanied by experiential subjective states, though this aspect will typically lie outside of the purview of psychotherapy to explore.

As already mentioned, while Islamic scholars typically discuss the soul's wide range of experiences with an acute focus on higher spiritual experiences that go deeper than mere emotional experience, this chapter will restrict the discussion to emotions, as it is beyond the scope of this chapter to consider more subtle spiritual experiences. A focus on spirituality and a deeper reflection on metaphysical truths is found in Chapter 10.

A Traditional Islamically Integrated Approach to Working with Emotions

Islamic scholars of the past have placed a great deal of emphasis on cognitive reconstruction as one of the main approaches to regulating or adjusting emotion. This top-down strategy is an important process, and it is perhaps necessary to cognitively internalize healthy beliefs in order to mitigate negative emotional reactions to environmental stressors. Abū Zayd al-Balkhī devotes a considerable amount of attention to this in his treatise on the sustenance of the soul (al-Balkhī, 2013). This top-down strategy has been demonstrated to be effective in cognitive therapies, but perhaps it is most effective as a preventative measure (Beck, 1967; Seligman, 2011; Seligman, Reivich, Jaycox, & Gillham, 1995). In contrast, Islamic ascetic scholars may at times opt to work in a more bottom-up fashion by working directly with the spiritual process through interventions like Islamic contemplative meditation (*murāqabah*). Similarly, emotion-focused psychotherapy places a great deal of emphasis on working in a bottom-up fashion, believing that using only a top-down approach for emotionally-laden problems can have limited efficacy. This is reinforced by research that demonstrates that cognition is almost always transformed when emotions are changed, while the converse does not necessarily hold true, i.e. emotional dysregulation can remain, despite cognitive change (Greenberg, 2004). Thus, effective emotional processing in sessions will ultimately evoke all that is associated and wired to the emotions that may not otherwise be knowable through pure cognitive processing. The essence of transformation in such experiential work lies in the activation of these emotions and by working through the process identified below.

The Emotional Process of Change

This section provides an explication of the general emotional unfolding process that can be induced in psychotherapy upon detection of emotions that require attention. As opposed to working cognitively or behaviorally, the therapist is working from the level of emotional experience and will consequently and indirectly also trigger cognitions and behavioral inclinations during this process. Figure 7.2 demonstrates this process or cycle of emotional experience. First, patients who present for therapy may describe emotional experiences without conscious awareness of their origins or underlying needs. During the process of working with patients, a trilectical constructivistic approach will entail attempting to gather more

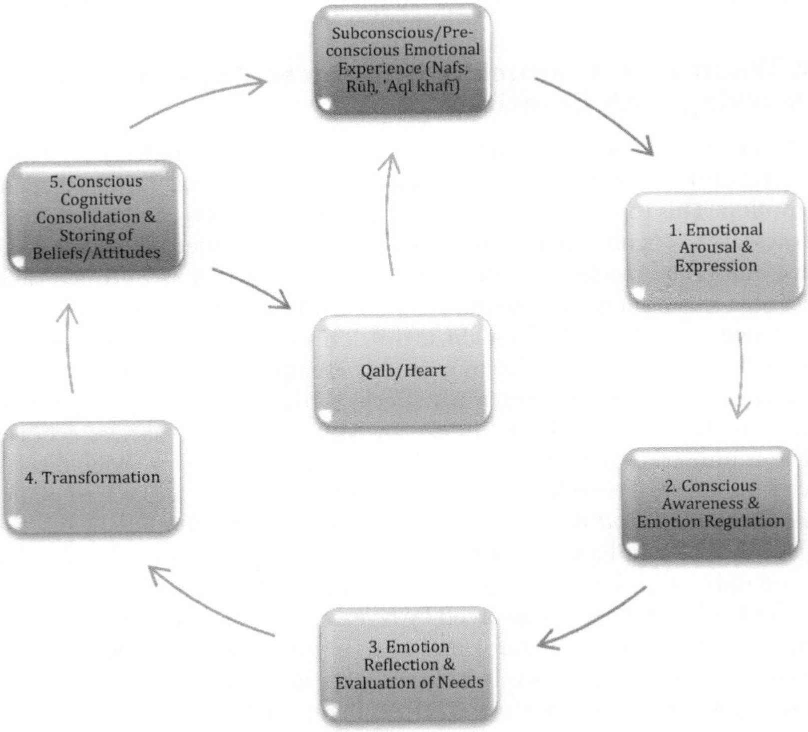

Figure 7.2 Process of emotional awareness and transformation.

information through evoking such emotions. It is important to note that in order to understand all that is associated with the emotions, the TIIP therapist must attempt to evoke them. Once emotions become expressed through the therapeutic process, the patient begins to become more consciously aware of their underlying origins, associated needs, memories, or thought processes. This is consistent with TIIP's goal of achieving introspective awareness (*inkishāf*). As EFT psychotherapy articulates, the pain compass is a useful tool in helping hone in on the most poignant experiences. In listening carefully for pain, the therapist, like the physician, will begin to press gently on the areas surrounding the pain until the wounds are identified. Full awareness of all that is associated with the patient's emotions cannot simply be attained cognitively or retroactively.

It is also useful for the practitioner to observe this process first hand rather than rely on a subjective report of emotional states that occur for the patient outside of the therapy room. After such awareness has been gained, the needs underlying the patient's emotions will begin to emerge during sessions. This is a critical juncture of the therapeutic process and is the bridge that leads to transformation. The therapist will not rush to discuss needs, but will patiently work with and explore the depths of the emotions, providing them full expression until the underlying needs begin to emerge naturally. After this process of need identification, the patient typically begins to move out of the subjective feeling or experience of emotions in a natural manner, as the intensity starts to subside. The therapist then works with the patient to evaluate their needs in the context of their origins (i.e. *rūḥ*, *nafs*, or *'aql*) and whether they can reasonably be acquired given the social context of the patient. For example, the patient may describe a sense of feeling neglected by their spouse and needing connection. The *nafs ammārah* may intensify this feeling, propelling a desire for retribution and aggression. However, the *rūḥ samāwī/nafs muṭma'innah* may demand selflessness, patience, and accommodation of the other, and encourage the patient to converse with their spouse to discuss how to balance these competing needs. These needs may also be checked against the patient's moral compass (*nafs lawwāmah*) and potential environmental constraints in meeting them. For example, the patient may realize that their spouse is unable to provide this need for connection in the way they desire, such as in the case where their spouse may have a disability. Thus, they may need to exercise patience (*ṣabr*), recognizing that their immediate temporal environment cannot meet this need.

This is where eschatology plays a role in coping with psychological distress in generating acceptance through the recognition of the limitations of the ephemeral world in meeting all of one's needs. 'Izz al-Dīn b. 'Abd al-Salām (d.660 AH/1262 CE), in his treatise *Fawā'id al-Balwā wa-l-Miḥan* or *The Benefits of Trials and Tribulations*, states that trials and tribulations can be reframed as an opportunity for divine connection during difficulty.

The believer will trust that His compassionate Lord decrees that which is good for him/her despite his/her lack of immediate awareness of it and the pain associated with the difficulty. This realization engenders a sense of contentment with the Divine decree (*riḍā bi-l-Qaḍā'*), eventual satisfaction, and gratitude (Ibn 'Abd al-Salām, 2005, p. 12). However, during emotionally oriented work, this realization can be achieved only after evocation of the emotional pain. After such emotional processing and emergence of needs, cognitive changes and consolidation may emerge to make meaning of one's suffering. A dry religious intervention of psychoeducation or preaching would prove ineffective as the patient must create a personal relationship and deeper experiential connection with such emergent experiences. Upon the completion of this process, it is theorized that the patient will a have a fuller awareness of self and ability to control these emotions that may be triggered by their environment in the future, thereby dampening the intensity of an unregulated emotional response that may be associated with maladaptive feelings and reactions.

Principles/Mechanism for Emotional Change

This section provides greater specificity on the first four processes mentioned above (see Figure 7.3) in order to provide four strategies for the facilitation of emotional activation and transformation. The activation of the aforementioned emotion schemes is necessary to access the

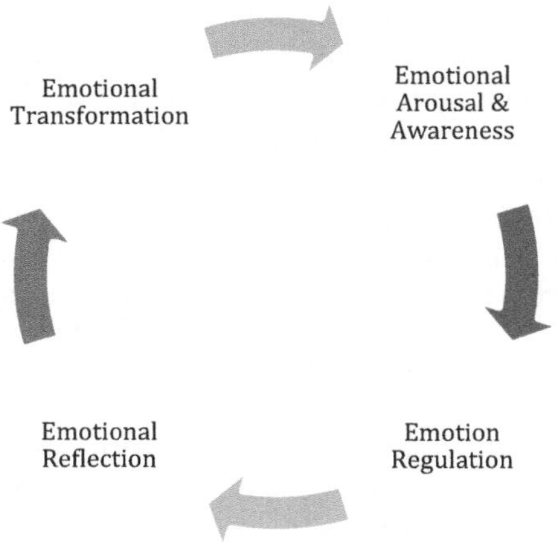

Figure 7.3 Mechanism of emotional change.

network of associated information for emotional processing. Processing emotions is necessary in the endeavor to reverse unhealthy emotional schemes that have been encoded over time. Therapists should aim to expand the patient's experiential range and depth, and the meaning that accompanies their feelings (Paivio & Pascual-Leone, 2010).

To identify the kind of processing necessary for the expression of a specific emotion, four strategies can be used. The first involves the attainment of **emotional awareness and increased emotional arousal**. Experiencing emotions deeply using empathic exploration achieves emotional arousal, which activates emotion schemes that can provide insight and awareness into patients' experiences (Paivio & Pascual-Leone, 2010). Once arousal is achieved, it becomes necessary to manage intense emotion. The second principle of emotional change requires **emotional regulation**. A patient's capacity for emotional regulation is assessed and the therapist provides self-soothing coping strategies that allow the patient to tolerate and explore painful emotions (Paivio & Pascual-Leone, 2010). Providing psychological distance affords patients the opportunity to examine and articulate their experiences by viewing them as useful information. Distressing experiences thereby not only become manageable, but are also reconstructed meaningfully (Pascual-Leone & Greenberg, 2006). The third principle of emotion change is **reflection on emotion**. Reflection encourages self-awareness and provides patients the opportunity to understand problematic or reactive feelings, and to make sense of emotional reactions that they find confusing. Reflection necessitates that both therapist and patient adopt a discovery-oriented approach to understanding client narratives and stories of emotion (Paivio & Pascual-Leone, 2010). It is during the reflection stage that the needs emerge. Lastly, **emotional transformation** occurs when the core concern of emotional suffering has been revealed. The maladaptively expressed emotions that have been aroused, expressed, and reflected upon start to subside during this phase of treatment, and the point of transformation can be facilitated. At this point, needs are evaluated and the therapist attempts to move the patient into emotional transformation. In order to facilitate emotional transformation, therapists continue to provide empathic attunement to distressing emotions while supporting the concurrent but contrasting development of adaptive emotions (Paivio & Pascual-Leone, 2010). Patients are therefore able to replace maladaptive response patterns with newly emerged adaptive emotions. Enactments and imaginary dialogues are tasks that are utilized to symbolically and experientially parse apart maladaptive from adaptive emotions (Paivio & Pascual-Leone, 2010). The use of these strategies leads patients to arrive at the identification of personal emotional needs and mobilizes them in striving to fulfill their adaptive emotions.

TIIP Assessment and Decision-Making on Doing Emotional Work

After initial sessions, prior to engaging in the above process, the TIIP practitioner must make a decision as to which aspects of the patient's psyche they plan on addressing first. If the practitioner opts to work with any of the non-emotion-focused domains, such as cognition or behavior, it is recommended that before venturing to offer any directive interventions, they utilize some initial emotion-focused relationship-building strategies such as therapeutic attunement. This will ensure that the cognitive work they provide will be strengthened as it rests upon the bedrock of a strong therapeutic alliance and understanding of the patient. The TIIP practitioner may lack some clarity in identifying the most salient locus of the problem and in deciding which component of the human psyche to focus on. Some indicators of a need to start with emotion are:

- If the patient demonstrates unclear, vague, or confusing content. This may be in the form of offering information about various different topics and having a difficult time focusing on or articulating their main problem(s). This is an indicator that, rather than attempting to organize the overwhelmingly abundant sum of thoughts or themes highlighted by the patient, the practitioner should venture to take a more bottom-up processing approach. This requires shifting the focus of the patient to their most salient emotional experiences by inquiring about the "experience" rather than the story. Gendlin's (1978, 1996) focusing task can help orient a patient to the most salient aspects of their psychological dilemmas. If the therapist takes a cognitive approach, they risk engaging in surface-level work, overwhelming the patient, or ignoring the more poignant emotions that are contained underneath the surface of the psyche of the patient.
- If the patient exhibits undifferentiated or unregulated emotions. In such circumstances, the patient may exhibit different emotions but it is unclear as to what seems primary or secondary, and this indicates a degree of emotional confusion. The patient may have a difficult time expressing or pinpointing the source of their issues, and feel surprised, overwhelmed, or unable to control and understand their seemingly random emotions. These are cues to the therapist to start phenomenological work with the patient, allowing the emerging emotions to surface in sessions that will, over time, facilitate unfolding and organization.
- If the patient describes a clear understanding of their problems and even has a rational evaluation and response to their feelings. For example, the patient may discuss losing a job but cognitively may have

an easy response by stating that they are coping by relying on Allah. Another example could be that the patient states that they should be grateful for all that they have in life, describing their privileged status relative to others, and yet still feels depressed. Despite cognitive clarity, the patient still feels unpleasant emotions and is visiting a therapist in an attempt to remove these unpleasant experiences. Such cases are commonplace in psychotherapeutic settings and require a bottom-up approach. The therapist may provide psychoeducation on the value of emotional expression and elicit the participation of the patient in their willingness to uncover emotional experiences that lie below the surface. Patients will need to be prepared to understand that, in order to feel better, they must go through potentially emotionally unpleasant feelings, as these will be triggered and heightened within the therapeutic encounter. Thus, the patient will not be able to get past emotions until they are processed.

- If the patient exhibits emotions rather quickly without being prompted for greater depth by the therapist. The patient may instantly start to tear up, display frustration or anxiety, or demonstrate shame. Such emotional expressions are clear signals that there are unresolved, emotionally-laden issues that must be addressed and that require expression. The instant ability to show such emotions is also an indicator that the patient is coming apart psychologically rather quickly. The evidence that the intensity of their distress is breaking through normative defenses and inhibitions by demonstrating vulnerable emotions prior to establishing a trusting alliance with their therapist.
- If the patient displays under-expression of emotions. Lack of expression of emotions is a signal that typically goes undetected. It is strange for the patient to discuss intense emotional pain without expressing it during a session. They may feel very comfortable intellectualizing their problems and be looking for cognitive interventions. However, their description of internal pain while demonstrating no expression of that pain is an indication that the therapist needs to start to penetrate the layers of experience to enliven and vivify the emotions being discussed in the session.
- If the patient discloses unresolved psychological trauma that impacts them in the form of traumatic symptoms. These include post-traumatic stress disorder (PTSD) or less pronounced trauma symptoms. The patient may easily dissociate as a protective mechanism or attempt to avoid their emotions for fear of becoming retraumatized. Such signals require careful treading and building of the therapeutic alliance toward eventual emotional reprocessing of such experiences within the safety of the therapeutic space.

Interventions

Emotional Attunement and Therapeutic Presence

Emotional attunement through an empathic prescence is necessary in order to be able to help facilitate the first process of emotional arousal and awareness. The Prophet of Islam (peace and blessings be upon him) is a great example of empathy and his attention to the emotional experiences of his subjects. Though he spoke little, when he did speak, his words were concise, comprehensive, and rich in meaning. His companions described him as *jawāmi' al-kalim* or the encompassor of speech (al-Tirmidhī, n.d., book 33, *Ḥadīth* 215). He selected his words carefully and had an acute awareness of the impact of speech upon others. Similarly, it is important for practitioners to note that the instruments of their interventions are their words. Thus, they must select the words they use and the timing of them carefully. The overall goal is to help move and facilitate the introspective and emotional journey for the patient. Thus, being too verbose can cause an interruption and disruption of processing for the patient. The Messenger of Allah (peace and blessings be upon him) advised his companion Mu'ādh b. Jabal (may Allah be pleased with him), "Verily, you will continue to be safe as long as you remain silent; if you speak, it will be recorded for you or against you" (al-Ṭabrānī, 1984, *Ḥadīth* 16591). The appropriate use of silence can be an important aspect of the attunement vehicle for the thoughtful selection of speech.

Additionally, therapeutic attunement to the most poignant and relevant emergent experiences are key in helping to facilitate deeper experiential work. This requires focus and an ear for hearing the emotions of the patient, and to provide empathic reflections that help symbolize this for the patient. A concept coined "listening with the third ear" (Reik, 1948) is described as allowing oneself to be touched by the depth of patient's experience by relying on all senses and being completely attuned to verbal and non-verbal expressions and exchanges in therapeutic encounters (Geller & Greenberg, 2012).

Presence, considered foundational for effective therapy, is defined as being engaged in the moment and using one's essence to attend and respond to patients (Clarkson, 1997; Kempler, 1970; Lietaer, 1993; Robbins, 1998; Vanaerschot, 1993). The Messenger of Allah (peace and blessings be upon him) used to attend to each individual that he interacted with. 'Ā'ishah (may Allah be pleased with her) relates to her surprise that, on one occasion, a deceitful person asked permission to see the Prophet (peace and blessings be upon him) and the Prophet (peace and blessings be upon him) spoke to him in a very gentle and kind manner. He gave them his complete attention by facing them, and not withdrawing his hand from their hand after a handshake until they let go (al-Tirmidhī, 1970, *Ḥadīth* 37, 2678). Each person that interacted with him believed that they were the most important and beloved person to him. This was irrespective of the age of the person. He exemplified the characteristic of compassion, and empathy was found in his transformative personality and presence. He showed empathy to the womenfolk of his household in his ability to capture their emotions, and to children by inquiring about details of events, such as his empathizing with a child's loss of a pet bird (al-Tirmidhī, n.d., book 35, *Ḥadīth* 226). The Messenger of Allah (peace and blessings be upon him) once said to his wife 'Ā'ishah (may Allah be pleased with her): "I know when you are pleased with me or upset with me." She replied, "How do you know that?" He said, "When you are pleased with me, you say, 'No, by the Lord of Muhammad, but when you are angry with me, then you say, 'No, by the Lord of Ibrahim'" (al-Bukhārī, 2010, *Ḥadīth* 5228). This empathic attunement to the experiences of others, and even the labeling of their internal experiences, is a key aspect of empathy and building a connection. The Messenger of Allah (peace and blessings be upon him) empathized to the degree that he felt the pain of others. The Qur'ān describes his character in saying, "Verily a Messenger has come to you from among yourselves. Your suffering distresses him: he is deeply concerned for you and full of kindness and mercy towards the believers" (9:128). He was described to have been continuously in a state of internal grief and concern (al-Tirmidhī, n.d., book 33, *Ḥadīth* 215) and he prayed for the relief of the believers (al-Bukhārī, 2010, book 60, *Ḥadīth* 683). Upon hearing the stories of others or seeing pain inflicted upon them, at times he could not help but shed tears himself (al-Bukhārī, 2010, book 23 *Ḥadīth* 63).

This aspect of attuning to the pain of others through the pain compass is essential to emotionally oriented therapy, as it alerts therapists to the most poignant aspects of the patient's experience, thus formulating the focus of therapy (Greenberg, 2002). Given that emotions are central to the client's experience, the pain compass (Elliot et al., 2004) is used to uncover the emotion schemes that most often have some adaptive origins. A common sequence is for patients to start by attending to external events, then move back and forth between reflection on meaning and accessing and expressing emotions (Angus & Greenberg, 2011).

Deepening/Heightening of Emotions

The articulation of distressing and difficult emotions can trigger emotional avoidance responses from the patient. Therapists must remain carefully attuned to patient experiences and maintain the focus in sessions to deepen and heighten experiences, in order to successfully explore and process emotions. While it may seem counterintuitive, exploring painful emotions will facilitate a process by which patients will be able to overcome blocks and obstacles to letting go of maladaptive emotions and forming new adaptive patterns. When emotions appear in the form of a feeling but the patient struggles to articulate the experience, a focusing task (Gendlin,

1978, 1996) can help patients to direct their concentration inward to symbolize, to feel internal bodily experiences, and to understand what they want to do (Elliot et al., 2004). Alternatively, guided imagery known as *taṣawwur* (see case illustration) can also be utilized. There are many response modes that can be used to enable patients to effectively engage with their experiences and facilitate moment-to-moment processing. A foundational strategy involves the use of empathetic understanding, reflection, and affirmation in the form of validation to communicate to patients that the therapist is understanding and supportive of the patient's difficulties. Empathetic responses demand that the therapist approach the divulging of sensitively shared information with genuine care (Elliot et al., 2004).

Having created a safe and collaborative space for patient experiences to emerge, empathetic exploration of responses can occur. This can entail exploratory reflections delivered tentatively to ensure the therapist has understood the patient. Leading open-edge responses is one strategy that allows patients to build upon complex aspects of experience (Elliot et al., 2004). Additionally, evocative reflections can be used to draw upon vivid imagery and powerful, dramatic, or expressive language to intensify and heighten experiencing (Elliot et al., 2004). Therapists can offer metaphors that relate to patient experiences, such as describing an open wound when discussing feelings of emptiness. In doing so, it is appropriate to ask exploratory questions as well as checking in with patients—asking questions such as "does that fit?"—to encourage patients to evaluate the accuracy of the therapist's understanding of their experience (Elliot et al., 2004). Process observations throughout the interaction assist with orienting the patient to their non-verbal cues, such as commenting on a patient's clenched fists when discussing emotions of anger. Acknowledgement of non-verbal cues often encourages the exploration of blocked feelings not yet articulated.

Using empathic conjectures also offers patients the opportunity to formulate feelings that have not been expressed, and deepen experiencing by putting words to their feelings (Elliot et al., 2004). Often, it is easier for patients to recognize words that fit their experience from conjectures made by the therapist, rather than having to recall them from memory. As patients endeavor to express and make meaningful sense of experiences, it is not uncommon for them to get lost in thought and disengage from emotional vulnerability, explaining external events with plot and characters. It is the therapist's task to maintain patient's focus and orient them inward. It is important that patients stay in the present moment and remain at the level of their experiences. Therapists can use the insight and information uncovered through deepening experiences to begin process-guiding (Elliot et al., 2004). Process-guiding responses can be experiential formulations that underscore important aspects of client experiences that inform the conceptualization of patient difficulties (Elliot et al., 2004). Furthermore, process-guiding also includes a more directive approach of experiential teaching or the introduction of structuring tasks, whereby therapists suggest therapeutic strategies, after identifying a marker, in order to prime patients for a specific activity (Elliot et al., 2004).

Marker-Oriented Emotion-Focused Psychotherapy

This section highlights some of the markers that can serve as helpful cues for appropriate interventions to accompany the marker. However, note that all interventions described are to be viewed simply as tools to heighten and facilitate emotional expression, processing, and transformation.

Self–Self

During the course of work with the patient, several competing voices may emerge. One such voice may be that of the *nafs ammārah*, the more pleasure-seeking aspect of the self. Though the lower *nafs* is motiviated by *shahwah* (desires), which serves as the underlying base appetitive drives, not all of its desires should be completely subdued or repressed. In fact, appetitive drives are necessary for basic survival, and when these are not excessive, then they are referred to simply as *nafs* (al-Ghazali, 2011, pp. 16–17). This is especially the case when the patient reports feeling overly constricted or suffocated. Therefore, the patient may start to express the themes of feeling constrained, burdened, heavy, or needing to be freed. This may be the result of an inability simply to have leisure time, free time, or to enjoy the pleasures of permissible hobbies. Thus, the therapist must stay closely attuned to the theme of feeling trapped, attempt to give voice to this feeling, and use heightening mechanisms to extract and arrive at the call for the softening of some of the grips of the *nafs lawwāmah*.

Alternatively, the voice of the *nafs lawwāmah* or *wā'iẓ* is typically among the loudest voices in the psyche for those who have internalized a strong consciousness that has been learned through their environment, such as religious education or parental upbringing. This voice typically is the voice of the critic. Its adaptive function is to promote propriety and to restrain appetitive drives. It is focused on personal development, excellence, and productivity. However, when this voice becomes overgeneralized, it can induce a sense of *qabḍ* or shrinking and seizure. It can feel like it is choking the sense of self or the inner personality composition of the self or *mizāj*. Abū Zayd al-Balkhī illustrates this in his saying that individuals have varying predispositions contingent upon their original makeup or inherent composition (*aṣl tarkībi-h*). In the face of environmental triggers, some are quick to become emotionally agitated while others may have a cooler temperament (al-Balkhī, 2005, p. 115). Thus, for someone who may have certain predispositions, overly repressing this energy can lead to a sense of constriction or feeling of suffocation. Al-Birgivī relates that character formation interacts with the varying temperaments of individuals, whereby some aspects of character may be easily achieved in some people, while acquisition proves more challenging for others (al-Birgivī, 2011, p. 154). Thus, if the *nafs lawwāmah* is overactive, it may overcompensate and, rather than simply restrain the *nafs ammārah*, exert undue pressure upon even stable personality characteristics. This can cause the self to become silenced, feel worthless, and experience intense internal shame. Alternatively, the patient may feel *basṭ*, or times of feeling freed from the grips of the *nafs lawwāmah* or calls of the *nafs ammārah*. The capacity to move toward integration that transcends this internal tension is what is desired, as mentioned above.

This marker is a signal to transition into chair work, where the critic is put in one chair and the *mizāj* or experiencing self is put in the other chair. This approach is ultimately an Islamic adaptation of EFT chair work that is more consistent with a TIIP orientation. A chart that highlights this process is provided in Figure 7.4. The process entails heightening maladaptive shame by allowing the critic to shame the self. After sufficient shaming, eventually assertive anger emerges from the self that serves to counterbalance and equalize the two sides. This causes the critic to begin to withdraw, engendering a greater sense of cohesion between the two parts, leading the critic to a greater acceptance of some of the inherent personality needs.

Alternatively, the patient may voice a sense of emptiness or lack of meaning emerging from the spirit (*rūḥ samāwī*)—an overall sense of a void, depletion, and isolation. This lack of connection to the divine can be a very lonely experience. The therapist can work with the patient's experience in order to give voice to this feeling, which may lead to the expression of the need to engage in more meaningful activities or to draw greater meaning from life. The key therapeutic intervention here is therapeutic attunement and heightening of the feeling of isolation and accompanying sadness, while patiently awaiting for signs of need emergence. This is characterized by the feeling of distance or departure from one's Beloved, i.e. Allah. Just as there are psychological developmental milestones that require the nurturance of a mother in order to generate a sense of security and self-confidence, so are there spiritual milestones that can lead to spiritual developmental arrest in the absence of spiritual connection with Allah. These signs may emerge in the form of emotions that signal an internal void and spiritual disconnection.

During emotion work prior to the consolidation phase, maladaptive attitudes encoded into the *'aql* may appear to serve as a roadblock of

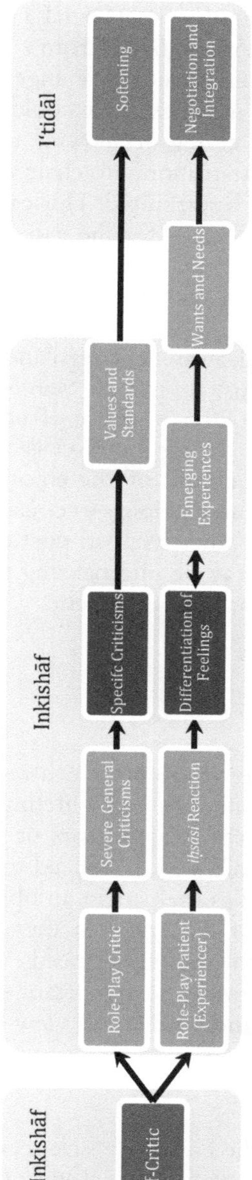

Figure 7.4 Process of change in self-criticism chair work.

emotions and inhibit their expression. For example, this could occur with someone who views feeling sadness as a sign of weakness. This is termed as the self-interruption split in EFT work. These can occur in instances where the patient is moving from secondary emotions to more primary ones, such as from maladaptive anger that serves as a cover for internal primary sadness. A key example could be where the patient starts to question the value of crying or allowing emotions to emerge. When such a marker appears, a transition into chair work with the cognitive self and the experiencing self is warranted. This can be useful in order to help address these cognitive blocks—for the experiential self to ask the cognitive self to step aside for the moment and to reintroduce itself during the phase of cognitive consolidation. Emotional expression needs to be valued during this process.

After emotional arousal, awareness, regulation, and reflection have been experienced, the conscious *'aql* may be reintegrated into the therapeutic process. This is the consolidation phase of emotional work. During this process, the *'aql* emerges during the discussion of needs or the attempt to make sense and meaning out of the emotional expressions exhibited thus far. This can be useful in helping to consolidate adaptive growth and enhance transformation. This type of post-experiential, cognitive processing can be a useful way of internalizing gains and insights acquired during the experiential phase of treatment.

Self–Other

UNFINISHED BUSINESS

At times conflicts can be experienced as a result of unfinished business or work with significant others in one's lifetime. This can include parents, who may be alive or deceased, aggressors or perpetrators of aggression, a former spouse, etc. Chair work is utilized to allow for closure of these events. Chair work provides the patient an opportunity to construct their internal representation of the other in therapy sessions with which to create a dialogue for resolving unmet needs. The patient is able to have an explicit conversation with the significant other that leads to a newly formed, more adaptive, and synthesized view of the self and the other.

TASAWWUR

Islamic scholars of the spiritual sciences utilize various spiritual interventions in psychospiritual care. One of the exercises utilized that is analogous to guided imagery is known as *taṣawwur*. This exercise is a way of enhancing spiritual connection in an experiential manner and can be emotionally powerful, evocative, and transformational. One such guided-imagery experiential exercise is known as *tasawwur al-shaykh*. This is the concept of utilizing imagery to envision the presence of a spiritual mentor sitting across from the patient, and is a spiritual exercise used by various spiritual orders (*ṭarīqah*). Although this exercise is designed primarily to activate the spirit and generally fits more neatly within spiritual interventions, it can also be used as a source of emotional evocation.

Shaykh Ḥusayn Aḥmad al-Madanī, a nineteenth-century renowned traditionist, jurist, and ascetic scholar of the Indian subcontinent, writes in his collections of letters, *maktūbāt*, (n.d., vol. 4, p. 83):

> To establish and bring a figure in the mind is linguistically called "*taṣawwur*"; this is regardless of whether it is of an animate or inanimate object, or of a famous or ordinary person, or of a saint and *walī*, or one's *shaykh*, father or mother. However, *Taṣawwur al-Shaykh* is the name commonly given to [the concept] of bringing and establishing the figure of a pious saint in one's mind, particularly the personality and face of one's spiritual guide (*murshid*) … to establish and bring the picture of one's *murshid* is beneficial and recommended by the noble Companions and the Prophet of Allah (peace and blessings be upon him). Sayyidunā Ḥasan (may Allah be pleased with him) established the picture and figure of the Messenger of Allah (peace and blessings be upon him) after repeatedly asking his maternal uncle Hind b. Abī Hālah (may Allah be pleased with him) about his features" [Qāḍī 'Iyāḍ, 2008, p. 103].
>
> (al-Madanī, n.d., vol. 4, p. 83)

This inherently Islamic intervention introduced into TIIP can be a powerful exercise for use during times of intense isolation, needing direction/advice or reassurance, or a sense of spiritual connection. For example, its can be very powerful when combined with imagery such as that of a spiritual mentor healing the psychological wounds of the patient, which can be facilitated through guided imagery. Alternatively, it can be utilized through chair work by imagining the presence of a spiritual figure sitting in the other chair and rotating between chairs, in order to arrive at a resolution, reconciliation, or transformation of one's experience.

Consolidation Phase of Gains: A Co-Constructivist Approach to Meaning-Making

In the consolidation phase of emotionally oriented psychotherapy patients naturally progress toward a desire for the cognitive evaluation of these emotional needs within their sociocultural contexts. The evoking of emotion typically renders a patient very vulnerable, and as they move toward emotional regulation and resolution of unmet needs, cognitive processing starts to emerge naturally. This aspect of meaning-making is critical in the transformation or restructuring of emotion schemes. Human beings have the potential for significant cognitive and behavioral transformation that follows the activation of emotion. This is the juncture at which the patient has emptied or exhausted emotional expression and is prepared to make decisions about how to make sense of or meet their needs. This is analogous to the idea of *takhallī* or emptying used by spiritual practitioners, and entails internal removal of the maladaptive in order to replace it with the adaptive. The successful internalization of newly acquired cognitions (*taḥallī*) will be re-embedded within a new emotion scheme that was formerly maladaptive. For example, excessive anxiety that manifests as cowardice may be replaced by assertive anger. Thus, emotions will be rewired with new memories and new cognitive evaluations that make up this new emotion scheme. Therefore, the cycle of grief being triggered by memory cues in the environment or internally will no longer evoke the same degree of intensity formerly associated with those memories. Much like the reprocessing and reconsolidation seen in trauma therapy, once the emotions have been sufficiently explored and reprocessed within a healthy therapeutic context, they will cease to contain the intensity of unregulated or dissociative reactions to emotional triggers.

The way in which one constructs meaning is very flexible and contains a diversity of creative new meanings that patients may acquire upon nearing the completion of emotional processing. The therapist is not required to transplant their own evaluation or constructed meanings into the patient, but rather is required only to help facilitate this process. This is the dance of collaboratively helping to co-construct new meaning. The therapist largely attends to the subtle expressions of growth and meaning that the patient is beginning to emit. An overall demeanor and feeling of relief, peace, and release of tension and intensity are indicators of a successful settlement into the consolidation phase. During this phase, a less pathological and more positive orientation to constructing meaning is desirable. It is not recommended that the therapist simply feed these positive reframes to the patient. Rather, the lack of the patient's ability to find positivity is an indication that they may still be blocked or stuck, and that there is still more emotional processing left to do. Thus, this process should not be rushed. In the interests of a semi-directive approach, the therapist should listen for signs of further emerging positive evaluations or experiences of the previously undergone emotional experiences. For example, the therapist may witness the emergence of adaptive anger, adaptive shame, adaptive grief, adaptive joy, etc. The key here is that the tone of the emotional expression within the context of consolidation of meaning is growth-promoting and adaptive. Once the therapist hears such voices emerging, the therapist should attend acutely to and accentuate such voices to help facilitate the consolidation of meaning-making.

The reason why this approach is seen as constructivist is on account of the fact that an event can have multiple perceptually true possibilities. This is embedded within the concept of *ḥusn al-ẓann* or positive perception of the divine or other people. For example, one can adopt a view of God as a punishing God or as a loving God, while Allah has both attributes of justice and forgiveness. Over-reliance on either of these attributes or perceptions of Allah can lead to imbalance and pathological thinking and emotions. Both perceptions are inherently true, but where the therapist directs the patient's attention will impact their emotional experience. Thus, achieving the right perceptual balance (*i'tidāl*) for the facilitation of both hope and adaptive anxiety (*khawf*) is what is desired. Another example is chair work for unfinished business with someone who has betrayed the patient, in which the patient may move to a more empathic evaluation of the perpetrator, thereby leading to forgiveness and relief. Thus, pathological emotions are countered with their adaptive opposite (al-Birgivī, 2011, p. 155). For example, excessive shame in the form of self-criticism requires assertive anger at the internal critic and self-compassion or words of self-affirmation. Excessive fear of God may require attending to verses of affirmation and compassion to counterbalance such overly activated emotional experiences. Thus, the therapist ultimately helps to uncover more adaptive reconsolidations of emotions that counter and transform both the cognitive and emotional schemes of patients.

Case Illustration

Case Summary

Aysha Gul is a 25-year-old female Turkish student who came to a college clinic at a local university in Turkey seeking out Islamically integrated psychotherapy. She identifies strongly with her faith and wears the *ḥijāb*, or headscarf. She is an undergraduate student in the School of Sociology and sought psychological services on account of her inability to "forget" her historical experiences of being persecuted for wearing the headscarf prior to recent Islamic governmental reforms that have taken place in Turkey. She describes flashbacks, dreams, and generally uneasy feelings such as nervousness or mild anxiety when congregating publicly with other Muslim women wearing headscarves. She states that this is irrational given that religious expression has become more open recently, and Muslim women no longer face the threat of public persecution. She reports that these intrusive memories and feelings can be triggered from time to time and make it difficult for her to concentrate or focus on her studies. Aysha also reports feeling quite frustrated and upset at herself for being preoccupied with these historical events and can be quite harsh with herself if she is not able to persevere or excel in her studies.

Case Conceptualization and Diagnosis According to TIIP

Aysha's psychological experience is at the level of her *iḥsās* on account of a history of trauma associated with persecution for religious expression. The dominant source of her psychological distress is emotional. The patient has unresolved feelings of sadness and anger associated with her historical experiences. The impact of her distressing experiences and rumination about her trauma on an emotional level impacts the various facets of her internal psyche, including her *ʿaql*, *rūḥ*, and behaviors in the following ways. Her irrational thoughts regarding congregation in public spaces on a cognitive level maintain her avoidant behaviors and impact her ability to fulfill her need for social and religious connection. Furthermore, self-critical thoughts of being weak and feeling as though she should get over her fears impede her ability to become aware of, regulate, and process her emotions for transformation (i.e. self-interruption split). Her self-criticisms act as a hindrance to adaptive needs for healing and spiritual connection. The result is destructive tendencies from the pain-averse aspect of her psyche, i.e. *nafs* for behavioral avoidance of social connection and religious practices, that would otherwise trigger her emotional pain. This leads to isolation and neglect of prayers and *du'ā'*. The spiritual repercussions on her *rūḥ* therefore result in a lack of religious connection, which renders her spiritually depleted as she describes a vague sense of a spiritual void. In order to fill the void, she spends a significant part of her time on social media, watching movies, and comfort-eating. The culmination of these experiences have emotional consequences of shame, guilt, depression, anxiety, and anger.

Treatment

During session five, while helping the patient unfold her emotions of feeling sadness regarding her past experiences of religious persecution, the therapist noticed that she was blocking her experiences. The therapist prompted the patient to pay attention to and focus on what was going on in her body. The patient described feeling really sad inside but could not elicit the sadness; she said that it was hard to access. The practitioner asked her to indicate where she felt the sadness while focusing on her body. The patient described feeling it in the pit of her stomach, but that there was also a block in her chest. With the practitioner's support, she described feeling that the sadness underneath the block needed expression and release. The therapist asked her if she could metaphorically remove the block, and prompted her to close her eyes and imagine going inside and removing the block if she felt comfortable enough to do so. The patient complied and reported, while her eyes were closed, that the block had been removed and she could feel the sadness coming up. She reported that the soreness of the wound emerged in the form of sadness on account of removing the block. The practitioner asked her to "stay with the sadness". The patient immediately began to cry profusely; she stated that she had thought she would feel relief, but rather the memories of the past came flooding in and that she felt really sad, hurt, and vulnerable. While remaining with the sadness, the patient began to describe her experience of having an underlying wound that she had never given expression to in the past. Through further emotional processing, the patient reported finding that the need of the emotion was to be expressed and that she needed to allow herself to remember the negative memories.

The patient also stated that she needed divine healing, since justice could never be fully achieved in this world, and therefore her wounds needed to be healed spiritually. The therapist asked whether she would like to do a guided imagery exercise entitled *taṣawwur* that would utilize a religious figure to heal her. She agreed and the therapist began by asking her to imagine a radiating divine light emanating from the heavens and entering her body through her mouth. That this light would go through her and eventually centralize itself around her heart, where she described the wound existed. Then she was asked to imagine an important spiritual figure who would join her in helping her heal, and gave her some time to allow this to formulate in her mind. The patient then began to sob profusely and signaled that she had identified someone. The practitioner asked the patient to imagine that this spiritual figure would extend his/her hand and rest it upon the wound, which would concentrate the divine light around her wound. She was asked to feel the warmth of the touch of the individual and to try to visualize his/her appearance. This exercise proceeded for the next few minutes until the patient started to report feeling immense tranquility and peace. She opened her eyes unprompted and stated that she felt really comfortable. The practitioner asked her to describe her experience and she reported that she envisioned that the Prophet of Islam (peace and blessings be upon him) had come to her in a vague form, while not visualizing his face. She reported that he brought immense comfort to her and she imagined he had put his hand up toward her chest, though not touching it, to soothe and quiet her inner pain and struggles. She described feeling immense connection to him and that she now felt spiritually rejuvenated. The practitioner closed out the session with the helpful reminder that the patient could access such guided imagery when needed as a healthy psycho-spiritual coping tool.

Conclusion

This chapter has outlined the importance of emotions and their significance in emotion theories and Islamic scholarly works. Convergences between Islamic scholarly works and modern psychological perspectives on the importance of emotions were demonstrated, as well as their significance in guiding a core aspect of the human experience. Thus, the need to explore, address, and understand emotions to expand upon the experiential repertoire of patients is outlined as an essential component of the therapeutic process. The theistic trialectual constructivism conceptualized within the TIIP model demonstrates how experiences are internalized to form emotion schemes that are activated to foster adaptive functions, in order to achieve positive therapeutic outcomes. Interventions that draw upon principles of attunement and presence, as prescribed by emotion-focused theory and the teachings of the Prophet of Islam (peace and blessings be upon him), target conflicts within the self and with others to achieve a therapist–patient co-constructed, meaningful consolidation of the elements of the internal human psyche, comprising the *'aql*, *rūḥ*, and *nafs*. Thus, the TIIP model provides practical ways of integrating Islamic principles with emotion theory.

References

Abū Dāwūd, S. (2009). *Sunan Abī Dāwūd*. Beirut: Dār al-Rasā'il al-'Ā lamiyyah.

al-'Aynī, B. (2011). *'Umdat al-Qārī li Sharḥ Ṣaḥīḥ al-Bukhārī*. Beirut: Dār Iḥyā' al-Turāth al-'Arabī.

al-Balkhī, A. Z. (2005). *Maṣāliḥ al-Anfus wa-l-Abdān*. Cairo: Ma'had al-Makhṭūṭāṭ al-'Arabī.

al-Balkhī, A. Z. (2013). *Sustenance of the soul*, trans. M. Badri. London: International Institute of Islamic Thought.

al-Bayjūrī, A. (2002). *Ḥāshiyat al-Imām al-Bayjūrī 'alā Jawharat al-Tawḥīd*. Cairo: Dār al-Salām.

al-Birgivī, M. (2011). *Al-Ṭarīqah al-Muḥammadiyyah wa-l-Ṣirāṭ al-Aḥmadiyyah*. Damascus: Dār al-Qalam.

al-Bukhārī (2010). *Ṣaḥīḥ al-Bukhārā*. Riyadh: Darussalam.

al-Ghazālī, A. H. (1990). *Mukhtaṣar: Iḥyā' 'Ulām al-Dīn*. Beirut: Mua'ssas al-Kutub al-Thaqāfiyyah.

al- Ghazālī, A. H. (2011). *Iḥyā' 'Ulūm al-Dīn*. Vol 5. Riyadh: Dār al-Minhāj.

al-Jawziyyah, I. (2002). *Kitāb al-Rūḥ*. Cairo: Dār al-Qadd al-Jadīd.

al-Kalābādhī, A. M. (2001). *Al-Ta'arruf li Madhhab Ahl al-Taṣawwuf*. Beirut: Dār al-Ṣādir.

al-Khaṭṭābī, H., (2012). *The important status of du'ā'*. Beirut: Dār al-Nawādir.

al-Madanī, H. A. (n.d.). *Maktūbāt Mawlānā Husayn Aḥmad al-Madanī*. Faisalabad, Pakistan: Malik Sons Booksellers.

al-Muḥāsibī, H. (1986). *Al-'Aql wa Fahm al-Qur'ān*. Beirut: Dār al-Kutub al-'Ilmiyyah.

al-Rāzī, F. (2008). *Al-Tafsīr al-Kabīr*. Damascus: Dār al-Fikr.

al-Qasṭallānī, ibn H. (2015). *Fatḥ al-Bārī, Sharḥ Ṣaḥīḥ al-Bukhārī*. Beirut: Dār al-Ma'rifah.

al-Suhrawardī, S. (1993). *'Awārif al-Ma'ārif*. Cairo: Dar al-Ma'rif.

al-Suhrawardī, S. (2000). *Philosophy of illumination.* Provo, UT: Brigham Young University.

al-Ṭabrānī, S. (1984). *Al-Mu'jam al-Kabīr.* Iraq: al-Jumhūriyyah al-'Irā qiyyah, Wizārat al-Awqāf.

al-Taftāzānī, A. H. (2000). *Sharḥ al-'Aqā'id al-Nasafiyyah.* Karachi: Maktabat al-Bushrā.

al-Tirmidhī, M. (1970). *Jāmi' al-Tirmidhī.* Riyadh: Darrusalam.

al-Tirmidhī, M. (n.d.). *Shamā'il al-Tirmidhī/Muḥammadiyyah.* Karachi: Dār al-Ishā'at.

al-Ṭūsī, A. S. (1914). *Al-Lama' fi-l-Taṣawwuf.* London: Brill Publishers.

Angus, L. E., & Greenberg, L. S. (2011). *Working with narrative in emotion-focused therapy: Changing stories, healing lives.* Washington, DC: American Psychological Association.

'Aṭṭār, F. (1905). *Tadhkirah al-Awliyā'.* London: Brill Publishers.

Barlow, D. H. (2000). Unraveling the mysteries of anxiety and its disorders from the perspective of emotion theory. *American Psychologist, 55,* 1247–1263.

Bear, M. F., Connors B. W., & Paradiso, M. A. (2007). *Neuroscience, exploring the brain.* 3rd ed. Philadelphia, PA/Baltimore, MA: Lippincott, Williams & Wilkins.

Beck, A. T. (1967). *The diagnosis and management of depression.* Philadelphia, PA: University of Pennsylvania Press.

Clarkson, P. (1997). Variations on I and thou. *Gestalt Review, 1,* 35–49.

Dolcos, S., Hu, Y., Iordan, A. D., Moore, M., & Dolcos, F. (2016). Optimism and the brain: trait optimism mediates the protective role of the orbitofrontal cortex gray matter volume against anxiety. *Social Cognitive and Affective Neuroscience, 11*(2), 263–71.

Elliott, R., Watson, J. C., Goldman, R. N., & Greenberg, L. S. (2004). *Learning emotion-focused therapy: The process-experiential approach to change.* Washington, DC: American Psychological Association.

Geller, S. M., & Greenberg, L. S. (2012). *Therapeutic presence: A mindful approach to effective therapy.* Washington, DC: American Psychological Association.

Gendlin, E. T. (1974). Experiential psychotherapy. In R. J. Corsini (Ed.), *Current psychotherapies* (pp. 317–332). Itasca, IL: F. E. Peacock.

Gendlin, E. T. (1978). *Focusing.* New York, NY: Everest House.

Gendlin, E. T. (1996). *Focusing-oriented psychotherapy.* New York, NY: Guilford.

Greenberg, L. S. (2002). Integrating an emotion-focused approach to treatment into psychotherapy integration. *Journal of Psychotherapy Integration, 12,* 154–189.

Greenberg, L. S. (2004). Emotion-focused therapy. *Clinical Psychology and Psychotherapy, 11,* 3–16.

Greenberg, L. S., & Iwakabe, S. (2011). Emotion-focused therapy and shame. In R. L. Dearing & J. P. Tangney (Eds.), *Shame in the therapy hour* (pp. 69–90). Washington, DC: American Psychological Association.

Greenberg, L. S., & Paivio, S. C. (1997). *Working with emotions in psychotherapy.* New York, NY: The Guilford Press.

Greenberg, L. S., & Safran, J. D. (1987). *The Guilford clinical psychology and psychotherapy series. Emotion in psychotherapy: Affect, cognition, and the process of change.* New York, NY: Guilford Press.

Ibn 'Abd al-Salām, I. (2005). *Fawā'id al-Balwā wa-l-Miḥan.* Damascus: Dār al-Fikr al-Mu'āṣir.

Ibn Abī al-Dunyā (1998). *Al-Riqqah wa-l-Bukā'.* Beirut: Dar Ibn Ḥazm.

Ibn al-Qayyim, M. J. (2013). *Rawdah al-Muḥibbīn*. Mecca: Dār ʿĀlam al-Fawā'id.

Ibn Ḥazm (2014). *The Ring of the Dove*. Trans. A. R Nykl. Eastford, CT: Martino Fine Books.

Ibn Ḥibbān, M. (2010). *Al-Majrūḥīn li Ibn Ḥibbān*. Aleppo: Dār al-Waʿy.

Ibn Mājah, M. (2007). *Sunan Ibn Mājah*. Trans. N. Al-Khattab. Riyadh: Darussalam.

Izard, C. E. (1977). *Human emotions*. New York: Plenum.

Izard, C. E. (1992). Basic emotions, relations among emotions, and emotion-cognition relations. *Psychological Review*, *99* (3), 561–565.

Jabin, F. (2011). A guiding tool in Unani Tibb for maintenance and preservation of health: A review study. *African Journal of Traditional Complementary and Alternative Medicines*, *8*(5), 140–143.

Johnson, S. M., & Greenberg, L. S. (1985). Differential effects of experiential and problem-solving interventions in resolving marital conflict. *Journal of Consulting and Clinical Psychology*, *53*(2), 175–184.

Kempler, W. (1970). The therapist's merchandise. *Voices: The Art & Science of Psychotherapy*, *5*, 57–60.

Lietaer, G. (1993). Authenticity, congruence, and transparency. In D. Brazier (Ed.), *Beyond Carl Rogers* (pp. 17–46). London: Constable.

Muslim, A. (2017). *Ṣaḥīḥ Muslim*. Riyadh: Darussalam Publishers.

Ortony, A., & Turner, T. J. (1990). What's basic about basic emotions? *Psychological Review*, *97*(3), 315–331. https://doi.org/10.1037/0033-295X.97.3.315.

Paivio, S. C., & Pascual-Leone, A. (2010). *Emotion focused therapy for complex relational trauma: An integrative approach*. Washington, DC: American Psychological Association.

Pascual-Leone, A., & Greenberg, L. S. (2006). Insight and awareness in experiential therapy. In L. G. Castonguay & C. E. Hill (Eds.), *Insight in psychotherapy* (pp. 31–56). Washington, DC: American Psychological Association.

Plutchik. R. (1980). *Emotion: A psychoevolutionary synthesis*. New York, NY: Harper & Row.

Ragab, A. (2018). *Piety and patienthood in medievil Islam*. Abingdon, UK: Routledge Studies in Religion.

Reik, T. (1948). *Listening with the third ear*. New York, NY: Farrar Straus.

Resick, P. A., Monson, C. M., & Chard, K. M. (2016). *Cognitive processing therapy for PTSD: A comprehensive manual*. New York, NY: Guilford Press.

Robbins, A. (1998). *Therapeutic presence: Bridging expression and form*. London: Jessica Kingsley.

Safi, O. (2018). *Radical love: Teachings from the Islamic mystical tradition*. New Haven, CT: Yale University.

Seligman, M. (2011). *Flourish*. New York, NY: Free Press.

Seligman, M. E. P., Reivich, K., Jaycox, L., & Gillham, J. (1995). *The optimistic child*. New York, NY: Houghton Mifflin.

Thānwī, A. A. (1971). *Anfās-e-ʿĪsā*. Deoband, India: Idārah Ta'līfāt-e-Awliyā'.

ʿUthmānī, M. T. (2001). *Spiritual discourses*. Karachi: Dār al-Ishāʿat.

Vanaerschot, G. (1993). Empathy as releasing several microprocesses in the client. In D. Brazier (Ed.), *Beyond Carl Rogers* (pp. 47–71). London: Constable.

Chapter 8

The Use of the Intellect (*'aql*) as a Cognitive Restructuring Tool in an Islamic Psychotherapy

Asim Yusuf and Heba Elhaddad

Chapter Summary

This chapter takes as its starting point two givens. First, what makes a psychology Islamic is the metaphysical framework within which its subject (the subjective human self) is situated and studied. Second, the difference between Behavioural Therapy and Cognitive Behavioural Therapy (CBT) is precisely the recognition of the human capacity for rationality, and that the nature, purpose, and use of this capacity should not be assumed but interrogated. It therefore focuses on cognitive approaches to psychotherapy from first principles: that is to say, the very idea of the "human being" as denoting an animal governed not merely by instinctual urges, but also an intellectual faculty.

The first part of the chapter explores this fundamental notion in terms of how the perception–decision–response loop manifests in humans as opposed to other living beings, focusing on the nature and role of "intellect" within it. The chapter then explores the concept of the rational intellect, as viewed within the idealist metaphysical scheme of traditional Islam.

Thereafter, the chapter gives an overview of how the intellect has been classically understood to operate within this frame of reference by al-Ghazālī and others. It then elaborates various approaches to cognitive therapy, including a new theoretical model (RIDA—recognition, identification, denial/decoupling and alternate formulation) that can be usefully employed within the TIIP framework—which explicitly premises both human instinctual/behavioural urges (*nafs*) and the presence of a rational faculty (*'aql*) that may modify these behaviours. It closes with a case study detailing a practical example of the TIIP cognitive therapy approach, including the use of RIDA.

Introduction

> The paradox of mortality is to seek eternity in full recognition of the inability to achieve it. The doomed-to-perish (*fānī*) seeks immortality (*baqā'*). Everything is perishing save only His Essence.
>
> (Asim Yusuf)

In order to properly understand the place of rational approaches in psychotherapy, it is worthwhile stepping back to first principles. The underlying assumption of this chapter is merely that the human being is a living entity, endowed with a rational faculty and existing within a cosmos. As far as possible, the philosophical commitments that underpin how one approaches this assumption—whether regarding epistemology, cosmology, or anthropology— will be précised.[1] However, the trajectory of the argument is that one cannot properly understand human behaviour without considering intellect, and that one cannot properly understand intellect without adopting some metaphysical or cosmological framework.[2] The chosen framework for this chapter is the Islamic conceptualization that underlies TIIP.

Scaffolding Behaviorism, Cognitivism, and Metaphysics

The first section of this chapter explores the rationale behind the involvement of the intellect in the process of healing the self (i.e. psychotherapy). The human, as an animal, is governed by the same basic instincts as any other animal—the need for self-preservation and perpetuation—and is possessed of the same basic faculties as any other animal—the ability to perceive and respond to changes in its internal and external environment.[3] It was such recognition that fuelled the popularisation of Behaviorism in the early–middle twentieth century: Models of stimulus-response were scaled up from animal experiments on the theoretical premise that the human being was simply an organism like any other, albeit with more involved responses to stimuli (Smith, 1986).

What made this approach inadequate was the fact that humans are more complex than this—they are possessed of an innate intellect (Chomsky, 1959). This is the separating characteristic (*faṣl*) distinguishing humans and other animals. Behavioural Therapy approaches thus largely gave way to Cognitive Behavioural Therapy and other forms of rational-based therapy, which explicitly took into consideration the subjective, rational aspect of the human psyche and its role in determining response. In doing so, though, they generally remained either agnostic or determinedly naturalist about the ontic nature of the intellect and the human being.

Understanding what precisely is the nature of this intellect, and the metaphysical assumptions underpinning it, becomes critical in evaluating or developing forms of rational therapy. Depending on those metaphysical commitments, secular and non-secular forms of rational therapy may be developed. These, in turn, may have varying degrees of relevance and utility for those who do not subscribe to that metaphysical outlook.

The most obvious example of this in current practice is mindfulness, which is largely based on *sati*, a classical Buddhist meditative technique that primarily refers to constant recollection of the true (illusory) nature of reality, and which in turn is etymologically derived from *smṛti*, a Sanskrit term that originally referred to the memorization and inculcation of the Vedas (Sharf, 2014).[4] Thus mindfulness, originally an intrinsic aspect of attaining enlightenment within a Buddhist cosmology, has both been shorn of its transcendental basis and also found to have useful application in a different metaphysical framework.

In Muslim religious thought, the fundamental nature of the human being—and creation in general—is inexplicable without reference to the Divine. "Self" is a relational concept, comprehensible only in relation to God—the Ultimate Reality (*al-Ḥaqq*). According to this understanding, God has created all life with a fundamental instinct to preserve or perpetuate itself, but also an innate recognition of its own incapability to do so in and of itself. This is expressed most pithily in the Qur'ānic verse, "O Mankind, you are (existentially) dependent on God, while He is utterly independent and worthy of all praise" (Sura Fāṭir 35:15).

In all animate beings, this preservation instinct[5]—in its most basic form—manifests as harm avoidance and benefit acquisition. In order to accomplish this, all living beings are possessed of sensorimotor functionality: the capacity to detect and respond to their internal and external environments (al-Bajūrī, 2002, p. 175).[6]

In animals, this primordial instinct is managed through highly complex nervous systems, which enable the inputting of information, the processing of it, and the execution of an appropriate response. In humans, the process of assimilation of multi-source sensory data into a unitary percept, affording salience, evaluation, and storage for recall, is managed via the "intellect". In its broadest sense, this intellect may be conceived of as having multiple elements: rational, emotional, memory, associative, discriminating, imaginative, abstracting, and deciding (Avicenna, 1959, pp. 57–59). Some or all of these processes occur—virtually instantaneously—upon receipt of a stimulus, and result in an observable behavior.

For example, a person might see a four-legged object moving swiftly towards them and hear a repeated sharp, loud noise. These sensory inputs would be combined into the percept of a barking dog, given salience from among thousands of other inputs, associated with past memories and imagined consequences, conjoined with the emotion of either fear or happiness—depending on one's discrimination of a friendly or unfriendly dog—resulting in the abstraction of the notion of physical danger or

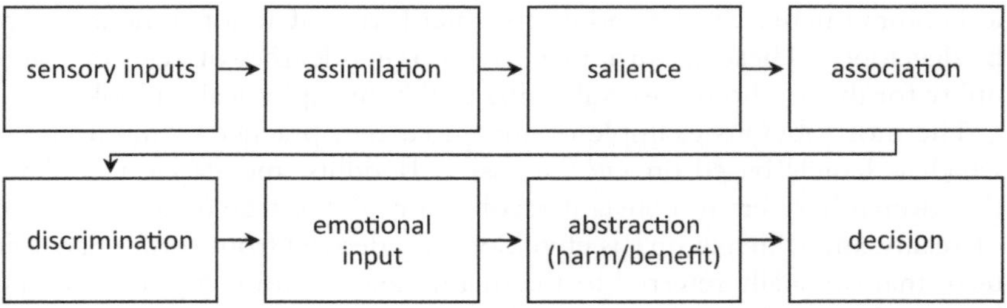

Figure 8.1 Internal processes relating to the broad definition of intellect in decision-making.

emotional benefit, and therefore in a decision to run either towards or away from it (Figure 8.1).

All of the above relates to the (oversimplified) mechanism by which the internal environment of the human self responds to a stimulus, via processes that cumulatively can be considered "intellect". The Islamic framework adds a critical rationale for why self-preservation is the fundamental instinct of living beings (it is an innate response to God's transcendent immortality). However, notwithstanding the advances in human neurobiology since the beginning of the twentieth century, it differs in few other base aspects from a secular approach to the *mechanics* of rationality.

A more significant difference relates to the understanding of the true nature and purpose of the intellect: Is it merely a survival aid, facilitating the benefit–harm calculus, or is it something more than this? Given that we are approaching therapy within an Islamic conceptual framework, it is worthwhile exploring how the nature and purpose of the intellect are viewed within it.

The 'Aql *in Islamic Thought*

As noted earlier, understanding the intellect requires a metaphysical frame of reference from within which to view it. How one views the nature, purpose, and hence use of the rational faculty of humans from a naturalist perspective is different in crucial ways to how one views it from a theistic one. We have already discussed the place of humans in a broader cosmology, so we will now consider how the nature and purpose of the intellect was discussed within classical Islamic discourse. Core to this discussion is the consideration that humans are classified in Islamic philosophy as "the rational animal". To put that another way, the intellect is part of the essential definition of the human being.

The most commonly utilized term for intellect in Islamic discourse is the *'aql*. Its lexical meaning is intriguing, in that its original etymological sense denotes "tying down" and "holding in place" (it is very close in meaning to its phonetic sister *'aqd*—to knot or fasten[7]), but it also appears from the very outset to bear a strong moral and ethical connotation: restraint of the passions, of non-normative or disapproved-of behavior, emotion, or speech (Ibn Manẓūr, 2013, vol. 6, p. 371). Additionally, it carries the secondary meaning of directed action on the basis of discriminating knowledge; it is this latter meaning that has become primary for many scholars and which is especially relevant to us. The word thus entails a holding back of the natural human instincts (*nafs*) and passions in order to direct their energies towards a morally and rationally praiseworthy output. The famously cited classical analogy is that of the horse (*nafs*) and the rider (*'aql*): the former powerful, surging, but potentially destructive if unrestrained; the latter either guiding and directing the former's strength towards a goal of which the former is unheeding and insensible, or else a prisoner to it (al-Ghazālī, 2001). This is, of course, uncannily similar to Freud's description eight centuries later (Freud, 1964).

The concept of the *'aql* has been much studied in Islamic discourse and, given that there are over a thousand years of writings relating to it,[8] even a superficial literature survey would be beyond the scope of this chapter. However, it is edifying to briefly examine some of the scope and foci of this millennium-long intergenerational conversation. In overview, discussions about the *'aql* can be broadly grouped into a number of categories, cited here in rough chronological order.

The Intellect in Scripture

The *'aql* is mentioned nearly fifty times in the Qur'ān, largely in its verbal form ("do you/they then not think/consider/ratiocinate?", "[this message is sent to] people who think"). Intriguingly, such intellection is primarily expected in relation to recognition of the *ghayb* (the metaphysical reality that lies beyond the observable world) through the *ḥāḍir* (the observable world), and hence to deduction of the idea of an ordinarily imperceptible and unitary Creator who transcends the multiplicity of the perceptible world.

It is here that one finds the primary connotation of the *'aql* within an Islamic framework: A perceptive or reflective faculty whose ultimate purpose lies in being able to abstract unity from multiplicity and reason the existence and attributes of the Ultimate Existent from its manifestation in contingent, perceptible time and space. As such, in the primary Islamic scripture *'aql* refers not just to practical, or even moral intellect, but also to theological intellect.

The Moral Intellect

Directly following on from such scriptural usages, as well as the primary lexical connotation of the word *'aql*, very early discussions focused on the role of the intellect as a means by which to both distinguish the ultimately beneficial from the harmful and to have the self-control to then choose it: the intellect as moral arbiter and guide. The intellect was considered a metaphysical light from God, wired into human nature (*fiṭrah*) alone of all creatures, that allowed the two-fold functions of *tamyīz* (discriminative evaluation) and *imtinā'* (restraint of instinctual or emotional urges) (al-Shawqī, 1987, p. 94). For early Muslim ethicists such as al-Muḥāsibī, therefore, it was not the precise nature of the intellect that was important but its critical role in human salvation. This conjoining of the base function of the intellect (discriminating benefit from harm) and its implication for volitional ethical action (distinguishing good from evil), as well as its impact on behavior, is critical in understanding the role of the intellect in both psychology and ethics—the two halves of human inner life.

The Intellect in Islamic Law

Closely linked to ethical discussions about the intellect, early jurists found practical application in the idea of legal and moral capacity. A fully functioning—hence adult—intellect was considered a prerequisite in order for a person to be both legally (in terms of worldly consequences) and morally (in terms of consequences in the life-to-come) capacitous (al-Ghazālī, 2012, pp. 116–117). Absence or impairment of this intellectual faculty (a continuum exists)[9] was considered to necessitate the involvement of a legal guardian in a worldly transaction (hence a "power of attorney"). It could also remove the responsibility to perform a purely next-worldly act (such as the obligatory prayers, fasting, or pilgrimage) or, in extreme cases, lift the liability for a criminal act ("defense of insanity") (Chaleby, 2001, pp. 37–48).

The touchstone of moral capacity was demonstration of the capacity to evaluate benefit and harm (Ibn 'Ābidīn, 2010, vol. 3, p. 306)—which links the "base" intellect (the evaluative faculty) with its moral dimensions. This in turn indicates that morality is fundamentally a benefit–harm estimation measured in the ethical scales of the hereafter.

The Metaphysical Nature of the Intellect

As the nascent Islamic world came into contact with (and to inherit, via the translation movement of the eighth to the tenth centuries) ancient Greek, Persian, and Hindu philosophy, discussion moved on to the nature of the intellect itself. It was first considered in traditionalist circles by the theologian al-Muḥāsibī, as briefly noted above, and tackled dialectically by the Ash'arī, Māturīdī, and Mu'tazilī discursive theological schools. A summary of the positions can be found in al-Taftāzānī's *Sharḥ al-'Aqā'id*, where he settles on the definition of al-Muḥāsibī: "the intellect is an innate faculty allowing perceptions and acquisition of compound knowledge" (al-Taftāzānī, 2007, pp. 44–45).

However, the question of the metaphysical nature of the intellect was most expansively dealt with by the great Islamic philosophers al-Kindī, al-Fārābī, and especially Ibn Sīnā (Avicenna). The latter was a renowned physician who documented many forms of mental illness—including psychosis—and postulated neurological explananda for them. He also laid out the mechanics of the intellect, as noted earlier (see Figure 8.1), assigning the various functions to the ventricles of the brain. Nonetheless, his primary interest in the *'aql* was philosophical.

Ibn Sīnā effectively constructed his entire cosmological and metaphysical system around the human soul, in which the "higher intellect" was the only discriminator of humans from the rest of creation and a direct link to metaphysical reality. This higher intellect was, in turn, divided into an abstracting intellect and a practical one—the former for understanding the theoretical sciences such as metaphysics and mathematics, and the latter for navigating the universe and one's life within it (hence ethics, among other things) (Avicenna, 1959, pp. 57–59). Via al-Ghazālī (2011, vol. 6, p. 18) and al-Rāzī ('Aṭṭār, 2014, pp. 63–69), this effectively became the approach adopted by the late classical Islamic theologians.

Although even a cursory presentation of any of these views is beyond the scope of this chapter, it is worthwhile considering how discourse on the nature of the intellect morphed as it passed through different explanatory frameworks and terminologies. In modern times, therefore, what is required is a faithful transmission of this rich heritage into terminological frameworks that allow engagement with current discussions—such as those of neuroscience and modern philosophy of mind (see Chapter 4).

The Salutary Function of the Intellect

Lastly, we will address historical approaches to the role of intellect in acquiring mental health and well-being, which is of course the primary purpose of this chapter. The relationship between the two has been a well-recognized aspect of both Islamic psychology and spirituality for over a thousand years, and will be explored further in the next section. In summary, there are two approaches to this: the intellect's role in clinical psychotherapy, and its role in moral psychology, which in turn impacts on psychological contentment.

The former approach is exemplified by Abū Zayd al-Balkhī, a celebrated tenth-century physician from Baghdad who can well lay claim—by several hundred years—to being the first documented cognitive therapist. He dealt with mental health and well-being in the last chapter of his multi-volume encyclopedia of medicine, *Maṣāliḥ al-Abdān wa-l-Anfus*. In this short section, which has been translated into English, al-Balkhī lays out a typology of anxiety, a classification of mental illness (intriguingly excluding psychosis), and a holistic approach to what can only be described as CBT. He considers preventative cognitive techniques for ensuring good mental health and self-administered cognitive "first aid", and discriminates conditions that require "professional help" on the basis of both severity and typology (Badri, 2013). The layout and presentation is fascinatingly modern, especially for those used to dealing with the stylistics of medieval texts. Central to his approach is the role of the *'aql* in mental health—the idea that, except in very serious presentations, one can "think oneself better".

Apart from this clinical approach to the cognitive dimensions of psychological well-being, the great Muslim ethicists recognized the critical role of the intellect in bringing about an internal moral transformation which would result in profound mental well-being. The relationship between moral virtue and psychological welfare, and the role of the *'aql* within it, can be traced back to the Prophet Muḥammad (peace and blessings be upon him) himself. It is affirmed in several well-known *Ḥadīths*, including:

- "goodness brings tranquility to the heart, whilst evil brings about restless agitation" (Muslim, 2012, *Ḥadīth* 2553);
- "the truly intelligent is one who subdues his nafs and works for what is after death" (al-Tirmidhī, 1970, *Ḥadīth* 66);
- his equating of the saved and the damned with "the happy (*al-sa'īd*) and the wretched (*al-shaqī*)" (al-Bukhārī, 2007, *Ḥadīth* 3208).

However, it was perhaps al-Ghazālī, above all, who most clearly explicated the relationship between virtue and worldly happiness. Indeed, his Persian reworking of his most famous work—an unrivalled masterpiece of Islamic ethics called *The Revival of Religious Knowledge*—is explicitly titled *The Alchemy of Happiness*. In both these works he basically tackles the ultimate Aristotelian good of Eudaimonia[10] (Aristotle, 2004, pp. 6–20) from an organic and naturalistic Islamic perspective, seamlessly fusing scriptural exhortations, inherited moral wisdom, genuine mystical experience, and laser-sharp rational analysis. He demonstrates, perhaps better than any other author on the subject, how a life lived according to the Muḥammadan Sunnah—crucially, when understood via its native rational lens—brings about not only salvation in the next life, but tranquility and peace in this current one, as well as providing the opportunity for definitive, direct knowledge of God and the metaphysical realms.

The key to both psychological welfare and moral virtue, therefore, is the utilisation of the intellect in understanding how virtuous acts both express and nurture salvific qualities, which in turn need to be developed in order to bring about psychological contentment. The final discussion in the first book of the *Iḥyā'*, *Kitāb al-'Ilm* (Book of Knowledge), is in fact an analysis of the intellect itself—the crucial tool that the other 39 books will rely upon—and the final discussion of the last book of the *Iḥyā'*, *Kitāb Dhikr al-Mawt wa mā Ba'dahū* (Book of Eschatology), relates to the highest manifestation of the higher intellect: the Vision of God Himself. It is a mark of al-Ghazālī's seminal impact that, after him, most classical discourse on the intellect related in some way to his holistic conceptualization of the active mind: the link between the metaphysical soul and physical body, navigating the world, harnessing scripture via both abstract and practical reasoning, to bring about moral virtue, psychological welfare, and finally true perception and knowledge of Ultimate Reality (*al-Ḥaqq*).

Summary

Throughout Islamic history, then, the nature and function of the intellect has been understood in several interconnected ways. It is, in many ways, the essence of the human being, a faculty whose reality is a metaphysical light allowing higher abstract perception. Its primary function is to enable recognition of the reality that lies beyond the ordinarily perceptible, and secondarily, navigation of the psyche in such a way as to bring about the psychological and moral virtues that, according to scriptural guidance, allow such recognition to occur.

It achieves this via recognition of one's innate behavioural responses to internal and external stimuli (*inkishāf*) and guided control of those impulses (*mujāhadah*), which brings about mental well-being and internal harmony (*i'tidāl*), which in turn ultimately leads to the fulfilment of one's purpose of perceiving reality (*ittiḥād*). The function of the intellect to ameliorate mental distress, when viewed from within an Islamic metaphysic, is therefore not merely commendable but inevitable—yet tertiary.

The Use of the Intellect in Therapy

Perhaps the most practically useful overview and guide to cognitive therapy within an Islamic framework is that provided by al-Ghazālī in his *Marvels of the Heart* (al-Ghazālī, 2001). This work is the core—literally and figuratively—of the *Iḥyā'*, and contains his topography of human psychology. An overview is beyond the scope of this chapter, but he avers that the human volitional construct consists of three basic components: cognition

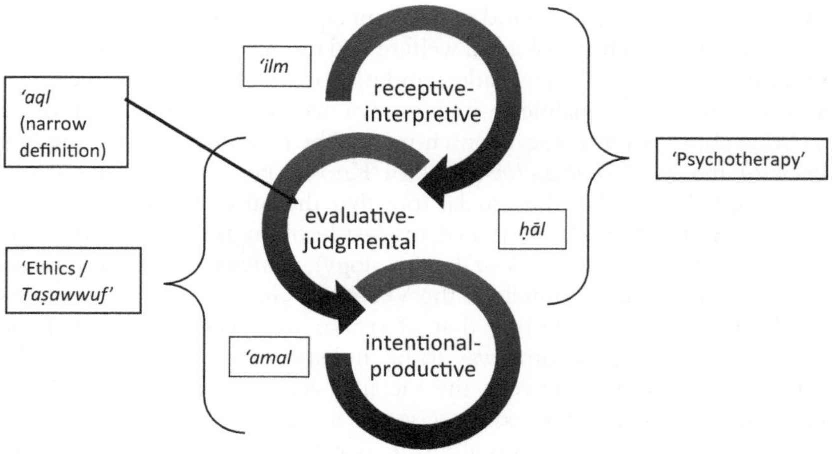

Figure 8.2 Components of the '*aql* (broadly defined) in relation to the functioning of the "human internal environment", and its relationship to psychotherapy and ethics.

(*'ilm*), emotional state (*ḥāl*), and behaviour (*a'māl*)[11] (al-Ghazālī, 2003, vol. 2, p. 722). Shown in Figure 8.2, these in turn roughly correspond to the three facets of internal experience: (1) stimulus reception–interpretation, (2) evaluation–judgment, and (3) volition–production (of actions). They are also related to the three theological predicates of life, respectively knowledge, will, and power (al-Maydānī, 2005, p. 42).

It is through the complex interaction of the three components explored by al-Ghazālī that the human soul (or unitary self) engages in a dialectic relationship with itself, the external world, and the unseen metaphysical reality that undergirds both. The product of such an interaction is itself an incremental evolution of the soul, which manifests as new cognitions and emotional memories, which in turn can manifest as new behaviours. These can be either beneficial or detrimental to the self, whether in terms of their "this-worldly" psychological or "next-worldly" moral consequences. As such, psychological learning can be both positive or negative.

It is important to note that, from within an Islamic framework, the psychological and ethical spheres of the human internal environment (i.e. the psyche) are thus virtually co-identified, with the former relating more to the mental health perspective and the latter to a classical *taṣawwuf* (Islamic mysticism) perspective, though this division is an oversimplification.[12] Respectively, these two spheres also roughly correlate to the receptive–interpretive (1) and volitional–productive (3) elements of the internal state, both of which are processed through the element for

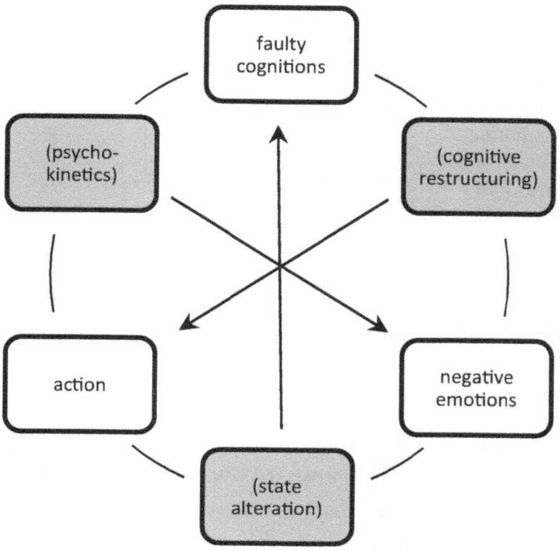

Figure 8.3 Ghazālian psycho-ethical interventions at each stage of the process.

evaluation–judgement (2). It is this last-mentioned, central element of the internal process that corresponds to the more narrow definition of *'aql*.

A crucial insight of al-Ghazālī, however, is that the three components do not necessarily work in a linear causative fashion (i.e. a cognition causes an emotion, which causes a volitional action), but are entwined: Emotions and actions affect cognitions; actions and cognitions can affect emotions (al-Ghazālī, 2003, vol. 2, p. 757). As such, the process of "course-correction" of this volitional process—potentially via psychotherapy—when it has resulted in self-detriment can have a number of diverse starting points.

Put another way, there are interventions that can be attempted at the various stages of the (usually subconscious) process of constructing a volitional experience which can alter its outcome, as shown in Figure 8.3. These include: challenging a negative cognition, soothing anxiety or sadness (via meditative practices like *dhikr*), emotional expression within an empathic relationship, or employing the "positive opposites" of unhealthy negative cognitions (such as supplicating on behalf of the object of one's jealousy). Further scriptural examples include ritual ablution, which is recommended as a behavioural diffuser of the emotional state of anger, or the act of giving to the needy, which is both motivated by—but also stimulates—emotions such as pity, compassion, and gratitude, as well as reflection on the nature of wealth and need (al-Ghazālī, 2011, vol. 3, p. 40).

This ameliorative effect is perhaps most potently observed in the ritual acts of Islamic worship, such as the psychodrama[13] of the Muslim

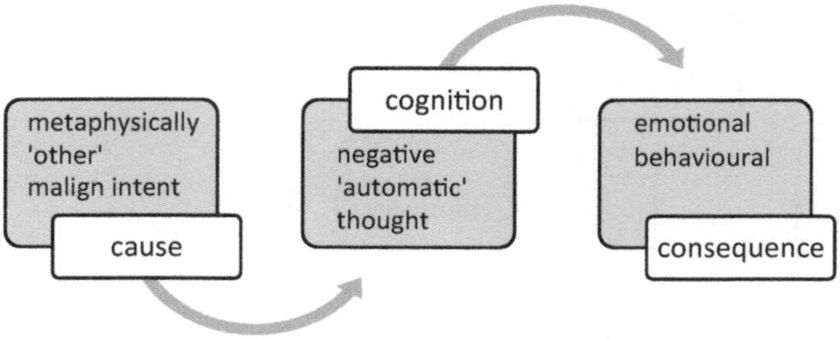

Figure 8.4 Challenging the cause and consequence of negative cognitions.

pilgrimage to Mecca, (*Ḥajj*) and the daily prayer. This latter act comprises a series of incantatory phrases and bodily postures which, when viewed in isolation, might possibly bring about an altered emotional state, but when conjoined with reflection on the meanings of the phrases and their relationship to the postures, becomes a transformational experience. As such, by unifying cognition, emotion, and action, the ritual prayer may be viewed not merely as an ordinance (from an outward ethical perspective), but also as a psychotherapeutic intervention (from an inward psychological perspective), or even as a sacrament[14] (from an ultimate spiritual perspective).

This chapter, however, focuses on the intellect as a therapeutic tool, both in terms of understanding the nature of the internal rational dynamics and processes of the human being, and also its subsequent utilization in cognitive restructuring. In other words, the intellect may serve to course-correct human cognitive–emotional processes at the stages of both consequence and cause (Figure 8.4). The former involves a re-examination of already problematic processes; the latter involves mounting a direct challenge to the very basis of their formation—hence being curative and preventative respectively. While the addressing of consequence is familiar to any secularly trained therapist, the tackling of cause is a model possibly unique to religious, and specifically Islamic psychology, drawing directly on theological resources in developing a practical understanding of human nature at a metaphysical level.

Cognitive Reframing to Alleviate Negative Consequences

There are a number of approaches one can take to the consequence aspect, including reframing the issue in more metaphysical terms by drawing on scriptural, theological, or spiritual resources, which in turn can be formulated along the concept that might be termed "the piety of hardship" (*al-ṣabr 'inda-l-baliyyah*) (al-Jazwiyyah, 1998, p. 18). This might take the form of cognitively reframing the issue via a positive interpretation of the Divine Decree (*taqdīr*) as being that of an all-benevolent deity, the recompense of the afterlife, and trusting in a loving and merciful God, or the concept of worldly life as primarily a cognitive–emotional lesson about the relationship between the self and God. There is a wealth of literature on the ameliorative effects of belief in an afterlife on mental health (Flannelly, Koenig, Ellison, Galek, & Krause, 2006), and one or other of these approaches were commonplace in Muslim history (Ragab, 2018).

One might also utilize a form of bibliotherapy in drawing strength from the hardships of exemplary figures such as the previous Prophets in the Qur'ān, the Muḥammadan biography, or the trials of the righteous. Alternatively, one might directly imbibe lessons from the formulation of these concepts by traditional scholars such as Ibn al-Qayyim al-Jawziyya and others.

The Process of 'Nafs-Reconciliation'[15] in Islamic Cognitive Psychotherapy

In this context, it is also beneficial to reconsider the basic Qur'ānic trifold division of the psyche (*nafs ammārah–lawwāmah–muṭma'innah*), classically (and correctly) interpreted as stages in the moral development of the self from "evil-commanding" through "self-critiquing" to "tranquil in righteousness" (al-Ghazālī, 2001, p. 8). This formulation has comprised the conceptual basis of the "behavioral ethical transformation program" of the believer (*tazkiyat al-nafs*) throughout most of Muslim history, with different thinkers adducing a number of sub-stages and approaches at each level.

More appropriately for the purposes of mental health therapy, and the utilization of the intellect within it, is to reformulate this as a (less-judgmental) three-stage process of cognitive therapeutic engagement with a difficulty. In this, one moves from a baseline—habitual, unreflective, and detrimental emotional responses to negative life circumstances (*ammārah*)—through a guided therapeutic interrogation of the negative cognitions underlying them (*lawwāmah*), to positive reformulation of these cognitions, leading to acceptance, strength, and tranquility (*muṭma'innah*).[16] This is actualized in TIIP via the process of *inkishāf*, *mujāhadah*, and *i'tidāl*, ultimately leading to *ittiḥād*.

Outlined in Figure 8.5, this guided cognitive therapeutic process—which in the case study relates to grief and bereavement—can also be conceptualized for a number of other psychological difficulties, all of which return to identifying and moving forward the "stage" in which a person finds themselves: (a) powerless, at the mercy of distressing inward or unhelpful outward behaviours at the behest of unexamined base cognitions (*nafs ammārah*), (b) struggling, engaged in the often difficult process of self-examination and reframing (*nafs lawwāmah*), and (c) at peace, having resolved the tension in a positive and psychologically helpful way

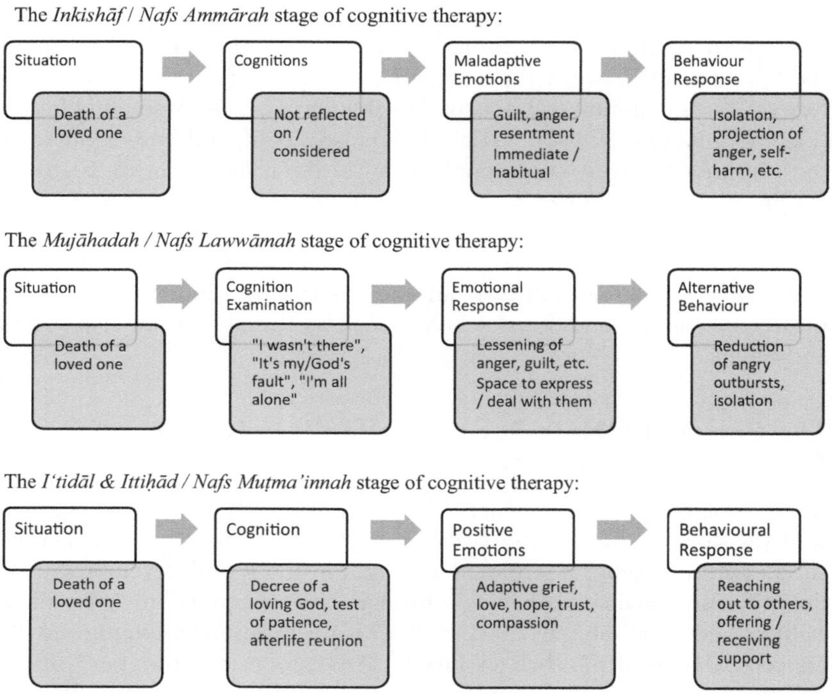

Figure 8.5 TIIP stages of therapy in accordance with the *ammārah-lawwāmah-muṭma'innah* paradigm.

(*nafs muṭma'innah*). This may be accomplished through cognitions such as acceptance or intervening in another element of the human psyche, such as emotional processing, behavioral reformation, or spiritual exploration.

Cognitively Reframing the Cause of Negative Cognitions

Following the process detailed above leads to the role played by the intellect in interrogating and challenging the *cause* of problematic cognitive–emotional processes. This can be achieved through the technique of mounting a direct cognitive challenge to negative inward states via a fourfold path: recognition, identification, denial/decoupling, and alternate formulation (RIDA). It is founded on the primary Islamic psychological concept of the positive and negative "inward voices" (*khawāṭir*). From a psychotherapeutic perspective, these voices map directly on to positive and negative automatic (or autochthonous) thoughts.

In such a formulation, explicitly derived from scripture and explicated in depth by psychological thinkers such as al-Ghazālī, the human self is understood to be subject to unconscious drives, which precede conscious thought, will, or determination of intent (al-Ghazālī, 2011, vol. 6, p. 97). Crucially, these arise not from the individual themselves, but from distinct metaphysical entities: one's protecting angels (*malā'ikah al-ḥafaẓah*) and devil-companion (*jinn qarīn*). They are traditionally referred to as "the angelic inspiration" (*nafs al-Rahmān*) and "the demonic suggestion" (*nafs al-shayṭān*). Though denoting "whisper" in this context, it may be that the signification of the word *nafs* here—which, as has already been seen, also means "self"—possibly indicates that these inward voices arise from metaphysically distinct entities (al-Ghazālī, 2001, vol. 6, pp. 76–78).

Once again, a detailed analysis of this seminal concept in Islamic psychology is beyond the scope of this chapter. Suffice to note, however, that these "third-party" impulses manifest in the form of "whispers", which are perceived—crucially—as first-person automatic cognitions, hence not "*you* are unworthy of love", but "*I* am unworthy of love". These then interact with the subject's subconscious memories, emotions, imagination, and instincts in specific ways to produce conscious thoughts, beliefs, and motivations.

RIDA (see Figure 8.6) is an approach aimed squarely at challenging the very genesis of such destructive negative cognitions via the exercise of intellect. It is grounded in a sound theological basis and has been informally practiced by traditional shaykhs in a variety of historical settings. It has several similarities to Acceptance and Commitment Therapy, such as externalization of negative thoughts, observing the self, and cognitive defusion (Harris, 2006). There are, however, significant differences, primary

RIDA	TIIP	Aspect	Example
Recognition	*Inkishāf*	Emotional awareness	I am feeling depressed, so the *nafs al-shayṭān* must be speaking to me
Identification	*Inkishāf*	Cognitive awareness	The negative thought inciting this is, "it's my fault all this happened"...
Decoupling	*Mujāhadah*	Cognitive diffusion	...but this means: the devil is saying that it's my fault this happened...
Denial	*Mujāhadah*	Cognitive challenge	...but the devil is a liar out to harm me, so I can reject the thought as a lie
Alternate Formulation	*I'tidāl / Ittiḥād*	Cognitive reframing	In reality, whatever God wills, happens for a good reason contained within the infinite wisdom of God, so I am not to blame

Figure 8.6 The RIDA process of challenging and reframing negative cognitions

of which is that the siting of this therapy within the Islamic cosmological system (i.e. its metaphysics) entails the actual—not imaginary—attribution of negative cognitions to malign external actors. It is the process of:

- recognizing when the *nafs al-shayṭān* has spoken (via one's experience of negative emotions, like anxiety, guilt, or hopelessness, which effectively act as a sensor),
- identifying the negative "automatic" cognition (the "whisper" itself) and the purpose of the devil-companion in voicing it (to cause distress, despair, etc.),
- decoupling and distancing the cognition by "changing the person from first to second to third"—i.e. attributing it not to oneself but to a separate malign source—and denying its truthfulness, for the devil is a liar (most easily accomplished by adding the word "not" to the thought), and
- alternative formulation of the circumstance—inserting a new, positive base cognition, on the basis of a therapeutic understanding of the self, the Divine, and destiny, and rebuilding the cognitive–emotional process on this basis instead.

The critical contribution of the RIDA model is that it allows a theological side-stepping of one of the most malign aspects of destructive psychological processes—the idea that the negative automatic cognition (and everything subsequently arising from it) must be true because it is "my own thought". It is effectively a conscious cognitive reversal of the process of the satanic thought: From "*I* am unworthy of love" to "*you* are unworthy of love" to "*the devil*, who is a liar and wants to harm you, is saying that you are unworthy of love, but this is a lie, because you are worthy of God's immortal love (*raḥmah*)".[17]

Guiding a patient through the process of reformulating negative cognitions and their consequences becomes significantly easier if one is not having to battle against the (often unstated) belief that "my therapist is trying to convince me otherwise, but I *know* this to be true about myself because *I'm* the one who thinks it". The theology-strengthened affirmation that the base negative cognition is to be understood as an externally sourced, deliberately malign opinion of one who wishes to harm you has been shown to be tremendously liberating for a patient suffering from it.

Conclusion

The broad approaches set out above—whether various approaches to alleviating the emotional and behavioral consequences of negative cognitions like implementing the piety of hardship, acceptance of destiny, or bibliotherapy, the process of aligning the TIIP stages of therapy to the Qur'ānic model of the self, or challenging negative cognitions via RIDA—are all reliant on the use of the intellect. This function of the intellect, in turn, is merely tertiary, allowing the safe and harmonious navigation of the human experience of the life journey in such a way as to facilitate the development of such ethically virtuous and tranquility-inducing character traits in the ultimate preparation for the purpose of existence: to witness—and bear witness to—the glory of God.

Case Summary

Salma is a 15-year-old female of Arab descent, who wears the headscarf despite going to a public high school with low ethnic diversity, and considers herself to be a practicing Muslim. She is a diligent student who has consistently maintained a high GPA and is currently enrolled in the 10th grade. Salma had a younger sibling who unexpectedly passed away at a young age, and currently has one older sibling. She witnessed her younger sibling experiencing sudden difficulty in breathing and was made to accompany her parents to the hospital, where her sibling passed away shortly thereafter. Salma did not have an opportunity to gain closure as her parents prevented her from seeing her sibling's body as a means of protecting her. There are no other salient psychosocial factors within the family to consider. Salma says that she has several friends who are supportive of her, and that she is part of a girls' weekly spiritual study group from which she also draws social support during challenging periods of her life.

Case Conceptualization and Diagnosis According to TIIP

Salma began the process of therapy after several visits to her psychiatrist during which she was diagnosed with Generalized Anxiety Disorder. She struggled with feelings of exhaustion despite her sleep exceeding the recommended 7–8 hours necessary to function well. Her feeling of being drained was compounded with ruminations, fear over the possibility of losing her loved ones, difficulty concentrating, increased irritability, and decreased appetite. Salma's ruminations were also hindering her spirituality and ability to connect with Allah, as her fatigue and compulsive worrying rendered her spiritually depleted. Salma reported lingering feelings of grief and guilt relating to the sudden passing of her sibling. Salma also struggled with feelings of anger towards life and her parents for decisions they had made that prevented her from getting the closure she yearned for.

Treatment

Utilizing cognitive therapy within a TIIP framework, the patient focused initially on the automatic thoughts and beliefs that are problematic and disruptive in nature. After a few sessions, some particularly problematic automatic thoughts were identified:

- "Why would this happen to my family?" "I feel like there's no purpose to my life and that I should have died instead of him",
- "Why would my parents take me to the hospital with them instead of sending me to a friend's house?", and
- "The world is a horrible place and things will never get better for me".

The patient was further weighed down with adverse cognitions about the purpose of creation being futile and comprising much suffering and deprivation. Her past unresolved trauma kept her at a standstill and inhibited her ability to recognize the goodness that is manifest in her life.

Although all areas of the patient's ontological existence were affected, the dimension of her being that needed to be engaged immediately was her *'aql*. Her unrestrained automatic thoughts and beliefs were driving her further and further into a dark abyss, and by focusing on engaging her *'aql* in more depth through cognitive restructuring and interventions from Acceptance and Commitment Therapy (ACT), this would alter her feelings of pessimism and general quality of life. Emphasis was placed on integrating spirituality into the therapeutic process based on the patient's request for assistance with coping with and acceptance of the new reality she had long been resisting. The patient transitioned from the initial state of feeling powerless to a state of struggling, to a final state of heightened inner peace and acceptance.

To build a requisite foundation with the patient upon which supplementary religious concepts could be added, the purpose of a believer's existence was addressed. In chapter 51, verse 56 of the Qur'ān, Allah states: "and I did not create the jinn and mankind except to worship me". The patient's understanding of this verse was evaluated for the clinician to gain insight as to the spiritual point of reference for the patient. The patient's interpretation of this verse was found to be superficial in nature. She believed that the primary objective behind life as a Muslim was to fulfill the five core pillars of the Islamic faith and to avoid the prohibited acts. To encourage more depth in contemplating (*tafakkur*) one's purpose, the patient was introduced to the concept of faith in behaviors guided by her thoughts. The patient was asked to revisit her thoughts/intentions behind her actions and consider modifying her thoughts into those that catered to her spiritual existence.

A conceptualization of the nature of worldly life, which is presented in Badri's translation of Abū Zayd al-Balkhī's *Sustenance of the Soul*, was shared with the patient: "This world (*dunyā*) is the abode of anxiety, sadness, worry and calamity. So, it is only normal for man to expect, in spite of his efforts, the onslaught of misfortune or even calamity to disturb the calmness of his soul" (Badri, 2013, p. 34). In coming to learn the intent behind one's existence and addressing the patient's thoughts surrounding her purpose in life, it was imperative for the patient to comprehend the nature of this temporal abode and how to exist within it constructively. Reflecting on al-Balkhī's conceptualization, it becomes evident that the nature of life is fleeting, with all its joy and sadness, ease and adversity, luxury and austerity. Through guided discovery, a technique stemming from cognitive therapy, a question was posed to the patient as to whether she was the only one who faced hardships, or if she was aware of others who also experienced a wide array of trials and tribulations. After some introspection the patient realized that nobody has managed to completely evade pain and suffering, and that tests of varying forms and intensities will touch the lives of every being.

To further aid the patient in developing a new lens through which to view her struggles, she was prompted by the practitioner to evaluate her need for social comparison through a spiritual lens, based on a saying of Prophet Muḥammad (peace and blessings be upon him), as quoted by Badri:

> In matters of this world look around to see those who are less than you or those who suffer more, and in matters of the akhirah or Hereafter, look at those who are better than you in their worshipping of Allah. This would cause you not to belittle what Allah has given you in this world and would motivate you to do more for your hereafter (al-Bukhārī).
>
> (Badri, 2013, p. 52)

This *Ḥadīth* enables one to cultivate gratitude in the face of every situation. The patient was asked what things that were present and manifest in her life she was grateful for, since gratitude has been linked to positive mental health (Wood, Froh, & Geraghty, 2010). She made mention of friends whose lives she perceived to be worse than hers, and she was grateful not to be in the same position as them. Young and Hutchinson (2012) affirm the benefits of gratitude in their article and state that gratitude allows one to experience an increase in positive emotions, results in an increase in optimism, serves as a buffer against stress, augments resilience, and aids patients in reinterpreting negative incidents through a more adaptive lens. Through psychoeducation, the clinician helped the patient to become aware of some of the aforementioned benefits of gratitude, and by utilizing the process of cognitive rehearsal, worked with her to "rehearse" new ways of perceiving various "problem: areas in her life through the lens of gratitude.

During the session, the practitioner was asked by the patienthow one can perceive loss in a healthier, theologically affirming way. The clinician attempted to cognitively reframe the patient's outlook by quoting an aphorism by Ibn 'Atā' Allāh al-Iskandarī (2014, p. 163): "If you want the door of hope opened for you, then consider what comes to you from Him; but if you want the door of sadness opened for you, then consider what goes to Him from you." A cognitive decision is made when one focuses on that which comes from God, rather than on that which is subtracted from one's life and returns to Him. Salma was previously unfamiliar with this approach to observing the events in her life. Recognizing that what is seemingly lost may not in fact be a "loss" was a crucial realization. What one loses could be a means for one's salvation, such as one's attachment to detrimental influences, possessions, or individuals. By reframing her thoughts to the idea that Allah has sole proprietorship over all things, and whether He gives or takes, a believer comes to understand that it is all in the best interest of the individual, she was able to move towards acceptance. Being exposed to this mode of thinking (*fikr*) helped facilitate the patient's understanding of the loss of her sibling; she broke down crying as she allowed for this recent awareness to sink in.

To address the automatic thoughts of "why would this happen to my family" and "I should have died instead of him", the essence of trials and tribulations along with their significance were discussed within the therapeutic setting. Before delving into this topic, however, it is vital to note that predictability is a modulator of anxiety and that by having the ability to predict aversive incidents or circumstances, one is equipped with the power to mitigate anxiety-related responses (Grillon, Lissek, Rabin, McDowell, Dvir, & Pine, 2008). A few of the patient's recurring automatic cognitions were addressed through an explanation given by Imām 'Izz al-Dīn 'Ābd al-Salām (n.d., p. 17), who mentions that tribulations and difficulties protect one from "evil, vanity, boastfulness, arrogance, ostentation and oppression". The patient sought to find meaning amidst the pain of her loss. Her anxiety was intricately tied to a diminished sense of control, and the absence thereof occasioned anxiety. Thus, the practitioner attempted to discuss the human need for control and how it paradoxically ends up making one feel less in control and apprehensive, resulting in anxiety and depression (Moulding & Kyrios, 2006). The patient's questions thereafter began to reflect her transforming perspective on the relationship between her anxiety and the manner in which it could manifest as states of need. She began to cognize that her symptoms of ruminations and fear, which she had long exerted every effort to avoid, could be utilized as a means of connecting her back to God, the ultimate refuge. The patient was asked if she felt a sense of need that could not be fulfilled by any of her family members or loved ones, to which she replied yes. The patient was then supported in finding her own pathway back to Allah, which had been severed for some time due to her overwhelming symptoms and her perceived inability to cope with them.

It was evident in sessions with the patient that she carried feelings of resentment and anger that were directed towards her parents for the manner in which they had handled her sibling's death. These feelings were associated with her negative attribution bias. Her negative attributions caused her to reconstruct her benign memories through a catastrophic and guilt-laden lens. The practitioner therefore attempted to work actively on assisting the patient in identifying her negative attribution bias and its accompanying adverse effects on her mental well-being and quality of life.

After the identification process took place, the practitioner prompted the patient to attempt to "act as if" there could be a positive interpretation of the incident with regards to her automatic thought of "Why would my parents take me to the hospital with them instead of sending me to a friend's house?" The patient was guided in the direction of shifting her mentality towards a positive attribution incorporating the Islamic conception of *Ḥusn al-ẓan*. This refers to having a good opinion of others and of Allah, despite the turmoil that may be present within one's life. It is a powerful tool in the face of adversity, and aids one in developing a strong belief in Allah's plan and trusting that the outcome is in the best interest of the believer. An exercise titled "components of awareness" (McKay, Rogers, & McKay, 2003) facilitates the development of *ḥusn al-Ẓan* towards others in real-life situations that may have triggered a considerable amount of anger or resentment. The exercise necessitates that the patient thinks of an individual whom they may have blamed for some action that they took. In this particular scenario, the patient was to think of her parents. The impactful decision that was selected by the patient for this exercise was the parents' choice to take her with them to the hospital during the time of family crisis. The patient had to reconstruct this decision specifically from her parents' vantage point. She had to note her parents' physiological and emotional state at the time of the crisis along with factoring in their beliefs, needs, background, strengths, and limitations. This exercise was an attempt to expand the patient's knowledge of both the reasoning behind her parents' decision and why the unfortunate sequence of events unfolded the way it had. This exercise also achieved the purpose of transporting the patient from viewing the situation from her own perspective to that of her parent's, which she had not been exposed to previously.

Throughout the exercise the patient's anger began to soften, as she mentally assumed the role of her parents for the duration of the session.

For the first time in years, she attempted to perceive the situation in its entirety from their perspective as opposed to solely her perspective. Considering her parents' physiological and emotional states contributed to a significant diffusion of built-up anger, as evidenced by a softening of her posture, as she was better able to channel feelings of empathy for her parents through perceiving the loss through their eyes. Incorporating this exercise into the therapeutic process was an attempt to dismantle the faulty one-sided lens that had been shaping the patient's perspective and contributing to her anxiety-related symptoms by adding an entirely new viewing field. The patient reported with tears in her eyes that she had an increased sense of clarity and inner peace following the completion of the exercise. Cognitively, the patient journeyed from introspective awareness (*inkishāf*) to psycho-spiritual equilibrium (*i'tidāl*) to the end result of integrative wholeness by the completion of the exercise (*ma'rifah*) (Keshavarzi & Khan, 2018). And arriving at the station of *ma'rifah* would not be attainable in the absence of the metaphysical *'aql*, according to al-Muḥāsibī (1987). Keshavarzi and Khan (2018, p. 182) assert that "through achieving this unity of being, the believer achieves a unification of their total being and the will of God such that their actions become directed by what God desires of them". Salma mentioned that she was unaccustomed to the mode of thought in which one's cognitions and actions are in complete alignment with God's will. She shared that she found some relief in training her mind to think this way, as being less consumed by her own thoughts and what they were directing her to do and feel alleviated some of her anxiety.

One's inner mechanism of interpretation is influenced by one's upbringing, beliefs, culture, experiences, and faith, alongside other factors. From a psychotherapeutic standpoint, however, the individual's unconscious drives must be recognized to discern between *nafs al-shayṭān* and *nafs al-Raḥmān*, as discussed earlier in the chapter. By engaging the *'aql* dimension of the patient's psyche to decipher the whispers adversely impacting her mechanism of interpretation, the first step of the RIDA process—recognition—is initiated. It was established that the *nafs al-shayṭān*'s inward voice had a more dominant presence in the patient's past and present due to the degree that her internal aspects of functioning had been disturbed. The first-person automatic cognition "the world is a horrible place and things will never get better for me" (much like the internal, stable, and global negative attributions found in most depressed/anxious individuals) was aligned with many of the patient's aforementioned cognitions that had been provoking her symptoms and generating flare-ups of excessive fear about her future (*faza'*)—recognition. Salma was able to identify the distorted aspects of her thoughts that were heavily influenced by the *nafs al-shayṭān* (identification). By utilizing guided questions, along with the integration of cognitive defusion originating from ACT, the clinician proceeded to demonstrate the process of switching the patient's negative automatic thoughts from first person to second person in order to dissociate from the devil-companion's external impulses that manifest in the form of whispers.

Cognitive defusion teaches the patient to alter the relationship they have with their maladaptive cognitions by learning to observe them as mere thoughts, in contrast with cognitive therapy, which aims to teach the patient to challenge and control their thoughts (Larsson, Hooper, Osborne, Bennett, & McHugh, 2016). The authors assert that by adding an initial prefix of "I am having the thought that …" to one's negative self-referential thoughts, these defused cognitions were found to be more comfortable and believable. Salma began identifying her thoughts using this technique by stating "I am having the thought that the world is a horrible place and things will never get better for me", which was then reformulated and broken down into smaller, believable statements (decoupling) consisting of "the world is a horrible place", "the world is made up of both good and evil", "the world can be a good place", and resulting in "the world is not a horrible place and things will eventually get better for me". Essentially, part of the therapeutic process was to demonstrate to the patient *how* to think from a more adaptive and healing viewpoint that engenders enhanced psychological well-being and peace of mind. By implementing the defusion intervention, once tyrannical negative thoughts were attenuated and began to loosen their grip on the patient's life.

Steering Salma through the process of placing her automatic cognitions under scrutiny by following the RIDA model assisted her in becoming aware of the significance and benefits behind reformulating her negative thoughts into more positive ones. Integrating the RIDA model, however, meant that the practitioner would take the process one step further from that which was incorporated through the ACT cognitive defusion method, by externalizing the detrimental thoughts to a greater extent. The patient began with "things will never get better for me" and transitioned that into "I am having the thought that things will never get better for me", then into "things will never get better for you", and then into the final stage of "the devil who is a liar and wants to cause you harm is saying that things will never get better for you". Becoming more cognizant of the devil-companion's influence on her mind and externalizing it was revelatory for the patient. This had previously been an unfamiliar concept to her, and learning about it relieved her of much of the shame and spiritual apathy associated with what she had once considered to be her own dark thoughts. Salma's overall demeanor and posture in sessions transformed from being slumped in her seat and making infrequent eye contact to sitting upright and being fully engaged, with a metaphorical load seemingly having been lifted from her.

Conclusion

In conclusion, after an exploration of the various definitions and attention scholars and the Islamic tradition have allocated to the role of the intellect, an inherently Islamic cognitive therapeutic lens is deemed to provide a richness of options towards the goal of restructuring belief, thereby leading to an accompanying alteration of human experiences. By modifying the negative cognitions that lead to pathological human occurrences, this can allow a transformation in the perceptual lens that permits one to view experiences through a more adaptive cognitive filter. It has become evident that the *'aql* plays a crucial role in influencing one's outlook on the world and all that occurs within it. Without a proper understanding of Islamic theology and the mechanisms by which it is integrated into life, an imbalanced lens will likely formulate, showing a lack of depth and meaning in relation to one's life. This may result in one's framework becoming weak and susceptible to misinterpretation of life events, cognitive distortions, and a lack of fulfillment of one's direction and purpose.

Notes

1 For a further exploration of the philosophical underpinnings of secular and theistic psychology, see Yusuf 2019.
2 Indeed, the difference between religious and secular approaches to psychology is not that the former adopts unverifiable metaphysical givens and the latter does not, but that the former is explicit about what they are whilst the latter is not. Every approach to any knowledge is ultimately premised on what Koperski calls "meta-theoretic shaping principles" which are not empirically verifiable (Koperski, 2015, p. 26).
3 As has been seen previously, in a TIIP framework these drives are known as the pleasure-seeking drive (*quwwat al-shahwa*) and the aggressive drive (*quwwat al-ghaḍab*). The authors prefer to term these the "benefit-acquisition" and the "harm-avoidance" instincts respectively.
4 These in turn, within an Islamic framework, map almost directly onto *tafakkur* (contemplation) of nature and *tadhakkur* (bringing-to-mind) of the Divine and His logos (the Qur'ān).
5 The perpetuating, reproductive instinct is what minimally defines life according to the majority of scientists—see Koshland (2002) as an example. There is, of course, much controversy about how precisely life might be defined.
6 Islamic theologians tend to discuss the nature of life insofar as it is a pre-eternal attribute of God, the Necessary Existent. As such, this definition of life (sensori-motor capacity) is explicitly adduced for *created* animate beings, thus excluding the Divine. A more inclusive classical definition, also in al-Bajūrī (2002, p. 175), is "the attribute that allows knowledge, will and power to subsist within a being".
7 As often found in trilateral root-based Semitic languages, phonetically similar roots tend also to be semantically related. In classical Arabic, this is studied in the science of *ishtiqāq kabīr* (greater derivation).

8 See, for example, al-Shawqī (2008).
9 See, for example, Kitāb al-Ḥajr (Interdiction) in the works of law, which relates to when and how much a person's right to dispose of their assets can be removed on the basis of impaired intellectual capacity.
10 A state of happiness and flourishing that arises from a lifetime of moral virtue, practical wisdom, and rationality.
11 Perhaps it is critical to note here that, for al-Ghazālī, all three components would be considered "*a'māl al-qalb* – the 'actions' of the heart/human essence" (al-Ghazālī, 2003, vol. 2, p. 722). In the *Iḥyā'* especially, his phraseology tends to be quite legalistic, and he explicitly refers to any guidance relating to the internal mental/emotional working of the human as *fiqh al-bāṭin*, which he contrasts with *fiqh al-ẓāhir*: guidance relating to physical or verbal acts.
12 This has been detailed previously when considering historical Islamic approaches to the intellect, specifically the overlapping but distinct concerns of al-Ghazālī and al-Balkhī when considering the salutary dimensions of intellect.
13 Here intending: a set of ritual actions performed in congregation, involving a re-enactment of pivotal incidents within the lives of three Prophets (Ibrāhīm, Ismā'īl, and Muḥammad—peace and blessings on all of them) designed to transform the inner state by evoking powerful emotions.
14 A term with a specific reference in Catholicism, but here intending a transformational act of receiving divine grace.
15 It is important for the unwary reader to note that the term *nafs* is used in three senses in this chapter, following the usage in traditional texts. The first, found as a single word, is the chosen sense within TIIP: instinctual, unreflective behavioural responses. The second, as here, is to denote the subjective self or psyche (the 'I') in one of its stages of healing/refinement. The third will be discussed later.
16 With due acknowledgement to Dr. Rabia Malik, from whom the authors first heard the original formulation of this idea.
17 This is explicitly indicated in the Qur'ān and used by figures like al-Ghazālī to demonstrate the idea of the *nafs al-shayṭān*, in verses such as 'the Devil threatens you with poverty and commands you to vileness, while God promises you forgiveness from His own presence and grace – God is All-Encompassing, All-Knowing' (Sūrat al-Baqarah 2:268).

References

al-Bajūrī, I. (2002). *Tuḥfat al-Murīd 'alā Jawharat al-Tawḥīd* [A gift for the aspirant (or "the aspirant's gift": "Being a marginalia" on "The Essential Creed"]. Damascus: Dar al-Bayruti.

al-Bukhārī, M. (2007). *Ṣaḥīḥ al-Bukhārī*. Beirut: Dār al-Ma'rifah.

al-Ghazālī, A. (2001). *al-Ghazali's Kitab Sharh Aja'ib al-Qalb: Marvels of the heart, Book 21 of the Ihya Ulum al-Din*. Trans. W. J. Skellie. Louisville, KY: Fons Vitae.

al-Ghazālī, A. (2003). *The alchemy of happiness: Kimiyā' al-Sa'ādah*. Trans. J. Crook. Chicago, IL: Kazi Publications, Inc.

al-Ghazālī, A. (2011). *Iḥyā' 'Ulūm al-Dīn*. Jeddah: Dār al-Minhāj Publications.

al-Ghazālī, A. (2012). *al-Mustaṣfā min 'Ilm al-Uṣūl.* Beirut: al-Maktabah al-'Aṣ riyyah.

al-Iskandarī, I. A. (2014). *The book of wisdoms: A collection of Sufi aphorisms.* Trans. V. Danner. London: White Thread Press.

al-Jawziyyah, I. (1998). *'Uddat al-Ṣābirīn wa Dhakhīrat al-Shākirīn. Patience and gratitude.* Trans. N. Al-Khattab. London: Ta-Ha Publishers.

al-Maydānī, 'A. (2005). *Sharḥ al-'Aqī dah al-Ṭaḥāwiyyah.* Damascus: Dār al-Bayrūtī.

al-Muḥāsibī, H. (1986). *Sharaf al-'Aql wa Māhiyyatuhu.* Beirut: Dār al-Kutub al-'Ilmiyya.

al-Shawqī, I. (2008). *'Ilm al-Nafs fi-l-Turāth al-Islāmī.* Cairo: Dār al-Salām.

al-Tirmidhi, M. (1970). *Jami al-Tirmidhi.* Riyadh: Darrusalam.

Aristotle (2004). *The Nicomachean ethics.* Trans. J. A. K. Thomson. London: Penguin Books.

'Aṭṭār, M. F. (2014). *Fakhr al-Dīn al-Rāzī on the Human Soul: A study of the psychology section of al-Mabahit al-mashriqiyya fi 'ilm al-ilahiyyat wal-tabi'iyyat* (unpublished Masters thesis), McGill University, Montreal, Canada.

Avicenna (1959). *Avicenna's De Anima: Being the psychological part of Kitâb Al-Shifâ'.* Trans. F. Rahman. London: Oxford University Press.

Badri, M. (2013). *Abu Zayd Al-Balkhi's Sustenance of the Soul: The cognitive behavior therapy of a ninth century physician.* Richmond, VA: International Institute of Islamic Thought.

Chaleby, K. (2001). *Forensic psychiatry in Islamic jurisprudence.* London: International Institute of Islamic Thought.

Chomsky, N. (1959). Review of language behavior. *Language, 35*, 26–58.

Flannelly, K. J., Koenig, H. G., Ellison, C. G., Galek, K., & Krause, N. (2006). Belief in life after death and mental health: Findings from a national survey. *The Journal of Nervous and Mental Disease, 194* (7), 524–529.

Freud, S. (1964). *The standard edition of the complete psychological works of Sigmund Freud. Volume XIX (1923–26) The Ego and the Id and Other Works.* Trans. S. James & A. Freud. London: Hogarth Press.

Grillon, C., Lissek, S., Rabin, S., McDowell, D., Dvir, S., & Pine, D. S. (2008). Increased anxiety during anticipation of unpredictable but not predictable aversive stimuli as a psychophysiologic marker of panic disorder. *American Journal of Psychiatry, 165*(7), 898–904.

Harris, R. (2006). Embracing your demons: an overview of acceptance and commitment therapy. *Psychotherapy in Australia, 12*(4), 2–8.

Ibn 'Ābd al-Salām, I. (n.d.). *Trials and tribulations: Wisdom and benefits.* Riyadh: Dar Salam.

Ibn 'Ābidīn, M. A. (2010). *Radd al-Muḥtār: al-Ḥāshiyah 'alā al-Durr al-Mukhtār.* Damascus: Dar Thaqat al-Turath.

Ibn Manẓūr, M. (2013). *Lisān al-'Arab.* Cairo: Dār al-Ḥadīth.

Keshavarzi, H., & Khan, F. (2018). Outlining a case illustration of traditional Islamically integrated psychotherapy. In C. York Al-Karam (Ed.), *Islamically integrated psychotherapy: Uniting faith and professional practice* (pp. 175–207). West Conshohocken, PA: Templeton Press.

Koperski, J. (2015). *The Physics of Theism.* Chichester, UK: Wiley Blackwell.

Koshland Jr., D. E. (2002). The seven pillars of life. *Science, 295*(5563), 2215–2216.

Larsson, A., Hooper, N., Osborne, L. A., Bennett, P., & McHugh, L. (2015). Using brief cognitive restructuring and cognitive defusion techniques to cope with negative thoughts. *Behavior Modification, 40*(3), 452–482.

McKay, M., Rogers, P. D., & McKay, J. (2003). *When anger hurts: Quieting the storm within.* Oakland, CA: New Harbinger Publications.

Moulding, R., & Kyrios, M. (2006). Anxiety disorders and control related beliefs: the exemplar of obsessive–compulsive disorder (OCD). *Clinical Psychology Review, 26*(5), 573–583.

Muslim (2012). *Ṣaḥīḥ Muslim.* Dār Mu'assasat al-Risālah.

Ragab, A. (2018). *Piety and Patienthood in Medieval Islam.* London: Routledge.

Sharf, R. (2014). Mindfulness and mindlessness in early Chan. *Philosophy East & West, 64*(4), 933–996.

Smith, L. (1986). *Behaviorism and logical positivism: A reassessment of their alliance.* Stanford, CA: Stanford University Press.

Taftāzānī, S. (2007). *Sharḥ al-'Aqā'id al-Nasafiyyah.* Damascus: Dār al-Bayrūtī.

Wood, A. M., Froh, J. J., & Geraghty, A. W. (2010). Gratitude and well-being: A review and theoretical integration. *Clinical Psychology Review, 30*(7), 890–905.

Young, M. E., & Hutchinson, T. S. (2012). The rediscovery of gratitude: Implications for counseling practice. *Journal of Humanistic Counseling, 51*(1), 99–113.

Chapter 9

Behavioral (*Nafsānī*) Psychotherapy

Character Development and Reformation

Hooman Keshavarzi and Rami Nsour

Chapter Summary

This chapter provides a TIIP conceptualization of working on the *nafs* or behavioral inclinations. Islamic discourses outlining the various discussions of the Islamic spiritual scholars on the competing drives and categories of the *nafs* are examined. In general, the *nafs* contains both predatory and appetitive drives. In its primitive state it inclines towards temporal pleasures and needs to be trained in order to develop the capacity to delay gratification and to progress to the stage of *iṭm'inān* or tranquility. A central TIIP principle of *mukhālafah* or opposing its maladaptive primitive drives is utilized in order to habituate it to incline toward that which is adaptive and consistent with the dictates of the rational self (*'aql*). Various approaches to training the *nafs* are provided as demonstrations of practical interventional tools that can be utilized by a TIIP practitioner. The Six M's model is outlined as a modality of reaching optimal behavioral goals identified by the practitioner and the patient. The Six M's are derived from the Islamic spiritual literature dealing with behavioral modification and they are: (1) *mushāraṭah* or goal-setting, (2) *murāqabah* or self-monitoring, (3) *muḥāsabah* or self-evaluation, (4) *mu'āqabah* or consequences, (5) *mu'ātabah* or self-reprimand, and (6) *mujāhadah* or exertion. Finally, a case illustration of the Six M's as applied to a case of obsessive compulsive disorder (OCD) with religious scrupulosity (*waswasa*) is provided.

Introduction

A great deal of attention has been afforded to the reformation of human behavior (*tadhhīb al-nafs*) and inculcation of good character (*akhlāq*) within the Islamic scholarly tradition. The scholars of Islam have recorded several prescriptive treatises on the modification of human behavioral inclinations in the interest of promoting good character. It is worth mentioning at the outset of this chapter that there is a great degree of fluidity and a continuum of health between clinical and non-clinical expressions of human behavior. The overall principles of character promotion or behavioral reformation share much in common and have not typically been viewed as discrete categories by Islamic scholars. In fact, behavioral modification for psychiatric maladies discussed by the celebrated physicians of the Medieval era, such as Abū Yūsuf al-Kindī (d.259 AH/873 CE), Abū Bakr al-Rāzī (d.313 AH/925 CE), Abū Zayd al-Balkhī (d.322 AH/934 CE), Abū 'Alī b. Sīnā (d.428 AH/1037 CE), when compared to the Ṣūfī scholars' discussion of spiritual dysfunctions, show a significant overlap in conceptualization and treatment, since both identify optimal character functioning as a central indicator of health. Sometimes this type of medicine is referred to as *ṭibb rūḥānī* or *tahdhīb al-akhlāq* (Ragab, 2018) by the physicians or philosophers and *taṣawwuf* by the Ṣūfīs. Ultimately, this code of behavior is inspired and derived from the Prophet of Islam himself (peace and blessings be upon him). The Prophet (peace and blessings be upon him) said: "I was exclusively sent to perfect good character" (al-Bukhārī, 2010, Adab al-Mufrad, book 1, *Ḥadīth* 273). Ṣūfīs have attempted to enumerate and specify these positive virtuous traits and outline the evil ones. For example, a treatise by the ninth-century Ṣūfī, Ibn al-Ḥusayn al-Sulamī (d.399 AH/1021 CE) utilizes the concept of *futuwwah*, a commonly used term of the Sufis to indicate the expression of positive virtues that arise out of the inculcation of this all-encompassing trait. Throughout his treatise, he describes the positive traits that must be embedded within the behavioral repertoire of the believer to nurture and develop *futuwwah*.

Alternatively, the renowned scholar-mystic and Islamic reviver Abū Ḥāmid al-Ghazālī (d.510 AH/ 1111 CE) in his *Iḥyā' 'Ulūm al-Dīn* (Revival of the Religious Sciences) categorized behaviors and traits into those that nurture salvation (*munjiyāt*) as opposed to the destroyers of human character (*muhlikāt*). Good character is viewed as arising out of an intentional process of continuous and lifelong behavior reformation and regulation (*tarbiyah*). This process begins in childhood with parents encouraging gradual but increasing degrees of self-exertion upon their children in accordance with their developmental capacities. The necessity to consider developmental capacity is captured in the statement of the Prophet of Islam (peace and blessings be upon him): "Speak to individuals in accordance with their cognitive capacities" (al-Bukhārī, 2010, book 1, *Ḥadīth* 199). The sixteenth-century Ottoman Islamic scholar and spiritual master Imām al-Birgivī (d.958 AH/1573 CE) describes good character as an acquisitional faculty that become habituated behaviors (*af'āl nafsāniyyah*) overtime and eventually emerge with an automaticity that does not require deliberation. He goes on to emphasize that this is a faculty that can be acquired through training while acknowledging that inherent personality dispositions (*mizāj*) interact with this process. A main element of this process is the application of significant restraints upon the lower ego until it becomes automated and habituated to virtuous and positive behaviors (al-Birgivī, 2011, p. 155).

Through this process, the child forms positive habits while learning to distinguish between good and bad actions and matures in their decision-making. Once their rational capacities are completely established, they can continue the process of behavioral training independently given that their cognitive capacity now possesses the ability to inhibit and regulate impulses on their own. This intentional behavioral training process continues typically into adulthood and is designed to maintain the conformity of the *nafs* to the demands of the *ʿaql*.

Al-Ghazālī illustrates that the cognitive capacity with its energy source originating in the metaphysical heart (*qalb*) of the individual should reign supreme among the other elements of the self, forming and internalizing healthy beliefs and directing its subjects to act in accordance with virtue and expressions of good character. Having said this, strong emphasis is placed on continuous mentorship by the scholars of Islam. Imām al-Ghazālī states that in order to continue to maintain an objective observant eye over the *nafs* and prevent it from slipping or regressing, one should adopt spiritual mentorship (al-Ghazālī, 1990). Abū Bakr al-Rāzī (d.313 AH/925 CE), an early prominent medieval physician, similarly echoed the necessity for continuous supervision a wise mentor, given the limitations of the self to objectively assess its functioning independently (Arberry, 1979). Ultimately, the goal of acquiring positive character is to become an upright and moral person (*ʿādil*). Being an upright person is a very important aspect of human functioning in the Islamic tradition, whereby the admissibility of even religious information such as recounting Islamic knowledge or one's court testimony hinges on possessing a minimum degree of uprightness. Uprightness (*ʿadl*) is defined by legal jurists as giving precedence to the faculty of reason over one's whims and impulses, such that it propels an individual to avoid major sins and the continuous performance of minor ones (al-Ḥaṣkafī, 2006; see also Ibn ʿĀbidīn', Haskafi, and Nasafi's (2006) marginalia on al-Ḥaṣkafī titled *Nasamāt al-Asḥār*). Once the *ʿaql* has internalized positive beliefs, it can be used in reasoning and directing of action.

In this chapter the authors will further illustrate the instinctual inclinations of the *nafs*, its competing drives, and methods of modifying them. At the end of this chapter a case illustration demonstrating the practical application of such principles of behavioral modification is provided.

Competing Drives

Despite being born from a primordially good essence vis-à-vis the *fiṭrah*, possessing the capacity to recognize and desire the good, the human being also has competing drives in the *nafs* that work against this *fiṭrah* in its untrained state. The *nafs* has two predominant drives that are natural and instinctual. These are (1) aggressive/predatory (*ghaḍab*) and (2) appetitive/pleasure-seeking (*shahwah*). These correspond to Freud's conception of the two main drives of the psyche: (1) Eros (life/pleasure) and (2) Thanatos (death/aggression) (Freud, 1961). However, an important distinction with the Freudian conceptualization is that these drives in the Islamic tradition are neutral and only have a propensity to be evil if they are under- or overregulated. In fact, these basic drives can be transformed into to praiseworthy protective instincts, thereby deriving pleasure in the worship of God and virtuous behaviors. Muftī Taqī 'Uthmānī, a contemporary jurist and spiritual scholar, describes the aggressive instinct as a natural inclination that contains an adaptive function for protection ('Uthmānī, 2001, vol. 3, p. 39). Imām al-Ghazālī states that subduing this instinct completely will result in cowardice, and that this is not praiseworthy (al-Ghazālī, 1990). Rather, reformation of these aggressive drives is necessary for survival. In fact, possessing such protective traits that lead to *ghayrah*, a protective instinct for one's possessions and loved ones are desirable (al-Birgivī, 2011, p. 254). The appetitive drives, that desire sexual gratification and to indulge in sensual pleasures, are also part of the animalistic essence of the human being and should not be completely eradicated. Rather, the redirection of these sexual impulses within the acceptable context (e.g. intimacy through marriage) is praiseworthy and even rewarded in the afterlife (see Muslim, 2006, book 12, *Ḥadīth* 66). The regulation of the intake of food, drink, and other sensual pleasures is also praiseworthy. Redirection of these animalistic drives towards promoting survival and providing the strength to perform spiritual exercises such as prayer and remembrances of God is meritorious.

In this way, the animalistic element can be used to transcend a beastly life, and through continuous behavioral refinement, attain *kamāl* or spiritual perfection. Conversely, the absence of training of the two desires, according to Imām al-Ghazālī, can cause these states to mutate into and breed satanic desires that arise out of the perversion and progressive feeding of these insatiable drives (al-Ghazālī, 1990). The successful development and training of these two essences leads to an angelic drive that derives great pleasure in the sacred. Al-Ghazālī provides the analogy of the horse in his reference to the training of the *nafs*, in that an untrained wild horse is neither useful as a riding beast, nor is it useful for reaching one's desired destination. Only after taming and training will the horse both facilitate transportation, and even begin to love its rider and the journey. According to a tradition, the Prophet (peace and blessings be upon him) said: "This religion is hard, so immerse yourselves in it gently and do not make worship of Allah something that you dislike, for verily the riding animal driven into the ground (*munbatt*) does not cross any land, nor does it remain something that can be ridden" (al-Bayhaqī, 2003, vol. 3,

p. 8). Therefore, the process of training the *nafs* is ultimately an attempt to make its aims consistent with the primordially good essence or *fiṭrah*.

Foundations of Behavioral Reformation

The behavioral training process is known as *tarbiyah* or *Mu'ālajah* in the context of psychotherapy. The ultimate aim of behavioral training is to develop an equilibrium (*i'tidāl*) that balances or routes the instinctual energy or impulses emitted from the *nafs* to accord with psycho-spiritual health. The middle path is considered to be optimal in this regard, as an Islamic tradition relates: "The best of actions is the path of moderation" (al-Bayhaqī, 2003, vol. 3, p. 273). Imām al-Birgivī provides a concise section in his *al-Ṭarīqah al-Muḥammadiyyah* (The Muḥammadan Way) on the need to be judicious in the performance of ritual worship. He dispels the notion that piety should lead to extreme asceticism or monasticism (al-Birgivī, 2011, p. 63). He urges individuals not to overly deprive themselves of sleep, food, or sexual inclinations. Thus, a complete repression of the natural instincts of the *nafs* is unreasonable and is believed to lead to either apathy and despondency or a counter-reaction of overindulgence and intense desire to engage in prohibited behaviors. This can produce a rubber band effect—when stretched too far back, it will either break or retract with intense force. Rather, a steady stretching out of the rubber band is necessary to eventually reshape it to the desired size without either over-exerting its capacity or leaving its potential resistance untapped. This path of resistance is intended to subjugate the *nafs* and mold it into its desired form.

Such a process of reformation must not be applied to inherent personality traits or dispositions (*mizāj*) that are the unique stable traits that make up individuals, for there is beauty in diversity of personalities. Character formation does not mean engendering a uniform monolithic personality or repertoire of behaviors. In fact, the temperament of each person must be considered in the development of character and behavioral modification (al-Birgivī, 2011, p. 154). The Prophetic example is one in which he reformed his companions while valuing and praising the variability found among their different personalities. The Prophet (peace and blessings be upon him) said: "my companions are like shining stars in the sky; whomever among them you follow, you shall be guided" (al-Bazzār, n.d., vol. 2, p. 924). Therefore, after consideration of inherent capacities, a moderate path of character formation is the most optimal path toward habituation to healthy behaviors.

Three Schools of Thought about Changing the Nafs

The polymath Aḥmad Zarrūq (d.871 AH/1493 CE), in his book *'Uddat al-Murīd al-Ṣādiq* (The Support of the Sincere Seeker) (2006), identifies three theories of how the *nafs* can be adopted in order to effect change. The first is the way of the Western Muslim lands (*maghrib*): their theory is based in the Prophetic tradition of the ores that states, "People are ores, like the ores of gold and silver; the best of them before Islam, is the best of them after Islam if they gain understanding" (Muslim, 2006, *Ḥadīth* 2638). Therefore, the job of the practitioner and whoever is guiding him/her is to identify their patients' unique personality traits, strengths, and deficiencies in order to extract the full potential of the person. The second approach is of the Yemeni school. Zarrūq notes that they based their theory on the prophetic traditions and Quranic verses that speak of different types of land and the effect that rain has on them. So, the job of the practitioner is to identify the type of land (fertile soil, rocky soil, solid rock, etc.), then to identify the type of seed that would best grow therein, thereby matching one's behavioral prescriptions that accord with the unique potential of the patient. The third outlook is the way of the non-Arabs, who used a *Ḥadīth*: "There are vessels from the inhabitants of the earth that are for Allah and the vessel of your Lord is the hearts of His righteous slaves. The most beloved of them to Him are the softest and most tender (hearted)" (al-Ṭabrānī, 1984, vol. 1, p. 40). So the practitioner would work to identify what type of vessel the person is and what would be the most beneficial action for them to take to fill that vessel.

One possible distinction between the three perspectives of change described above is the source of change, either emerging predominantly from the patient or from the interventions of the practitioner. The other aspect that differentiates them is the degree of change perceived to be achievable in the patient. The latter two views that liken the self (*nafs*) to soil or a vessel assume that change cannot occur independently in the patient but is practitioner-dependent. The practitioner plays a critical role and serves to provide the environment for growth, so that the seed will develop, given appropriate nourishment. However, the soil and vessel analogy also present an individual as having a limited capacity for change, with internally predisposed upper and lower limits of change that cannot be surpassed. On the other hand, the ore analogy sees human growth as boundless and achievable both with the intervention of a guide or semi-independently. The Maghribis, who see the self (*nafs*) as like an ore, believe it can be purified and refined, and can have multiple capacities, such as transforming into a piece of jewelry, a conductor of electricity, or one of many other countless possibilities, since ore is very malleable.

In exploring the above theories, the commonality to be found between them is their recognition that every person is unique and that the goal of the practitioner is to extract that which is within each patient. Ibn 'Ajībah (d.1194 AH/1809 CE) says in his exegesis of the Qur'ān (*al-Baḥr al-Madīd*) that the struggle against the self (*jihād al-nafs*) is not a struggle to "break" the self; rather, it is the struggle to identify one's strengths and inclinations and then work within the context of the individual (Ibn 'Ajībah, 2002). Despite al-Ghazālī's emphasis on prescribing exercises designed to break the two hedonistic and predatory inclinations of the *nafs*, practitioners must be keenly aware of the potential risk of being too rigourous in this regard resulting from an inadequate assessment of the individual characteristics of their patients. 'Ajībah points out that once a thorough evaluation of the strengths of an individual is conducted, resistance exercises should be within the parameters of their capacities, taking into consideration and placing emphasis on personal strengths equally. So, for example, if a person finds extensive prayer at night easier than charitable work, they should work to develop the strength of their prayers and reduce their focus on the time they spend praying. Or if a person finds studying or doing charity work easier than fasting and devotional prayers, they should develop this area of strength. All of this is done while keeping the basic obligatory actions in mind. When guiding or advising a patient who feels a remorseful insufficiency in development and growth in a certain area, the practitioner can help them identify whether or not such an expectation is rooted in attempting to change stable or highly resistant inherent traits. This would ensure consistency of behavioral goals being formulated within the context of the patient's reasonable abilities.

In a statement of the Prophet (peace and blessings be upon him), he said: "Know that the most beloved actions to Allah are those that are most consistent, even if they are few" (al-Bukhārī, 2010, *Ḥadīth* 6465). Thus, rather than pile up a lot of action on the *nafs* and risk driving it into the ground, or creating the rubber band effect mentioned above, the practitioner may assist their patient in building up small consistent actions, focusing first on what is achievable with minimal effort and increasing that amount only once consistency of habit has been achieved.

In sum, the process of behavioral modification requires a strong work ethic and will (*himmah*) to change. Practitioners attempting to facilitate this change must first develop a strong relationship (*murābaṭah*) with their patients. The absence of this relationship will both undermine the prescriptions to undergo discomfort and significantly decrease treatment compliance (*inqiyād*). When significant rapport has been established, one can move into the *mu'ālajah* stage of engendering resistance (*mukhālafah/ mujāhadah*). Once a behavioral addiction or avoidance behavior is identified, then incremental prescriptions of this uncomfortable behavior can be given. These prescription of exercises (*riyāḍāt*) are designed to apply pressure and intrapsychic pain upon the unhealthy avoidance or performance impulses of the lower ego (*nafs*). Muftī Taqī 'Uthmānī describes this in the form of the analogy of a folded piece of paper. In order to straighten the paper, one must fold it in the other direction ('Uthmānī, 2001). This entails not only constricting the impulse toward the center, but some overcompensation is also desirable in order to anticipate the rebound effect. Although the rebound effect is taken into account, applied prescription must also consider the fine balance between application of resistance training and keeping within the bounds of achievable change for the patient so that they do not overexert themselves. Thus, in considering these prescriptions of opposition, it is important that a thorough collaborative assessment and uncovering (*inkishāf*) of the patient's psychological functioning, capacity, and limitations is carried out, such that goal-setting and treatment plans are reasonable.

Stages of Change of the Nafs

The *nafs* progresses through several stages. The three stages of the nafs are the tranquil self (*nafs muṭma'innah*) mentioned in Qur'ānic verse 89:27–28, the reprimanding self (*nafs lawwāmah*) in verse 75:2, and the self that incites evil (*nafs ammārah*) in verse 12:53.

The term self (*nafs*) is used to refer to the inherent drives associated with the faculties of anger (*ghaḍab*) and appetence (*shahwah*), and is what the Ṣufī scholars intend when they refer to the "struggle against the self" (*jihād al-nafs*). It is this definition of the self (*nafs*) that is used when describing the first of the three types of *nafs*, namely the self that, over indulges in appetitive and aggressive desires known as the *nafs ammārah*.

The stages of the self (*nafs*) are sometimes presented in a way that suggests they are sequential and mutually exclusive. Some scholars have even mentioned that a person may oscillate between the stages multiple times a day or even in a single hour (al-Jawziyyah, 2016). The developmental stages of the *nafs* can also occur in parallel to one another—a person's self (*nafs*) may be both tranquil and inciting evil at the same time. This can be illustrated by looking at any person who, in one respect, may have very bad habits or do bad things, but in another respect excel. If, for example, an individual has a great relationship with a spouse, parent, or sibling, but in financial transactions cheats others, then it could be stated that the person is tranquil in one respect but inciting evil through their financial cheating. This categorization may be helpful when guiding a person to recognize their particular areas of character strengths and weaknesses, as opposed to an absolutist, all-or-nothing approach to the self, such as viewing the self categorically as "that which incites evil". This categorical self-perception can lead to a fatalistic view of the self, which can result in an abandonment of treatment on account of the very poor view of the self. This understanding can be helpful for practitioners in challenging patients who have an absolute fatalistic view of themselves, and is achievable through a demonstration of the multiple layers of the self (*nafs*). Finally, it is also important to note that the stages of change and character reformation are not irreversible. In other words, it is possible for a person to move forward and backward between these stages. According to al-Ghazālī, the diseases of the heart are a part of human nature and their traces can never be removed fully (al-Ghazālī, 1990).

The above categorization of the three stages are what is generally found in the Islamic literature surrounding the discussion of the *nafs*. Other sources have listed seven stages of the *nafs* and they are (in order of their development): the self that incites evil (*ammārah*) (Qur'ān, 12:53), the reprimanding self (*lawwāmah*) (Qur'ān, 75:2), the self which is given thoughts (*mulhima*) (Qur'ān, 91:8), the tranquil self (*muṭma'inah*) (Qur'ān, 89:27), the content self (*rāḍiyah*) (Qur'ān, 89:28), the approved self (*marḍiyyah*) (Qur'ān, 89:28), and finally the perfected self (*kāmilah*).

This wider categorization of the nafs provides a more elaborate illustration of the process of developmental growth from the lower stage of *nafs ammārah* toward tranquility that arises out of complete submission, contentment with the decree of Allah, and an acquired habituation for that which God desires of the servant. A Prophetic tradition encapsulates the completion of this process in saying:

> My servant continues to draw near to Me with supererogatory works so that I shall love him. When I love him, I am his hearing with which he hears, his seeing with which he sees, his hand with which he strikes and his foot with which he walks.
>
> (al-Bukhārī, 2010, *Ḥadīth* 6502)

Strategies of Behavioral Modification

The Islamic spiritual practitioners and Muslim scholars in general have described several strategies and prescriptions to be utilized by seekers of the spiritual path. However, prior to the application of any behavioral interventions, some cognitive work must be done in order to reshape the potentially faulty cognitions or irrational beliefs that promote or rationalize unhealthy behaviors (Engle & Arkowitz, 2006). Thus, once significant cognitive dissonance has been created whereby the patient recognizes that their behaviors are unreasonable or create a vicious cycle that maintains their dysfunction, then a natural progression to behavioral exercises is appropriate. However, at times the practitioner may choose to invest in behavioral modification even before complete cognitive restructuring has been achieved. This may be appropriate in light of the fact that change in either element of *'aql* or *nafs* is bidirectional, and a modification of one element may promote or spark a change in the other. For example, a patient with a fear of public speaking may not achieve confidence or complete removal of their inhibitions until they have been plunged into the discomforting task of public speaking itself. Thereby, by acting in a confident manner, and a few repeated attempts at successful completion of the task, will also promote a change in cognitions that may become weakened by virtue of behavioral modification.

Additionally, as discussed above, it is important to consider that the *nafs* is like a muscle, and applying significant weight beyond its capacity will damage growth. A study performed by Baumeister, Bratslavsky, Muraven, and Tice (1998) divided a group of people into two groups and gave both groups a plate of radishes and a plate of freshly baked chocolate chip cookies. One group was permitted to eat the cookies while the other was instructed to exert restraint and eat the radishes. Afterwards, both groups were given an unsolvable problem to work on. The group that ate the radishes spent 9 minutes on the exercise before quitting, while the group that ate the cookies spent 19 minutes on the problem. This demonstrated the finite nature of impulse control and the need to moderate resistance. Therefore, after a treatment plan has been devised, any exercise that engenders discomfort should be discussed with the patient. The task should be challenging but should not feel impossible. For example, in the case of behavioral addictions, the practitioner may ask the patient to create a behavioral log that assesses the number of occurrences of the illicit or unhealthy behavior. Based on this, the practitioner will evaluate and discuss with the patient what seems like an uncomfortable yet manageable change for the week. This repeated incremental process is known as *istidrāj*.

It is also important to inform patients of the potential for natural burnout and relapse, and that this is anticipated. The Prophet of Islam (peace and blessings be upon him) stated that "for every action there are motivators, and for every (feeling of) motivation there is (eventual) exhaustion/depletion, and whoever's exhaustion remains within (the bounds of) my way (sunnah), is rightly guided and whoever's exhaustion is other than that, is destroyed" (Ibn Ḥibbān, 2012, vol. 1, p. 186).

Assessment of Spiritual Diseases

This section focuses on approaches to self-awareness and change that have been used in West Africa, primarily Mauritania, for the last 150 years. Much of the presented information comes from the work "*Maṭharāt al-Qulūb*" (The Purifier of the Hearts) by Shaykh Muḥammad Mawlūd (d.1905 CE). This book is predominately a book on the science of purification and was not written as a text on psychology. Thus, his writing assumes that a person has established a basic understanding of theology (*'aqīdah*) and law (*fiqh*) and his classification of health and pathology is largely within the context of spiritual/pastoral care. Despite this, the authors felt it would be important to present an unfiltered view of his writing that intertwines psychology and spirituality. According to Shaykh Mawlūd, the heart is the ultimate receiver of health and dysfunction, as is consistent with the TIIP framwork. It is also the seat of the metaphysical essence (*laṭīfah rabbāniyyah*) that fuels the drives and faculties of the other elements. Al-Birgivī adds that it is the actualizing agent/force of all of the other faculties that contains central executive functions fulfilled through the other elements. Mawlūd developed a manual that is accessible and has a practical implementation. In this he follows, and draws extensively from, the works of al-Ghazālī and Zarrūq. This book can be seen as both an introduction and a key to accessing the more extensive works on this subject.

The first step in behavioral change that Mawlūd focused on is knowing the diseases of the heart. For each of the 30 diseases that he lists, he mentions their signs, symptoms, and treatments (see Table 9.1). The treatments he mentions are either preventative or interventional once the disease appears. The treatments can be both actions (*'amalī*) (behavioral) and/or knowledge-based reflections (*'ilmī*) (cognitive). The diseases are presented in a way that shows links between them, as some lead to others and some treatments work for multiple related diseases. The process of identifying and treating diseases is referred to as removal (*takhallī*) and the negative characteristics or diseases are referred to as *awṣāf dhamīmah* (al-Birgivī, 2011, p. 156). Mawlūd then lists, defines, and explains how to attain the stations of excellence (*maqāmāt al-iḥsān*) (Table 9.2). This is referred to as the process of adornment (*taḥallī*) and the adorned positive characteristics are known as *awṣāf ḥamīdah* (al-Birigivī, 2011, p. 157). In many traditional manuals, the process of removal (*takhallī*) and adornment (*taḥallī*) is presented as happening sequentially. An example is sometimes given that one cannot perfume a garment until they have washed it. We would argue that this process, like the stages of the self, is happening to various aspects of the self in a parallel fashion. So, one may be washing one element of their self while perfuming another element, due to a strength and a weakness in each domain respectively.

The process of *takhallī* provides an orientation for categorizing character defects following the work of scholars of the Islamic spiritual sciences. One will notice a combination of behavioral, cognitive, emotional, and spiritual aspects, as these are all typically interwoven in the writings of the scholars of the spiritual sciences. The authors of this chapter have opted not to separate these elements and have preserved Mawlūd's classification in Table 9.1. This was done in an attempt to provide an illustration of the inseparability and interconnected nature of understandings of psycho-spiritual illness in the writings of Islamic scholars. However, for the purposes of creating a typology suitable for modern psychological application, the TIIP framework has separated and classified these aspects

Table 9.1 *Takhallī* (removal) of spiritual diseases

Name of Disease	*Transliteration of Arabic*	*Definition*	*Cause*	*Cure**
Stinginess	*Bukhl*	The prevention of and fear of obligatory spending	Love of worldly things in and of themselves or to achieve desire through them	Reflection on the reality of wealth, considering the state of stingy people in the eyes of others
Blameworthy joy	*Baṭr*	Extreme joy	Love of worldly things, love of position	Hunger, *dhikr*, and verse 28:76
Hate	*Bughḍ*	Hate for other than the sake of Allah	Arrogance, asserting the right of the self (*intiṣār al-nafs*)	Supplication (*du'ā'*) for the one who is hated
Transgression	*Baghy*	Harming another person	Ignorance (*jahl*) of the rights of others, disregard for their rights, rationalization (*ta'wīl*) that the rights can be removed, arrogance (*kibr*)	Learning about the rights and responsibilities of others, reflecting on the stories of the transgressors, humility, doing good for others
Love of position	*Ḥubb al-riyāsah*	The desire to be recognized by others	Lack of seeking the acceptance (*riḍā*) of Allah, covetousness (*ṭama'*)	Reflection on those who gained everything and then lost it or died, realizing that this is a distraction from Allah, doing things that could elicit the critique of people, isolation (*i'tizāl*).
Love of worldly things	*Ḥubb al-dunyā*	Loving worldly things in and of themselves – note that not all love is prohibited as love can fall within five categories (prohibited, disliked, permissible, recommended, obligatory)	This is the root disease of all diseases according to some scholars. Others have considered conceit (*riḍā bi-l-nafs*) as the root cause.	The cure for stinginess can be used here, certainty (*yaqīn*), reflecting on death, increasing rejection of worldly things (*zuhd*), treating conceit as a possible root cause

(*continued*)

Table 9.1 Cont.

Name of Disease	*Transliteration of Arabic*	*Definition*	*Cause*	*Cure**
Love of undue praise	*Ḥubb al-madḥ bi mā lam yaf'al*	Wanting to be praised for something that they did not really do	Religious showing off (*riyā'*), covetousness (*ṭama'*), love of worldly things, love of position	Increasing sincerity (*ikhlāṣ*)
Envy	*Ḥasad*	The desire to have a blessing removed from another person	Enmity, vying for love, arrogance, vying for position, vanity, love of position, and extreme stinginess (*shuḥḥ*)	Actions that are contrary to what one desires to do, reflecting on the harm in harboring these feelings
Blameworthy shyness	*Ḥayā' dhamīm*	Shyness which prevents changing wrongdoing or asking a question that needs to be asked	Coveting things (*ṭama'*), fear of criticism (*karāhat al-dhamm*)	Increasing courage (*shajā'ah*), increasing certainty (*yaqīn*) in the truth of their beliefs or ideas
Blameworthy thoughts	*Khawḍ fī mā lā ya'nī*	Reflecting on matters prohibited by the Sacred Law	Covetousness (*ṭama'*), transgressing the limits (ḥudūd) of God, ignorance (jahl) of the limits of God, love of worldly things	*Dhikr*, seeking refuge in Allah (*ta'awwudh*)
Fear of poverty	*Khawf al-faqr*	Fearing the loss of what one has and/or not getting what one needs	Having a negative opinion about God in that He cannot provide, excessive hope (*ṭūl al-amal*)	Having a positive opinion about God and His ability to provide, reflecting on the storehouse of God never being diminished
Sycophancy	*Mudāhanah*	Sacrificing one's religion to serve a worldy need	Covetousness (*ṭama'*) and religious showing off (*riya'*)	Treatment the root causes of both covetousness (*ṭama'*) and religious showing off (*riyā'*)
Religious showing off	*Riyā'*	Performing an act of worship other than for the sake of God, for a benefit, to seek praise or to prevent harm	Covetousness (*ṭama'*), love of position, love of worldly things	Reflecting on the true nature of where harm and benefit come from, reflecting on the harm it causes in this life and the next, doing acts of worship in private, *sūrat al-ikhlāṣ, sayyid al-istighfār*

Fearing things other than God	*Khawf ghayr Allah*	Fear that prevents one from fulfilling their obligations	Decreased *yaqīn*, fear of poverty (*khawf al-faqr*), decreased dependence (*tawakkul*) on Allah	Increasing *yaqīn* and *tawakkul*
Resentment of Divine ordainment	*Sakhaṭ a-qadr*	Opposing Divine ordainment (*qadr*) by saying things like "I didn't deserve this" or "What did I do to deserve this?"	Not having sufficient certainty (*yaqīn*)	Increasing acceptance (*riḍā*), reflecting on the *Ḥadīth* "The pens have been lifted"
Religious bragging	*Sum'ah*	Telling others about an act of worship after it was completed without any deficiencies like showing off	Some of the same reasons for religious showing off (*riyā'*)	Hiding actions, not speaking about one's good actions, praising the actions of others, reading about the humility of the prophets and the righteous
Covetousness	*Ṭama'*	Constantly wanting and never being satiated by what one attains	Heedlessness (*ghaflah*), doubt about Divine ordainment (*qadr*)	Reflecting on the true nature of the *dunya*
Excessive hope	*Ṭūl al-amal*	Acting as if one will live forever	Heedlessness (*ghaflah*), ignorance of the reality of life	Reflecting on death
Belief in omens	*Tiyarah*	Having a negative belief due to the occurrence of a specific thing	Ignorance of the fact that all things are in the control of God, negative opinions (*sū' al-ẓann*) about God	Having a good opinion (*ḥusn al-ẓann*) about God
Negative opinions	*Sū' al-ẓann*	Having certainty about another person without any evidence	Arrogance, satisfaction with one's own opinion (*i'jāb al-nafs bi-l-ra'y*)	Having a good opinion (*ḥusn al-ẓan*) about the person, praising them publicly, supplicating (*du'ā'*) for the person
Vanity	*'Ujb*	Being overly impressed by a blessing while forgetting that it is from God	Being heedless of the true source of blessings (*nisyān al-ni'mah*)	Reflecting on the fact that God is the Creator and Giver of Blessing, reflecting the fact that one is truly unable to create benefit or harm

(*continued*)

Table 9.1 Cont.

Name of Disease	*Transliteration of Arabic*	*Definition*	*Cause*	*Cure**
Cheating	*Ghish*	Hiding something harmful, whether a religious matter (*deen*) or worldly matter (*dunya*), making what is not the best seem like it is the best	Arrogance, giving victory to the self (*intiṣār al-nafs*), love of worldly things, coveting things (*ṭama'*)	Reflecting on brotherhood (*ukhuwwah*)
Anger	*Ghaḍab*	Unreasonable anger when things do not go their way	Strong belief in the right of the self	Preventative cure: reflecting on the lofty status of the forbearing ones and of humility. Treatment when angry: Reflecting on who is ultimately in control, washing with cold water, silence, sitting or laying down, and seeking refuge in God (*ta'awwudh*)
Heedlessness	*Ghaflah*	Being heedless of the commands and prohibitions of God	Excessive joy (*baṭr*), making light of religion (*tasāhul bi-l-dīn*), ignorance (*jahl*)	Seeking forgiveness (istighfār), visiting the righteous, prayers on the Prophet (*ṣalawāt*), reading the Qur'ān
Deceit	*Ghill*	The heart's resolution to deceive or be treacherous	Anger, hate, arrogance, love of worldly things	Be kind to the person, reflect on the forgiveness given to those who make amends
Boasting	*Fakhr*	Self-praise of one's own characteristics or accomplishments	Arrogance, vanity (*'ujb*), belief that one is complete, believing oneself to be better than others (*ru'yat al-faḍl*)	Humility, hiding one's blessings

Arrogance	*Kibr*	Grandyfying oneself while belittling others	Love of position	Being clear about the true status of God and one's status as a human, working on the station of gratitude and humility
Self-abasement	*Dhull*	Placing oneself in a situation where others belittle them or take their right	Discounting blessings (*nisyān al-ni'mah*)	Increasing healthy pride (*'izzah*)
Disdain of criticism	*Karāhat al-dhamm*	Fear of being criticized by people and seeking out their praise	Love of position, arrogance	Reflecting on where benefit and harm ultimately come from
Fear of death	*Karāht al-mawt*	Fear of death to the point that one is bothered if it is merely mentioned	Love of worldly things, negative opinion about Allah (*sū' al-ẓann*)	Reflecting on death and what is beyond death, increasing hope (*rajā'*) in Allah, good opinion about Allah (*ḥusn al-ẓann*)
Discounting blessings	*Nisyān al-ni'mah*	Being heedless of one's blessings and not showing gratitude for the giver of the blessing	Arrogance, heedlessness (*ghaflah*) specifically of the fact that all blessings from Allah	Counting one's blessings, increasing gratitude (*shukr*), reciting the verses about blessings (specifically 14:7 and 13:11), thinking about those who are less fortunate, the *dhikr* of gratitude (*al-ḥamdu li-llāh*)
Mockery	*Haz'*	Pointing out faults in a manner that causes humour and laughter	Arrogance	Use the treatment for arrogance (*kibr*)

* Note: If a cause is another disease, treatment should also include addressing the root disease(s)

Table 9.2 Adornment (*Taḥallī*) with the stations of excellence (*Maqāmāt al-Iḥsān*)

Name of Station	*Transliteration of Arabic*	*Definition*
Repentance	*Tawbah*	Remorse over what has transpired, a firm resolution to never return to that matter, leaving the matter (if currently engaged in it), and righting wrongs if another person if the sin affected another person.
Patience	*Ṣabr*	Steadfastness in preserving the rulings of God from both the Qur'ān and Sunnah during times of affliction and blessing.
Gratitude	*Shukr*	Humbly expending the blessings of God in that which would please Him while being happy for the Giver of the blessing (i.e. God) and not the Blessing in and of itself.
Hope	*Rajā'*	Hope along with actions that are means to what is hoped for. Otherwise, it is vain hopes (*amal*) and desires (*ṭama'*).
Fear	*Khawf*	The fear here is not referring to mere feelings of fear and dread, but rather actual actions and avoidances in fulfilling the commands of and avoiding the prohibitions of God.
Intimacy	*Uns*	The elation of the heart as it observes the beauty of God.
Positive thinking	*Ḥusn al-ẓann*	The firm belief of the heart that good will come from God.
Detaching from the world	*Zuhd*	Intentional detachment from worldly matters while considering them lowly.
Depending on God	*Tawakkul*	Taking the normal means of cause and effect while recognizing that ultimately everything is controlled by God.
Accepting fate	*Riḍā' bi-l-qadr*	Being free, outwardly and inwardly, from disputing the ordainment of God.
Love	*Maḥabbah*	A reality in the heart that causes a person to obey the One Who is loved (i.e. God).
Sincere intention	*Ṣidq al-niyyah*	Focusing attention, with presence of heart, on the One being worshipped (i.e. God).

as cognition, emotion, behavior, and spirit, even though such a separation is atypical in the scholarly writings. It is also important to note that many of the "spiritual diseases" mentioned may be beyond the scope of psychotherapy. Having said this, it may still be useful to consider some of these character ills as contributors to some issues that may be within the purview of the psychotherapist. This is especially so when doing relational work or opting to focus on developing resiliency and psycho-spiritual growth. For example, in the context of marital therapy one may be able to utilize this relationship as an avenue for working on character traits that could potentially both enhance and serve the patient in their marital life and increase the quality of relationships in general.

General Strategies

Reciprocal Inhibition

Reciprocal inhibition, though a behavioral concept in modern psychology thought to have been identified (or conceptualized) in Western Europe by Joseph Wolpe in the 1950s, is a concept that is well known within the Islamic tradition. Abū Zayd al-Balkhī has discussed this very concept in his works (al-Balkhī, 2005). It is the process of utlizing an alternative replacement behavior that serves to inhibit the undesirable behavior on account of its incompatibility when performed simultaneously. For example, an individual who has a habit of surrounding themselves with bad company that may promote their addictive behaviors, may be asked to attend a religious weekly *halaqah* or group during the time that they would usually spend time with friends. Additionally, this can be combined with reinforcements for positive opposite actions, whereby the practitioner promotes and highlights alternative positive behaviors. For example, an anxious patient who was asked to speak in public may make light of their achievement, assuming they should not be congratulated for performing actions they feel they should be doing naturally. In response, the practitioner may spend some time discussing and drawing attention to their achievement.

Change the Environment, Change the Behavior

Islamic scholars have placed a great degree of emphasis on the need for *ṣuḥbah* or good companionship in facilitating change. At times, it is important to consider the intense pull, craving, or urge to fall back into automated unhealthy behaviors. An Arabic proverb states "all things regress back to their original state", or put another way, "regression to the mean" (Prochaska, DiClemente, & Norcross, 1992). Once the balance or mean is altered, then automated behaviors become consistent with healthy behaviors. Therefore, in order to moderate the natural urge for repetition, it is important to facilitate and examine aspects of the patient's environment that may exacerbate those temptations. Associated behavioral responses are wired neurologically and can be triggered by environmental cues (Bernheim & Rangel, 2004). These include the presence of particular objects, times of day, people, and so on. For example, an individual may be triggered to overeat by the contextual cue of being in their room alone in the evening. This can even induce a physiological hunger response. In a study cited by Wansink in his book on *Mindless Eating*, researchers provided participants attending a movie with two large containers of popcorn in a quantity too great to be consumed entirely. One group was given a slightly smaller container than the other. The group that was given the very large container ended up eating a greater amount popcorn than those given the slightly smaller container, despite both groups not finishing all the popcorn. Therefore, external cues and environmental adjustments can facilitate transformations in one's behaviors (Wansink, 2006, pp. 16–19).

Change the Behavior, Change the Thinking

Research demonstrates that individuals strive to regulate the tension accompanied by cognitive dissonance (Aronson, 2019). Cognitive dissonance is when an individual experiences anxiety or distress on account of their behaviors being misaligned with their beliefs (Festinger, 1957). Thus, a typical approach is to focus on adjusting the beliefs that enable or reinforce unhealthy behaviors. However, the converse is also true, and this is a bidirectional relationship. That is, after cognitive re-evaluation of behaviors, sometimes automated behaviors still persist and prove resistant to change (Miller & Rollnick, 2004). Therefore, focusing on behavioral modification can also have a reciprocal impact on cognitions, which can then be adjusted, given that individuals typically seek congruence. Persistent behavioral modification and continual behavioral performance of the desired behaviors will automatically start to soften and challenge the cognitive beliefs that maintained the destructive behaviors in the first place (Harmon-Jones, 2000). In fact, the converse will begin to manifest itself, whereby new cognitive rationalizations will form in order to alleviate the tension created by the cognitive dissonance, thereby generating new neurological links between the newly acquired behaviors and cognitions (Albarracin & Wyer, 2000; Craske, Treanor, Conway, Zbozinek, & Vervliet, 2014). For example, if a patient is to behave more consistently with the idea of self-confidence or the belief that they are a good Muslim, even if they do not wholeheartedly subscribe to this notion or the aspiration to acquire it, over time the continued behavioral consistency with this notion will begin to internalize this belief system that did not resonate completely with the patient at the outset.

Exposure Response Prevention

Exposure response prevention (ERP) is a form of cognitive behavioral therapy (CBT) that is used particularly in the treatment of anxiety disorders that carry a very strong behavioral avoidance or compulsive response (Hezel & Simpson, 2019). Typically, anxiety-prone patients tend to engage in avoidance behaviors. For example, in the context of OCD this involves confronting obsessional triggers and preventing associated neutralizing behaviors, where the patient is permitted to have the intrusive thoughts and is made to realize that these thoughts are of no consequence, irrespective of the content of the obsessions (Hezel & Simpson, 2019). This is mostly helpful for patients who focus a lot of energy on trying to block out thoughts that they consider intrusive and distressing. Once the patient suspends all efforts to block out thoughts, this often leads to a reduction in intrusions, instead of a surge in thinking these undesirable thoughts, which is what most patients expect to happen (Himle, Chatters, Taylor, & Nguyen, 2011). Similarly, Abū Zayd al-Balkhī describes the necessity of facing or being exposed to irrational phobic fears (Awaad & Ali, 2015). This is in essence an opposition (*mukhālafah*) to the obsessional pull to avoid the feared stimulus by facing it head-on. This type of exposure response prevention can be used in the context of any anxiety-laden behaviors. Repeated exposure to the feared stimuli will soften and reduce physiological arousal when those stimuli are experienced. This can include the treatment of *waswasah* or OCD scrupulosity, whereby the therapist accompanies the patient in repeating their ritual ablution (washing before prayer), restricting them to only one cycle of washing and preventing the inclination to wash again. During such exposure activities the strengthening of more rational cognitions is encouraged through cognitive processing during and after exposures. The general idea of exposure to any discomforting behavior can be applied beyond OCD in order to soften resistance and the associated cognitive fears that serve as barriers to change.

The Six M's Model of Behavioral Change

The "Six M's" model can be used by practitioners to help guide the process of behavioral change. They are: *mushāraṭah* (goal-setting or stipulation), *murāqabah* (self-monitoring), *muḥāsabah* (self-evaluation), *mu'āqabah* (consequences), *mu'ātabah* (self-reprimand), and *mujāhadah* (exertion). These six tools do not have to occur sequentially, simultaneously, or even at a specific time of day; however, the general recommendation is to perform the goal-setting at the beginning of the day and the self-evaluation in the evening. A practitioner can create a workbook or a printout of these Six M's as a daily ritual for the patient to fill out, accompanied by a frequency or behavioral log mentioned above that monitors progress on behavioral goals (see Tables 9.3 and 9.4).

Mushāraṭah (goal-setting) has two aspects: (1) knowledge of the desired goal that is consistent with the dictates of the rational self or *'aql*, and (2) knowledge of the triggers, cues, and variables that maintain or enable

Table 9.3 The six M's—daily log

	Beginning of the Day	*End of the Day*	*Score**
Mushāraṭah (goal-setting or stipulation)	What is the action or non-action that is desired?		
Murāqabah (self-monitoring)	List the triggers, cues and thought processes that lead to both success and failure.		
Muḥāsabah (self-evaluation)	How many times during the day will you stop and evaluate yourself?	How would you rate your achieving of the goal you set today?	
Mu'āqabah (consequences)	What consequence will you give yourself for not achieving the goal?	Did you give yourself the consequence for not achieving the goal?	
Mu'ātabah (self-reprimand)	What will you say to yourself when you are not achieving the goal?	Did you use this self-talk/reminder?	
Mujāhadah (exertion)	What do you need to do in order to fulfill your goal throughout the day?		

* For each of the M's, one can self-grade themselves using the 3 levels of actions from Qur'ān 35:32 which are:

0 Fell short (*ẓālimun li nafsihī*)
1 Practiced it most of the time (*muqtaṣid*)
2 Went beyond the goal (*sābiqun bi-l-khayrāt*)

Table 9.4 The six M's—weekly log

Day	*Mushāraṭah (goal-setting or stipulation)*	*Murāqabah (self-monitoring)*	*Mu'āqabah (consequences)*	*Mu'ātabah (self-reprimand)*	*Mujāhadah (exertion)*	*Muḥāsabah (self-evaluation)*
1						
2						
3						
4						
5						
6						
7						

pathological behaviors. After an appropriate assessment of behaviors and a potential holistic evaluation of the self have been carried out, a behavioral plan should be developed.

Murāqabah (self-monitoring) is a desirable goal that allows the individual to develop better consciousness and mindfulness of the variables that trigger behavioral reactions or impulses in them. This process of observing the self allows the individual to put a bit of distance between themselves and their behaviors. Additionally, it allows them to have a better understanding of the steps or stages that lead to the undesirable behavioral outcomes. This increased mindfulness will allow them to interrupt or intervene in order to break the vicious cycle. Patients are often unaware of the process they undergo that leads them to these behavioral outputs. Thus, behavioral monitoring through psychotherapy should be aimed at helping the patient to understand this process and nurturing continuous mindfulness. Such monitoring requires understanding the various sources of thoughts, impulses, or drives. For each occurrence, patients may want to record (1) the trigger, (2) the associated cues in the environment, (3) the thoughts before, during, and after the action, (4) the place, and (5) the time of day in their daily Six M's chart.

Muḥāsabah (self-evaluation) requires that patients analyze their actions and the associated thoughts of that day, period, or moment and see how they align or not with the goals that were set. For goals that were met or surpassed, gratitude (*shukr*) should be shown, which is one of the stations of excellence (*maqāmāt al-iḥsān*). For the goals where a person falls short, these have to be made up (*qaḍā'*) or corrected, or a consequence needs to be administered either at that time or set as a goal to be met at a later time. In their Six M's log, the patient may want to record whether they met their goals or fell short, and then record how and when they would make up any shortcomings, and write down how grateful they were for those goals they achieved.

Mu'āqabah (constructive consequences) is something that one does in response to not having met a goal or having transgressed the limits of the set goals. Reinforcement cycles utilize both reward and punishment; thus it is recommended that during the therapeutic encounter, one also considers rewards for successes. Operant conditioning is rooted in the idea of reinforcements and punishments in shaping behaviors. Islamic scholars, too, have identified this as a mechanism of change. Abū 'Alī b. Miskawayh (d.421 AH/1030 CE) discussed the necessity to punish the *nafs* for overstepping the limits set by the *'aql* (ibn Miskawayh, 2003). Thus, the practitioner may employ this strategy in order to train the *nafs*. Conceptually, the *nafs* is driven to enjoy pleasures and, by virtue of depriving alternative pleasurable behaviors through punishment or administering other pleasures, the *nafs* is more likely to comply with these incentivized requests. However, it is noteworthy that the punishment, i.e.

deprivation of another pleasurable behavior or reward, should be significant or strong enough to facilitate change. For example, mandating a rich individual to pay to a charity a sum of money that is insignificant to him or her may not be a significant deterrent to make them comply with the request to give up the undesirable behavior. The administration of these punishments or rewards should be discussed with the patient and a reinforcement schedule decided upon. Review of the frequency of the behaviour or charts of change should be conducted intermittently and there should be consistent evaluation as to whether the deterrents are leading to the intended results.

Another method of choosing a consequence is to have something that relates to the limb that fell short. Two common examples of *mu'āqabah* are mentioned by both al-Ghazālī and Mawlūd: (1) self-imposed hunger as a response to having eaten something one should not have, and (2) averting one's gaze from permissible things after having looked at something prohibited. In the first example, it was the stomach (considered a "limb" in Islamic writings) which fell short, so some amount of permissible food would be avoided as a consequence. If a person is working to avoid prohibited (*ḥarām*) food, unhealthy food, or overindulgence in permissible food, then the consequence would be to hold back from eating something that the *nafs* enjoys. The exact nature of the consequence should be discussed with the patient to ensure the prohibition is appropriate.

Mu'ātabah (self-reprimand) is closely related to the previously described tool of consequence, as it is used as a response to having fallen short on set goals. Once an identified goal has not been met, patients should reprimand themselves. Emotion theory places some importance on the adaptive utility of shame (Greenberg & Pavio, 1997). Shaming oneself decreases the likelihood of behavioral repetition. One of the names of the *nafs* discussed earlier is the reproaching self (*nafs lawwāmah*). The *lawwāmah* is the soul which is aware of its faults and is critical of them. This seems to be the distinguishing factor between this self and the self which is only inclined towards evil (*nafs ammārah*) in that the latter is devoid of criticism of its state. It could also be that the *lawwāmah* is completely unaware of its fault, which is a root disease called *ghaflah* (heedlessness). *Mu'ātabah* is distinguished from *mu'āqabah*, in that *mu'ātabah* is generally conceived as self-examination that is used to keep oneself in check critically. It typically is designed to be preventative and is to be utilized as a deterrent to acting in undesirable ways.

However, it is crucial to avoid the utilization of this 'M' to prevent the introduction of unhealthy shame. The overactivation of the *nafs lawwāmah* can engender maladaptive shaming that further depletes and depresses the individual. Therefore, such self-critique must be moderated and used within the appropriate context of the patient. Often excess guilt can serve as a demotivator of behavior and can lead to despondency. Therefore, in order to counter this experience, one may need to emphasize self-compassion. The practitioner can prescribe a proactive approach of having a normative routine of general repentance once after every prayer, as is typical of normative Islamic religious practice, bringing to mind that God forgives all sins. It is a resignation of the patient's self to the imperfection of being human, and that such imperfection combined with repentance is one of the reasons for the elevation of the human rank even above the angels. These positive reframes can help to solidify an alternative cognitive orientation that shifts a negative attribution bias to a positive and optimistic one filled with hope (*rajā'*).

Mujāhdah is emphasized as one of the key principles of change in TIIP. It is the element of self-struggle and is sometimes referred to as *jihād al-nafs* (struggle against the self), or the greater struggle or *jihād akbar* (Haddad, 2005). The linking of the term *jihād* with struggle against the self is also found in the Qur'ān which states: "And those who struggle in our cause, We will surely guide them to Our ways" (29:69). The overall goal of the process of self-exertion is to embrace the path of resistance by performing good actions, avoiding the blameworthy, and constantly recycling through the process of the "Six M's". Mawlūd mentions that any method that a person chooses to use in the struggle against the self must be in accordance with the tradition (*sunnah*) of the Prophet Muḥammad (peace and blessings be upon him). This is where it is important that an individual choosing a practice to implement in their personal struggle consults with someone familiar with the limits and advice of the tradition of Islam.

Case Illustration of Implementation of the Six M's

Case Summary

Ahmed was a 30-year-old Eastern European Muslim male who sought out religiously integrated therapeutic services on account of his obsessions and compulsions that were of a religiously oriented (scrupulous) nature. This included excessive washing for his daily prayers, whereby he believed that he continuously nullified his ritual purity and repeatedly returned to wash his limbs over and over again. These behavioral compulsions alleviated his immediate anxiety but contributed to a vicious cycle of reinforcing his obsessive fears of nullifying his ritual purity and invalidating his prayers, which strengthened his compulsive reactions to these thoughts.

Case History

Ahmed Abdullah reported that his grandfather had also demonstrated obsessive compulsive-type behaviors, though they were not of a scrupulous nature due to him not being very religious. Ahmed reported growing up in a family that was characterized by turmoil and instability. His family was relatively poor, causing them to move around a lot from neighborhood to neighborhood. Mr. Ahmed's parents' marital relationship was turbulent and he witnessed a lot of this conflict in the home. He also experienced hypervigilance related to things potentially "going wrong", or continually had a general feeling that bad things would happen. When he was 18 years old and had completed high school, Ahmed started to practice Islam and internalized Islamic beliefs, despite not having actively identified with his faith previously. The impetus for his religious "conversion" was attending a religious sermon where the Imam discussed the punishments for those who neglect their religious duties. This greatly impacted him, engendering in him a resolve to rectify his lifestyle and turn to God. He began to learn the ritual rules of Islam and felt that his religious beliefs brought a lot of comfort, stability, predictability, and order to his life. However, after reading further about the details of the punishments of the grave for sinners and those negligent of prayer, and also about some of the "nullifiers" of ritual purity (*wuḍū'*), he started to feel intense nervousness. He began to repeat his prayers whenever he "felt unclean" or that he had nullified his prayers out of "precaution". This behavior become gradually more and more repetitive, whereby religious practice started to feel like a burden upon him and overwhelmingly frustrating. This resulted in him feeling "down" after several hours of repeating his ritual washing and prayers, fearing they may still not have been accepted. It also reduced his capacity to be "present" during his prayers, as he wass continuously hypervigilant and focusing acutely on whether he had nullified his purity, being concerned with "doing it right".

Case Conceptualization and Diagnosis According to TIIP

Based on the assessment by the clinician, Ahmed clearly exhibited obsessive compulsive symptoms that fitted the criteria for a formal DSM V diagnosis of OCD. The manifestations of the OCD symptoms were of a religious scrupulous subtype. Although his obsessive thoughts were considered to be from his *'aql*, Ahmed's compulsive behaviors originated out of his *nafs* and these behaviors were the predominant problem. This was evident from his recognition of the unhealthy and irrational nature of his behaviors and the overwhelming intensity of his compulsive behavioral drives or impulses.

At the outset, his *'aqlānī* catastrophic thoughts were characterized by fears of not having his prayers accepted due to the absence of ritual purity. These thoughts were easily debunked during initial sessions of cognitive therapy that helped him to restructure his thinking and to challenge his irrational cognitive distortions. In a relaxed and unagitated state, he was able to demonstrate insight and maintain rational thinking. However, when triggered by the habituated feared stimuli—in this case prayer-time and washing—he would cognitively regress and his irrational fears would return immediately. During this state of hypervigilance, his anxiety would escalate and cognitions would snowball to thoughts of being questioned in the afterlife and being punished severely. Additionally, he began to selectively recall verses of the Qur'ān and prophetic narrations regarding punishments for those who neglect prayer. This is reflective of overactive negative cognitive ruminations that are characteristic of obsessional thinking, particularly when triggered. At times this would progress even further to the belief that praying without being in a state of ritual purity (on account of his "invalidation of purity") may even result in blasphemy. These cognitive escalations heightened his fear, and such anxiety propelled him into an aroused physiological state that intensified his compulsive urges to repeat ritual washing and prayer in order to extinguish this anxiety. With regard to the spiritual dimensions of his functioning (*rūḥ*), he felt overburdened by prayer, and did not derive any peace or sense of spiritual connection during the course of his prayers on account of his preoccupations with potentially violating Islamic sacraments.

Additionally, after struggling with "perfecting" his ritual ablution and prayers, by the end of the day he felt depleted, along with experiencing a sense of hopelessness that he would ever get better. This further led to him feeling despondent and he began to sink into a state of "doom and gloom", whereby he would at times neglect his religious duties, feeling completely spiritually disconnected, incompetent, and unforgivable.

Treatment

His TIIP practitioner started off his treatment by doing a preliminary assessment in the form of an initial interview while building their relationship. Keeping consistent with TIIP treatment goals, the practitioner first empathically followed the patient, probing for further details about the nature of his behaviors, history, and associated triggers, and attempted to identify the nature of his cognitions, emotions, and spiritual experiences. After a few preliminary sessions, the patient and practitioner were able to identify and have a better awareness (*inkishāf*) of the vicious cycle of behaviors described in the case conceptualization.

The practitioner then spent a session helping to construct treatment goals and oriented the patient to the Six M's model of behavioral change. This would be implemented in the *mu'ālajah* phase of therapy, after establishment of sufficient rapport and therapeutic alliance (*murābatah*). Once these goals were agreed, the practitioner started sessions with finalizing and solidifying them (*mushāraṭah*), the first step of the Six M's model. The practitioner then moved on to describe the concept of *murāqabah*. The therapist helped the patient to recognize that his compulsive behaviors reinforced his cognitive ruminative fears. These cognitive ruminative fears were the direct cause of the escalation of his physiology. The practitioner taught Ahmed that he could learn to identify the early emergence of these unhealthy cycles by being better attuned to early signals of increased physiological arousal, such as an increased heart rate or breathing. Such physiological cues could help him transition into actively utilizing learned self-soothing cognitive remedies, such as reassuring himself that his thinking was due to satanic whispers (*waswasah*) that were religiously inconsequential, and that his ritual purity could not be invalidated due to a subjective "feeling" of nullifying ritual purity. Such cognitive defusion skills and externalization of the source of his thinking were reinforced by teaching the patient that, under Islamic law, subjective feelings are inconsequential.

The practitioner worked with the patient to help him identify more objective indicators of invalidation of ritual purity, such as passing gas out loud that could clearly be heard or smelt. The practitioner then worked with the patient to discuss the concept of *mujāhadah*. He discussed with the patient the necessity to consider healthy progress as objectively measurable through his behaviors and not his inconsequential thoughts. Although his thoughts activated his anxious feelings, he was taught to allow his thoughts to pass through his mind, to accept his thoughts, and to commit to not performing his compulsive reactions. Through this process he could begin to break and soften the intensity of this negative cycle. The therapist and patient then transitioned to start interoceptive exposures in order to extinguish and dishabituate the patient's compulsive behaviors, i.e. exposure response prevention therapy used intermittently throughout sessions. Repeated successful attempts at ritual washing and praying without repetition engendered a quieting and diffusion of the power of his impulsive urges.

The therapist transitioned the patient into developing a *muḥāsabah* chart. They collectively created a frequency notebook that attempted to document the number of repetitions in ritual washing and prayer as an objective monitor of gains. The therapist and patient together then identified constructive punishments and reprimands (*mu'ātabah* and *mu'āqabah*) for falling short of set goals. The concept of reciprocal inhibition was introduced into this process. If the patient washed himself too much, at a level decided upon by the patient and therapist, then he would be responsible for increasing in-sessional exposures, which were psychologically unpleasant for the patient. This punishment served to inhibit and counterbalance his impulsive urges to exceed the maximum allowable repeated washes for the week. The therapist and patient made a plan to have progressive reductions in allowable washing repetitions towards the goal of normalcy.

While the Six M's method was utilized continuously, the therapist also introduced the concept of compassion into sessions. He described the patient's cognitive style as being oriented to a negative attribution bias, signaling an imbalance in thinking. Therefore, the therapist helped the patient come up with compassion-inducing rituals that would help shift this orientation. He was given prescriptions of performing a set number of litanies of remembering or pronouncing the names of God that carried the attributes of Mercy, such as al-Ra'ūf al-Raḥīm. Guided imagery was introduced as a mechanism of heightening the value of such an intervention. During the course of imagery, he was to imagine that God was accepting his prayers and worship and that the Light of God was entering his heart and quieting his catastrophic thoughts and impulses. Through the utilization of the Six M's the patient and therapist were successfully able to diminish his symptoms, and this treatment lead to full remission.

This case demonstrates a holistic approach to working with OCD. The intentional focus of this case was to demonstrate a strong *nafsānī* or behavioral impulsive inclination that could not simply be eradicated by cognitive restructuring, spiritual exercises, or emotional processing. The disorder, despite being influenced by these aforementioned factors, was predominately maintained and enabled by the compulsive rituals that needed to be dishabituated and extinguished. By virtue of working behaviorally, the cognitions and anxiety that were triggered by the associated environmental stimuli of washing/prayer could be disentangled through behavioral exposures and cessation of compulsive rituals. Successful behavioral reformation would then lead to the solidification of cognitive beliefs formed outside a triggered emotional state.

Conclusion

In sum, an intentional and focused approach to modifying character traits from undesired behaviors (*dhamīmah*) to positive behaviors can engender holistic health and balance. This is especially true in the case of Muslim patients seeking religiously oriented intervention. Both the theoretical framework and practical applications presented in this chapter draw extensively from the Islamic spiritual tradition, showing that they can continue to be a source of extracting sound methods of intervention and treatment. Although the case provided is more clinical in focus, the behavioral principles outlined above can be extracted and are equally applicable, as demonstrated in the case presentation. It is the authors' hope that practitioners can appreciate Islamic scholarly writings and develop the faculty for extracting the utility of particular interventions or principles for use in a psychological treatment context, despite their original intent to engender purely spiritual health.

References

Albarracin, D., & Wyer Jr., R. S. (2000). The cognitive impact of past behavior: Influences on beliefs, attitudes and future behavioral decisions. *Journal of Personality and Social Psychology, 79*(1), 5–22.

al-Balkhī, A. Z. (2005). *Maṣāliḥ al-Anfus wa-l-Abdān*. Cairo: Ma'had al-Makhṭūṭāṭ al-'Arabī.

al-Bayhaqī, A. (2003). *Al-Sunan al-Kubrā*. Beirut: Dār al-Kutub al-'Ilmiyyah.

al-Bazzār, A. A. (n.d.). *Jāmi' Bayān al-'ilm wa Faḍluhu*. Damascus: Mu'assasah al-Risālah.

al-Birgivī, M. (2011). *Al-Ṭarīqah al-Muḥammadiyyah wa-l-Ṣirāṭ al-Aḥmadiyyah*. Damascus: Dār al-Qalam.

al-Bukhārī (2010). *Sahih al-Bukhari*. Darussalam: Riyadh.

al-Ghazālī, A. H. (1990). *Mukhtaṣar: Iḥyā' 'Ulūm al-Dīn*. Beirut: Mua'ssas al-Kutub al-Thaqāfiyyah.

al-Ḥaṣkafī (2006). *Ifāḍat al-Anwār with al-Nasafī's al-Manār fī Uṣūl al-Fiqh*. Istanbul: Irshad Kitabevi.

al-Jawziyyah, I. Q. (2016). *Ighāthat al-Lahfān*. Mecca: Dār 'Ālam al-Fawā'id.

al-Ṭabrānī, S. (1984). *al-Mu'jam al-Kabīr*. Baghdad: al-Jumhūriyyah al-'Irā qiyya, Wizārat al-Awqāf.

Aronson, E. (2019). Dissonance, hypocrisy, and the self-concept. In E. Harmon-Jones (Ed.), *Cognitive dissonance: Reexamining a pivotal theory in psychology* (pp. 141–157). Washington, DC: American Psychological Association.

Arberry, A. J. (1979). *Sufism: An account of the mystics in Islam*. New York, NY: Harper & Row.

Awaad, R., & Ali, S. (2015). Obsessional disorders in al-Balkhi's 9th century treatise: Sustenance of the body and soul. *Journal of Affective Disorders, 180*, 185–189.

Baumeister, R. F., Bratslavsky, E., Muraven, M., & Tice, D. M. (1998). Ego depletion: Is the active self a limited resource? *Journal of Personality and Social Psychology, 74*, 1252–1265.

Bernheim, B. D., & Rangel, A. (2004). Addiction and cue-triggered decision processes. *American Economic Review, 94*(5), 1558–1590.

Craske, M. G., Treanor, M, Conway, C. C., Zbozinek, T., & Vervliet, B. (2014). Maximizing exposure therapy: An inhibitory learning approach. *Behaviour Research and Therapy, 58*, 10–23.

Engle, D. E., & Arkowitz, H. (2006). *Ambivalence in psychotherapy: Facilitating readiness to change*. New York, NY: Guilford Press.

Festinger, L. (1957). *A theory of cognitive dissonance*. Stanford, CA: Stanford University Press.

Freud, S. (1961). *Beyond the pleasure principle*. New York, NY: W. W. Norton.

Greenberg, L. S., & Paivio, S. C. (1997). *Working with emotions in psychotherapy*. New York, NY: Guilford Press.

Greenberg, L. S., & Watson J. C. (2006). *Emotion-focused therapy for depression*. Washington, DC: American Psychological Association.

Haddad, G. F. (2005, February 28). Documentation of "Greater Jihad" hadith. Retrieved from www.livingislam.org/n/dgjh_e.html.

Harmon-Jones, E. (2000). Cognitive dissonance and experienced negative affect: Evidence that dissonance increases experienced negative affect even in the absence of aversive consequences. *Personality & Social Psychology Bulletin*, *26*(12), 1490–1501.

Hezel, D. M., & Simpson, H. B. (2019). Exposure and response prevention for OCD: A review and new directions. *Indian Journal of Psychiatry*, *61*(1), 85–92.

Himle, J. A., Chatters, L. M., Taylor, R. J., & Nguyen, A. (2011). The relationship between obsessive-compulsive disorder and religious faith: Clinical characteristics and implications for treatment. *Psychology of Religion and Spirituality*, *3*(4), 241–258.

Ibn ʿĀbidīn, M. A. (1992). *Radd al-Muḥtār ʿalā al-Durr al-Mukhtār*. Beirut: Dār al-Fikr.

Ibn ʿĀbidin, M., Haskafi, M. A., & Nasafi, M. (2006). *Sharhu sharh al-manar*. Karachi: Idaratal Quran.

Ibn ʿAjībah, A. (2002). *al-Baḥr al-Madīd*. Beirut: Dār al-Kutub al-ʿIlmiyya.

Ibn Ḥibbān, A. M. (2012). *Ṣaḥīḥ Ibn Ḥibbān*. Beirut: Dār Ibn Ḥazm.

Ibn Miskawayh, A. (2003). *The refinement of character*. Trans. Constantine K. Zurayk. Chicago, IL: Kazi Publications Inc.

Mawlūd, M. (1996). *Maṭharat al-Qulūb*. Nouakchott, Mauritania: Aḥamdū Sālik Publications.

Miller, W. R., & Rollnick, S. (2004). Talking oneself into change: Motivational interviewing, stages of change, and therapeutic process. *Journal of Cognitive Psychotherapy: An international Quarterly*, *18*(4), 299–308.

Muslim, M. (2006). *Ṣaḥīḥ Muslim*. Riyadh: Dār Ṭaybah for Publishing and Distribution.

Prochaska, J. O., DiClemente, C. C., & Norcross, J. C. (1992). In search of how people change: Applications to addictive behaviors. *American Psychologist*, *47*(9), 1102–1114.

Raghab, A. (2015). *The medieval Islamic hospital: medicine, religion, and charity*. New York, NY: Cambridge University Press.

Ragab, A. (2018). *Piety & patienthood in medieval Islam*. New York, NY: Routledge.

ʿUthmānī, M. T. (2001). *Spiritual discourses*. Karachi: Dār al-Ishāʿat.

Wansink, B. (2006). *Mindless eating*. New York, NY: Bantam Dell.

Zarrūq, A. (2006). *ʿUddatul Murīd al-Ṣādiq*. Beirut: Dār Ibn Ḥazm.

Chapter 10

Spiritually (*Rūḥānī*) Focused Psychotherapy

Hooman Keshavarzi, Asim Yusuf, Paul M. Kaplick, Tameem Ahmadi, and Amin Loucif

In recent modern history a growing body of literature has suggested that the mental and behavioral effects of religiously and spiritually based practices can be operationalized, and reveal that such practices positively impact psychological well-being (Koenig, King, & Carson, 2012). More specifically, a study on Muslims demonstrated that Qur'ān recitation can be linked to a reduction of withdrawal symptoms in tobacco consumers (Zainudin, Ahmad, Ishak, & Yusoff, 2018) and lower anxiety symptoms in athletes before competition (Mottaghi, Esmaili, & Rohani, 2011). The psychology literature has targeted the association between Islamic positive religious coping methods and health indices in Muslims (Abu-Raiya, Pargament, Mahoney, & Stein, 2008): Regardless of whether a link was established between positive religious coping and desirable (positive association) or undesirable health outcomes (negative association), only a small and almost negligible portion of research demonstrates that spiritually based practices have no effect at all (Abu-Raiya & Pargament, 2015). Here, a key assumption is that models of the dynamics of the human entity, articulated by spiritual scholars, can be psychologically operationalized, though not mechanized (Abu-Raiya, 2012; Rothman & Coyle, 2018; Skinner, 1989/2018). This body of literature is related to the growing spiritually integrated psychotherapies movement that is seeing increasingly greater recognition and mainstream acceptance in the scientific community (Richards, Sanders, Lea, McBride, & Allen, 2015).

Given this shift, in recent years Muslim psychologists have also shifted their focus from a conflict hypothesis on the relationship between the Islamic intellectual tradition and contemporary psychology to a harmonizing hypothesis that emphasizes the complementarity of both knowledge systems. Since the early days of the emergence of contemporary Islamic psychologies (IPs), the existence of a spiritual domain within the human entity has been proffered as perhaps the most critical theoretical assumption of the nascent discipline. During the 1980s and 1990s in particular, Muslim psychologists frequently recognized that consideration of the spiritual domain in health and disease in psychology and psychotherapy entails stripping off some of the ultra-materialist and ultra-reductionist orientations of psychology and psychotherapy (Kaplick & Rüschoff, 2018).

In this chapter we rearticulate an explanation of the *rūḥ* (the spiritual domain of the human psyche) within the context of TIIP spiritually focused psychotherapy before we proceed with a case illustration. The theoretical section covers the definition and conceptualization of the spiritual domain of the human psyche and its dysfunctions. The various possibilities for positive modulation of the spiritual domain through motivated behaviors ("Islamic mechanisms") that utilize *dhikr* (spiritual exercises and litanies of remembrance of the Divine) are described. The therapeutic concept for TIIP spiritually integrated or *rūḥānī*-based psychotherapies specifies how these Islamic mechanisms can be rendered into potential spiritually based psychotherapeutic interventions.

Interrogating the Efficacy and Mechanisms of Spiritual Therapies

There are two broad approaches that may be taken to the question of the efficacy of spiritual approaches to therapy, both of which allow integration of such therapies into psychotherapeutic practice. The first is that of the TIIP model, which, as has been noted previously and as will be reiterated below, affirms the essentially dualist integrative nature of the human as being comprised of a closely interconnected body and soul. The second, however, does not require assent to this metaphysical position—that is to say, one can affirm the efficacy of spiritual approaches to therapy without needing to affirm the existence of the human soul.

In terms of this latter position, which might well be adopted by non-Muslim practitioners dealing with Muslim (or more broadly, religious) patients, spiritual therapies such as those detailed in this chapter can be generally beneficial on the basis that they comprise behaviors that exert powerful cognitive and emotional effects on those who engage in them, along much the same lines as noted in the previous chapters of this book.

As an example, Yusuf and Elhaddad in Chapter 8 described the *Ḥajj* pilgrimage as "a set of ritual actions performed in congregation, involving a re-enactment of pivotal incidents within the lives of three Prophets (upon them be peace), designed to transform the inner state by evoking powerful emotions". This explanation could be expanded to note that the physical exertion involved in the re-enactment cannot help but evoke powerful cognitions, such as remembrance of the hardships endured and sacrifices made by such revered and respected figures, together with their sincerity and dedication. This in turn puts the performer's own life circumstances into context, enabling a cognitive reframing and restructuring that is paired with their emotional connection to the sacred places and persons in whose footsteps they tread.

As such, the (admittedly much less strenuous) spiritual exercises described in this chapter could be viewed as merely specific culturally or religiously framed forms of therapy that work—perhaps via the creation of a theologically constructed "emotional safe-space" in which to cognitively reframe one's difficulties—to alleviate the distress caused by negative cognitions and emotional states. This is especially so when, as is sometimes the case, those negative states are themselves derived from pathological spiritual dispositions or negative religious expressions, such as "God is punishing me", or "I am sinful and nobody loves me, including God", or "there is no hope that I will ever be free of this". This effect is also magnified when such spiritual therapies are conducted in congregations of the like-minded individuals who often characterize religious communities. Studies that would indicate such findings are numerous and well known (Rausch, Gramling, & Auerbach, 2006), and congruent with the explanatory model adopted in mainstream psychology in regard to spiritual therapies.

The approach taken in this present work, however, is not this latter one, but the former, which positively affirms the existence of a transcendent soul at the core of the human construct. This is affirmed not on the basis of prima facie empirical evidence (the soul, as a metaphysical entity, is by definition empirically unmeasurable), but rather on the basis of (1) rational possibility,[1] (2) empirical inference, such as the folding of the soul into an explanation for a particular psychological phenomenon, and (3) the scriptural resources of Islam. On the basis of this, the Islamic scholarly tradition recounts in profuse detail—and in accordance with various theoretical models, such as the TIIP paradigm—the precise manner in which body, mind, and soul interact. It also delves into the manner in which what are referred to in this chapter as "spiritual therapies" bring about salutary psychological effects, such as relief from depression, anxiety, and obsessionality, as well as the engendering of hope, connection, identity, meaning, and purpose.[2]

At this point, Ockham's Razor may be deployed to question whether there is any need whatsoever to positively affirm the existence of a soul, even in the context of spiritual therapies. If their effect on the soul cannot be directly and empirically measured, and they can be shown to be efficacious even in the purported absence of a soul via more prosaic emotional and cognitive means, what added advantage is there to affirming the soul except as a matter of sensitivity to believing patients? This is an important question and deserves closer exploration.

The TIIP model, as with the majority of classical and modern Islamic theoretical frameworks, posits a close interactionism between body and soul, in which each fundamentally affects the other. The previous chapters of this work demonstrate that an Islamic psychotherapy can work closely with the cognitive and emotional elements of the human psyche to ameliorate distress. Those chapters further explain that these elements have their effect by the influence that they in turn have on the soul itself. As such, one could posit that spiritual therapies work in a manner indistinguishable from others, through their indirect effect on the soul via human cognitive, emotional, and behavioral modifications. These are, hypothetically, just as empirically demonstrable as anything else in psychology. However, the Islamic models delve further than this, proposing that spiritual therapies, unlike other forms of therapy, have a direct effect on the soul that is over and above any indirect cognitive or emotional action. In order to understand this further, the concept of a "transcendent spiritual/mystical experience" (TSE) needs to be briefly unpacked.

Mystical Experiences

Throughout the nineteenth and twentieth centuries the study of religion became sporadically interested in the concept of a TSE—whether "revelatory" experiences, "ecstatic states of union", or other variations of this. The Harvard psychologist William James ([1902] 2016, pp. 113–117) provided the first (and probably best) modern definition of a mystical experience, describing its unifying features as being "transient, ineffable, noetic and passive".' In other words, they were discrete, temporary experiences that arose unexpectedly and sporadically (whether as the result of mediated actions such as prayer or meditation, or completely spontaneously). They were of such a nature that they could not be adequately expressed in words, but were authoritative such that they induced an utter certainty impossible to convey to others. These were both states of feeling and knowledge, but unlike either of them, plumbing depths of insight unfathomable to the ordinary discursive intellect, and tended to be experienced as if personal wills were in abeyance and at the command of a higher power (James, [1902] 2016, pp. 113–117).

Such experiences may range from being wholly overpowering to almost imperceptible, and relate to the most profound of human concerns as well as more mundane matters. It is such experiences that many therapists may describe as a "spiritual" moment, or therapeutic moments that are very "deep" and almost metaphysical. Carl Rogers once stated to Paul Tillich that "I feel at times when I'm really being helpful to a client of mine … there is something approximating to an I–Though relationship between us, then I feel as though the forces of the universe are operating through me" (Mouladoudis, 2008, p. 19). An anecdotal example from the contemporary clinical practice of one of the authors (Yusuf) further illustrates such experiences. It was the case of a woman who for decades had been traumatized by a toxic relationship with her mother. The woman said that one day, completely out of the blue and unprovoked or explainable by her therapy, she was overwhelmed by a feeling of "complete peace":

> It was as though I was living my mother's life through her eyes, and I instantly understood exactly why she was as she was and treated me the way she did. I was flooded by an instantaneous, overpowering sense of empathy that brought an irresistible forgiveness. It was gone as soon as it came and took me some time with my shaykh to process it. I didn't understand what had happened, but all the hurt dissipated in that instant and has never returned. I don't know why or how I was able to forgive my mother, but I know absolutely that I did. Its effect on my psychological issues was incredible.[3]

This experience fulfills all of James' criteria: transient, passive, noetic, and ineffable, and demonstrates the salutary effect of such TSEs on mental health.

To this, Rudolph Otto ([1923] 2010, pp. 8–31) added the idea of the encounter with the "Other"—a dualist experience—as being "numinous", which he defined as *sui generis* (an experience that was in a category of its own, unlike any other that had been experienced) and *mysterium tremendum et fascinans* (an indescribable experience of "encountering" that filled the mystic experiencer with a sense of overwhelming awe and dread, but also unutterable love).

Both of these typologies of spiritual experience emphasize the otherness of the experience, as well as the powerful cognitive and emotional effects that are—crucially—consequent to the experience, rather than being the cause of it. There have been various attempts to construct a typology of mystical experience in the Islamic tradition, including that of al-Dihlawī in his *Tafsīr 'Azīzī* (al-Kandihlawī, n.d., pp. 9–10), which discusses the notion of *tawajjuh* (coming face to face). He categorizes them in levels of intensity, beginning with "common-place" ineffable occurrences (*tawajjuh ilqā'ī*), and ascending to what he terms a unitary experience (*tawajjuh ittiḥādī*).[4] The more powerful versions of such experiences tended to be life-changing and paradigm-shifting for experiencers, frequently being accompanied by feelings of utter peace and tranquility that are palpable to others. Such mystics are often subsequently sought out by others for "blessings and healing"—which effectively entails a desire to experience such states by proxy (Beauregard & O'Leary, 2007, pp. 235ff).

The Neurobiology of Spirituality

Other typologies have been purported, but discussions about TSEs were largely restricted to the field of philosophy of religion until the late twentieth century, when interest was piqued once again in the newly developed field of neuroimaging and cognitive neuroscience. Research conducted via advanced brain imaging techniques such as fMRI and SPECT scans were able to significantly reduce the "Cartesian trialism" that had existed between pharmacotherapy, psychotherapy, and spirituality—or brain, mind, and soul. It demonstrated, firstly, that psychotherapy and medication were both able to affect brain functioning and, in some cases, structure: for example, Baxter showed that both reduced the metabolism of glucose in the right caudate nucleus, improving outcomes in obsessive compulsive disorder (Baxter et al., 1992, cited in Gabbard, 2000). Additionally, similar imaging research indicates that the spiritual practice of meditation up-regulates activation in the ventro-lateral prefrontal cortex, which then reduces activity in the amygdala, improving emotional regulation in response to negative thoughts (Schaefer et al., 2002).

Both spiritual techniques and psychotherapy can thus have empirically demonstrable effects on brain function and structure similar to—or more powerful than—those observed with psychotropic medication. Indeed, research demonstrates that long-term meditation mitigates against precisely those changes in the brain seen in severe, treatment-resistant depression—the type that is least susceptible to both medication and psychotherapy—by increasing the gray matter volumes and activity in the right orbito-frontal cortex and hypothalamus (Luders, Toga, Lepore, & Gaser, 2009).

TSEs, however, would appear to produce entirely different, but equally demonstrable neurological effects. SPECT studies on Carmelite Nuns and experienced Buddhist meditators during states of *unio mystica*, which were then correlated with their subjective experience (using Hood's mysticism scale; Hood & Francis, 2013), demonstrated increased activation of many different regions of the brain. These included regions as widely spaced as the inferior and superior parietal lobules, right prefrontal cortex and right thalamus, and the left-brain stem. This would indicate that TSEs are highly complex experiences involving a number of remote brain regions working together (Beauregard & O'Leary, 2007). Findings such as these, combined with the subjective sense of either temporary or permanent peacefulness and tranquility that obtains from such practices, demonstrate the potential of TSEs (at any level of Hood's scale) in promoting mental wellness, as well as the distinctness of spiritual approaches to mental health as opposed to other forms of cognitive or emotional psychotherapy.

In summary, the spiritual techniques used as part of an Islamic psychotherapy are posited to operate on a number of levels, from variant psychotherapeutic approaches acting on emotions and cognitions, to direct action on the spiritual reality of the human. These have the potential to bring about changes in the state and trait of the practitioner (or *ḥāl* and *maqām*, as they are termed in Islamic texts). Both of these can be understood

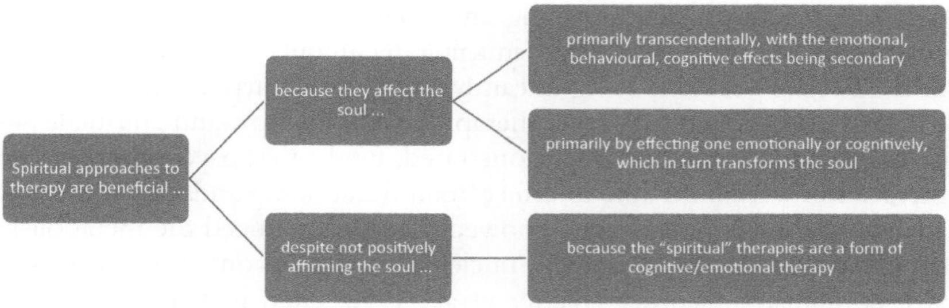

Figure 10.1 Explanatory approaches of the efficacy of spiritual therapies.

to relate—either causally or consequentially—to the brain structure and functioning of the human being via the integrationist dualist approach to the human being that is the premise of virtually all Islamic theories of anthropology (see Figure 10.1).

TIIP Disciplinary Assumptions

TIIP is one developing strand of Islamically integrated psychotherapy and constitutes a classically integrative approach to psychotherapy that combines indigenous psycho-spiritual concepts rooted in the Islamic intellectual heritage with the rigorous standards of modern psychotherapy. The TIIP framework considers the cognitive, behavioral, experiential/emotional, and spiritual needs of the human entity—the latter being the focus of this chapter. Spiritually integrated psychotherapies can be understood as a summary of psychotherapeutic treatment approaches which share the recognition that religion and spirituality constitute integral elements in the life of patients and therapists, and that these can be utilized meaningfully in the therapeutic encounter (Pargament, 2007).

The development of spiritually integrated psychotherapies in a TIIP context is associated with fundamental challenges as to why spiritually based practices might work. Consideration of the spirit as a therapeutic target builds upon disciplinary assumptions about the system of belief in the unseen, which is impossible to qualify mechanistically through the scientific method exclusively, but which is critically important to the spiritual orientation and epistemological and ontological foundations of an Islamic psychology, as illustrated above. An Islamic psychological explanation goes beyond the mere physical to include metaphysical explanatory notions rooted in Islamic cosmology. For example, although the *Sunnat Allah* (order of God based on cause and effect, or system of Allah) does operate in a normatively mechanistic fashion, Muslim prayer (*du'ā'*) can change behavioral outcomes through Divine intervention, which does occasionally interrupt the system. These notions are perhaps seen to cause the greatest divergence in an explanatory model of a spiritually oriented approach to psychotherapy and mainstream psychotherapeutic practice as a science. Thus, a leap of faith is necessary in incorporating spiritual concepts within a psychological framework.

Having said this, as with other psychological measures, such a notion does not negate the capacity to identify measurable indicators of spiritual change. Ibn Khaldūn states that the internal metaphysical aspects of the *nafs* cannot be observed spiritually, but rather that human behavior is an indicator of its internal state (Ibn Khaldūn, [1377] n.d.). Similarly, Shāh Walī Allah in his *al-Qawl al-Jamīl* states that inner obscure notions such as human belief can be judged and qualified through subjective human testimony and verification, that for the purposes of worldly functionality takes the place of its inner true reality (Walīallah, 2010, p. 33). Therefore, indicators of the positive effects of spiritual remedies can be measured through subjective self-reports as well as observed behavioral/psychological adjustment or maladjustment in patients, since it cannot be stated that all types of spiritual interventions are always beneficial for every patient.

While putting aside an entirely mechanistic explanation of this metaphysical process, Muslims can faithfully embrace spiritually oriented psychotherapy and even measure change through observed human behavior and subjective patient self-reports. Though this is in essence the staple of the overall field of psychology as a "soft science", which relies extensively on subjective self-reports and observable behavior, the major distinction is that Islamic spirituality embraces true divine metaphysical experiences informed by Islamic revelation that lie outside of the human psyche itself. For example, *dhikr* may bring down *barakah* or divine blessings upon the heart of the believer that can be self-reported by the patient as calmness. This is corroborated by the Prophet's (peace and blessings be upon him) response to to Ubay b. Ka'b's comment that he will engage only in the recital of *ṣalawāt* upon the Prophet (peace and blessings be upon him) for his supererogatory worship: "If you do so, then all your worries and concerns will be relieved and all your sins will be forgiven" (al-Tirmidhī, 2000, *Ḥadīth* 3265, vol. 2, pp. 628–629). This demonstrates a relationship between spiritual practices that bring down unqualified metaphysical radiances that contribute to emotional relief. Therefore, Islamic belief would not attempt to measure or prove this notion of *barakah* or "divine blessings", but would rather affirm its scripturally transmitted reality. Several other examples can be thought of, including belief in the presence of protective angels after Qur'ānic recitation or the proliferation of the devil's whispers in the human psyche after engaging in evil actions.

The richness of the Islamic tradition and the work of the spiritual scholars demonstrate a comprehensive and nuanced approach to the application of spiritual interventions. For example, reciting the different names of Allah is believed to have different effects on the human soul (al-Ghazālī, 2008). Additionally, scholars have also mentioned that an unmindful and careless administration of spiritual prescriptions can lead to worsening of the psychological condition of an individual, and even to insanity. This observation is critical, especially in terms of the discussion above about the "mode of action" of spiritual techniques: i.e, are they merely cognitive or emotional salves for the individual, or do they bring about discrete changes in the individual that may be harmful as well as beneficial? It was well understood in the classical literature that certain prescriptions—or intensities of spiritual experience—were not for everyone. The words of God, especially, were deemed to have an ontic power of their own, and many of the "holy madmen" (*majānīn*) were considered to have become that way through precisely such unauthorized delving into these powerful litanies (Dols & Immisch, 2011, p. 350). The author (Yusuf) has anecdotal experience of a patient developing (and being monitored for) mood changes, sleep disturbances, and even physical symptoms during a time-limited spiritual exercise under the close guidance of a spiritual master, which symptoms resolved upon its completion.

It should also be noted that spiritual exercises do not work in a linear fashion, nor in vacuum, since some potential targeted spiritual changes can simultaneously affect other aspects of the psyche, such as the *'aql*. In working with the spirit, multiple aspects of the psyche may be activated. Thus, it is supposed that multiple processes, including external spiritual aspects, may be at play in promoting change. For example, a conscious and attentive recitation of particular prayers will impact the subject based upon the language or cognitive orientation that is being promoted by the prayer, in addition to its inherent spiritual potency.

In sum, empirical investigation of the utility of spiritual interventions can be welcomed on the condition that the mechanism of change is not solely reduced to mere psychological variables or brain pathways of change. This consideration is instrumental in informing the principal foundational differences between a faith-based orientation to psychotherapy and a purely scientific one.

Paradigmatic Assumptions of Spiritually Integrated Psychotherapies in a TIIP Context

As mentioned in previous chapters (see Chapters 1, 4, and 7), Islamic scholars generally agree upon the view of the human being as a dualistic entity, comprising both a body (*jasad*) as well as a metaphysical element. This was referred to as the *laṭīfah rabbāniyyah* or divine subtle essence in

Chapter 1. One of the aspects of the *laṭīfah rabbāniyyah* discussed was the *rūḥ*. Its two alternative expressions in the *rūḥ ḥayawānī* and *rūḥ samāwī* was highlighted, with the former fueled by animalist drives and the latter by a celestial attraction for the Divine. In essence, as mentioned by al-Suhrawardī (see Chapters 1 and 7), the tension between the two competing drives fueled by these animalistic and divine impulses can be softened through the reformation of the lower *nafs* by usage of *riyāḍāt* or spiritual exercises that are designed to tame and train these animalistic impulses. These positive opposite interventions induce pain in the lower *nafs*, forcing its growth and compliance (see Chapter 9). Alternatively, the celestial essence or *rūḥ samāwī*, given its affinity for the Divine, requires nourishment in the form of worship and the constant remembrance of the Divine (*dhikr*). This is saliently captured by the Qur'ānic verse that states: "Verily the hearts find rest in the *dhikr* or remembrance of Allah" (13:28). Imām al-Suhrawardī proposes that intrapsychic tensions can be removed by transcending above the animal plane of existence. This leads to the development and transformation of the *nafs* into the *nafs muṭma'innah*, which is a by-product of both nurturing the *rūḥ samāwī* through divine remembrance (*dhikr*) and opposing (*mukhālafah*) the hedonistic desires of the lower *nafs*. Additionally, the Qur'ān states that the absence of *dhikr* and spiritual nourishment has a resultant effect of hardening the heart, by stating: "Whomsoever Allah endows his breast with faith, so he is upon a divine light from his Lord, so woe be upon their hardened hearts from (the absence of) the remembrance of Allah (*dhikr*)" (39:22). Additionally, the Prophet of Islam (peace and blessings be upon him) is known to have stated that "the example of the one who does *dhikr* of Allah (remembrance of Allah) compared to the one who does not, is like the example of the dead person and the living" (al-Bukhārī, 2000, *Ḥadīth* 6482, vol. 3, p. 1301). Thus, taken together, the statements of revelation (*naṣṣ*) clearly draw a relationship between the application of *dhikr* and spiritual life, spiritual radiance, and divine tranquility.

The eighteenth-century Indian theologian and mystic Shāh Walī Allah's (d.1175 AH/1772 CE) offers a complementary explanatory model of the *rūḥ* by providing an integration of views on the *rūḥ* from different disciplinary slants, Ṣūfī orders, and scholarly eras. Shāh Walī Allah outlines lower and higher planes of existence and functioning. Each component of the metaphysical essence could be expressed either in a lowly, unrefined, primitive form or a more developed and celestial form. The lowest expression of the spirit (*rūḥ*), says Shāh Walī Allah, is the airy spirit (*rūḥ hawā'ī/ rūḥ ḥayawānī*) and constitutes the life force at its basic level, while the elevated angelic spirit (*rūḥ malakūtī, ruūḥ rabbānī, ruh 'ulwī,* or *rūḥ samāwī*) is nourished by the remembrance of the Divine. Thus, this aspect of Shāh Walī Allah's conceptualization of the spirit reinforces the notion of two opposing tendencies needing nourishment from the human components of the psyche to reunify the diffused *rūḥ* back into the *rūḥ malakūtī* or *rūḥ samāwī* (Hermansen, 1988).

The initial TIIP internal framework of the human psyche put forward by Keshavarzi and Haque (2013) identifies the spiritual domain (*rūḥ*) as an intricate part of the expression of the *laṭīfah rabbāniyyah*, in conjunction with the *'aql* (cognitive processes) and *nafs* (behavioral inclinations) that are one unitary metaphysical entity with different functions that originate out of the *qalb*. All components of the human entity operate as a unit, and a change in any domain of the human psyche will ultimately have consequences for the health or pathology of the heart (*qalb*). Furthermore, from an Islamic perspective, psychological dysfunctions are not exclusively indicated by impaired individual and social functioning, but also extend to include such character traits and behaviors that may potentially compromise the believer's afterlife, alluded to in the aforementioned verse as "The Day" [of Judgment]. Thus, the spiritual and the physical aspects of the human psyche and the body are interwoven into an irreducible unity. The behavioral expressions of human volition (*aʿmāl*—actions or motivated behaviors), the source of which may be allocated to the spiritual domain itself, return to affect the heart, with strong residual effects on the psyche and the body. These assertions certainly stand in contradistinction to the ultra-reductionism that passes as a sound psychology today.

In the nomenclature of the Islamic spiritual discourses, the "*qalb*" refers not to the biological *cardia*, but to the subtle spiritual domain of the *laṭīfa rabbāniyyah* that is addressed in regard to Divine commands and injunctions, held accountable when committing evil, and reproached when it commits rebellion (al-Ghazālī, 2001). The spirit's most central feature is its psychological predisposition, or *fiṭric* (primordial good-natured dispositional) need for the Divine. Due to this longing, it has a predilection for the sacred, for that which transcends the temporal. However, the spirit's activity can be down- or upregulated, just as the body can. Just as the latter requires appropriate exercise and nutrition for the maintenance of its healthy, homeostatic state (*iʿtidāl*), so does the former. A functional spirit is a well-nourished spirit, and this healthful spirit manifests temporally as the attainment of gnosis of the Divine, and eternally as being in the Divine presence itself. As such, the primary modulator of the spirit, as we will elucidate further below, is human actions (*aʿmāl*).

Motivated Behaviors (Aʿmāl) Modulate the Spiritual Domain

In general, actions can be characterized as being both (1) volitional and (2) intention-based mental processes and behaviors, in order to actualize the primordial spiritual purpose of human beings.

A'māl, which are actions or motivated behaviors, are those behaviors and mental processes that will either maintain the human being's lower plane of existence in the *nafs ammārah* and *rūḥ ḥayawānī* or conversely elevate it to *rūḥ samāwī*. Both gravitational pulls and exhibiting actions feed back to and affect all aspects of the psyche, as well feed forward to and have ultimate effects in the afterlife. "Action" here relates to events occurring within the human being, whether somatic (related to the body) or mental (related to the mind). Each of these can be two-fold: volitional (*ikhtiyārī*) and non-volitional (*iḍṭirārī*).

Non-volitional behaviors are those that occur spontaneously and without conscious thought. This of course includes all of the neuromuscular, endocrinological, and immunological processes relating to the autonomic nervous system (such as the actions of the internal organs and their interactions with the central nervous system). The theological texts usually mention "shivering due to the cold" as their example of a non-volitional action (al-Ṣāwī, 1999, p. 240). In medical terms, disturbances in such non-volitional behaviors would fall within the domain of a physician or neurologist, rather than a psychologist. However, also included are complex physical actions that mimic volitional ones, such as those that occur in the context of altered mental states like sleep-walking, delirium, passivity, complex partial seizures, or—for that matter—ecstatic spiritual states. The key aspect that we are concerned with from a psychological perspective is that such actions are not capacitous—not directed by the conscious self. Hence the individual is not considered morally accountable for the consequences of these actions (Farfūr, 2002 pp. 124–130).

Equally from an Islamic perspective, mental processes (cognitions) are understood to be divided into non-volitional and volitional. Sufi scholars categorize these internal mental processes into four (or five) ascending layers of volition—the passing thought (*hājiz*), the lingered-on or imaginal thought (*khāṭir*), the deliberated-upon thought (*Ḥadīth al-nafs*), the decision (*niyyah/hamm*), and the determination (*'azm*) (Ibn 'Allān, 2006, vol. 1, p. 48). It is understood that, morally, one is rewarded for the latter two processes, as in the *Ḥadīth* "one who intends a good action but does not act on it is rewarded as though they had performed it … one who intends an evil deed but does not act on it is also rewarded" and "God has overlooked for my community what their hearts whisper to them as long as they do not act on it or give it voice". The scholars also indicate that one is morally accountable for the determination to perform an evil deed—such that only something external prevented it from occurring. In terms of beneficial and harmful effects on the psyche, however, it is the latter three levels that can exert a positive or negative effect on the soul.

Volitional Mental Processes and Behaviors

As such, both types of *a'māl*—mental processes and physical actions—can be "volitionized" (or "volitionally committed to") and the deliberate, conscious allocation of attention to an initially spontaneous mental process (or behavior) such as sudden insights or fleeting thoughts can exert a positive or negative effect on the spirit. The quality of this effect depends on the type of process and the context within which it occurs, with residual effects on the overall psyche. This can manifest as simply maintaining a thought in one's conscious "workspace" or attentional focus, ruminating upon it, using it as a basis for or as a component of one's rational activities, reflecting upon it, analyzing it, or transforming it into a behavior. In Islamic literature this process is referred to as *tafakkur* or contemplative/meditative reflection. An illustration of how this differentiation between positive and negative modulation of the spirit can be leveraged for psychological well-being is provided below.

Intention-Based Mental Processes and Behaviors (Motivated Behaviors)

In most cases, for a mental process and behavior to qualify as an "action" (*'amal*) and thus be capable of affecting the spirit, it must be not only volitional but also intention-based. The intention—the reason or purpose behind a volitional mental process or behavior—is the key component in determining whether an action will strengthen (nourish) or weaken the spirit. This is reiterated by the prophetic statement "Indeed, actions (*a'māl*) are only by intentions and each person will only attain that which he intended" (al-Bukhārī, 2000, vol. 1, *Ḥadīth* 1). Intention is the essence of the activity of the spirit, and it links the spirit to the Divine, thus nourishing it, if it is associated with the lofty purposes and meanings afforded human beings through revelation. If it is associated with base purposes, those that run counter to the ones provided by revelation, then it has a detrimental effect.

In his discussion of the virtues and benefits of certain formulations of *dhikr*, al-Ghazālī (2011, vol. 2, pp. 367–368) explains how it is that such a seemingly minor act, involving a minimum amount of effort, can have such powerful consequences for the soul. From a practical perspective (*'ilm al-mu'āmalah*), it is precisely the process of intellectually and emotionally engaging with the act (*ḥuḍūr al-qalb*) that powers the transformative effect of the act on the soul, both in this world and the hereafter. An illustrative example of this occurs in his preceding book (al-Ghazālī, 2011, vol. 2, p. 291 onwards) when he discusses the ten inward transformative actions (*ādāb*) relating to the Qur'ān, most of which revolve around the process of engaging both intellectually and emotionally with the text and its recitation, such as contemplating its meanings, personalizing it, being moved by the emotional "currents" of the text, and imagining oneself as the recipient of the Divine address.

Righteous Mental Processes and Behaviors and the Nature of Intentions

There is a sub-class of mental processes and behaviors that can qualify as "actions" even without intention (an example will be provided shortly); however, the more explicit their intention, the stronger their effect. In general, however, mental processes and behaviors that are volitional and that are intended for God either directly (e.g. "I intend to pray to God as He has commanded it") or indirectly (e.g. "I intend to enjoy this meal because it will increase my gratitude to God"), are classified as "righteous actions" or *a'māl ṣāliḥah*, and they attract an increase in divine gnosis and the likelihood of permanent divine presence in the afterlife. This attraction of divine gnosis contains both a metaphysical and unobservable cause–effect relationship observable in the afterlife, and beneficial positive psychological orientation such as in the case of gratitude, as a mental process, that is associated with psychological well-being (Bonelli & Koenig, 2013).

The increase in divine gnosis may be explained by the effect that righteous actions have on the spirit. This is explained, for the lack of a better psychological term, as an "enlightenment", in the literal meaning of the word. A righteous action casts a spiritual light upon the *qalb* or metaphysical heart, thus nourishing it, whereas a sin, the opposite of righteous actions increases darkness, thus weakening it. The illumination or darkening of the heart/spirit then affects all aspects of the human psyche, including cognition and emotions, as well as the *nafs*—light causing it to become more refined, darkness causing it to reduce to its more animalistic tendencies. As a result, righteous actions have a positive residual effect throughout the psyche and engender psychological well-being.

Mental processes and behaviors that are volitional and that are intended for other than God, or are otherwise sordid or intended for the temporal sphere alone, result in a decrease in divine gnosis, and may jeopardize the opportunity for permanent divine presence in life and the afterlife. As a result, they have a negative residual effect throughout the psyche, tending towards psychological dissonance and ultimately ill health, as understood from an Islamic framework even if not observable in a worldly context. For example, narcissism that is "functional" for one's worldly life may prove detrimental in the afterlife. It is important to mention that this category is not meant to stigmatize those who may not always involve God in their intentions, particularly believing Muslim patients whose dysfunctions are related to ritual practices. Rather, our intention is to demonstrate that the idea of continuous remembrance of the Divine and intentionality is important. For instance, dealing kindly with one's spouse in emulation of the Prophet (peace be upon him) may be gradually habituated. However, even though it might be a subconscious rather than conscious intention, it may still be rewarded and contribute to health on account of the initial personal psychological training being the initial cause for the habituated behavior.

Therapeutic Concept for TIIP Spiritually Integrated Psychotherapies

Various righteous actions can have a positive effect on the spirit. The most essential of these is *dhikr*, the remembrance of Allah or recitation of litanies. Others are prayers, fasting, giving to charity, *murāqabah* (intimate meditation upon Allah's attributes or presence), and other *waẓā'if* (spiritual practices)—all of which come with their own unique manifestation of light, allowing for different kinds of actions to be prescribed for different psycho-spiritual dysfunctions. All of these actions illuminate the spirit/heart, and this "enlightenment" goes on to affect the entirety of the human psyche and serves as an Islamic explanation for the psychological, and even potential neurophysiological effects that are associated with spiritual practices (Newberg et al., 2015).

The following section, firstly, expounds upon *dhikr* as the key spiritually based practice that acts directly on the spirit and that forms one of the four core interventions of TIIP, and, secondly, discusses how these mechanisms can be rendered into potentially reproducible psychotherapeutic applications. The psychotherapeutic setting is particularly ripe for providing an environment in which the spirit can be (re-)acquainted with the ability to compete with hedonistic drives, and in which it can be guided through its developmental stages of change towards the state of *rūḥ malakūtī/samāwī* (angelic spirit) and the realization of a sound heart (*qalb salīm*), as outlined by TIIP. As such, spiritually focused interventions in an Islamic context draw heavily from the main historical precursor of modern Islamic psychology—that is *taṣawwuf*. The spiritually based interventions described in this chapter focus on the affinity for divine nourishment through *dhikr* and the formation of spiritual meaning and divine connection, as opposed to taming the *nafsānī* impulses, or restructuring human beliefs, or the regulation of emotions, as outlined in previous chapters. Such spiritual dysfunctions according to TIIP may be indicated by the experience of spiritual depletion, exhaustion, and fatigue, intentional incongruence with religious tenets, and religious despondency (Keshavarzi & Khan, 2018). Often patients may describe sensing a void, or a total lack of meaningful contentment or satisfaction.

The case studies that follow are examples of how spiritually oriented practitioners can assist patients in their spiritual development by integrating spiritually based interventions into the TIIP framework. In TIIP, initial sessions can be categorized into: (1) spiritual and psychiatric assessment—building the therapeutic alliance, assessment of religiosity, diagnosis and conceptualization, assessment of internal and external psycho-spiritual functioning, psychoeducation and setting therapeutic goals, and assessment of the stage of change, and (2) establishment of agreement upon treatment goals and furthering the therapeutic alliance. *Rūḥānī*-based psychoeducational sessions may be conducted before any directive prescriptions are provided. This can facilitate spiritual momentum in the patient that can function as positive motivation and increase compliance with treatment goals (Keshavarzi & Haque, 2013; Keshavarzi & Khan, 2018).

Dhikr

Elevation and transcendence of the spirit is intricately related to the performance of *dhikr*, as stated by Maḥmūd Ḥasan Gangōhī (d.1996 CE), the Grand Muftī of Dār al-'Ulū m Deoband and a spiritual master of the Chishtiyyah-Imdādiyyah Ṣūfī order. He emphasizes that anyone who gains anything on this spiritual path has acquired it through the blessing of *dhikr*. *Dhikr* falls into the sub-class of mental processes and behaviors that are considered actions even without intention because of the strong, stand-alone effect upon the *dhākir* (the one remembering) of uttering the names of God. Ṣūfī practitioners note, however, that the stronger one's intention and the deeper the reflection upon meanings, the stronger the effect upon the spirit, with stronger residual effects on cognition and behavioral impulses or *nafs*, manifesting as balance.

Dhikr *Balances/Counterbalances the Animalistic Drives*

Dhikr can have specific effects on the *nafs*. The illumination of *dhikr* has the capacity of refining the *nafs* to its higher levels and bringing inner *nafsānī* drives into balance, hence facilitating congruence within the psychological system. The Ṣūfī sage Ibn 'Aṭā' noted that *dhikr* attenuates the basic, animalistic desires of human beings by balancing the effect of *dhikr* upon the cardinal faculties that serve as a source of all other character states. Most importantly, as Shaykh Ibn 'Aṭā' al-Baghdādī further describes, at the same time the spiritual (*rūḥānī*) desires increase and the lure and attraction to *nafsānī* desires decreases (al-Sarrāj, 2016). The strong effects of *dhikr* in reducing animalistic desires is demonstrated by Mawlāna Ashraf 'Alī Thānwī, an Islamic scholar, reviver, and spiritual master in early ninteteenth-century India, in his prescription for a disciple struggling with a sexual disorder at his spiritual lodge (*khānqah*): *khalwah* (solitude), silence, attending to the spiritual discourses of the shaykh, fasting, routine recitation of litanies (*waẓā'if*) and *istighfār* (repentance) (Ilāhabādī, n.d., vol. 1, p. 141). He asked the disciple to continue in this behavior for 40 days, and reported that the disciple was not only cured of his spiritual ailment after this 40-day period, but that he also felt an abhorrence towards his previous addiction and described feeling as if his heart had become "enlightened".

Another anecdotal case of one of the authors (Yusuf) from his recent practice is that of a woman struggling with the breakdown of her marriage, who was experiencing low moods, anxiety symptoms, and strong feelings of guilt and worthlessness. In addition to standard psychotherapy, she was taken through the Names of Allah and asked to meditate on whichever ones occurred to her through her experiences that day. She chose *al-Ẓāhir al-Bāṭin* (The Manifest, the Hidden), on the basis of an identification with a mother feeding her child. She said that, for the first two days, her feelings of anxiety, detachment, and worthlessness intensified, but she was advised to continue. On the third day she described a "breakthrough", experienced as she observed a flock of birds wheeling in the sky, in which she:

> felt I caught hold of a string of *lā Ilāha illa-llāh*—as creation, our outward and inward are in conflict and opposite, but God is One in both the inward and the outward … it was like the lighting of a log on a cold winter's day … I was filled with a deep sense of gratitude'

It is, however, critical to consider as a disclaimer that, for maximal benefit, such spiritual interventions that target lowering behavioral drives should be utilized alongside other normative therapeutic interventions that target the other domains of the human psyche. An exclusive application of spiritual remedies divorced from a holistic protocol can potentially be detrimental in psychotherapeutic settings.

Group-Mediated Effects of Dhikr

Group *dhikr* has long been considered by spiritual practitioners to be particularly effective in the mediation of positive psychological and spiritual effects for both active and passive participants. A long *Ḥadīth* in al-Bukhārī (2000, *Ḥadīth* 6407) details that circles of *dhikr* emit a metaphysical light that shines up to the dwellers of the heavens like stars shine down to dwellers of earth. This in turn is related to the *Ḥadīth* (prophetic narration) that tranquility (*sakīnah*) will descend on those groups of people that remember God (Ṣaḥīḥ Muslim 7030, 2/1139 in al-Naysābūrī, 2000). 'Allāmah Ālūsī (may Allah have mercy on him), in his exegesis of the Qur'ān *Rūḥ al-Ma'ānī*, comments on the meaning of the word "*sakīnah*", namely that it is a "light that descends from Allah, that becomes absorbed into the heart, fixes one's attention on the Divine, and saves a person from internal distraction and scatteredness" (Ālūsī, 1999). A contemporary spiritual master explained further that participants in group *dhikr* are creating two outputs: the vocalizations, which are perceptible on earth and bring about emotional changes in the participants' psyches, and a metaphysical light, perceptible to the angels and directly affecting the souls of the participants. It is the combination of the two that is the "tranquility" that God associates with *dhikr*.

One illustrative case of the group-mediated effects of *dhikr* is as follows. A middle-aged man complained to Mawlānā Ḥakīm Akhtar (a Ṣūfī Master of the Chisti, Imdādiyyah-Ashrafiyyah order, d.2013 CE) of having a decreased appetite and depressed mood, of crying excessively, and having difficulty sleeping and thoughts of suicide. He was advised to attend the daily *dhikr* gatherings at the *khānqah* of the shaykh, where other students would regularly gather to learn and engage in *dhikr* in the shaykh's presence, and to not remain alone at any time. After approximately two weeks of adhering to this regimen, the individual reported an uplifted mood, no further suicidal thoughts, a decrease in frequency of inexplicable tearfulness as well as an overall decrease in negative thinking. From a spiritual perspective, the proposed effect of the tranquility (*sakīnah*) descending upon the heart of this individual and enlightenment as a result of partaking in *dhikr* as part of a group was far-reaching, balancing his emotions, focusing his cognitions on positive thoughts, and uplifting his spirit. This case shows that (1) spiritually based practices can be sufficient to reduce depressive symptomatology and that (2) they should be accompanied by treatment by a qualified psychotherapist or psychiatrist.

Tawbah *and* Istighfār *as Special Forms of* Dhikr

Other righteous actions that can elicit a positive effect on the spirit, and which may serve as a mechanism for *rūḥānī*-based psychotherapy, are *tawbah* and *istighfār*. Contrary to simplistic views of these concepts, *tawbah* and *istighfār* do not merely mean "repenting" to make amends and to "ask forgiveness" for an unlawful transgression of the divine law committed by an individual. A deeper understanding that has potential for spiritual therapeutic interventions has been adopted by the Ṣūfī shaykhs. This deeper meaning and concept of *tawbah* and *istighfār* has been extracted from the following verse of the Qur'ān: "Except for those who make *tawbah* (repent), believe, and do righteous work. For them Allah will replace, change, transform, their (desire and inclination to commit) evil deeds with (desire and inclination to perform) good. And ever is Allah Forgiving and Merciful" (25:70). Mawlānā Ashraf 'Alī Thānwī (n.d.) explains in reference to this verse that compensation for transgressive behavior is provided by *tawbah* and *istighfār*. Initially, *tawbah* can change the desire to sin into the desire to exhibit righteous actions, by enhancing the spiritual domain with righteous actions that counteract the influence of behavioral inclinations (*nafs*). This is facilitated by mental as well as behavioral implementation of *tawbah*: this may involve the performance of ablution and two units of voluntary (*nāfilah*) prayer, which replaces the initial transgressive behavior. Subsequently, one is encouraged to cry to and implore Allah for forgiveness, because once *istighfār* has been achieved, it leaves behind illumination and light in the heart, or an enhanced spiritual domain in light of a prophetic narration (Ibn Raslān, 2016) that suggests *tawbah* and *istighfār* after sinning and guarantees forgiveness, which obliterates the sin and related effects. The two units of prayer, as described above, must follow a deep and devotional recital of the *Sayyid al-Istighfār*, which is considered to be the most prominent and comprehensive prayer of repentance in the prophetic traditions:

> O Allah! You are my Lord! None has the right to be worshipped but You. You created me and I am Your slave, and I am faithful to my covenant and my promise as much as I can. I seek refuge with You from all the evil I have done. I acknowledge before You all the blessings You have bestowed upon me, and I confess to You all my sins. So, I entreat You to forgive my sins, for nobody can forgive sins except You.
>
> (al-Bukhārī, 2000, Ḥadīth 6379, book 16, p. 1556)

However, this practice will only be of benefit if it is coupled with volitional, deliberate decision-making towards righteous actions. Mere recitation of empty litanies will not give the desired effect. This is illustrated by a query from a disciple of Mawlānā Ashraf 'Alī Thānwī,who complained about lustful glances, and that although he resorted to *tawbah* and *istighfār*, his heart "remains as filthy as ever". The Shaykh's response clarified that the heart cannot be purified so quickly by verbal *istighfār* and that purity and light return only when the disciple restrains himself and withholds the desire by means of volitional decision-making.

The following case illustration demonstrates an alternative, predominately spiritual approach to the reformation of a behavioral addiction that can be applied in conjunction with *nafsānī* or behavioral modification approaches.

Case Illustration

Case Summary

Muhammad Bilal is 30-year-old unmarried male who attended Islamically oriented psychotherapy, complaining predominately of a pornography addiction. The patient reported having very little motivation to reduce his pornography usage despite the guilt associated with his behavior. He said that he recognized that it was immoral behavior and felt internal dissonance as a result. However, he described feeling depleted and unmotivated, expressed feelings of hopelessness in life, and felt that he was living a purposeless existence. He reported that he did not have much to look forward to in life, and thus pornography use accompanied by masturbation seemed to be "all he had to look forward to". The patient reported social isolation, depressive feelings, fatigue, low motivation, hopelessness, reduced interest in normative social and familial activities, and difficulty concentrating at work.

Case Conceptualization and Diagnosis According to TIIP

Despite an initial indication that Muhammad's issues stemmed from a *nafsānī* problem of impulse control, his spiritual depletion, sense of purposelessness, and hopelessness seemed to indicate a significant problem with his spiritual (*rūḥānī*) functioning. The *nafsānī* sexual impulses and self-gratification appeared to play a secondary function of deriving some form of pleasure while living a depressive life. Cognitively, the patient believed these impulsive behaviors to be unethical and thus experienced cognitive dissonance. There was an incongruence between his professed beliefs in his *'aql* and the *nafsānī* behavior that he engaged in. This lead to feelings of shame and guilt that exacerbated his sadness on the functioning of his *iḥsāsī* and furthered his spiritual depletion and sense of purposelessness. The patient seemed to be experiencing a sense of spiritual death and void, leading to a routine animalistic way of living that was devoid of deeper meaning. Thus, as the patient reported, he did not seem to find much "point" in engaging in the routine functions of his life, whether social or familial activities, and had to "drag" himself to work everyday. This overall experience lead to a diagnosis of major depressive disorder, since it had persisted for over 6 months and had impaired his functioning.

Treatment

During initial sessions, the TIIP practitioner focused on forming the initial relationship with the patient (*murābaṭah*), while helping him to identify that the vicious cycle and nature of spiritual depletion was closely linked to his *nafsānī* impulsive "self-medicating" behavior. Thus, through this mutual process of co-conceptualizing his case (*mukāshafah*), the patient was able to experience better self-awareness of his own state of functioning and the sources of his overall dysfunction (*inkishāf*). Since the patient had very little motivation to change his behavior, given his inability to see the "point" of this change, the practitioner worked with him on identifying and generating motivation. This was done through the *rūḥānī* exercise of *tafakkur* and *ta'mmul*, or contemplative reflection on the overall purpose of life and personal meaning of his life. This *rūḥānī* intervention also activated his *'aql*, as it was supposed that through this reflection he would arrive at spiritual insights or unveilings that would guide and enlighten his heart.

Follow-up sessions and therapeutic processing of his derived personal meaning created for Muhammad a renewed sense of purpose. He reported that his function in life was to uncover his God-given talents and strengths, and identify avenues to utilize these strengths for God's sake. This entailed a thorough examination of his current life, choices, career, extracurricular activities, and the overall vision that he might have for his life. Following such processing, the patient began to exhibit a renewed sense of life that was clearly noticed by the practitioner. The practitioner attempted to increase and play to this new motivation for a God-centered living by asking the patient to start to focus on building an experiential spiritual connection with Allah that would nurture his newfound purpose. This connection would remain alive in him, regenerating his motivation for actualizing his goals.

The patient also inquired about how to treat his impulsive *nafsānī* desires and behaviors. Instead of dealing with this directly, the practitioner decided to redirect the patient's focus to generating and strengthening spiritual connection as an alternative vehicle for attenuating his unhealthy sexual drives. This was on account of the practitioner's initial conceptualization of the pornography use as a secondary gain to cope with a meaningless existence. The practitioner did this in conjunction with normalizing sexual desires to be with a woman given the patient's bachelor status, since not all of his porn usage could be attributed to psychological coping alone. Therefore, separate from the spiritual interventions, the patient and practitioner together discussed marriage in follow-up sessions.

However, the spiritual intervention primarily utilized, in addition to *tafakkur* as previously prescribed, was the intervention of *tawbah* (ablution, *nāfilah* prayer, recital of the *Sayyid al-Istighfār*). The Islamic spiritual explanation for using this prayer is that *istighfār* removes the effects of darkness, increases light, and transforms the *nafsānī* inclination to commit sin to a spiritual inclination to do good. Additionally, the protection prayer for the morning and evening (three times *sura* 112, 113, 114, and one time *āyat al-kursī*) and the prayer of Yūnus (peace be upon him) (al-Tirmidhī, 2000, *Ḥadīth* 3383) were used: "There are none worthy of worship besides You. Glorified are You. Surely I am from the wrongdoers" (Qur'ān 21:87). This process was carried out in conjunction with normative *nafsānī* behavioral modification and harm reduction principles. The patient routinely used these spiritual litanies in the form of *tawbah* and *istighfār* while also creating an inventory/log of behaviors, employment of frequency reduction from high to low frequency (multiple times a day—daily—weekly—every two weeks—none) and quality (photos ofgroup engaging—one couple—one nude female—picture of nude female—none) was applied. After each relapse, the *isthighfār* payer, the *dua* of Yūnus, and other *dhikr*, such as saying *lā ilāha illa-llāh*, were used with increased intensity.

After three months a stable reduction of porn consumption (at most once a month) was achieved, and after around seven months a level of complete abstinence was reached. Further positive effects manifested in a better relationship with Allah, beginning with regular prayers, and an overall reduction in the depressive feelings reported earlier. The patient was able to resume familial and social activities, feel subjective motivation and increased energy, and was able to concentrate at work, with minimal shame or sadness. After solving his addiction problem, he investigated marriage prospects. Thus, cognitive dissonance was removed, and there was a greater integration of all aspects of the human psyche, which became balanced and served the same aims. More specifically, he began experiencing better emotional regulation, behavioral control, cognitive realizations, a contemplative orientation, and spiritual contentment.

Conclusions

In this chapter we have attempted to provide a reconciliatory sketch of the Islamic conceptualization of the spirit within the broader context of the human psyche in a TIIP framework. An integrative approach has been employed to illustrate how this conceptualization can be utilized towards garnering a felicitous afterlife via the application of techniques that exert an effect on the spirit and that are embedded within a holistic psychotherapeutic framework. In providing an Islamic psychological explanation of the spiritual domain, the key points are that the composition of the human psyche requires unity, with the *rūḥ*/spirit playing a critical role in the entire psychological system of the human psyche. Any effect upon the spirit will have residual effects upon all aspects of the psyche. We demonstrated that mental processes or behaviors that are committed volitionally and with an intention attached to revelatory aims is classified as a righteous action (*a'māl ṣāliḥah*) that will modulate the spirit positively. Additionally, we demonstrated how spiritual exercises can reduce appetitive desires. Certain spiritually focused behaviors, such as *dhikr*, *istighfār*, *tawbah*, and *ṣalawāt* can have such an effect regardless of intention. Finally, we demonstrated this process through a case illustration to exemplify how *dhikr* can be a means to improve mental health.

Through the case conceptualizations provided, we have demonstrated the usefulness of spiritually based interventions in psychological functioning. Collaboration between scholars of *taṣawwuf* and psychotherapists is essential! We conclude that Islamic spirituality can inform spiritually integrated psychotherapies in a TIIP framework in a collaborative fashion. Caution should be exercised with the application of spiritual remedies, as they should be prescribed in consultation with spiritual scholars in order to ensure appropriate Islamic usage. Spiritually based intervention should be employed in a complementary fashion within a TIIP framework with those individuals who are deemed appropriate to receive such treatment during initial assessment sessions and during the spiritual and religious anamnesis (for most part highly religious Muslims—see Chapter 2). This will ensure its beneficial features are used to their advantage and simultaneously reduce the risk of patients feeling scared by or uncomfortable with overtly "religious" interventions. Additionally, it would be useful for Muslim researchers and practitioners to explore the use of varying spiritual remedies to treat a variety of psychological problems to test their efficacy.

Notes

1 Some would argue rational necessity—the existence of the subjective, conscious self (the 'I') being inexplicable otherwise.
2 The question of what "recovery" or "health" entail—whether a subjective sense of well-being (*'āfiyah*), the absence of pathology or symptoms, or something else entirely—is a critical point.
3 This incident and much of the next section is taken from anecdotal clinical notes of the author (Yusuf).
4 Originally from 'Abd al'Azī z al-Dihlawī, *Tafsīr 'Azīzī*, Sura Iqra—now lost.

References

Abu-Raiya, H. (2012). Towards a systematic Qura'nic theory of personality. *Mental Health, Religion & Culture, 15*(3), 217–33.

Abu-Raiya, H., & Pargament, K. I. (2015). Religious coping among diverse religions: Commonalities and divergences. *Psychology of Religion and Spirituality, 7*(1), 24–33. doi:org/10.1037/a0037652.

Abu-Raiya, H., Pargament, K. I., Mahoney, A., & Stein, C. (2008). A psychological measure of Islamic religiousness: Development and evidence of reliability and validity. *International Journal for the Psychology of Religion, 18*(4), 291–315. doi:org/10.1080/10508610802229270.

al-Bukhārī, M. I. (2000). *Ṣaḥīḥ al-Bukhārī.* Stuttgart: Thesaurus Islamus Foundation.

al-Ghazālī, A. H. (2001). *Iḥyā' al-Ulūm*. Beirut: Dār al-Kutub al-'Ilmiyyah.
al-Ghazālī, A. H. (2008). *Al-Maqṣad al-Asnā fī Sharḥ Ma'ānī Asmā' Allah al-Ḥusnā*. Cairo: Dār al-Salām.
al-Ghazālī, A. H. (2011). *Iḥyā'*. Jeddah: Dār Minhāj.
al-Kandihlawī, Z. (n.d.). *Mashāykh-e-Chisht*. Cape Town: Majlis al-'Ulamā' Productions.
al-Naysābūrī, I. H. (2000). *Ṣaḥīḥ Muslim*. Stuttgart: Thesaurus Islamica Foundation.
al-Sarrāj, A. N. (2016). *Kitāb al-Luma'*. Amman: Dār al-Fatḥ.
al-Ṣāwī, A. (1999). *Sharḥ Jawhart al-Tawḥīd*. Damascus: Dār Ibn Kathīr.
al-Tirmidhī, M. I. (2000). *Sunan al-Tirmidhī*. Stuttgart: Thesaurus Islamicus Foundation.
Ālūsī, S. A. (1999). *Rūḥ al-Ma'ānī*. Beirut: Dār Iḥyā' al-Turāth.
Beauregard, M., & O'Leary, D. (2007). *The spiritual brain*. New York, NY: HarperCollins.
Bonelli, R. M., & Koenig, H. G. (2013). Mental disorders, religion and spirituality 1990 to 2010: A systematic evidence-based review. *Journal of Religion and Health, 52*(2), 657–673. doi:10.1007/s10943-013-9691-4
Dols, M. W., & Immisch, D. E. (2011). *Majnun: the madman in medieval Islamic society*. Oxford: Clarendon Press.
Farfūr, M. A. (2002). *Al-Zād min Uṣūl al-Fiqh al-Islāmī*. Beirut: Maktabat Dār al-Bayrūtiyyah.
Gabbard, G. (2000). A neurobiologically informed perspective on psychotherapy. *British Journal of Psychiatry, 177*, 117–122.
Hermansen, M. K. (1988). Shāh Walī Allāh's theory of the subtle spiritual centers (Laṭā'if): A Sufi model of personhood and self-transformation. *Journal of Near Eastern Studies, 47*(1), 1–25. doi:10.1086/jnes.47.1.3693678
Hood, R. W., Jr., & Francis, L. J. (2013). Mystical experience: Conceptualizations, measurement, and correlates. In K. I. Pargament, J. J. Exline, & J. W. Jones (Eds.), *APA handbooks in psychology. APA handbook of psychology, religion, and spirituality. Vol. 1: Context, theory, and research* (pp. 391–405). Washington, DC: American Psychological Association. doi:10.1037/14045-021
Ibn 'Allān, M. (2006). *Dalīl al-Fāliḥīn Sharḥ Riyāḍ al-Ṣāliḥīn*. Beirut: Dār al-Kutub al-'Ilmiyya.
Ibn Khaldūn, A. M. ([1377] n.d.). *The Muqaddimah*. Trans. F. Rosenthal. Retrieved from: https://asadullahali.files.wordpress.com/2012/10/ibn_khaldun-al_muqaddimah.pdf.
Ibn Raslān, S. A. (2016). *Sharḥ Sunan Abī Dāwūd*. Fayyum, Egypt: Dār al-Falāḥ.
Ilāhabādī, S. M. (n.d.). *Anfās-e-'Ī sā*. Karachi: H.M. Sa'id Company Publishers.
James, William, ([1902] 2016). *The Varieties of Religious Experience*. London: Crossreach Publications.
Kaplick, P. M., & Rüschoff, I. (2018). Islam und Psychologie – Gegenstand und Historie. In P. M. Kaplick & I. Rüschoff (Eds.), *Islam und Psychologie – Beiträge zu aktuellen Konzepten in Theorie und Praxis* (pp. 25–84). Münster: Waxmann.
Keshavarzi, H., & Haque, A. (2013). Outlining a psychotherapy model for enhancing Muslim mental health within an Islamic context. *International Journal for the Psychology of Religion, 23*(3), 230–249. doi:10.1080/10508619.2012.712000
Keshavarzi, H., & Khan, F. (2018). Outlining a case illustration of traditional Islamically integrated psychotherapy. In C. York Al-Karam (Ed.), *Islamically*

integrated psychotherapy: Uniting faith and professional practice (pp. 175–207). West Conshohocken, PA: Templeton Press.
Koenig, H., King, D., & Carson, V. B. (2012). *Handbook of religion and health*. 2nd ed. New York, NY: Oxford University Press.
Luders, E., Toga, A. W., Lepore, N., & Gaser, C. (2009). The underlying anatomical correlates of long-term meditation. *Neuroimage*, *45*(3), 672–678.
Mottaghi, M. E., Esmaili, R., & Rohani, Z. (2011). Effect of Quran recitation on the level of anxiety in athletics. *Quarterly of Quran & Medicine*, *1*(1), 1–4.
Mouladoudis, G. (2008). Paul Tillich and Carl Rogers conversation: Review with commentary. *The Person-Centered Journal*, *15*(1–2), 13–28.
Newberg, A. B., Wintering, N. A., Yaden, D. B., Waldman, M. R., Reddin, J., & Alavi, A. (2015). A case series study of the neurophysiological effects of altered states of mind during intense Islamic prayer. *Journal of Physiology – Paris*, *109*, 214–220.
Otto, R. ([1923] 2010). *The Idea of the Holy*. Mansfield Centre, CT: Martino Fine Books.
Pargament, K. I. (2007). *Spirituality integrated psychotherapy: Understanding and addressing the sacred*. New York, NY: Guilford Press.
Rausch, S. M., Gramling, S. E., & Auerbach, S. M. (2006). Effects of a single session of large group meditation and progressive muscle relaxation training on stress reduction, reactivity and recovery. *International Journal of Stress Management*, *13* (3), 273–290.
Richards, P. S., Sanders, P. W., Lea, T., McBride, J. A., & Allen, G. E. K. (2015). Bringing spiritually oriented psychotherapies into the health care mainstream: A call for worldwide collaboration. *Spirituality in Clinical Practice*, *2*(3), 169–179. doi:org/10.1037/scp0000082
Rothman, A., & Coyle, A. (2018). Toward a framework for Islamic psychology and psychotherapy: An Islamic model of the soul. *Journal of Religion and Health*. doi:10.1007/s10943-018-0651-x
Schaefer, S. M., Jackson, D. C., Davidson, R. J., Aguirre, G. K., Kimberg, D. Y., & Thompson-Schill, S. L. (2002). Modulation of amygdalar activity by the conscious regulation of negative emotion. *Journal of Cognitive Neuroscience*, *14*(6): 913–921.
Skinner, R. (1989/2018). Traditions, paradigms and basic concepts in Islamic psychology. *Journal of Religion and Health*. doi:10.1007/s10943-018-0595-1
Thānwī, A. A. (n.d.). *Da'wat-e-'Abdiyyat*. Karachi: Maktabat Thānwī–Daftarul-Ibqa.
Walī allā h, S. (2010). *Al-Qawl al-Jamīl fī Bayān Sawā' al-Sabīl*. Cairo: Dar al-Jawdiyyah.

Index

Note: Entries in **bold** denote tables; entries in *italics* denote figures.

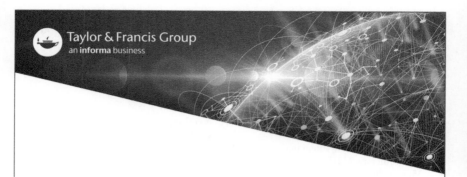